D1591312

THE GOSPELS IN THE SCHOOLS

c.1100 – c.1280

THE GOSPELS IN THE SCHOOLS

c.1100 – c.1280

BERYL SMALLEY

THE HAMBLEDON PRESS

LONDON AND RONCEVERTE

Published by The Hambledon Press 1985

35 Gloucester Avenue, London NW1 7AX (U.K.)

309 Greenbrier Avenue, Ronceverte,
West Virginia 24970 (U.S.A.)

ISBN 0 907628 49 4

History Series 41

British Library Cataloguing in Publication Data

Smalley, Beryl
    The Gospels in the schools c. 1100 – c. 1280
    – (History series; 41)
    1. Bible – Study – History
    I. Title
    220'07   BS600.2

Library of Congress Cataloging in Publication Data

Smalley, Beryl.
    The Gospels in the schools, c. 1100 – c. 1280

    Includes bibliographical references and index.
    1. Bible. N.T. Gospels – Criticism, interpretation, etc.
    – History – Middle Ages, 600-1500. I. Title
    BS2555.2.S57 1985   226'. 06'09021 85-5550
    ISBN 0 907628 49 4

Printed and bound by Hartnoll (1985) Ltd,
Victoria Square, Bodmin, Cornwall

Contents

Acknowledgements

The first four chapters of this book appeared first in the following places and are reprinted here by the kind permission of the original publishers.

1   *Recherches de Théologie ancienne et médiévale*, xlv (1978), pp. 147-80.

2   *Recherches de Théologie ancienne et médiévale*, xlvi (1979), pp. 84-129.

3   *'Sapientiae Doctrina': Mélanges de Théologie et de Littérature médiévales offerts à Dom Hildebrand Bascour O.S.B.*, *Recherches de Théologie ancienne et médiévale*, Numéro Spécial I, Louvain (1980), pp. 299-311.

4   *Franciscan Studies*, 39, Annual xvii (1979), pp. 230-54; 40, Annual xviii (1980), pp. 298-369.

Foreword

. . . audaci promere cantu
mens congesta iubet.
(Claudian, *De raptu Proserpinae*)

The Old Testament predominated in my *Study of the Bible in the Middle Ages*; I gave only passing glances at study of the New. Curiosity has driven me to fill in the gap, at least partially, by examining some Gospel commentaries of the twelfth and thirteenth centuries. The Gospels posed different problems from those of the Old Testament books to the medieval schoolmen. A different type of book confronted them, calling for new kinds of evidence. The persons and events described there belonged to the new age, the last of St. Augustine's ages before the seventh would bring the Last Things to the world. The schoolmen's Church, as they perceived it, prolonged the Church founded by Christ and his apostles. The Gospels belonged to their era, whereas the Old Testament merely foreshadowed it. How did this difference affect exegesis? Perhaps I should have quailed at the task, had I foreseen the fog of uncertainty lying over the commentaries and glosses of the early twelfth century, the elusiveness of an Alexander of Hales and the flood of new sources let loose by John of Wales and Albert the Great. My rash attempt has resulted in a bare survey. Age and ill health have prevented me from travelling far afield. I have had to rely on such manuscripts, microfilms and printed editions as came to hand. To make a thorough study of each commentary was 'not on'. The comforting thought is that one person's end may mark another's beginning, and that my struggles with the subject may offer guide-lines to future researches.

The amount of technical detail involved even in such a survey may daunt some readers. The reasons for its presence are first that one has to ask 'who, when and where?' before discussing a commentator; the question may be difficult or impossible to answer, given the number of anonymous or unascribed commentaries. Second, one has to track down and isolate the sources, since commentaries tend to be derivative. Success in this painful task will tell us or hint at two facts about the author; which sources appealed to him and what choice he had among the books available to him; what personal or original comments he made. Knowledge of his sources is all the more needed in that he often made unacknowledged borrowings from them. No student of medieval exegesis can avoid these queries, nor can he ignore changes in the techniques employed. What others he chooses to make are his own business. Mine, which would not be everyone's, are how far he interpreted the Gospel in terms of his own experience and how he reacted to

Gospel teaching in so far as it compared or contrasted with the Church's doctrine and practice in his own day and age. For instance, did his milieu and his profession as a secular clerk or as a member of a religious Order affect his interpretation of the Gospels?

My last query is the most difficult to answer, and yet it is basic. It concerns the fourfold interpretation: Scripture had a literal-historical, an allegorical, a moral or tropological and an anagogic sense; the last three were often subsumed under the heading 'spiritual' or 'mystical'. Admittedly, the spiritual senses of Scripture belonged to the divine economy as a patristic or medieval exegete saw it. Admittedly, it followed that the literal-historical sense could be singled out for disregard as the lowest. Quite apart from its perception as a kind of servant-master relationship, it blocked or could block any sense of historical continuity: a person or event was isolated from the context in order that a 'spiritual' construction could be built upon it.[1] Yet there was room for development within this immovable framework. The tradition handed down by the Fathers did not make a clear-cut distinction between the literal-historical and the spiritual senses. The signified would push its way into its sign. St. Augustine's treatment of the raising of Lazarus illlustrates the muddle. In the spiritual sense Lazarus signified a sinner, dead to virtue; his raising signified his repentance through grace and the loosing of his grave cloths his forgiveness and absolution (John 11. 1–44). Augustine forestalled an objection here:

Someone says: how can Lazarus signify a sinner and be so beloved by the Lord? Let him hear the Lord saying: *I am not come to call the just, but sinners*(Matt. 9. 13). For God would not have descended to earth from heaven if he had not loved sinners.[2]

A friend of Jesus, nowhere blamed for sin in the Gospel, has to be a sinner in the literal sense because that is what he signified in the spiritual.

There was also a trend (we shall see examples later) to deny *any* literal sense to a passage if it would have been shocking or seemingly impossible, had it been accepted. In that case there was no literal sense, but only a spiritual. Further, the spiritual sense could distort or enlarge the literal even more than in the case where Augustine makes the historical Lazarus a sinner; Old Testament predictions became part of New Testament history, although not mentioned in the latter. The ox and ass in the nativity scene is a classic example; we shall meet others. Contamination or cross-fertilization? That depends on one's attitude to medieval Bible studies. It seems to me that the literal-historical sense had to be rescued from its shackles before progress in its understanding could happen. 'Progress' here obviously refers to the limited extent to which it could be made in the middle ages.

Lest I seem to show misunderstanding of medieval schoolmen in

---

[1] See E. Panella, 'La "Lex nova" tra Storia ed Ermeneutica. Le occasioni dell'esegesi di S.Tommaso d'Aquino', *Memorie Domenicane*, N S 6 (1975), 25.

[2] *In Iohannis Evangelium Tractatus* xlix, 5 (CCSL 36, 422).

expecting them to see the point of distinguishing between the senses, it may be said in my favour that many of them faced up to the problem and made bold to tackle it.

From a literary point of view, schoolmen trained in grammar and rhetoric must have noticed and puzzled over their heritage of muddle. John of Salisbury's account of tropes, metaphors, figures and other modes of expression warned the critic against taking words at their face value instead of looking to the minds of speakers. Otherwise the Fathers will quarrel even in the canonical Scriptures and even the evangelists will seem to contradict one another.[3] Surely a schoolman with this background training could hardly shirk the question of what the evangelist meant to say either in plain words or according to rhetorical rules of speech?

Theologically, he had to decide on the question, raised from at least the time of Andrew of St. Victor: which of the Old Testament prophecies were christological according to the prophet's first intention, in which case they would belong to the literal sense, and which referred to the prophet's immediate or near future situation, in which case the spiritual sense would be built on them. The Gospels would raise the same kind of question on the evangelist's first intention. We shall see that some at least of our commentators accepted the challenge.

These are abstract questions. The historian who studies characters has to establish some sort of contact with them. He has to come clean about his subjective impressions of them as persons. Many commentaries originated in lecture courses. Sitting in on a lecture cannot but make him admire or like, criticize or dislike the lecturer as such. I shall be quite open on my reactions to my commentators.

A foreword must end with thanks to all the librarians and scholars who have helped me to struggle through the thicket. I owe a special debt to Fr. Ignatius Brady O.M. for his help and encouragement throughout and to Dr. James Weisheipl O.P. of the Pontifical Institute for sending me his book and offprints on St. Thomas and St. Albert.

My translations from the Latin Vulgate come from the Douai version. In transcribing published texts I have followed the editors' punctuation and spelling. In transcribing manuscript texts I have used my own punctuation and slightly altered the spelling to make for readability.

As a postscript I must explain why the prolific Oxford Fransciscan Thomas Docking has got left out. A research student began to work on him, though she has given it up now.

---

[3] *Metalogicon*, ed.C.C.I.Webb (Oxford, 1929), 47: 'Siquidem, ut Hilarius ait, intelligentia sumenda est ex causis dicendi; alioquin etiam in scripturis canonicis rixabuntur patres, sibique erunt etiam Euangeliste contrarii, si iudex insulsus ad solam dictorum superficiem et non ad dicentium mentes aspiciat.'

TO SUSAN HALL WITH GRATITUDE

1

Some Gospel Commentaries of the Early Twelfth Century

The scarcity of twelfth-century commentaries on St Matthew surprised the late Father D. Van den Eynde :

> La scolastique naissante, si riche en gloses et commentaires sur les Psaumes et les Épîtres de saint Paul, n'en connaît que très peu sur l'Évangile de saint Matthieu [1].

Early medieval commentaries on the other gospels were also few and far between. Burgundio of Pisa gave as a reason for translating St John Chrysostom's homilies on the fourth gospel that the Latins, as far as he knew, possessed no continuous exposition of it apart from St Augustine's [2]. Burgundio finished his translation in 1174 [3]. As his editor points out, the Pisan did not know of the commentary of Rupert of Deutz, written about 1115; but Rupert's commentary on this book never circulated widely [4].

Van den Eynde contrasted the dearth of gospel commentaries with the number on the Psalter and St Paul. The contrast reflects school teaching. Lectures on the Psalter and St Paul became part of the curriculum at an early date. A letter in a model letter collection from Hildesheim, 1054-1085, is written by a student, probably studying at a school in northern France, dissuading a friend from going to fight in Saxony. The student entices his friend to come to the schools instead, by telling him that his

---

1. *Autour des "Enarrationes in Evangelium S. Matthaei" attribuées à Geoffroi Babion*, in *Rech. Théol. anc. méd.* 26 (1959) 50.

2. '...tum quia huius Iohannis evangeliste expositionis penuria apud Latinos maxima erat. Nullum enim alium nisi sanctum Augustinum eum continue exponentem inveni'. See P. CLASSEN, *Burgundio von Pisa Richter-Gesandter-Übersetzer*, in *Sitzungsberichte des Heidelberger Akademie der Wissenschaften, Philos.-hist. Kl.* 4 (1974) 84.

3. *Ibid.* 52.

4. RUPERTI TUITENSIS *Commentaria in Evangelium Sancti Iohannis*, ed. R. HAACKE (*Corpus Christianorum, Contin. med.* 9) Turnhout 1969, vii.

master has now finished the Psalter and is going on to the
Pauline Epistles, on which he is thought to surpass all other
masters[5]. The letter witnesses to common practice in the late
eleventh century schools. Fame as a master of the sacred page
depended on one's performance in lecturing on the two set texts
of the Old and New Testament.

Custom changed during the twelfth and thirteenth centuries.
The gospels took a more central place in the syllabus. The aim
of this paper is to trace the steps of the change and to suggest why,
as well as how, it happened. In a later paper I hope to examine the
contents of these new gospel commentaries more closely.

Two reasons for the older tradition stand out from the beginning.
The Psalter's place in the liturgy and St Paul's in theology go far
to explain why masters preferred them to the gospels. But it does
not go far enough. The patristic tradition presented the Bible as
a whole. Old and New Testaments alike mirrored the divine light
of revelation[6]. Gospel truth shone forth from all parts. Not only
did the Old Testament foreshadow the New; it added concrete
details. The christological psalms belonged to the gospel story:
'Christ's Passion is narrated as clearly here as in the gospel', wrote
St Augustine on *Ps*. 21. 'It is less prophecy than history', echoed
Cassiodorus[7]. We see how a psalm was read as history in the
story of Judas Iscariot. A thief as well as a traitor (*Ioan*. 12,6),
he stole the money in his charge to give to his wife and children.
How do we know that Judas had a family? Because it says so

5. 'Audiens, quia magister noster, iam finito psalterio, epistolas Pauli sit
incepturus, in quibus ipse ultra communem omnium magistrorum valentiam valere
dicitur, et volo et opto te eisdem, si tibi placuerit, interesse'. See C. ERDMANN
and N. FICKERMANN, *Die Briefe der deutschen Kaizerzeit* 5: *Briefsammlungen
der Zeit Heinrichs IV*. (*Mon. Germ. Hist*.) Weimar 1950, 93-95. The Saxon wars
began in 1073.

6. 'Speculum namque nostrum scriptura tua sacra, quae nobis lucet in nocte
huius vitae'. From JEAN DE FÉCAMP, *Confessio theologica*, ed. J. LECLERCQ and
J. P. BONNES, *Jean de Fécamp*, Paris 1946, 163. On the 'mirror' of Scripture see
H. J. SPITZ, *Die Metaphorik des geistigen Schriftsinns* (*Münsterische Mittelalter-
Schriften* 12) München 1972, 115-119.

7. AUGUSTINE, *Enarrationes in Psalmos* (CCSL 38) 123: 'Passio Christi tam
euidenter quasi euangelium recitatur'. CASSIODORUS, *Expositio Psalmorum* (CCSL
97) 189: 'Nam cum multi psalmorum breuiter de Domini passione meminerint,
nemo tamen eum tanta proprietate descripsit, ut non tam prophetia quam
historia esse uideatur'.

in *Ps.* 108,9 : *May his children be fatherless : and his wife a widow.* St Peter's quotation of the preceding verse (*Act.* 1,20) proved that the psalm referred to Judas[8]. The traditional mode of exegesis according to the four senses also tended to put both Testaments on a level. A learned and devout reader could find Christian doctrine in either, or indeed in all books of the Bible[9]. The monk could choose any text for his prayerful meditation. An abbot would treat of the gospels to his brothers to exhort rather than to teach them[10].

It was different in the schools. Secular masters were there to teach, and came to think that their pupils ought to leave the classroom with a wider, if more superficial knowledge of *sacra pagina*. The Psalter and Pauline Epistles kept their honoured place, but more books were lectured on, to the benefit of the gospels. The custom of expounding the whole Bible began in the school of Laon, like so many other novelties. Master Anselm and his colleagues and pupils equipped the whole Bible with the Gloss which came to be known as *Ordinaria*[11]. Peter Lombard expanded the Anselmian Gloss on the Psalter and St Paul to make 'the Great Gloss'. Anselm's Gloss on the Psalter was sometimes distinguished from the Lombard's as 'Psalterium de parva glosatura Anselmi'[12].

To review our evidence for the authorship of the Gloss on the gospels : we know most about that on St John's. Anselm himself

8. AUGUSTINE, *ed. cit.* 40, 1583; 1590. PETER COMESTOR, *Historia scholastica* (PL 198, 1598) : 'Iudas vero propter lucrum, quia fur erat, et loculos Domini habens, quae mittebantur portabat, id est non solum ferebat, sed asportabat. Habebat enim uxorem et filios, sicut scriptum est de eo : 'Fiant filii eius orphani, et uxor vidua'. Uxori ergo et filiis dabat quae furabatur'.

9. H. DE LUBAC, *L'exégèse médiévale. Les quatre sens de l'Écriture*, Paris 1959-1964.

10. PASCHASIUS RADBERTUS, Prologue to his commentary on St Matthew (PL 120, 31) : 'Dum sacrae professionis obedientia, coram fratribus Evangelium, uti consuetudinis est, diebus solemnibus, licet limate loquendi genere, exhortandi magis gratia quam docendi tractaretur ...'.

11. For recent surveys see B. SMALLEY, *Les commentaires bibliques de l'époque romane*, in *Cahiers de Civilisation médiévale* 4 (1961) 15-22; R. WASSELYNCK, *L'influence de S. Grégoire le Grand sur les commentaires bibliques médiévaux*, in *Rech. Théol. anc. méd.* 32 (1965) 186-192.

12. A thirteenth century title in MS *Hereford Cathedral O.vi.12*, fol. 1. Mr. N. R. KER pointed this out to me. On the glosses of Gilbert Porreta and Peter Lombard, see now I. BRADY, *Magistri Petri Lombardi Parisiensis Episcopi Sententiae* I, 1 *Prolegomena (Spicilegium Bonaventurianum* 4) Quaracchi 1971.

compiled it; we even know something of his methods as a compiler[13] : he drew on John Scot Erigena's commentary as well as on the Fathers. Peter Comestor is our best witness to the authorship of the Gloss on the other gospels, and also to subsequent lecturing on the gospels in the Paris schools. Although it means jumping forward, I shall have to start from our data concerning him, and then work backwards from his teaching period in the 1160s and '70s.

Petrus Comestor or Manducator became dean of Troyes in 1147. He was already a canon of the abbey of Saint-Loup at Troyes (Augustinian from 1135/6). After studying under the little-known Master John of Tours, himself a pupil of Anselm and therefore a link between Comestor and Laon, he heard Peter Lombard's lectures at Paris; Comestor is our best informant on the Lombard's teaching. He taught at Paris in the decade following the Lombard's election to the bishopric of Paris, 1159, holding the office of chancellor of Notre-Dame 1168-1178. He died Oct. 22, 1178, soon after retiring to spend his last days at the abbey of St Victor. His classic *School History* was probably finished 1169-1173[14]. Faithful to his master, he quotes the Sentences on baptism there[15]. His unprinted lectures on the four gospels survive as *reportationes*. F. Stegmüller has listed the MSS[16]. I have chosen for convenience to work from MSS *Durham Cathedral Library A.I.9* (*D*), *Cambridge Pembroke College 75* (*P*), *Oxford Bodl. 494* (*B*) and *Laud. misc. 291*

13. S. MARTINET, *Montloon*, Laon 1972, 103-104; JEAN SCOT, *Commentaire sur l'Évangile de Jean*, ed. É. JEAUNEAU (*Sources chrétiennes* 180) Paris 1972, 57-62.

14. I. BRADY, *Petrus Manducator and the oral teachings of Peter Lombard*, in *Antonianum* 40 (1966) 454-490; J. LONGÈRE, *Œuvres oratoires des Maîtres Parisiens au XIIᵉ siècle* (*Études augustiennes*) Paris 1975, 20-21 and *passim*. COMESTOR's *De sacramentis* was one of the first theological treatises to use the Sentences as a basis; see R.-M. MARTIN, *Pierre le Mangeur « De sacramentis »*, appendix to H. WEISWEILER, *Maître Simon et son groupe* (*Spicil. sacr. Lovan.* 17) Louvain 1937, xxviii.

15. PL 198, 1554 : 'De vi enim et institutione baptismi duplex est opinio, ut in Sententiis habetur'. See *Sent.* IV, iii, 5.

He refers to the same passage in his lecture on *Mt.* 3,15, MS *Oxford Bodl. Laud. misc. 291*, fol. 18ʳᵃ : 'quia tres sunt opiniones de institutione baptismi, quas habemus in sententiis distinctas, et nulli earum volo me arctare'. Peter Lombard does in fact give three opinions.

16. *Repertorium biblicum Medii Aevi* (Madrid 1950-1976) nos. 6575-8. I shall refer to Stegmüller's work as RB.

(*L*). These MSS will be described in a later article. Our only clue to the date of Comestor's lectures is that they must belong to his teaching period from 1159 to sometime before his retirement in 1178. He probably lectured on the gospels consecutively, since he says 'ut dixi vobis super Marcum', when commenting on *Lc*. 8,43 (*D*, fol. 104vb).

Comestor tells us that neither Master Anselm nor Master Ralph, his brother, glossed St Mark's gospel. The passage is known, but will bear repetition in the light of what follows; Comestor is commenting on the prologue to St Mark :

> *Marcum pene intactum, quia pedissecus est Mathei*; etiam pro difficultate eum reliquerunt antiqui, nec legit eum magister Anselmus nec magister Radulfus frater eius (*L*, fol. 93rb).

It seems, therefore, that Comestor ascribed the Gloss on the other gospels to the two brothers, and that on St Mark to some unknown collaborator, who finished their work subsequently. He ascribes the Gloss on St Matthew to Master Ralph. Comestor queries the original authorship of an excerpt contained in the Gloss on *Mt*. 1,12 :

> De hoc habes glosam Rabani. Non tamen habes hanc glosam intitulatam cuius auctoris sit, et ideo incertum est unde magister Radulfus, frater magistri Anselmi, qui glosaturam ordinavit, eam assumpsit... (*L*, fol. 5vb)[17].

Confirmation of Comestor's ascription comes from a detailed study of the Gloss on St Matthew by Fr. H. Weisweiler. He has shown that the Gloss in its present form must be post-Anselmian, and therefore probably compiled by Ralph, as Comestor says. Weisweiler found that much of the Gloss on Matthew derived from the commentary of Paschasius Radbertus (d. *c*. 865), combined with Raban Maur and patristic sources[18]. That is not surprising, seeing that Gilbert the Universal drew the Gloss on Lamentations, which he compiled, largely from Paschasius on Lamentations, and that John the Scot's fragmentary commentary passed into the

---

17. A. LANDGRAF first noticed this text, *Familienbildung bei Paulinenkommentaren des 12. Jahrhunderts*, in *Biblica* 13 (1932) 67.

18. H. WEISWEILER, *Paschasius Radbertus als Vermittler des Gedankengutes des karolingischen Renaissance in den Matthäeuskommentaren des Kreises um Anselm von Laon*, in *Scholastik* 35 (1960) 363-402, 503-536. I shall refer to this paper as WEISWEILER.

Gloss on the Fourth Gospel. The Fathers reached the glossators through, and enlarged by, Carolingian commentators.

Comestor says nothing of the authorship of the Gloss on St Luke or St John. Since Anselm's authorship of that on St John is known from other evidence, Comestor leaves us to assume that one or other of the two brothers compiled that on St Luke; perhaps they collaborated or worked with pupils.

Comestor's references lead us to infer that the masters of Laon read the Gloss as a lecture course, which is even more interesting than his hints on its authorship. Thus he says 'nec *legit* eum', when speaking of the Gloss on St Mark. Better evidence appears in his comment on *Mt.* 21,7-8. Comestor took pains to 'order' the glosses when he read them to his pupils, explaining the correct punctuation and distinguishing one gloss from its neighbour on the page. The Gloss gave two interpretations of the entry into Jerusalem : (1) the apostles' clothing, set upon the ass which Jesus rode, signified that the apostles would preach divine commands to the world; the crowd strewing clothes on the road signified martyrs for the faith; (2) the crowd signified the Jews, since Christians would trample down their legal precepts, signified by the clothes strewn on the road. The glosses stating these two interpretations, Comestor said, must be kept separate and not run together so as to confuse them :

> Prosequere litteram usque ibi : *Alii autem*, et necesse est hic legere glosas incisive, sicut legebatur in glosatura magistri Anselmi. Glosa *Sic et apostoli*, usque ibi *et imposuerunt vestimenta*; que autem *vestimenta* apostoli mundo *imposuerunt* principium alterius glose ostendit : *Vestes apostolorum etc.* usque ibi : *Minor turba*. Postea resume glosam ubi dimisisti : *sed et cetera turba etc.* (*L*, fol. 76[rb-va])[19].

Comestor does not ascribe the compilation of the Gloss on St Matthew to Master Anselm; he does tell us what he knew, or thought he knew : it used to be read out *incisive*, in such a way as to separate two component glosses. We have evidence for the reading aloud of a gloss on the Psalter. An early copy of Gilbert Porreta on the Psalter has the explicit :

19. The incipits of the glosses mentioned by Comestor on *Mt.* 21,7-8, are found in the Gloss *ad loc.* I have used the Lyons 1589 edition of the *Glossa ordinaria*, printed with the Postills of Nicholas of Lyre and other additions.

Explicit glosatura magistri Giliberti Porretani quam ipse recitavit coram suo magistro Anselmo causa emendationis[20].

Abelard lectured on Ezechiel at Laon with an *expositor* to guide him, to show off his powers to his fellow students[21]. Comestor stretches our evidence to cover the Gloss on the gospels; it, too, was read aloud to pupils. Where it was read is not stated. Presumably Comestor meant lectures in the school of Laon, which contined to function at least until the death of Ralph, 1131-1133; Anselm had died in 1117[22]. Weisweiler points to other scraps of evidence for the practice of lecturing on Scripture in Anselm's school[23].

There is more to follow. The Laon tradition passed to Paris. Comestor quotes his master Peter Lombard on St Luke so clearly as to leave no doubt that the Lombard lectured on the third gospel. At this point Peter the Chanter comes on stage, since he confirms Comestor in his gloss on *Unum ex quatuor*, a conflated text of the gospels. Its date can be fixed between autumn 1187, that is, after news of Saladin's capture of Jerusalem on October 22, 1187 had reached the West, and before the Chanter's death in old age in 1197[24]. He knew Comestor's lectures on the gospels

20. R. MYNORS, *Catalogue of the MSS of Balliol College, Oxford*, Oxford 1963, 26.

21. *Historia calamitatum*, ed. J. MONFRIN, Paris 1959, 69 : 'Assumpto itaque expositore statim in crastino eos ad lectionem invitavi'.

22. O. LOTTIN, *Psychologie et morale aux XIIᵉ et XIIIᵉ siècles* 5, Gembloux 1959, 183-184.

23. WEISWEILER, 534-535, citing titles in MS copies of commentaries ascribed to Anselm : 'Secundum lectionem magistri Anselmi' etc.

24. On the Chanter's career and writings see J. W. BALDWIN, *Masters, Princes and Merchants. The Social Views of Peter the Chanter and his Circle*, Princeton 1970, 3-11; and his review of my *The Becket Conflict and the Schools*, in *Speculum* 51 (1976) 358-359. For a list of MSS of his *Unum ex quatuor* see RB 6504-7. I have used MS *Oxford Merton College 212*. The Chanter writes on *Mt.* 8,20 :'*Vulpes foveas habent* : Sepulchrum habuit, sed alienum, que due modo magis alienata sunt, quia *exterminavit* crucem *aper de silva et singularis ferus depastus est eam*' (fol. 48ʳᵃ). Another copy, *London British Library Royal 2.C.IX*, fol. 72ᵛᵇ, has a marginal note 'Saladinus' to the quotation *aper de silva etc.* (*Ps.* 79,14). His *Unum ex quatuor* came after his also undated Psalter commentary, since he refers back to it on *Mt.* 7,3, on the question whether a prelate sins if he rebukes sinful subjects, when guilty himself : 'Hec planius dicta sunt super psalmum *Peccatori autem dixit Deus*' (fol. 39ʳᵇ). There is in fact a *quaestio* on the subject in his comment on *Ps.* 49,16 (MS *Oxford Bodl. Hatton 37* (S.C. 4091), p. 61.

and quoted them, sometimes by name and sometimes anonymously. Comestor quotes his master on three texts of St Luke. On the first the Chanter identifies Comestor's master with Peter Lombard. He does not help us on the other two; but the identification can be assumed. I transcribe the passages, adding the Gloss on the first, since Comestor appeals to it as supporting his master's view on the meaning of *donavit* (*Lc.* 7,43) as implying 'condonavit'. Comestor's reporter wrote 'inquid' *tout court*, when reporting the lecturer's personal comments. 'The master' is not the reporter's master, but Comestor's, as quoted by him in his lectures. The first quotation shows that Peter Lombard lectured on a glossed text, just as Comestor did, since he supported his exposition from a gloss. A reading of the quotations will carry conviction that they come from a lecture on St Luke and would make nonsense in any other context.

COMESTOR ON LUKE

MS *Pembroke College, Cambridge, 75*, fol. 32rb (on *Lc.* 7,43: '*Respondens Simon dixit: Aestimo quia is, cui plus donavit. At ille dixit ei: Recte iudicasti*'):

Sicque maiori dilectione maiorem offensam redimatur, sed generaliter est verum: qui amplius debuit, amplius diligit. Ergo Magdalena amplius dilexit quam beata Virgo, quia amplius debuit et amplius est ei dimissum. Hoc, inquid, solent ita determinare... In expositione, inquid, huius loci gloriabatur magister, quia omnes ante tempus suum pertransibant; ipse longe melius exposuit; et expositionem suam voluit habere ex quadam glosa, sicut ego ostendam. Voluit ergo adherere illi verbo *cui plus donavit*. Nam donare interdum pro dare ponitur, interdum pro condonare. Hic ergo utramque significationem importat, ut ita intelligatur: *cui plus donavit*, id est cui plus dedit et condonavit, et ex hac causa verum est: cui plus donatur plus diligit, id est cui plus datur et condonatur plus diligere tenetur... *Duo debitores*... Prosequere glosam secundum misticum sensum et nota quod finis consonat aperte expositioni magistri.

Gloss ad loc. Duo debitores duo populi sunt... Sed minus debet iudaeus, cui decalogus legis per servum datur; plus debet christianus, cui per filium gratiae vita committitur... Plus ergo diligit ecclesia gentium quam iudaeus, quia si secundum praesentem statum maior ei gratia confertur et secundum praeteritum de maiori feditate extrahitur, plus debet qui plus accepit. Nullus potest tantum diligere quantum ea que in pluribus diligit. *Is, cui plus donavit*: secundum homines plus fortasse offendit, cui plus debuerit, sed misericordia Domini causa mutatur, ut amplius diligit qui amplius debuit, si tamen gratia consequatur.

CHANTER ON 'UNUM EX QUATTUOR'

MS *Merton College, Oxford, 212*, fol. 115^{rb-va} :

> *Plus debet qui plus accepit. Secundum homines… consequatur.* Si generaliter verum est : qui amplius debuit amplius diligit, ergo Magdalena plus beata Virgine dilexit. Ad hoc ita solvit Petrus Lombardus : Donare interdum pro dare ponitur, interdum pro condonare. Hic utramque significationem habet, ut ita intelligatur : *cui plus donavit,* id est cui plus condonavit et dedit ; et secundum hoc verum est : cui plus condonavit de commissis et dedit de caritate plus diligit.

P, fol. 66vb (on *Lc.* 17,4 : '*Si peccaverit…*') :

> Sed verbum hoc disputabile est ; ideo hic diligenter est distinguendum… Hec ergo tria debemus generaliter omnibus qui in nos peccaverunt. Refert ergo an qui nos offendit veniam petat, an adhuc in malitia persistat, quia veniam petenti tenemur amplius quam in malitia persistenti, quia tam perfecti quam imperfecti petenti veniam tenentur dicere 'Ave' et ei communicare, sed in malitia persistenti neque perfecti neque imperfecti tenentur communicare ; immo etiam perfecti possunt excommunicare in ecclesia vel facere ut excommunicetur. Hic tamen distinguebat magister de quibusdam perfectis, asserens scilicet de speculativis quia nullo pacto debent [facere?] ut pro iniuria eorum aliquis excommunicetur. Ita visum est magistro.

fol. 75vb (on *Lc.* 20,47 : '*Qui devorant domos viduarum, simulantes longam orationem*') :

> Magister tamen aliter transibat hunc locum. Ita enim exponebat, pro ipsis orationibus pro promissione ipsarum orationum, quia scilicet fraudulenter promittebant se pro simplicibus viduis orare.

A fourth passage, this time from Comestor on *Mt.* 9,5, has a reference to his master's opinion. I mention it last because it needs to be read in the light of the other examples of Comestor's technique in quoting the Lombard. This quotation might conceivably come from the Lombard on *Lc.* 5,23, rather than on *Mt.* 9,5, since Comestor cites the Gloss on both texts, trying to square it with his master's interpretation. Again, the past tense is used for Comestor's master, whereas the reporter wrote 'inquam' for Comestor ; the first person stresses that Comestor speaks for himself. The text in question was : *Quid est facilius dicere : Dimittuntur tibi peccata tua, an dicere : Surge et ambula?* Comestor's master had argued that it showed greater divine power and mercy to justify a sinner than to create heaven and earth. The Gloss stated only that Christ showed no less power in remitting sin than

in healing the body. Comestor brought it into line with his master's
view by understanding 'vobis' in the text. Hence it became a matter
of which *seemed to men* to be the greater power, according to the
Gloss, whereas Comestor's master was discussing not which *seemed
to be* the greater power, but which actually *was* the greater.

MS *Laud. misc. 291*, fol. 48[ra-b] :

> *Quid est facilius*, supple 'vobis', id est quid videtur vobis *facilius*,
> scilicet an dicere : *dimittuntur tibi peccata tua*, id est solo verbo peccata
> dimittere, et ita sanare in anima, *an dicere : surge et ambula?*, id est
> solo dicto sanare in corpore...; et nisi, inquam, ita exponatis *quid est
> facilius* 'vobis'?, id est *quid* videtur vobis *facilius*, videbitur glosa obloqui
> opinioni magistri. Voluit enim quod et maioris potentie et maioris
> misericordie sit suscitare mortuum in anima quam in corpore... et in
> glosa super Lucam habes quod utrumque equalis est potentie, sed
> alterum maioris misericordie, scilicet iustificare impium. Magister voluit
> quod longe fuit maioris potentie iustificare impium quam creare celum
> et terram etc, super hoc reddens talem rationem : ideo enim videbatur
> ei maioris potentie esse iustificare impium quam creare celum et terram,
> quia iustificationi impii videtur iustitia reclamare... Unde visum est ei
> quod maioris esset potentie impii iustificatio quam celi et terre creatio...
> Vide quia glosa quam hic habes nec obloquitur nec videtur obloqui
> glose quam habes super Lucam. Videtur autem obloqui opinioni
> magistri, nisi caveas... Ecce hoc non obloquitur glose que est super
> Lucam, ubi dicitur equalis potentie, sed obloquitur opinioni magistri;
> ideo, ut salves eius opinionem, ubi in littera dicitur : *Quid est facilius*
> supple 'vobis'.

Gloss on *Mt*. 9,5 :

> *Quid est facilius?* Sed quoniam hoc spirituale non creditis, probetur
> signo visibili quod non minoris constat esse potentiae, ut in filio hominis
> latentem cognoscaris potentiam maiestatis, quae potest dimittere peccata
> ut Deus.

The Gloss on *Lc*. 5,23 is the same. The Comestor's copy may have differed
from the printed edition in stating that to heal the soul showed equal power,
but more mercy than to heal the body.

Two conclusions can be drawn from these passages. Firstly,
Comestor's quotations from his master the Lombard's lectures on
the gospel supply more evidence for the school tradition which
associated the Lombard with exegesis of biblical books other than
the Psalter and Pauline Epistles. Prologues to various books of
the Bible and other pieces were ascribed to him in late twelfth

and thirteenth century MSS. Fr. Brady has rightly rejected these ascriptions as unsupported and as too late to be authentic[25]. The prologue to Isaias ascribed to Peter Lombard takes a shape found only in the later twelfth century : it begins with a biblical text to be adapted to the book to be lectured on. Peter Lombard did not use this form, which later became standard, in his authentic works. On the other hand, the ascriptions, however spurious, point to a hazy memory of the Lombard as a teacher of Scripture in a broader sense than his extant works reveal. The technique of reporting lectures was still in its infancy during his teaching period : we need not wonder that his lectures survive (short of further discoveries) only in Comestor's quotations. Secondly, it sounds as though the Lombard had precursors. He used to pride himself *(gloriabatur),* according to Comestor, on being the first master to find a correct interpretation of *Lc.* 7,43 by taking *donavit* to include the meaning 'condonavit'. Hence he would not have been the first to lecture on a gospel text in the schools at Paris or elsewhere. But who anticipated him, and where, we do not know. Perhaps it had become a custom at Paris by the mid twelfth century or perhaps the Lombard was referring back to Laon, when he claimed to have surpassed his predecessors. Comestor's words *'solet tamen fieri circa hoc satis elegans distinctio magistralis'* (*L,* fol. 33[ra]) on *Mt.* 5, 44 suggest continuous discussion somewhere.

To Laon we must now return. The school made a centre, whence a number of commentaries on St Matthew radiated outward. One line led to the practice of lecturing on the gospel text with its Gloss, as witnessed by Peter Comestor at Paris. But there were others, also converging on Paris by different routes.

Fr. Weisweiler, building on the foundations laid by Lottin and Van den Eynde, has structured the outlines of the story[26]. The tale

---

25. B. SMALLEY and G. LACOMBE, *The Lombard's Commentary on Isaias and Other Fragments,* in *The New Scholasticism* 5 (1931) 123-162; see now *Catalogue général des MSS latins* 6, Paris 1975, 543-548 for a full description of MS *3705*: I. BRADY, *Prolegomena, op. cit.* above n. 12, 113*-117*.

26. *Op. cit.* above n. 18; O. LOTTIN, *La doctrine d'Anselme de Laon sur les dons du Saint-Esprit et son influence,* in *Rech. Théol. anc. méd.* 24 (1957) 267-295; D. VAN DEN EYNDE, *Autour des "Enarrationes in Evangelium S. Matthaei" attribuées à Geoffroi Babion,* in *ibid.* 26 (1959) 50-84.

begins with an abbreviation of Paschasius Radbertus on St Matthew (PL 120, 31-994). The anonymous abbreviator probably worked in the Laon milieu, since his book was used there. I shall call him *V*, in reference to the fact that Lottin, who first drew attention to him, found his commentary in a fragmentary form in MS *Valenciennes 14* (item 7). This MS is a collection formerly belonging to the abbey of St Amand, written in twelfth century hands. The incipit is 'Nomen libri evangelium grece...', the explicit on *Mt.* 6,14, the end of the Lord's Prayer, 'sine meritis ad beatitudinem pervenitur'. Weisweiler discovered the same fragment in a Stuttgart MS (*Landesbibliothek, Cod. theol. quart. 262*) originally from the abbey of Zwiefalten, also in a twelfth century hand. Stegmüller's *Repertorium* provided him with three more (no. 9947)[27]. I can add to these a copy in MS *Bodl. Laud. misc. 87*, twelfth century, from the Charterhouse of Mainz. The text corresponds exactly with *V*, as Lottin transcribed it, and breaks off at the same verse of St Matthew as *V* and the Stuttgart MS. I shall give a detailed description of the Laudian MS later. Lottin noted that *V* had much in common with the Gloss on St Matthew. Comparison of the two led him to suppose that *V*, although written out as a continuous commentary, had used the Gloss as his main source. Weisweiler's researches led him to the opposite conclusion : the Gloss copied *V*, and not *vice versa*, as Lottin thought. Recognising *V* as an abbreviation, often verbal, of Paschasius Radbertus, he showed that *V* was closer to the original than were the excerpts from Paschasius in the Gloss. Further, he delved into the manuscript tradition of the Gloss on St Matthew and found that some early copies of the Gloss lacked glosses taken from *V*. The latter belong to an expanded version of the Gloss, represented in our printed editions, as in later MSS. They must have been added to the original Gloss at an early stage in its history, since the first scholars of the twelfth century known to have used the Gloss had the fuller version before them. The additions from *V* explained certain discrepancies or contradictions in the Gloss in its fuller form, which had puzzled Lottin. All becomes clear if we postulate an early Gloss, drawn from Raban Maur and other patristic sources,

27. WEISWEILER, 364, 529.

directly or indirectly, which was expanded by insertions from *V*. The interpolator may well have been Ralph of Laon, improving on a Gloss compiled or used by his brother Anselm.

Unfortunately, two of the surprisingly rare mistakes in Stegmüller's *Repertorium Biblicum* have concealed the fact that *V* exists in a complete form, going to the very end of the gospel. Numbers 7494-7502 list various scriptural pieces ascribed to 'Robertus Wigorniensis (de Worcester)', with the statement : 'Floruit saec. XII, canonicus Wigorniensis' (no. 7495). Stegmüller misread the incipit of MS *Paris Bibl. nat. lat. 16794* (which he wrongly listed as *16784*). The tract in question (foll. 1^r-5^v) is the *De concordia et dispensatione evangeliorum* of Master Senatus, monk of Worcester; he held the offices of precentor and chamberlain before becoming prior in 1189; he resigned in 1196 and died in 1207. His *De concordia* survives in an autograph, prefaced by a dedicatory letter to his *socius* Master Aluredus :

> Dilecto amico suo et socio magistro Aluredo suus Senatus Wigorniensis ecclesie filius salutem ...[28].

'Robert canon of Worcester' (a monastic cathedral, which did not have canons) thus disappears into thin air. There is no reason to replace the fictitious Robert by Senatus of Worcester as the author of the following anonymous items in MS *lat. 16794* (no. 7496), nor is it clear why Stegmüller credited his 'Robert' with the other items listed under Robert's name. For the moment it will be enough to note that MS *lat. 16794* has a commentary on St Matthew, foll. 6ra-79rb, which begins with a prologue reminiscent of Comestor's : 'Fecit Deus duo magna luminaria...', followed by an exposition of St Jerome's prologue. Stegmüller helpfully gives long excerpts from both prologues and commentary. Comparison of his excerpts with Comestor's prologue and exposition of Jerome's prologue suggests that those in MS *lat. 16794* (foll. 6ra-7vb) are abridged from Comestor's (*L*, fol. 1^{ra-vb}). The incipits and excerpts

---

28. I am much obliged to Mr Stephen Ferruolo for investigating these items and clearing up the muddle. On Senatus see D. KNOWLES, C. N. L. BROOKE, V. C. M. LONDON, *The Heads of Religious Houses, England and Wales 940-1216*, Cambridge 1972, 84; C. H. TURNER, *Early Worcester Manuscripts*, Oxford 1916, xliii-lii.

from the commentary, on the other hand, correspond exactly to *V*, as far as he goes in the known copies, that is up to *Mt.* 6,14. After that the excerpts given by Stegmüller and his explicits can all be found in the Gloss on *Mt.* 10,1 and 28,20, with the exception of the last: 'Ex tribus testibus quatuor evangeliorum ... et mater Domini'. This is not in the printed edition of the Gloss. It does, however, appear in a copy of the Gloss in MS *Laud. misc. 69* (fol. 286ᵛ)[29]. The excerpts might have been drawn from Paschasius *via V*, with several additions[30]. It seems, therefore, that we have a complete text of *V*, perhaps expanded, prefixed by prologues lifted from Comestor. MS *lat. 16794* is twelfth century from S. Martin-des-Champs.

Part of *V* survives in another form: the prologue 'Nomen libri ... abyssi mergeretur' (a comment on *Mt.* 1,1) was often prefixed to the Gloss, especially in twelfth century MSS. There are numerous examples[31]. Indeed, it is surprising in view of its popularity that it did not pass into the Gloss prologues to St Matthew; the glossators willingly incorporated prefatory matter which was not patristic. Weisweiler lists many MSS containing the *V* prologue in addition to the Gloss. MS *Laud. misc. 69*, foll. 130ʳᵃ-133ʳᵃ, can join the collection. It is a twelfth century MS from St Mary Eberbach. Weisweiler found by making a minute comparison that the *V* prologue prefixed to copies of the Gloss represented a fuller version of *V*'s abbreviation of Paschasius than we have in the other form of it[32]. This prologue would have derived from a fuller abbreviation of Paschasius than we have in our copies of *V*, where the commentary, up to *Mt.* 6,14, follows the prologue 'Nomen libri ...'. Hence two versions of the abbreviations of Paschasius were available to the glossators and other scholars concerned with the transmission of the Gloss, a fuller and a shorter version. Neither need have been complete, unless we accept MS *lat. 16794* as giving the complete commentary, which is probable, but not very significant, since it did not circulate as widely as the two truncated forms, that is (1) the prologue prefixed to some copies

29. See below, p. 21.
30. See PL 120, 403-404 for parallels on *Mt.* 10,1, and for explicits 992-993.
31. WEISWEILER, 529-530.
32. *Ibid.* 530-533.

of the Gloss and (2) the prologue plus commentary up to *Mt.* 6,14.

I shall now thankfully take leave of *V*. He witnesses to the industry of the Laon scholars and throws light on their method in expanding earlier sets of glosses to include other matter. He makes no pretensions to originality, apart from occasional re-phrasing and development of his Paschasius commentary[33]. The long commentary on St Matthew, 'Cum post ascensionem...', found in MS *Alençon 26*, foll. 91ra-198vb, has attracted more attention than *V*. I shall call this commentator *A*. MS *Alençon 26* is written in fairly early twelfth century north French hands and has fine romanesque initials. It came from Saint-Evroul[34]. The often-quoted title reads as follows: 'Incipit expositio ex diversis auctoribus a domino Ansello laudunensis philosopho exquisitissimo collecta'. The ascription to Anselm of Laon does not carry conviction. Lottin, Van den Eynde and Weisweiler have all agreed in denying it to him. *A* used both the Gloss in its expanded form (therefore post-Anselmian and probably compiled by Ralph) and *V*; the latter is quoted in his commentary independently, as well as *via* the Gloss. The ascription to Anselm, though spurious, points to a Laon milieu for *A*. Regarded as a compilation of authors, it is an impressive achievement. *A* goes far beyond Raban Maur, *V* and the Gloss in his range of sources. Research on earlier *florilegia* might tell us where he found so much of Claudius, Hilary, Leo and Maximus, to set beside the four doctors of the Latin Church. He saw his work as something more than a mere 'up-ending' of authors, since he uses such phrases as 'exponamus', 'ut diximus' and 'ut expo-suimus' (foll. 108va, 109ra, 110^{rb-va}). Personal comments are rare; but one startling remark shows that he could introduce a novelty. He identified the child, whom Jesus set in the midst of the disciples to teach them humility (*Mt.* 18,2), with St Martial of Limoges, 'as many say':

> Multi dicunt illum parvulum, quem statuit in medio, fuisse sanctum Martialem Lemovicensem (fol. 185rb).

---

33. *Ibid.* 384.
34. H. OMONT, *Cat. gén. des MSS des bibliothèques publiques de France. Départements* 2, Paris 1888, 501. I have used a microfilm kindly supplied by the Institut de Recherches des Textes.

A's source for this statement was Pseudo-Aurelian's *Life* of St Martial of Limoges, forged by the monastic chronicler Adhémar of Chabannes (d. 1034). Adhémar forged the *Life* as part of his propaganda campaign to win acceptance for the apostolicity of his saint. According to 'Aurelian', the supposed successor of St Martial as bishop of Limoges, the child chosen by Jesus served as a waiter at the feeding of the multitude, handed towels for the washing of feet at the Last Supper, and then, at the bidding of St Peter, went to evangelise Gaul as one of the seventy-two apostles. He became the first bishop of Limoges[35]. *A*'s passing reference to St Martial as the child of the gospel, picked up by later commentators and lodging in Comestor's *School History*, testifies to the success of Adhémar's propaganda[36].

The manuscript tradition points to more diffusion of *A*'s text than Lottin and Van den Eynde suspected. Weisweiler, using Stegmüller's *Repertorium* (no. 1359), points to a thirteenth-century copy, anonymous this time and breaking off in the course of *Mt.* 27, in MS *Paris Arsenal lat. 87*, of unknown provenance[37]. Stegmüller also lists MS *Oxford St John's College 111*, which Weisweiler was not able to see. This MS is important enough to describe in full.

It is the only surviving book from the library of All Saints, May, Fife, a cell of Reading Abbey[38]. The *ex libris*, written in an early thirteenth century hand, is pasted on to the modern flyleaf. We do not know when or whence it came to May. Archbishop Laud gave it to St John's College. The MS, 25 × 15 cm., is written in hands of about the third quarter of the twelfth century, perhaps in northern France or Flanders, an impression borne out by the red and black initial, fol. 7ra. There is a fine twelfth century drawing of Christ on the cross, fol. 19^v. The items are (1) *A*'s commentary '[C]um post ascensionem Domini... coniungamur et ei adhereamus', foll. 1ra-4vb. The text corresponds closely

35. Les RR. PP. Bénédictins de Paris, *Vies des saints et des bienheureux* 6, Paris 1948, 518-523.

36. See the *Enarrationes in S. Matheum* (PL 162, 1406; PL 198, 1584). Comestor also refers to the legend in a sermon (PL 198, 1728), and in his commentary on St Matthew (*L*, fol. 71va).

37. Weisweiler, 387, 526-527.

38. N. R. Ker, *Medieval Libraries of Great Britain* (2nd ed.) London 1964, 130.

to that of MS *Alençon 26*, foll. 91ra-95rb, breaking off during the commentary on Christ's genealogy; the main difference is that the order of words in a sentence is sometimes changed. Three leaves have been cut out close to the margin after fol. 4; hence the MS may originally have included more of *A*, though not the whole commentary. (2) The prologue to St Matthew's gospel, 'Matheus ex Iudea', foll. 5^r-6^v. Spaces have been left in the margin for glosses, but only one short gloss has been written into the top left-hand margin : 'Cum multi scripsisse evangelia legantur, ... sibi ecclesie temporalis', fol. 5rb. This is an abridgement of the Gloss on the prologue 'Matheus cum primo... sacramentum'. (3) The text of St Matthew's gospel with glosses. They have much in common with the Gloss on this gospel, but differ in some respects. They represent one of the prestandardised copies of the Gloss, which circulated before the Gloss, as we know it, replaced the older versions. The layout of the text and glosses is untidy and badly spaced, as is usual in early copies. There is no contemporary capitulation. Modern chapters have been added in a later hand. (4) Short sentences in the same hand or one very like that of the *A* commentary and the glosses, fol. 112ra. They resemble the kind of miscellanea from the school of St Victor analysed by Lottin[39], and other collections of the same type. A summary may help to classify them at some future date :

> Sugillo a suggo, tractum a lamiis, id est trangulo (*sic*). From the Gloss on *Lc.* 18,5 : '*Sugillet* a suggero, tractum a lamiis, id est strangulo'. The Gloss itself is a garbled piece of grammar.
>
> Secularis sapientia quasi coluber per humum serpit, divina autem de celestibus, unde Moyses : Non est terra ad quam intratis sicut Egipto, sed de celo pluvias expectans (from *Deut.* 11,10-11).
>
> Tres mortuos, in consensu peccati, in opere, in consuetudine suscitavit Iesus; quartum vero mortuum audivit nuntiante discipulo, et tres ab expectatione precarentur; nuntii defuerunt. Dimitte, inquit, mortuos (*Mt.* 8,22), scilicet in spiritu, id est malivolos mali graventur laudibus, et quia non est iustus caput eorum. Derived from Gregory, *Moral. in Iob*, PL 75, 663, where gospel resurrection miracles are related to *Lc.* 9,60. The Gloss on *Ioan.* 11,25 reads : 'Tres mortuos suscitavit Iesus, unum in domo, id est in corde... consuetudine peccandi'. The

---

39. *Questions inédites de Hugues de Saint-Victor*, in *Rech. Théol. anc. méd.* 26 (1959) 177-263.

sentence 'Tres mortuos' occurs in collections from the school of Anselm of Laon[40].

Nomen Gehenne (*Mt.* 5,22) in veteribus libris non invenitur, sed prius ad novum ponitur. Cuius nomen occasio est : idolum Baal fuit iuxta Ierusalem ... Huius ergo loci nomine futura supplicia designantur. A similar note on 'Gehenna', though not in the same words, occurs in *quaestiones* ascribed to Hugh of St Victor[41].

Omnia non semper ad totum, sed ad partem refertur maximam, ut *omnes declinaverunt* (*Ps.* 13,3, *Rom.* 3,12) omnes qui venerant fures sunt ... omnia mea tua sunt.

Etiam angeli, sed lex prophete, quamquam illi nil negant quem ad esum ortatur vituli. Some line or lines must have dropped out here.

In ecclesiasticis rebus non queruntur verba, sed sensus, is est panibus vita sustenanda est, non siliquis.

Quatuor opiniones fuerunt de incarnatione animi ... etiam modo Deus facit. The same statement occurs in a collection of sentences which may derive from Anselm of Laon himself[42].

Augustinus in epistola ad Ieronimum : Non omnia orta occidunt, quia et caro Christi in tempore cepit, que iam non moritur[43].

A quocumque verum dicitur, illo donante dicitur, qui est veritas.

Basan confusio dicitur.

Probationes pennae in various hands, fol. 112[rb].

Verses from *Salve mater Salvatoris* (v. U. CHEVALIER, *Repertorium Hymnologicum* 3, Louvain 1897, no. 18051) with plainsong musical notation, square notes on four red lines, late twelfth or early thirteenth century, written in northern France or the British Isles, fol. 112[v 44].

Notes and *probationes pennae* in various hands, including 'Cantuariensis archiepiscopus fuit. Instituit (?) amorem', fol. 113[r]. The verso is blank.

40. H. WEISWEILER, *Das Schrifttum der Schule Anselms von Laon und Wilhelms von Champeaux in deutschen Bibliotheken* (*Beiträge Gesch. Philos. Theol. Mittelalters* 33) Münster 1936, 156, 358, ascribed to Augustine.

41. LOTTIN, *op. cit.* 179, no. 52. The source of *St John's College 111* version is verbally from JEROME, *Com. in Mat.* (CCSL 77, 71).

42. LOTTIN, *Psychologie et morale aux XIIe et XIIIe siècles* 5, Gembloux 1959, 124, no. 171. The sentences 'Omnia non semper ... non queruntur verba sed sensus' occur also as a gloss on the flyleaf of MS *Trinity College, Cambridge, 9* (B.1.10), prefacing the Gloss on St Matthew, twelfth century of unknown provenance. The sentences are written in the top left-hand corner, fol. 1[r], as though the scribe meant to leave enough space for others. On this MS see M. R. JAMES, *The Western MSS of Trinity College, Cambridge* 1, Cambridge 1900, 12-13.

43. A reference to AUGUSTINE, *Ep.* 166 (CSEL 44, 566-567).

44. My colleagues in the Faculty of Music at Oxford kindly gave me this information.

MS *St John's College 111* gives us a fragment of *A*, prefixed to a pre-Anselmian copy of the Gloss on St Matthew, followed by sentences, at least one of which derives from a possibly authentic Anselmian collection; the other sentences correspond to the type of miscellanea found in the early twelfth century genre. The fragment of *A* belongs to the kind of setting which we might expect. The sentences have something in common with those in MS *Laud. misc. 87*, to be described later in this paper.

A's prologue was rewritten, so as to turn it into a prologue to all four gospels, by an anonymous author. It forms part of a miscellany in MS *Oxford Bodl. Laud. misc. 5* (RB 8, 1359). This small manuscript has attracted the attention of some distinguished scholars by reason of its various components. It is written in a small, clear, probably English hand of the early thirteenth century, apart from flyleaves at the beginning and end, covered with notes on a variety of subjects, including some *exempla* and an astrological forecast, written in fourteenth century English hands[45]. The prologue, anonymous and without title '[C]um post ascensionem Domini... premii expletionem' (foll. 109^v-113^v), follows *A* exactly, only interpolating one sentence after *A*'s 'in partibus Achaie et Boetii', up to 'dicens: *In principio erat verbum etc. (A*, fol. 91^{ra-b}). After that the author of the prologue bases his matter and structure on *A*'s, but elaborates and abbreviates, adding more information on the other three evangelists than he found in *A*.

Quotations from *A* also prove that he enjoyed popularity as a commentator. The author of the *Enarrationes*, to be discussed presently, used *A* anonymously as a main source. The monastic commentator Hervey of Bourgdieu (d. *c.* 1150) also used him, as well as the Gloss, which he quoted independently of *A*, again without acknowledgement to *A*, in his homilies on St Matthew[46]. We still have not heard the last of *A*. Weisweiler noted that MS *Arsenal lat. 87* points to continuing interest in him in the thirteenth century. Alexander of Hales offers further proof by quoting 'Anselmus' frequently in his postill on St Matthew. I hope to show in a

45. H. O. COXE, *Quarto Catalogue II, Laudian MSS, reprinted from the edition of 1858-1885 with corrections and additions* by R. W. HUNT, Oxford 1973, 57-58, 543.
46. WEISWEILER, 504-526.

sequel to this paper that his quotations refer to *A* directly. To anticipate on his dates : Alexander's postills on the gospels probably date from his regency at Paris, *c.* 1220 to 1236, when he joined the Franciscan Order[47]. Hugh of St Cher, postillating the whole Bible during his regency at the Dominican *studium* at Paris, quoted Alexander on St Mark[48]. Hugh's regency lasted from 1230 to 1235. If he began at the beginning and worked through from Genesis to the Apocalypse, as seems probable, then he would have reached the gospel of St Mark towards 1235 — say 1233/4 at earliest. That would put Alexander's postills on the gospels into his regency as a secular master, that is before 1236, though he may perhaps have used his lectures again when teaching the friars. In any case his quotations from 'Anselm' fit nicely into the evidence of MS *Arsenal lat. 87.* A compilation ascribed to Anselm, identical or at least similar to the copy in MS *Alençon 26*, was available at Paris in the 1220s or early 1230s. Our Laon compiler, *A*, had a second life in the Paris schools as 'Anselmus'.

Our next offshoot of the Laon school, and the most interesting, is the author of the *Enarrationes in Evangelium S. Matthaei*, printed under the name of Anselm of Laon, PL 162, 1228-1500. Anselm's authorship has long been discredited. Some modern scholars ascribe the *Enarrationes* to Master Geoffrey Babion, with a query. Stegmüller listed the MSS that he knew under Geoffrey's name (no. 2604). I shall call the author *B*, without prejudice to the correctness of the ascription to Geoffrey Babion, which I incline to reject. Some forty surviving MSS appear on the list. To these may be added a copy of the prologue and part of the commentary on the

---

47. I. BRADY, *Sacred Scripture in the Early Franciscan School*, in *La Sacra Scrittura e i Francescani* (Pontificium Athenaeum Antonianum, Rome 1973) 70-73.

48. HUGH OF ST CHER, *Post. in Bibl.* (Paris 1530-1545) ad *Mc.* 1,7 : '*solvere corrigiam calciamenti*. Venit ad nos calciata deitas, dicit auctoritas, ex qua videtur quod deitas incarnata sit, et -ita si filius Dei incarnatus fuit, videtur quod in quantum est homo non sit quid, ergo nec aliquid, quod est contra Alexandrum'. ALEXANDER OF HALES on the same text, MS *Durham A.II.22*, fol. 75[ra] : 'Per calciamentum humanitas unita deitati, sicut pes sub calciamento et calciamentum apparet, sic humanitas. Glosa : Venit ad nos calciata divinitas'. I cannot find the quotation in Alexander's Sentence-Commentary or *Quaestiones disputatae antequam etc.* Therefore Hugh must have been referring to the postill on St Mark.

genealogy in MS *Trinity College, Cambridge, 70* (B.2.27), foll. 1^r-2^r[49], and an excerpt from the commentary going from *Mt.* 5,1-20,22 (PL 162, 1282-1420) in MS *Bodl. Laud. misc. 69*, foll. 1ra-128vb; it comes from the Charterhouse at Mainz and is written in a German hand of the late twelfth century. The excerpt is anonymous[50]. A thirteenth century *florilegium*, now MS *Paris Nat. lat. 3752A*, contains two sets of anonymous excerpts from *B*[51]. MS *Phillipps 438*, listed by Stegmüller, is now MS *Bodl. Lyell 66*. Here we have the complete commentary, anonymous, from Steinfeld, written in a German hand not long after the mid-twelfth century[52]. Most copies are anonymous. Of those which are not, excluding late or obviously false ascriptions, only two are ascribed to Anselm, as against five to Geoffrey Babion[53]. A systematic analysis of date and provenance of the MSS, where they can be recognised, might bring us closer to the author. At present we know more about the content and method of his *Enarrationes* than we do about his career or his name.

B used *A* as his principal source, while also drawing on the Gloss and *V*. He manipulated his texts, sometimes giving them a more scholastic phrasing. He used the term *continuatio* in preference to the earlier *sequitur* to connect his texts. He also introduced theological discussions foreign to his sources. Van den Eynde decided, after studying these theological passages, that *B* must have written towards the mid twelfth century and not earlier, since he was acquainted with problems debated in the milieux of Abelard and his contemporaries : *B* could not have been a pupil of Anselm of Laon 'de première heure'. His ecclesiology corresponds to his theology : he used the title *Vicarius Christi* for the pope on *Mt.* 16,18. 'Vicar of Christ' replaced the earlier 'Vicar of St Peter'

---

49. JAMES, *op. cit.* above n. 42, 86-88, twelfth century of unknown provenance. The scribe broke off in the middle of a sentence, '...moralitatem et allegoriam' (PL 162, 1230C). The verso has a series of piece: from the gospels with short expositions. There follows a copy of the Gloss on St Matthew.

50. O. PÄCHT and J. J. G. ALEXANDER, *Illuminated MSS in the Bodleian Library* 1, Oxford 1966, 9.

51. *Cat. gén.* 6 (see above n. 25) 749-750.

52. A. DE LA MARE, *Catalogue of the Medieval MSS bequeathed to the Bodleian Library by James P. R. Lyell*, Oxford 1971, 202-203.

53. WEISWEILER, 518.

towards the mid twelfth century. St Bernard and others brought it into use; it entered the terminology of the papal chancery under Eugenius III, 1145-1153. *B* makes the point forcefully, explaining that Christ set St Peter as chief of the apostles, and his vicar, in order to avoid schism in the Church :

> Sed ideo, quasi uni Petro eam [potestatem] concessit specialiter, ut ad unitatem nos invitaret. Ideo enim eum principem apostolorum institutit, ut Ecclesia quasi unum principalem vicarium Christi haberet, ad quem diversa Ecclesiae membra recurrerent, si forte inter se dissentirent, quoniam si diversa essent capita in Ecclesia, unitatis vinculum rumperetur per diversa schismata (PL 162, 1396).

It would be exceptional to find so clear a statement before the 1130s[54].

An anonymous copy of *B* in MS *Bodl. Laud. misc. 87* gives us a rough *terminus ante quem* on palaeographical grounds (listed RB no. 2604). The MS, 26 × 17 cm., came from the Charterhouse of Mainz[55]. It is written in German hands which could not be later than *c.* 1150, even allowing for a conservative German scriptorium. The commentary, fol. 1[r], is headed : 'Glose super Matheum, Dominus et redemptor noster... 'fol. 56[va]' ... euntem in celum'. The text is underlined in ink, but there is no contemporary capitulation. A thirteenth century hand has marked modern chapter numbers in the top and side margins. A hand contemporary with that of the text has noted the Sundays, weekdays and feast days and readings for the common of the saints in the margins, showing that the commentary was equipped for use in preaching or meditation. The scribe left occasional gaps where he could not read his exemplar; these have to be filled in from the printed edition. Otherwise the text is comfortingly close to the latter and sometimes helpful for emendation. The contents following *B* are (1) A homily headed 'In dedicatione secundum Lucam : In illo tempore *ingressus est Iesus... et ipse dives et reliqua* [*Lc.* 19,1-2]. Quotiescumque,

---

54. M. MACCARRONE, *Vicarius Christi. Storia del titolo papale*, Rome 1952, 92-100. The author quotes *B* as a strikingly early example, since the study by Van den Eynde on *B*'s dating had not yet appeared when he published his book.

55. COXE, *op. cit.* above n. 45, 96. This MS was bound together with another from Eberbach, foll. 86-240. These leaves need not concern us. On the initial see PÄCHT and ALEXANDER (above, n. 50) 5.

fratres karissimi... transmigratione perveniret. Per Dominum nostrum etc.' (fol. 57ra). I have not identified this homily. The incipit corresponds to Pseudo-Augustine (PL 39, 2166); but the development is quite different[56]. (2) Sentences from the Fathers: 'Ieronimus. Oratio est suavis... dubium habes eventu' (fol. 57^{ra-vb}). (3) The commentary on St Matthew by *V*, 'Nomen libri evangeli evangelium... ad beatitudinem pervenitur' (foll. 58ra-65rb). Here the commentary covers the text of St Matthew up to the end of the Lord's Prayer, as in the copy found by Weisweiler in a MS from Zwiefalten, now at Stuttgart, of the twelfth century, which also contains a copy of *B*[57]. (4) Short sentences: 'Gregorius: Qui perfecta desiderat cura (*sic*) necesse est ut non solum ad operationis latitudinem, sed etiam ad contemplationis culmina se extendat... Utiliter palee cum granis nutriuntur, ne nomen Domini in granorum paucitate coartetur' (fol. 65rb). (5) An introduction or prologue to the four gospels: 'Cum multi scripsisse evangelia legantur, soli quatuor evangeliste... conglorificationem, si non recusemus compassionem'. An isolated sentence follows: 'A quocumque verum dicitur illo donante dicitur qui est veritas' (see MS *St John's College 111*, fol. 112ra). The last five lines of the column are blank (fol. 65va). The first lines of the prologue *Cum multi* appear as a gloss to St Jerome's prologue in MS *St John's College 111*. I have not identified the source. (6) A mystical interpretation of Christ's genealogy: 'Tres thesseresce decades (*sic*) in generatione Christi mistice insinuant fidem sancte trinitatis... Maria maris stella, que tenebris huius amari et undulosi mundi addidit lucem' (foll. 65vb-66ra). (7) Sentences relating to the gospels, set out in no discernible order: (i) 'Sugillo a sugo ...'. (ii) 'Secularis scientia'. (iii) 'Tres mortuos... caput eorum'. These three correspond to sentences in MS *St John's College 111*, fol. 112ra, as does a later sentence: 'Nomen Gehenne... designantur'. The other sentences are peculiar to MS *Laud. misc. 87* and include some *quaestiones* on baptism etc.: 'Inferior natura... si convertantur' (foll. 65ra-66rb). (8) A prologue (?) to a gospel commentary on the four evangelists: 'Quoniam constat quatuor libros recte conscriptos gestorum et

---

56. Dr J. B. SCHNEYER kindly pointed the Pseudo-Augustine incipit out to me and informed me that the Laudian homily was not in his repertoire.

57. WEISWEILER, 364.

dictorum Domini, sciendum quis eorum ordo sit Evangeliorum ordo colligitur magis re quam tempore ... ipse aperte voce ostendere Dominum, dicens : *In principio erat verbum etc.*' (fol. 67[rb]). The verso of fol. 67 is blank.

MS *Laud. misc. 87* therefore gives us a copy of *B* written before *c.* 1150, plus part of *V* (no. 3) plus excerpts (?) from commentaries on the gospels (nos. 5-8). It represents an effort to assemble material for the study of all four gospels, and of St Matthew's in particular.

B's importance lies in the fact that he acted as a bridge between post-Laon teaching and lectures on St Matthew in the Paris schools. Peter Comestor and Peter the Chanter both quote him, sometimes by the name of Master Geoffrey Babion and more often anonymously. Just as *B* must be checked from *A* to decide whether a comment is personal or not, so Comestor must be checked from *B*. Comestor refers to *B* as Master Geoffrey Babion, 'whose glosses are solemn and authentic', and quotes him by name on several other passages. Van den Eynde pointed to unacknowledged borrowings too[58]. He did not pursue *B*'s influence as far as Peter the Chanter on *Unum ex quatuor*. Comparison of the three texts shows that Comestor and the Chanter quoted *B* independently, though the Chanter took something also *via* Comestor, whose lectures he knew. The following tables will illustrate their relationship. The Chanter quotes 'Babion' freely, summarising opinions and generally putting them in his own words. Text I shows him quoting 'Babion' without any parallel in Comestor. In II Comestor follows *B* without naming his source, whereas the Chanter does so. In III all rely on the Gloss; but the Chanter quotes 'Babion's' interpretation of it. In IV both Comestor and the Chanter follow *B*. The Chanter names him and quotes him independently of Comestor, who again does not name him. Comestor's quotations from 'Babion' have been printed several times and need not be included here (see Van den Eynde, 67).

---

58. *Op. cit.* (above n. 26), 67-69.

I

Mt. 5,24 : *...et vade prius reconciliari fratri tuo, et tunc veniens offeres munus tuum.*

B

PL 162, 1296 :

Et vade, si praesens est et humiliare ei, et fac quod ad te attinet. Si autem absens est, promitte et habeas bonam voluntatem, et quam citius invenies, humiliabis te illi et bene poeniteas in corde tuo, et tunc revertere ad oblationem tuam.

CHANTER

Merton College 212, fol. 32^{rb-va} :

Vade pedibus, si presens est frater, et fac quod te attinet ut ei reconciliaris... Si vero absens, *vade*, non pedibus, sed animo et gressibus fidei et caritatis. Gal. Gabion (*sic*): Licet, si vero absens, expectare quousque ipsum invenimus.

II

Mt. 5,31 : *Dictum est autem: Quicumque dimiserit uxorem suam, det ei libellum repudii.*

B

1298 :

Moyses propter duritiam cordis Iudaeorum permisit, non praecepit, dimittere uxores si displicerent, quia essent litigiosae vel foedae, vel propter multas alias causas, potius quam eas interficere. Levius enim erat dimittere quam interficere, et tunc qui dimittebant, peccabant, nec salvabant(ur).

COMESTOR

Laud. misc. 291, fol. 31va :

Non enim precepit iudeis Moyses dimittere uxores, dato libello repudii, sed propter eorum duritiam permisit, timens ne forte uxores que displicerent eis occiderent, si eas inviti haberent, et sic pro vitando homicidio sustinuit divortium.

CHANTER

M, fol. 33va :

Secundum magistrum Gal. Babium omnia sic : dimissis uxoribus et aliis ductis, adulteri erant.

III

Mt. 5,44 : *et orate pro persequentibus et calumniantibus vos...* Gloss : AUGUSTINUS : Non ait pro hoc fratribus in quibus sunt aliquando peccata persecutione inimicorum graviora, unde cum Iohannes dixisset : Si quis *scit fratrem suum peccare peccatum non ad mortem, petat, et dabitur ei vita*, subdit : *Est* autem *peccatum ad mortem, non pro illo dico ut roget quis* (*I. Ioan.* 5,16), ubi aperte ostenditur quosdam fratres esse pro quibus orare non iubemur.

1302-3 :

Iterum cum praecipiat orare pro inimicis, vide-

fol. 34vb :

Nota quod Dominus hic precipit orare pro perse-

fol. 35va :

Magister G. Bab. : Sic sancti pro hiis quos sciunt

tur Ioannes contrarium dicere : *Si quis … roget quis*, ubi aperte ostenditur quosdam fratres esse, pro quibus orare non licet … Sed non omnes cognoscunt eum nisi spirituales viri, ut Ioannes, et ideo non praecipitur nisi ei qui scit non orare pro eo …

quentibus. Iohannes in epistola canonica non audet dicere ut oretur pro omnibus fratribus, nedum pro inimicis. Hec enim non audet dicere …

per revelationem esse reprobos non orant, consentientes divine iustitie ; pro aliis tamen, etsi inimicis, orandum esse docuit.

IV

Mt. 6,34 : *Nolite ergo solliciti esse in crastinum …*

1313 :
Prohibuit sollicitudinem praesentium rerum temporalium, modo prohibet sollicitudinem ex vitio hominum provenientem, non ex rebus. Sed si quis abbas providens sibi et monachis suis colligeret annonam ad annum praesentem sufficientem hoc esset providentia, non sollicitudo vana. Sed si esset timens vel desperans de bonitate Dei, et ideo ad usum reliquorum annorum velit eam reservare, haec esset vana sollicitudo, et hoc esset cogitare de crastino. Praesentem enim diem vocat, scilicet hoc tempus, quod providentia nostra debet observare. Non metimus in anno nisi semel, et ideo quantum ad messes unus annus est quasi praesens tempus.

fol. 39vb :
sollicitudinem vitiosam prohibuit Dominus.
fol. 40rb :
Vide quia non prohibet providentiam in crastinum, id est in annum. Annus enim est crastinum nostrum, in quo licite possumus nobis providere necessaria, quia semel in anno metimus et vindemiamus. Si autem providentia ultra annum extenditur, iam in vitiosam sollicitudinem vertitur, et talis sollicitudo prohibetur a Domino. Conceditur ergo nobis a Domino providentia de presentibus, ut nomine presentis intelligamus annum, sed prohibet de futuris, id est ultra annum sollicitudinem protendi.

fol. 39vb :
G. Bab. : supra prohibuit sollicitudinem de presentibus, que scilicet sunt unius anni. Semel in anno metimus, serimus et colligimus, unde et que presentia dicuntur. Hic autem prohibet Dominus sollicitudinem de futuris. Si ergo providentia tua ultra annum extenditur vel vertitur, ut abbas qui usque ad tertium annum reservaverit annonam.

The identification of *B* with Babion by Comestor and the Chanter is positive; but can we trust them? To start from what we know of Babion : the one certainly documented fact is that he taught at the cathedral school of Angers 1103-*c.* 1110. The nickname 'stammerer' came from his speech. Dom J. P. Bonnes has built up an ingenious account of his subsequent career from scanty data[59]. He identifies Babion with Geoffrey du Loroux, archbishop of Bordeaux from his election in 1136 to his death in 1158. In the intervening period Geoffrey retired from teaching to go into a religious retreat of some kind. St Bernard called him by letter to leave his quiet in order to exert his influence in favour of Innocent II against Anacletus II in the papal schism of 1130. Perhaps his efforts had some bearing on his election as archbishop. M. Marcel Pacaut lists him as a canon regular in his account of the French bishops holding office under Louis VII[60]. Babion left a large number of sermons, which had a vast circulation; some were given by a prelate in synod[61]. The identification of Babion with Geoffrey du Loroux seems plausible enough; but it raises difficulties. Comestor showed himself to have been unaware of Babion's archiepiscopal rank. True, bishops were often quoted as 'Master' without their title[62]. On the other hand, one would have expected Comestor to add 'postea archiepiscopus' when quoting an author who lived until 1158, only a year before Comestor succeeded to the Lombard's chair at Paris. If we accept the identification, then we have to place *B*'s *Enarrationes,* following Van den Eynde's dating, in the period when he was archbishop and would hardly have had the leisure to write a long commentary. Van den Eynde queried the ascription of the *Enarrationes* to Babion on other grounds. One objection was that *B* referred to himself as a religious. Discussing the question of scandal on *Mt.* 5,29, he asks whether a religious is bound to obey a superior whose command might lead him into temptation :

59. *Un des plus grands prédicateurs du XII*^e *siècle, Geoffroy du Loroux, dit Geoffroy Babion,* in *Revue bénédictine* 51 (1945-6) 190-199.

60. *Louis VII et les élections épiscopales dans le royaume de France,* Paris 1957, 152; see also on the archbishop's activities 92, 109.

61. BONNES, 205-209.

62. VAN DEN EYNDE, 80-81.

> Vel si *abbas meus* me ad contraria opera mitteret, et ibi non possum me salvare, excusare me debeo. Si autem saepius me coegerit, nec aliter evadere possem, eum potius aufugere debeo (PL 162, 1298).

Comestor, following the same line of thought, changed the wording to : 'Roga abbatem *tuum*' (*L*, fol. 31rb). In a comment just above, *B* confirms Van den Eynde's view that he counted himself as a religious. *We* ought to undertake active work of some kind, if the leisure of contemplation tempts us to sin, as it does many monks :

> Si ergo illa scandalizat *nos* in desidiam mittendo, ut plures monachos facit, deseramus eam, et ad activam transeamus, et aliquem laborem faciamus, ut salvemur in ea, potius quam ibi lugendo pereamus (PL 162, 1297).

B found the gist of this comment in the Gloss (ad *Mt.* 5,29); but he applies it to himself in a personal way. Again, he takes the command to turn the other cheek (*Mt.* 5,39) as applying to an insulted Christian and/or religious :

> Si quis improperat tibi quod Christianus es *vel religiosus*... et vocat te ideo hypocritam, *quia religiosus es* (1301).

Even if Archbishop Geoffrey had worn a religious habit, as seems likely, he would hardly have identified himself with a religious, acting under obedience to his abbot, while he held office as prelate. This brings us back to *B*'s date : a man teaching as *scholasticus* in the first decade of the twelfth century could not have put forward such advanced theological and ecclesiological opinions as we find in *B*.

Van den Eynde raised another objection : he compared Babion's sermons on texts from St Matthew with the *Enarrationes* on the same texts, but could find no similarity other than what might be expected in two writers of the twelfth century, drawing on a common stock of ideas and sources. No argument can be deduced from style, since one was recording his sermons, the other writing a commentary[63]. But there is a serious difference in ecclesiology. We have seen that *B* called the pope 'Christ's Vicar'. One of Babion's sermons, preached during the Anacletan schism (1130-

---

63. *Ibid.* 65-66; WEISWEILER, 517. On Babion's sermons see BONNES, above n. 59, 175-190, 200-211, with a correction by G. CONSTABLE, *The Letters of Peter the Venerable* 2, Cambridge (Mass.) 1967, 184.

1138), refers to a division in the Church and urges the faithful to show reverence and obedience to the pope. Here we have an exposition of the same text, *Mt.* 16,18, where the pope is called 'Vicar of St Peter'. The doctrine is the same, but the papal title differs :

> Huius igitur unitatis observatione, fratres charissimi, voluit Dominus super unum aedificare Ecclesiam suam; super illum scilicet de quo ait *Tu es Petrus etc.* Petrus ergo est fundamentum cui unitur Ecclesia; fide enim illius omnia membra adhaerent... Quia, igitur, fratres, magister noster est Petrus, dominus noster est vicarius eius, ideo nos oportet... dominum nostrum papam visitare (PL 171, 795).

The sermon belongs to an earlier phase than the commentary in its attitude to the see of St Peter. Of course it might be argued that Babion's view developed; so that we could still identify him with *B*. Another argument against the identification is that Comestor and the Chanter may have worked on a copy of the *Enarrationes* wrongly ascribed to Babion and were misled by it into making a false ascription.

All in all, I incline to think that Van den Eynde was too hesitant in hesitating to accept the identification. Whether we follow Dom Bonnes in identifying Babion with Geoffrey du Loroux or not, we still cannot bring the *scholasticus* of Angers down into the period *c.* 1140. It seems wiser to leave *B* anonymous. We may guess that he studied and perhaps taught in some school or schools in northern France, before entering a religious house where he wrote his *Enarrationes*, using material which he had collected in the schools. His *Enarrationes* came to be regarded as 'solemn and authentic', to quote Comestor, under Geoffrey Babion's name. The reason was that they fulfilled a *desideratum*. The compilations deriving from Laon, *V*, the Gloss and *A*, were presented by *B* in a more scholastic form and equipped with theological *quaestiones*. Indeed, to anticipate a later study, I find that *B*'s originality comes out even more strongly than has been supposed, if one compares him with the three compilers just mentioned.

We have described a circle, beginning at Laon and ending at Paris, where Peter Lombard lectured on St Luke at least, and his pupil Comestor lectured on all four gospels, followed by the Chanter who lectured on a conflated text of the gospels. All three scholars used the Gloss. The *A* compilation and *B*'s *Enarrationes* plus some excerpts from *V*, linked them to Laon indirectly as well as directly. If Anselm of Laon left a commentary on St Matthew, it has disappeared and cannot be identified with our existing material[64]. Nevertheless, the Laon *équipe*, centred on the master, put the gospels 'on the map' of the school curriculum. They never attracted a *Magna glosatura*; but masters lectured on them more frequently.

One other chain connects Comestor and the Chanter to Laon and bears its own witness to renewed interest in the gospels. Zachary of Besançon, master of the cathedral school at Besançon, 1131-1134, and a canon of the Praemonstratensian priory of St Martin at Laon about 1157, wrote a commentary on a con-flated text of the gospels based on Tatian's *Diatesseron, In unum ex quatuor et expositio desuper continua exactissime diligentia edita* or *Unum ex quatuor seu concordia et desuper expositio continua*[65]. Van den Eynde dated it *c.* 1140-1145 on grounds of content. It survives in some hundred MSS, mainly of the thirteenth century, a witness to its continuing popularity. Zachary set out to make a compilation from the Fathers; but he thought that a 'continuous exposition' ought to include doctrinal teaching; hence he drew on such theological manuals as he had to hand, dipping into the collection known as *Sententiae Anselmi*, and making more use of the Victorine *Summa sententiarum* and the Abelardian *Sen-*

---

64. WEISWEILER, 534-535. Another unlikely candidate for Anselmian authorship, which remains to be investigated, is the commentary on St Matthew listed RB 1349 and 8, 1349. G. MEYER and M. BURCKHARDT compare the text of MS *Bâle B.VI.17a* with *B*; see *Die mittelalterlichen Handschriften des Universitätsbibliothek Basel* 1, Bâle 1960, 618-20. The Bâle commentary is longer than *B* and has variants. Since it contains the same theological matter as *B*, it must represent an expansion of *B*, and therefore must be post-Anselmian. The Bâle copy is dated *c.* 1200, the other, in MS *Paris Bibl. nat. lat. 2491*, late twelfth century; see *Cat. gén.* 2, *op. cit.* above n. 25, 487.

65. On his life and writings see O. SCHMID, *Zacharias Chrysopolitanus und sein Kommentar zur Evangelienharmonie,* in *Theologische Quartalschrift* 68 (1886) 531-547, 69 (1887) 231-275; D. VAN DEN EYNDE, *Les "Magistri" du Commentaire "Unum ex quatuor" de Zacharias Chrysopolitanus,* in *Antonianum* 23 (1948) 3-32, 181-220; B. DE VRÉGILLE, *Note sur la vie et l'œuvre de Zacharie de Besançon,* in *Analecta Praemonstratensia* 41 (1965) 292-309; RB no. 5699, 1-2, 8400. The commentary is printed in PL 186, 11-619.

tentiae Hermanni. A desire for orthodoxy balanced his marked leaning towards Abelard; he revised his book after Abelard's condemnation at the Council of Sens, 1140. For our present purpose his significance lies in his use of the Gloss, quoted anonymously[66], and his influence on Comestor and the Chanter. O. Schmid noted that Comestor referred to Zachary anonymously in his *School History*, to illustrate the diversity of opinions on chronological order in the gospels:

> Quidam enim scribentes unum ex quatuor, imitantes Ammonium Alexandrinum, Eusebium Caesarensem, Theophilum, qui septimus a Petro sedit Antiochiae, qui (*sic*) dicunt Dominum post ieiunium aperte praedicasse... Communior autem et veracior opinio est, Dominum post illud miraculum discipulos vocasse occulte,... et hunc ordinem prosequemur, sine alterius ordinis praeiudicio (PL 198, 1558).

This refers to Zachary's chronological sequence (PL 186, 41). Comestor both uses Zachary's book and prefers the more common opinion on gospel chronology to his[67]. The same kind of use appears in Comestor's prologues to the gospels, which were not accessible to Schmid, being unprinted and outside the scope of his enquiry. Zachary discussed the prefiguration of the four evangelists by the animals in Ezechiel's vision. Jerome saw the man as Matthew, the lion as Mark, the bull as Luke and the eagle as John. Zachary quoted Sedulius in support of Jerome. Iuvencus, however, made the eagle signify Mark and the lion John. Zachary quoted the relevant verses from Sedulius and Iuvencus in full. For himself, he preferred Augustine's rather different view: lion Matthew, man Mark, bull Luke, eagle John[68]. Comestor discussed the same

---

66. VAN DEN EYNDE, see above n. 65, 201, 204-205.

67. Comestor may have had Zachary in mind when he referred to the use of chapters: 'Expositores autem qui concordant evangelistas distinguunt eos per capitula; nos autem de huiusmodi distinctionibus non facimus mentionem' (*B*, fol. 4[va]).

68. PL 186, 14-15: 'De figuris evangelistarum non adversas, sed diversas Patrum sententias ponemus, ut lector eligat quod sibi potissimum videbitur... Sedulius: Hoc Mathaeus agens... astra Ioannes. Aliter Iuvencus: Mathaeus instituit... mysteria vitae. Augustinus vero... Unde mihi videtur probabilius attendisse illos qui leonem in Mathaeo, hominem in Marco, intellexerunt, vitulum vero in Luca, aquilam in Ioanne, quam qui hominem Mathaeo, aquilam Marco, leonem Ioanni tribuerunt'. See SEDULIUS, *Paschal. Carmin.* i, lines 355-358 (CSEL 10, 41-42); IUVENCUS, *Evangeliorum liber quatuor* (CSEL 24, xlvi).

problem. He betrays his debt to Zachary by quoting a few verses only from Sedulius and Iuvencus. Comestor did not quote verses as freely as Zachary did; his abridgement of his source, cutting down the full quotations to a few verses, proves that he had Zachary before him. Comestor differed from Zachary in preferring Jerome and Sedulius as the 'more certain' opinion on the correspondence between animals and evangelists[69]. I have not noted dependence on Zachary elsewhere, apart from similarities drawn from a common stock of material.

Peter the Chanter in his own *Unum ex quatuor* quoted Comestor anonymously on Zachary's chronological sequence, adding a few details; but he too preferred the sequence of the *School History* to Zachary's (MS *Oxford Merton College 212*, fol. 25[ra]). The Chanter may have had Zachary's book before him when he quoted Comestor's disagreement with it. He never mentions Zachary by name, though a careful collation might disclose some borrowings. The link between them is that Zachary drew on the Laon Gloss and was known to Comestor, while the Chanter used both the Gloss and Comestor, even if he did not use Zachary directly.

A recently discovered commentary on a gospel harmony may be mentioned, though not included in this study[70]. It survives in one MS, perhaps autograph, and ends unfinished. The author, Abbot Wazelin II of St Laurence of Liège, had studied under Rupert of

69. *L*, fol. 1va: 'Notandum autem quod premissa opinio de prefiguratione quattuor evangelistarum per figuras quattuor animalium Ieronimi est, cui concordat Sedulius, dicens: Hoc Matheus agens hominem generaliter implet etc. Iuvencus quoque de Matheo et Luca Ieronimo consonant, sed de Marco et Iohanne dissonat, dicens Marcum per aquilam designari, Iohannem per leonem sic. Marcus amat terras inter celumque volare, Iohannes fremit ore leo similis rugienti'. Comestor quotes the same verses in his prologues to St Mark and St John and expands his statement in his prologue to St Luke, *D*, fol. 81[rb]: 'Hinc est quod de prefiguratione aliorum trium varie (*sic*) auctores dissentiunt; in hoc tamen omnes conveniunt quod Lucas prefiguratus est per vitulum, tam in Ezechielis visione, quam in Iohannis revelatione. De aliis vero tribus auctores dissentiunt; nam Ieronimus dicit quod per hominem Matheus, per leonem Marcus, per vitulum Lucas, per aquilam Iohannes exprimitur, cui sententia attestatur ille versificator egregius dicens: Matheus agens hominem generaliter implet. Legite, inquid, Iuvencum, qui similiter fuit versificator egregius et invenietis quod per aquilam prefiguratus est Marcus, per leonem Iohannes; ait enim: Marcus amat... rugienti'.

70. H. SILVESTRE, *Le "De concordia et expositione quatuor evangeliorum" inédit de Wazelin II abbé de Saint-Laurent à Liège (c. 1150–c. 1157)*, in *Revue bénédictine* 63 (1953) 310-325.

Deutz, and died probably in 1157. He was a compiler, drawing on his master Rupert's works as well as on the usual patristic sources, though there are a few touches of originality. Wazelin did not use Zachary's commentary, nor is he recorded to have used the Gloss. His commentary shows a desire to study the gospels in the cloister at the same time as masters were beginning to lecture on them in the schools.

Turning back to the schools, we find that early gospel commentaries are fewer in number and scrappier in form than those on the Psalter and Pauline Epistles. The abbreviation of Paschasius Radbertus, *V*, survives possibly complete in one MS, hiding under the name of the non-existent Robert of Worcester (RB 7496); otherwise we have nothing but fragments. *A* survives complete in one copy only. We have to wait for *B* and Zachary of Besançon to find a complete commentary surviving in complete form and in large numbers of copies. Nevertheless the study of a few MSS, selected by chance, *St John's College 111* and *Laud. misc. 87*, confirms the findings of Lottin, Van den Eynde and Weisweiler; many MSS containing copies of the Gloss in its earlier and later forms include prologues and sentences, some relating to the gospels. Such miscellanea surely stem from teaching or aids to teaching. They support the evidence for the practice of lecturing on the gospels which began at Laon and continued at Paris.

The gospels fit into the pattern of a revived interest in separate books of the Bible. Hugh of St Victor stressed both the need to study all biblical books and the importance of establishing their literal historical sense before passing to a spiritual interpretation. Hugh and his pupil Andrew influenced Comestor to write his *School History*, which owed much to Andrew on the Old Testament[71]. Although we have no consecutive commentary on the gospels from St Victor, Hugh's teaching certainly made one seem to be wished for. These are external reasons for the increase in lectures on the gospels. We can compare modern academic slogans, familiar to all university teachers: widen the syllabus; provide

---

71. B. SMALLEY, *The School of Andrew of St Victor*, in *Rech. Théol. anc. méd.* 11 (1939) 146-151; *The Study of the Bible in the Middle Ages* (3rd ed.), Oxford 1983,

more options. But we must go deeper. If the gospels were lectured on more often, they also provoked more thought.

The Gregorian reform movement affected the schools. It aimed at purifying the Church in order that a better clergy might bring the laity to lead a more Christian life. The reformers succeeded in part; but they posed a question: how far did the Church, even after reform, obey Christ's precepts? Heretics answered: 'not at all'. Many seceded to form sects of their own, disgusted with the Church as a wealthy and litigious institution. A master lecturing on the gospels had to face the scandal. He had to justify contemporary practice, as sanctioned by Gregorian reform, though he would preach against abuses not so sanctioned. Individual conscience came into play in an age of increasing self awareness[72]. Could one really keep the command to love one's personal enemies and turn the other cheek? 'Nichil mirabilius in omnibus mandatis quam diligere inimicos et reddere bona pro malis', runs a sentence in the miscellany of MS *Laud. misc. 87*, fol. 65[rb]. Gerald of Wales was franker than most in stating his inability to obey the command, a defect which his career and writings bear out only too well:

> Utinam autem vindictam omnino nullam appeteremus, sed equanimiter omnia sustinere possemus, adeo ut in una maxilla percussi et alteram incontinenter preberemus, nulli malum pro malo reddentes...! Hanc autem doctrinam apostolicam sepius quidem audivimus, sed ad eius revera perfectionem nondum pervenire valuimus...; qui nostra tollit pro inimico reputantes et inimicos nostros... exosos habemus[73].

Gerald's characteristic outburst applied to his own conscience; he could not forgive his persecutors. But was it sinful to stand up for one's rights without personal malice, especially when the rights in question belonged to a church, and hence to its patron saints?

These and similar questions were debated in many contexts. Gospel commentaries made a natural focus for discussion. In my next chapter I shall describe the masters' ways of dealing with them.

---

72. COLIN MORRIS, *The Discovery of the Individual 1050-1200*, London 1972, gives a good background.

73. GIRALDUS CAMBRENSIS, *Speculum Duorum or A Mirror of Two Men*, ed. Y. LEFÈVRE and R. B. C. HUYGENS, English transl. by B. DAWSON, Cardiff 1974, 260. This letter was written about 1213; see xlvii. On the writer see M. RICHTER, *Giraldus Cambrensis. The Growth of the Welsh Nation*, Aberystwyth 1972.

ADDITIONAL NOTES

p.3, n.11: On the Laon origins of the Gloss see now R. Wielockx, 'Autour de la *Glossa Ordinaria*'. *Rech. Théol. anc. méd* 49 (1982) 222-228, and my forthcoming article "Glossa Ordinaria", *Theologische Realenzyklopädie*.

p.15, n.34: MS Alençon 26 was written by the historian Orderic Vitalis, who entered the Norman monastery of Saint-Évroul as a child from England in 1085 and remained there until his death at an unknown date; he finished his *Historia Ecclesiastica* in 1141 in his sixty-seventh year. He worked as a scribe for the abbey library as well as writing his *Historia*: see *The Ecclesiastical History of Orderic Vitalis* , ed. with English translation by Marjorie Chibnall 1 (Oxford, 1980) 1-23; 28; 202. Mrs Chibnall kindly pointed this out to me. She tells me that the whole MS, not only part, is now thought to be in Orderic's hand.

p.16, n.35: Add D.F. Callahan, 'The sermons of Adémar of Chabannes and the Cult of St. Martial of Limoges', *Revue Bénédictine* 86 (1976) 251-295.

p. 20, n.48: It now seems that Hugh of St Cher did not use Alexander's postills;　see　below, chapter 4, pp. 122-4.

p. 23, n.57a: For other anonymous copies of the prologue *Cum multi* see RB Suppl. 10, 190.

2

Peter Comestor on the Gospels
and his Sources

This chapter will describe Peter Comestor as a pioneer of lecturing on the gospels at Paris. It follows on 'Some Gospel Commentaries of the Early Twelfth Century'[1], where I dealt with commentaries emanating from the school at Laon. The nature of the subject forced me to dwell on questions of authorship and of relations between commentaries. Content and doctrine had to wait their turn. Comestor imposes himself as the starting point in studying them, since he was the first Paris master whose lectures on the gospels have come down to us. An account of his techniques as a lecturer and of his sources will provide a framework for his doctrine. I shall focus on his attitudes to the precepts of the Sermon on the Mount, to apostolic poverty and to ecclesiology.

On all counts it is necessary to begin with a sketch of patristic teaching on the gospels as it passed down to Comestor in the originals and through intermediaries such as the Gloss. What techniques of exegesis and what doctrine on gospel texts did he inherit from his predecessors?

I

The patristic technique of exegesis left a zone of uncertainty in the demarcation of the literal and spiritual senses. The 'letter' represented a veil, shell or rind, hiding the sweetness of the spiritual senses within[2]. This concept enabled the Old Testament to be read in the light of the New; but it was transferred to the New Testament also. Bede offers a striking example in his comment on the story

---

1. See above, chapter 1, pp. 1-35, where data on Comestor's career will be found.

2. H. J. SPITZ, *Die Metaphorik der geistigens Schriftsinns* (*Münstersche Mittelalter-Schriften* 12) 1972.

of Christ's healing of the sufferer whose friends *went up upon the roof and let him down through the tiles with his bed into the midst before Jesus* (*Lc.* 5, 19). Bede likens *the tiles of the roof* to the 'despicable veil of the letter': the divine grace of the spiritual sense can be uncovered if a doctor be at hand to disclose it[3]. He wrote of "the letter" of this miracle story as 'despicable'! This points to a traditional ambivalence. Veneration for the literal truth of the gospels, which Bede felt deeply, competed with a search for hidden meanings.

The gospels put special difficulties in the way of an exegete wishing to expound in the literal sense. Jesus spoke and acted in parables; the evangelists used metaphorical language; the gospels, St John's in particular, were meant to be read on two levels. St John invested his narratives of the wedding feast at Cana and Christ's talk with the Samaritan woman at the well with a spiritual significance. St Augustine's commentary on the fourth gospel accords with current New Testament scholarship in taking account of the two levels principle. Both Augustine and Jerome had a good understanding of metaphor, parable and figure as part of the literal sense; but they did not always observe the distinction in practice, to the confusion of their successors. Sometimes they would offer a literal interpretation, explaining the literal sense of their text and then passing explicitly from a literal to a spiritual interpretation *iuxta leges allegoriae* or *tropologiae*. Sometimes they prefaced their spiritual interpretation by writing that the literal sense was clear or self-evident. Sometimes, on the other hand, they omitted a literal interpretation without warning and passed straight to a spiritual. Augustine's *Quaestiones evangeliorum* and *Quaestiones XVII in Matthaeum* display a strange mixture. He answers· some of the questions raised by considering the literal sense and others by giving a spiritual interpretation only[4].

Another notion transferred from Old Testament exegesis was

---

3. CCSL 120, 120: 'Et bene domus Iesu tegulis contecta describitur, quia sub contemptibili litterarum uelamine, si adsit qui reserit doctor, diuina spiritalis gratiae uirtus inuenietur'.

4. PL 35, 1321-1376.

'l'absurdité signe de l'allégorie'[5]. Certain Old Testament precepts struck commentators as impossible to observe, contradictory, trivial or ridiculous. Such precepts pointed to a spiritual interpretation to *replace* the literal: God set a puzzle to confound the Jews and to stimulate Christian readers. Gospel texts could be forced into the same pattern, as we see from the history of *Mt.* 21, 12-13 in exegesis. Jesus cast out buyers and sellers from *the temple of God and overthrew the tables of the money changers and the chairs of them that sold doves*. Jerome explained the text as referring to punishment in store for those who presumed to sell the gifts of the Holy Spirit, symbolised by the doves, in exchange for money; but he went on to argue that the overthrowing of the dove-sellers' *chairs* was absurd, if taken in its 'simple sense': the doves were in cages, not in chairs, nor were chairs fitting for dove-sellers, since *cathedra* denotes the honourable seat of a doctor. The 'absurdity' of the text in its literal meaning sends us to the spiritual: a doctor's teaching comes to nothing if money is involved[6]. The rebuke to self-seeking doctors was too good to miss, even at the price of a distorted interpretation. Raban Maur quoted Jerome verbally here[7]. His quotation passed into the Gloss[8]. Rupert of Deutz jumped into the trap, giving sharper edge to the 'absurdity sign of allegory' notion; so did Zachary of Besançon[9]. Christian

5. J. PÉPIN, *A propos de l'histoire de l'exégèse allégorique*, in *Studia Patristica* 1 (1957) 394-413; B. SMALLEY, *Ralph of Flaix on Leviticus*, in *Rech. Théol. anc. méd.* 35 (1968) 35-82.

6. CCSL 77, 188: 'Iuxta simplicem intelligentiam columbae non erant in cathedris, sed in cuneis, nisi forte columbarum institores sedebant in cathedris, quod penitus absurdum est, quia in cathedris magistrorum maius dignitas indicatur, quae ad nihilum redigitur cum mixta fuerit lucris'.

See also ST GREGORY, *Hom. in Evang.* (PL 76, 1091-1092, 1145).

7. PL 107, 1041-1042.

8. I quote the Gloss from the Lyons 1589 edition, printed with the postills of Nicholas of Lyre and other additions. My quotations will be *ad loc.* unless otherwise stated.

'*Et cathedras.* Quae magistrorum sunt, id est sacerdotium eorum [Christus] destruit, qui de impositione manus, per quam Spiritus sanctus datur, pretium accipiunt. Hinc est quod haeresis Simonis damnatur. Ad litteram autem absurdum est dicere institores columbarum in cathedris sedere'.

9. On *Ioan.* 2, 16 (CCSL, *Contin. med.* 9) 126: 'Cathedras quoque uendentium columbas iuxta Matthaeum euertit, quod iuxta simplicem intelligentiam accipere absurdum est. Non enim columbae in cathedris erant, sed in caueis, nec colum-

of Stavelot, commenting on St Matthew in the mid ninth century, showed unusual concern to distinguish between the senses. He defended 'the letter' against the charge of 'absurdity' by explaining that the dove-sellers' function in the temple was important enough to entitle them to sit in chairs. The spiritual sense, which he distinguished from the literal, was that the doves signified the Holy Spirit, not to be put up for sale[10]. Christian's sane commentary was too little known to displace Jerome's and its derivatives on this gospel text.

The word *cathedra* misled commentators because it denoted magisterial dignity. Other words acquired 'guilt by association', confusing the matter further. Old Testament writers normally regarded sickness as a divine punishment for sin, to be cured by repentance, perhaps through the medium of a holy man. Later the blame for sickness was laid on demons, which a holy man could exorcise. Healing, exorcism and forgiveness of sins belonged to the same process[11]. The woman healed by Jesus had spent all her money on medical cures in vain (*Mc.* 5, 26). The Latin fathers accepted medical practice as a fact of life[12]; but they tried to harmonise it with the biblical equation of sickness with sin. Jerome commented on *Mt.* 9, 5, *Whether it is easier to say, Thy sins are forgiven thee : or to say, Arise and walk*: Many bodily ills result from sin, 'and so perhaps sins are forgiven first in order that health may be restored when the causes of sickness have been removed'[13]. The Old Law commanded that a leper must show

barum institores putandi sunt sedisse in cathedris, sed mystice in cathedris magistrorum dignitas indicatur, quae ad nihilum redigitur, cum mixta fuerit lucris'.

ZACHARY, PL 186, 366-367. On Zachary see above, pp. 30-32.

10. PL 106, 1432: 'Idcirco honorati viri erant, qui et cathedras ad sedendum habebant. Spiritualiter vero ...'

On CHRISTIAN DRUTHMAR see *Dict. de Spirit*. III, Paris 1954, 1721-1723.

11. G. VERMES, *Jesus the Jew*, London 1973, 58-82.

12. Jerome quoted Galen with approval; Augustine was attended by doctors in illness; J. N. D. KELLY, *Jerome. His Life Writings and Controversies*, London 1975, 184; P. R. L. BROWN, *Augustine of Hippo. A Biography*, London 1967, 432. For early medieval defence of medicine see L. C. MACKINNEY, *Medical Ethics and Etiquette in the Early Middle Ages*, in *Bulletin of the History of Medicine* 26 (1952) 9-11.

13. *Ed. cit.* 55: 'et idcirco forsitan prius dimittuntur peccata ut causis debilitatis allatis sanitas restituatur'.

On sickness regarded as a consequence of sin, see P. RICŒUR, *The Symbolism of Evil*, transl. E. BUCHANAN, Boston 1972, 27, 31-33.

himself to a priest, who decided whether he was cured. Jesus himself observed the precept when he told the man cured of leprosy to show himself to a priest (*Mt.* 8, 4). Hence leprosy became almost synonymous with sin, just as the raising of Lazarus and the loosing of his grave cloths became almost synonymous with the absolution of a repentant sinner. Symbolism ingrained itself in the text. To 'ascend a mountain' meant drawing nearer to God; to 'descend' meant drawing away from him or 'condescending' to one's fellow men.

All these pitfalls awaited masters of the sacred page when they tried to follow Hugh of St Victor's advice: begin by clarifying the literal, historical meaning of a text before starting on allegories and tropologies. Men trained in the arts course looked for precision, where their predecessors had chosen vagueness. Masters had to find their own way through a 'no man's land' between the literal and spiritual senses[14].

Turning from technique to content and beginning with the crucial matter of poverty, we see that the Fathers approached it with their own doctrinal problems in mind. They had to combat heretics who stressed Christ's divinity *versus* his humanity, or the other way round, by insisting on his two natures in one person. Hence the gospel record of his earthly poverty interested them less for its own sake than for its theological import as part of the mystery of the Incarnation: the Son of God renounced his divine richness in order to share our poor human condition. As Dom Jean Leclercq put it:

> C'est par ce qu'il est d'abord devenu 'un pauvre homme', qu'il a été aussi 'un homme pauvre'...[15]

The Fathers, therefore, dwelt more on inward poverty of spirit, meekness and humility, than on the external circumstances of Christ's life on earth. They agreed that material poverty carried no virtue in itself. Poverty of spirit means humility and the

---

14. For Old Testament exegesis see B. SMALLEY, *William of Auvergne, John of La Rochelle and St Thomas Aquinas on the Old Law*, in *St Thomas Aquinas 1274-1974 Commemorative Studies* II, Toronto 1974, 11-71.

15. *Études sur l'histoire de la pauvreté (Moyen Age au XVI*e *siècle)*, dirigées par M. MOLLAT, Paris 1974, 35-52.

realisation that whatever goods we have come from God. *Blessed are the poor in spirit* forbids vainglory and greed[16]. Poor men can be bad, whereas riches may incite their owners to virtue; Christ condemned only those who did not know how to use their wealth rightly[17]. *In spiritu* was added in case anyone might think that Christ preached poverty borne of necessity; he meant humility, not penury[18]. The poor in spirit were god-fearing and submissive to authority, not presuming to question the teaching of Scripture[19]. Christ called money *the mammon of unrighteousness* because wicked men put their trust in it, whereas good men, while owning money, put their hopes in heaven[20]. This teaching echoed through the ages.

None of the Fathers denied that Christ and his apostles had money. The reason why he chose unlettered fishermen to send out as preachers was that otherwise the faith of believers might have been thought to rest on eloquence and learning, rather than on divine virtue[21]. St Hilary of Poitiers merely stated that their calling as fishermen foreshadowed their mission to be fishers of men[22]. Christ's saying, *The foxes have holes and the birds of the air nests, but the Son of man hath not where to lay his head* (*Mt.* 8, 20) did not evoke a picture of destitution. St Hilary interpreted *the foxes* as false prophets and *the birds of the air* as devils; the Son of Man, whose *head* was God the Father, found no recognition

16. HILARY OF POITIERS, *Com. in Mat.* (PL 9, 931-932).

17. AMBROSE, *Expos. Evang. sec. Lucam* (CCSL 14, 152-153): 'Licet in pecuniariis copiis multa sint lenocinia delictorum, pleraque tamen sunt etiam incentiua uirtutum. Quamquam uirtus subsidia non requirat et commendatior sit conlatio pauperis quam diuitis liberalitas, tamen non eos qui habeant diuitias, sed eos qui uti his nesciant sententia caelestis auctoritatis condemnat'.

18. JEROME, *ed. cit.* 24: 'Ne quis putaret paupertatem, quae nonnunquam necessitate portatur, a Domino praedicari, adiunxit *spiritu*, ut humilitatem intelligeres, non penuriam ...'

19. AUGUSTINE, *De sermone Domini in monte* (CCSL 35, 10): '*Beati pauperes spiritu*, id est non inflati, non superbi ... Qui enim pie quaerit, honorat sanctam scripturam et non reprehendit quod nondum intellegit, et propterea non resistit ...'

20. AUGUSTINE, *Quaestiones Evangeliorum* (PL 35, 1349): 'Mammona vero iniquitatis ob hoc a Domino appellata est ista pecunia, quam possidemus ad tempus ... nec sunt istae divitiae nisi iniquis ... a iustis vero cum haec possidentur, est quidem ista pecunia, sed non sunt illis divitiae nisi coelestes et spirituales ...'

21. JEROME, *In Mt.*, *ed. cit.* 23.

22. PL 9, 931.

among men [23]. Bede summarised a less fanciful tradition when he explained the text as meaning that Christ forbad men to follow him for the sake of earthly gain by pointing to his poverty; but Bede added an alternative explanation : *the foxes* signified fraud and *the birds* signified pride; Christ was stressing his humility; he had no place with deceivers and the proud [24].

Patristic commentaries do not give the impression of having been written in a period when the cult of asceticism and renunciation was reaching new heights. The theme *Nudum Christum nudus sequi* is surprisingly absent. Nor do the Fathers as commentators show awareness that the increasing wealth of the Church as an institution caused moral problems, though they would attack the pomp and laxity of individual prelates. Bede's letter to the archbishop of York, written towards the end of his life, 734, voices his anxiety on the over-endowment of monasteries [25]; his gospel commentaries suggest nothing of the sort.

What we read in patristic commentaries stems from a reaction against extremism. The Fathers were teaching at a time when Catholicism was a state religion. Only a minority would seek to follow Christ's teaching literally; the majority need not despair of salvation. The Fathers realised too that literal obedience to the precepts of the Sermon on the Mount would bring organised life to a stop. Hence they had to interpret the precepts in such a way as to allow it to continue.

The concomittant to gospel poverty, *Nolite ergo solliciti esse in crastinum* (*Mt.* 6, 34), did not excuse improvidence. Christ granted that we might take thought for our present needs; *the morrow* referred to the future in general; we must not look too far ahead, especially not as regards superfluities. The apostles set an example by returning to their calling as fishermen before the Resurrection and Ascension [26]. Raban Maur summed up the tradition : the

---

23. *Ibid.* 957-958.
24. *In Lc., ed. cit.* 212-213.
25. *Epistola ad Egbertum Episcopum*, ed. C. PLUMMER in *Opera*, Oxford 1896, 414-423.
26. JEROME, *ed. cit.* 41 : 'De praesentibus ergo concessit debere esse sollicitos qui futura prohibet cogitare ...'
AUGUSTINE, *De sermone, ed. cit.* 150-153.

precept forbad anxiety but not labour[27]. Bede put forward his own answer. Writing as a monk, vowed to poverty, but living according to a rule, he took the precept in its context: *Nolite quaerere quid manducetis aut quid bibatis, et nolite in sublime tolli* (*Lc.* 12, 29). The precept, Bede wrote, perhaps with clause 49 of the Rule of St Benedict in mind, blames those who demand either more *or less* than the common portion, that is monks who want to behave differently from their brethren[28]. Christ's mission of the apostles to preach without taking provisions for their journey (*Mt.* 10, 9-10) was generally explained as meaning that preachers must neither seek for gain nor seem to do so. Jerome's comment that the precept not to take *two coats* and to go barefoot did not apply to preaching in a cold climate clung to the text all through the middle ages[29]. The need for forethought applied to almsgiving too (*Mt.* 5, 42). Hilary made the proviso that the giver must not give so freely as to prejudice the performance of duties imposed on him by his office[30]. Jerome pointed out that a rich man who gave too generously would soon be too poor to give anything at all[31]. Augustine praised almsgiving with the rider that if the command to give applied to necessities, then how much more to superfluities? His scruple on the question of whether one should give one's slave for the asking illustrates the moral difficulties involved in obeying the precept *Qui petit a te da ei* (*Mt.* 5, 42) or *Omni autem petenti te, tribue* (*Lc.* 6, 30). The Fathers never condemned slavery as an institution; it belonged to the established order of property relationships[32]; but Augustine doubted whether a slave should be included in the objects to be given to him who asked. A slave was a man, to be loved as a human being, even

27. PL 107, 837.

28. *Ed. cit.* 253 : 'Ubi mihi uidentur argui, qui spreto uictu uel uestitu communi, lautiora sibi uel austeriora prae iis cum quibus uitam ducunt, alimenta uel indumenta requirunt'. H. M. R. E.. MAYR-HARTING suggested this clause of the Rule as inspiring Bede's comment. See his *The Venerable Bede, the Rule of St Benedict, and Social Class* (*Jarrow Lecture 1976*), Newcastle-upon-Tyne, 1977.

29. *Ed. cit.* 66.

30. PL 9, 942 : '... ut boni gratùiti sit dispensatio gratuita ... semper sine habendi damno impertiendi ministerio functuri'.

31. *Ed. cit.* 34.

32. G. E.M. DE SAINTE CROIX, *Early Christian attitudes to property and slavery*, in *Studies in Church History*, ed. Derek Baker, 12 (1975) 19-35.

though he might cost less than a horse. Ought one to hand him over to a new master, who might care less for his soul's welfare? Augustine did not know what to say[33].

The precepts to forgive one's enemies (*Mt.* 5, 38-44) and not to reclaim one's goods, *ei qui aufert quae tua sunt, ne repetas* (*Lc.* 6, 30) would have subverted all discipline on a strict interpretation, just as the ban on swearing (*Mt.* 5, 34) would have debarred Christians from the law courts. Jerome and Augustine agreed that the obligation to forgiveness applied to one's fellow Christians only, nor did it preclude the correction of sinful Christians in a spirit of charity[34]. The question gave Augustine another occasion to point the way towards medieval casuistry. He set the text *orate pro persequentibus et calumniantibus vos* (*Mt.* 5, 44) beside St John's exception of prayer for a brother who has committed mortal sin : ... *Est peccatum ad mortem, non pro illo dico ut roget quis* (*I. Ioan.* 5, 16). St John clearly shows that there are some brothers for whom we are not to pray[35]. What is *peccatum ad mortem* or the sin against the Holy Spirit, and how do we know whether our brother has committed it? The question was left unsolved. The command to be reconciled to one's brother before offering one's gift to the altar (*Mt.* 5, 23-24) so baffled Augustine that he treated 'the letter' as absurd and took refuge in the spiritual sense : how could one be reconciled to a man who was overseas at the time? Must one delay offering one's gift until after making a long journey in search of him? Augustine explained that the *altar* signified faith. The precept meant that God would accept no offering of a spiritual gift, such as teaching, prophecy or prayer, unless it were upheld by true faith on the giver's part[36].

Neither Jerome nor Augustine applied the ban on swearing to legal procedure, relating it rather to private conversation. Jerome said that a Christian's word should suffice. Augustine stipulated

---

33. *De Sermone Domini in Monte, ed. cit.* 69-70.
34. JEROME, *ed. cit.* 25.
35. *Ed. cit.* 81-83.
36. *Ibid.* 27-29.

that a Christian should swear only if men would not otherwise believe what it was useful to them to know[37].

Naturally the Fathers gave little guidance on gospel texts which would later play a key part in the polemics of Gregorian reform. The relations between *regnum* and *sacerdotium* came to pose problems unforeseen by earlier exegetes.

Carolingian commentators mediated patristic teaching without much alteration. They were equally unforthcoming on relations between *regnum* and *sacerdotium*[38]. They seldom worried about the distinction between literal and spiritual senses: Paschasius Radbertus repeated Augustine's comment on the absurdity of the literal sense of *Mt.* 5, 23[39]. Poverty texts evoked no more response in the ninth century than earlier.

Gregorian reform breathed new life into exegesis, as we find it in the gospel commentaries of Bruno of Segni. Although they did not enter into the school tradition they deserve mention here both as a contrast to what went before and as a foretaste of what would follow. Bruno shows potentialities in exegesis which would be exploited later. He was bishop of Segni 1079-1123, holding it jointly with the office of abbot of Montecassino, which he had entered as a monk in 1103, until Paschal II ordered him to resign the abbacy in 1112[40]. Bruno commented on St Matthew, then on passages in the other synoptic gospels which do not appear in the first, and finally on St John. Their probable dedication to Peter of Albano, cardinal 1072-Sept. 1089, gives a tentative date for the commentaries; closer to 1089 seems the more likely.

As a strong partisan of Gregory VII Bruno stepped up the attacks on simoniacs: Jesus cast money changers out of the temple and

37. JEROME, *ed. cit.* 32-33; AUGUSTINE, *De sermone, ed. cit.* 58.

38. See R. E. MCNALLY, *The Bible in the Early Middle Ages*, Westminster (Maryland, USA) 1959, 69.

39. PL 120, 242: 'Unde constat quod haec omnia non secundum litteram religioni sacre conveniunt; sed potius spiritualiter accipiendum ...'

On Paschasius see H. WEISWEILER, *Paschasius Radbertus als Vermittler des Gedankengutes der karolingischen Renaissance in den Matthäuskommentaren des Kreises um Anselm von Laon*, in *Scholastik* 35 (1960) 363-402, 503-536.

40. On his life and works see R. GRÉGOIRE, *Bruno de Segni exégète médiéval et théologien monastique*, Spoleto 1965; *Notes sur Bruno de Segni*, in *Rech. Théol. anc. méd.* 37 (1970) 138-142. Dom Grégoire rightly stressed the mainly traditional character of Bruno's exegesis, but did not do justice to his flashes of originality.

overturned the dove-sellers' chairs in order to teach us that simoniacs are not bishops at all (their orders were invalid according to Gregorian theory). His exceptional violence in cleansing the temple showed that we too should use force against simoniacs without harming the Church, if no other means be available[41]. Bruno would have had the papacy in mind when he commented on *Mt.* 7, 1 : *Nolite iudicare* : Let none think that righteous judgments are forbidden by these words, if the proper persons make them (PL 165, 125). The ban on swearing does not apply to the practice of swearing on the gospels, when we take Christ and his words to witness (264). Contemporary ascetic movements may have led Bruno to give more weight to the merits of poverty than his predecessors : God provides for those who totally forsake the world without provision for the morrow, as he would for all men should they do so (125). Bruno dwelt in personal terms on the honour and reverence due to the poor, as members of Christ, who hungers, thirsts and suffers himself with the poor and sick (285). On the other hand, his experience as a bishop, active in the stormy period of Gregorian reform, while feeling the pull of monastic *otium*, suggested a thoughtful review of the action *versus* contemplation theme. Comparing Martha and Mary, he remarked that Martha worked for others, Mary for herself only. Both active and contemplative lives were necessary; Mary must sometimes bestir herself to help her worried sister. Here the reforming bishop speaks (391-392).

Less learned men could adapt patristic teaching to their own ends. A crude example comes from a story told about St Wulfstan bishop of Worcester (1062-1095) by the monk Hemming in his *Chartularium*. Hemming had known Wulfstan and wrote not long after his death. Aethelwig abbot of Evesham took the opportunity of the Norman Conquest to withdraw tenants and their lands from the Worcester estates. He died of gout without having made peace or received absolution from his bishop. St Wulfstan compassion-

41. PL 165, 244-245 : 'Audite haec, Simoniaci ... Horum autem cathedras evertit, ut per hoc eos non esse episcopos intelligamus'. 440 : 'Si igitur eum in hoc quoque imitari velimus, si aliter non possumus, violenter simoniacos ab Ecclesia pellere debemus, si tamen vires suppetunt, quibus hoc sine Ecclesiae detrimento facere valeamus'. For similar sentiments see 92-93, 100, 214, 232-233.

ately offered special and urgent prayers for his dead enemy, until
he was stricken with the same disease and his life was despaired of.
Then it was divinely revealed to him that his illness came as a
punishment for praying for the abbot's soul; he must cease if
he wished to recover; and so he did[42]. Hemming believed that
Aethelwig had committed the *peccatum ad mortem* by robbing the
cathedral monastery of its lands; St Wulfstan drew God's wrath
upon his head by praying for his persecutor!

II

We enter the new world of early scholasticism with the
Enarrationes in S. Matheum ascribed to Anselm of Laon in the
Migne edition (162, 1227-1500). Modern scholars now reject
Anselm's authorship. Geoffrey Babion has been suggested as the
author, wrongly it seems to me. I shall call our anonymous *B*;
he wrote c. 1140, as a religious, but had probably studied and
taught in some school or schools in northern France before
joining an Order. He used the Gloss and other Laon material
as well as later sources. The anonymous compiler of the commentary on St Matthew found in MS *Alençon 26*, whom I call
A, provided *B* with his basic matter. When quoting *B*, I have
taken care to collate him with *A*, to see whether his comments
were personal or derivative. *B*'s personality comes through clearly,
in spite of his anonymity and his reliance on *A*. He belongs to my
subject because Peter Comestor made so much use of him[43].

---

42. *Hemingi Chartularium Ecclesiae Wigorniensis*, ed T. HEARNE, Oxford 1723,
270-272: '... Pro cuius anima cum episcopus Wulstanus, compassione visceribus
permotus, orationes peculiares instantissime crebro faceret, subito et ipse podagri
dolore in crure et pedibus invaditur, in tantum ut... desperaretur, et a curatione
cessaretur. Qui mox... ad nota orationum confugit subsidia et (ut ipse nobis
referre sepius solebat) nocte quadam sibi oranti divinitus revelatum est, quod hanc
infirmitatem ideo incurrisset, quia pro ipsius abbatis anima preces peculiares
faceret, dictum est ei, ut, si curari vellet dimitteret... Unde colligere possumus,
quante dampnationis sit, terras et possessiones monasteriorum invadere et monasteriis
auferre, quando etiam pro ipsis raptoribus exorari Deus aversatur'.

On Hemming see N. R. KER, *Hemming's Cartulary*, in *Studies in Medieval History
presented to F. M. Powicke*, ed. R. W. HUNT, W. A. PANTIN, R. W. SOUTHERN,
Oxford 1948, 49-75. Miss Elizabeth McIntyre pointed the passage out to me.

43. See above, pp. 24-26. The Migne edition of *B* is incomplete, lacking the
prologue; see F. STEGMÜLLER, *Repertorium Biblicum Medii Aevi* (henceforward

B introduced topical theological *quaestiones* into his commentary[44]. He made an advance in exegetical technique by distinguishing clearly between the literal and spiritual senses : 'Littera non indiget expositione' or 'aliud tamen spiritualiter intelligendum' are common phrases (1444, 1427). *A*, his source, sometimes gave a lead; *B* went further. Where Augustine denied any literal interpretation as 'absurd', as on *Mt.* 5, 23-24[45], *A* wrote: 'Secundum litteram de oblationibus non est absurdum'; the intention counted if one's brother was abroad (fol. 112[vb]). *B* made the situation of the offerer more concrete, specifying that the gift to the altar might be material, such as a candle, or spiritual, such as a prayer. He did not even consider the idea that the literal sense might be 'absurd' (1296). *A* passed straight to the spiritual sense on the overthrowing of the dove-sellers' chairs :

> *Et cathedras vendentium columbarum,* id est gratiam spiritus sancti per impositionem manuum evertit, id est sacerdotium eorum destruit; qui de impositione manus, per quam datur spiritus sanctus, pretium accipiunt. Hinc est quod simonaica haeresis dampnatur (fol. 164[ra]).

B took this sense as 'figurative' :

> Dampnatur *in hac figura* simonaica haeresis (1427).

---

referred to as RB) no. 2604. Canon B. Merlette has discovered that *B* represents an abridgement, with alterations, of a commentary entitled 'Glose magistri Anselmi de Monte Leonis et Remensis archiepiscopi super Matheum' in MS *Paris, Bibl. nat. lat. 2491,* foll. 1-143. He takes this for 'le Commentaire "magistral" d'Anselme'. The fact that Master Anselm was never archbishop of Reims and that this manuscript is datable from the end of the twelfth century (*Catalogue général des MSS latins* 2, Paris 1940, 487) makes me wonder whether it was really the original and not an enlargement of *B*. Merlette does not question the doubtful ascription of *B* to Geoffrey Babion, nor does he consider the evidence for the late dating of *B*. If *B* depended on Anselm's 'magistral' commentary, he must have changed it drastically. See B. MERLETTE, *Enseignement et vie culturelle IXe-XVIe siècle. Écoles et bibliothèques,* in *Ministère de l'Éducation nationale. Comité des travaux historiques et scientifiques, Actes du 95e Congrès national des sociétés savantes, Reims, 1970. Section de philologie et d'histoire jusqu'à 1610,* 1 (1975) 44-46. This important discovery makes it necessary to reconsider the relationship between MS *lat. 2491* and *A* and *B*. Meanwhile, the outcome, whatever it may be, would not affect Comestor's use of *B*, which concerns us here. See also RB Suppl. no. 1349.

44. D. VAN DEN EYNDE, *Autour des «Enarrationes in Evangelium S. Matthaei» attribuées à Geoffroi Babion,* in *Rech. Théol. anc. méd.* 26 (1959) 50-84. I quote *A* from MS *Alençon 26* and *B* from PL 162.

45. See above, p. 45.

He broached the problem of the sin-sickness syndrome posed by
Mt. 9, 5 by listing five reasons for God's infliction of sickness:
to increase the sufferer's virtue by the exercise of patience, as
happened to Job and Tobias and to many martyrs of both
Testaments; to safeguard virtue, lest the sufferer be tempted by
pride, as in St Paul's case; to expose and correct sin, as when
Aaron's sister Mary was stricken by leprosy; this reason applies
to the palsied man healed by Jesus, 'whom we treat of here'; to
the glory of God as saviour, as when Christ healed the man blind
from birth; the blind man had not sinned, and neither had his
parents; the same applied to Lazarus. These healings showed forth
God's glory by means of his Son. Fifthly, sickness may forecast
the pains of hell in reprobates such as Antiochus and Herod, who
merited twofold punishment, as the prophet said (*Ierem.* 17, 18)
(1328-1329). *B* did not tackle the relationship between forgiveness
and medical care; but his analysis broke through the simplistic
notion that sickness must necessarily result from sin. He cited
biblical examples to the contrary. This passage shows his awareness of the need to demarcate the literal and spiritual senses. It
passed into a sentence collection of the school of Laon in shortened
form, a tribute to the value set on it[46]. *B*'s care to distinguish
between the senses must have endeared him to Peter Comestor,
who wrestled with the problem, as we shall see.

B made an enterprising use of non-exegetical sources. A pat
quotation from Lucan's list of Pompey's allies (*Bellum civile* iii,

---

46. Ed. H. WEISWEILER, *Das Schrifftum der Schule Anselms von Laon und
Wilhelms von Champeaux in deutschen Bibliotheken* (*Beiträge Gesch. Philos. Theol.
Mittelalters* 33, 1-2) Münster 1936, 317. The sentence clearly derives from the
Enarrationes and not *vice versa*. The sentence is shorter, it omits some of *B*'s
examples and his 'de quo tractamus' on the palsied man. For similar borrowings
see VAN DEN EYNDE, *op. cit.* 56-65. His pattern of 'sevens' imposed on the beatitudes,
the petitions of the Lord's Prayer and the gifts of the Holy Spirit has been
described by Lottin and Van den Eynde; it came *via* Paschasius Radbertus and
ultimately from St Augustine's *De sermone Domini in Monte.* For bibliography
see H. WEISWEILER, *Paschasius Radbertus als Vermittler des Gedankengutes der
karolingischen Renaissance in den Matthäuskommentaren des Kreises um Anselm
von Laon,* in *Scholastik* 35 (1960) 366. MS *Cambridge, Trinity College 70 (B. 2.27),*
twelfth century of unknown provenance, has a circular diagram illustrating the
'sevens' pattern, fol. 3ʳ; see M. R. JAMES, *The Western MSS in the Library of
Trinity College, Cambridge* I, Cambridge 1900, 87.

247) gave colour to his account of the Magi's journey from Arabia to honour the Christ child :

Ignotum vobis Arabes venistis in orbem (1253).

Commentators had often quoted the Christian poet Sedulius[47]; they cited pagan poets rarely, though it is worth recalling that glosses on Lucan have been ascribed to Anselm of Laon[48]. *B* also exploited the liturgy as a source more systematically than had been done before. Bede had mentioned the liturgy on the custom of anointing the sick and possessed, and on the use of plain linen vestments at mass[49]. He wanted to show that liturgical practice derived from the apostles. *B* cites it as proof of a theological opinion. He explains that the souls of the Holy Innocents went down to hell, although they were martyrs, and stayed there until Christ released them after his passion. That is why neither the *Gloria in excelsis* nor the *Alleluia* are sung on their feast day (1259). The passage was lifted from *B*'s commentary by compilers of sentence collections[50]. It gives further proof of his modernity. Early books on the liturgy gave respect for the sorrowing mothers as a reason for the omission of 'songs of joy' on the Holy Innocents' day. Amalarius, writing towards the mid ninth century, gave this as the only reason[51]. The first mention of *B*'s theological reason for the omission seems to come into the *Gemma animae* of Honorius Augustodunensis, who adds it to the reason given by Amalarius. The *Gemma animae* has been dated c. 1115; but the details of Honorius' career and writings remain uncertain[52]. John Beleth gave *B*'s as the only reason, quoting no

---

47. E.g. RABAN MAUR, PL 107, 744. A twelfth century copy of Raban on St Matthew (MS *Oxford, Bodl. 729*; *Summary Catalogue* 2706) has a marginal note on *Mt.* 28, 1, fol. 215[ra] : 'Sedulius : Hoc luminis... tumulum' from *Pasch. carm.* (CSEL, 10, i, 132); RUPERT OF DEUTZ on St John, *ed. cit.* 740.

48. B. BISCHOFF, *Living with the Satirists*, in *Classical Influences on European Culture A.D. 500-1500*, ed. R.R. BOLGAR, Cambridge 1971, 84.

49. *Ed. cit.* 183, 293.

50. VAN DEN EYNDE, see above n. 44, 57. For other references to the liturgy by *B*, see 1265, 1396.

51. AMALARII EPISCOPI *Opera liturgica omnia*, ed. I. M. HANSSENS (*Studi e testi* 139) Città del Vaticano 1948, 193.

52. PL 172, 646-647; Y. LEFÈVRE, *L'Elucidarium et les Lucidaires*, Paris 1954, 221. The question cropped up in sentence collections from the school of Laon; see H. WEISWEILER, *Das Schrifttum der Schule Anselms von Laon und Wilhelms von Champeaux, op. cit.* 76, 88, 160. Here the grief of Rachel is given as the reason.

authority, in his popular *Rationale divinorum officiorum.* Beleth wrote it 1160-1164, probably at Paris, and therefore too late for *B* to have used it as a source. Afterwards the reason for the omission became standard[53].

B, to his credit, fought shy of Apocrypha and legend, apart from quoting the tale that the child set in the midst of the disciples was St Martial of Limoges; and that came from his respected source *A*[54]. Weisweiler noted that *B* dismissed as 'frivolous' the story that the star of Bethlehem fell into a pond and was seen only by virgins afterwards (1254)[55]. *B* refrained from giving the names of the three Magi, remarking cautiously that we deduce their number only from that of their proferred gifts to the Christ child :

> Nec refertur in Evangelio quot reges fuerunt, sed numerus eorum ex numero munerum percipitur (1254).

On the signs foretelling Doomsday (*Mt.* 24, 26), *B* does not enumerate fifteen, nor speculate on the date to be looked for, contenting himself with a reference to the *Life* of St Martin of Tours, where it says that the devil may appear as an angel of light (1453)[56].

He feels his way towards clarifying the gospel story by putting it into post-biblical terms. The scribes were chancellors, he explains :

> Scribae erant cancellarii, qui legem exponebant et novas traditiones scribebant (1294).

This conforms to one early medieval use of the term 'chancellor' as one who wrote legal documents, or scribe employed in the king's chancery[57]. *B*'s account of the chancellor's function, on the

---

53. Ed. H. Douteil (CCSL, *Contin. med.* 41-41 A, 1976) 2, 132 : 'In festo Innocentium penitus subticentur cantica laetitiae sicut in XLa, quia ad inferos descenderunt'. On Beleth's career see *ibid.* 29*-36*; also N. Häring, *Chartres and Paris revisited*, in *Essays in Honour of Anton Charles Pegis*, ed. J. R. O'Donnell, Toronto 1974, 306. For later references to the reason given by *B* see Comestor, *Hist. schol.* (PL 198, 1544) and Praepositini Cremonensis *Tractatus de officiis*, ed. J. A. Corbett, Notre Dame (Indiana) 1969, 37. Praepositinus died in 1210.

54. See above, pp. 15-16.

55. For a useful account of apocrypha current in the middle ages, see now M. McNamara, *The Apocrypha in the Irish Church*, Dublin 1975.

56. Sulpicius Severus, *Vita sancti Martini*, ed. & transl. into French by J. Fontaine (*Sources chrétiennes* 133, 1) Paris 1967, 302-307.

57. J. F. Niermeyer, *Mediae Latinitatis Lexicon Minus*, Leiden 1954-76, 125-126.

other hand, seems to derive from a literary source rather than from current practice. The Gloss on *Mt.* 4, 5, telling how the devil took Jesus up to the top of the temple and tempted him to cast himself down, gave the traditional explanation that in Palestine the roofs of buildings were flat. The doctors of the Jews had their chairs on the temple roof, whence they spoke to the people. Their exalted position induced vainglory; the devil tempted Christ in that place where he had deceived so many. The comparison became a cliché, to be applied to modern doctors and preachers, whose status tempted them to pride[58]. *B* gives the usual derivation of 'chancellor' from *cancelli*, a grill or window. He goes on to say that chancellors, who speak of royal or imperial mandates to the people below, announce them from windows :

> ... et erant ibi sedes doctorum, ut inde loquerentur populo infra posito. Cancelli dicuntur illa in gyro muralia, unde prospiciunt homines. Inde cancellarii dicuntur, qui habent sermonem ad populum de mandatis regis vel imperatoris, quia iussa regis solent in cancellis praedicari. Cancelli similiter dicuntur fenestrae, de quibus prospicitur. Ideo duxit eum super pinnaculum templi, cum vellet eum de vana gloria tentare, quia ibi in cathedra doctorum multos deceperat in gloria; ideo putavit et istum positum in cathedra magisterii in vanam gloriam extollere posse (1273-1274).

We do not know how Capetian *mandata* or imperial edicts were promulgated in the early twelfth century. We do know that a royal or imperial chancellor would not have gone round proclaiming government commands from windows. *B*'s statement may echo some late-antique concept of the chancellor as intermediary between court and people. Honorius Augustodunensis, an older contemporary of *B*, tells much the same tale in his commentary on *Cant.* 2, 9 :

> Unde dicuntur cancellarii, videlicet procuratores regis, qui de cancellis edictum regis populo dicunt (PL 172, 391)[59].

---

58. J.W. BALDWIN, *Masters, Princes and Merchants. The Social Views of Peter the Chanter and his Circle* II, Princeton 1970, 270.

59. Quoted in *Mittellateinisches Wörterbuch*, Munich 1959, 1500. HONORIUS's Canticle commentary has been dated c. 1151-1158; but his dates are uncertain; see H. RIEDLINGER, *Die Makellosigkeit der Kirche in den lateinischen Hohenlied-kommentaren des Mittelalters (Beitr. Gesch. Philos. Theol. Mittelalters* 38, 3) Münster 1958, 136-139. CASSIODORUS refers to the chancellor, derived from *cancelli*, as an

The interesting point is that *B* looked further afield than his sources. His chancellor-scribes may not reflect contemporary officials; at least he tried to up-date them by finding a parallel.

On content, *B* marks himself out as a disciplinarian. He stressed papal headship over the Church, giving the pope the title of 'Christ's vicar' (1396)[60], while stating the traditional opinion that a pope who had preached heretical doctrine should be deposed. He does not say how this should be done. He refers *the salt of the earth* (*Mt.* 5, 13) to those chief pastors of the Church whose subjects cannot depose them. An alternative explanation is that the *salt of the earth* refers to all prelates : 'Note that any prelate is to be cast out and accused by men, should he deviate from the faith'; but he adds a caution : the prelate must be borne with, should his teaching be good, though his life be bad; but if a pastor's life be so bad as to corrupt those committed to his care, then he should be cast out, as Gregory and other saints have decreed (1291). The vague reference to St Gregory may perhaps derive from his *Regula pastoralis* I, ii, 12 (though it is not a verbal quotation) or perhaps from some canon law text. *B* teaches subjects to obey their prelates, who must be tolerated unless their teaching be heretical or their behaviour too openly scandalous. The ban on judgements, *Nolite iudicare etc.* (*Mt.* 7, 1-3) applied to judgements made by equals; Christ forbad judgement to equals, not to prelates (1313-1314). *Beati misericordes* (*Mt.* 5, 7) does not forbid us to correct rebels, though we must pardon the penitent (1287). Discipline had to be enforced by the secular power. *B* held the so-called Gelasian theory of the two swords, wielded respectively by the spiritual and secular powers acting in harmony. Vengeance is not wholly forbidden, he writes on *Mt.* 5, 38 : the secular powers are God's vicars, who condemn evildoers in God's place, both for their own good and to frighten others. It is allowed to take vengeance on evildoers through zeal for justice, but not

intermediary between the court and the people, *Variae* xi, 6 (CCSL 96, 432-433). On the imperial chancery see H. W. KLEWITZ, *Cancellaria. Ein Beitrag zur Geschichte des geistlichen Hofdienstes*, in *Deutsches Archiv für Geschichte des Mittelalters* 1 (1937); on the Capetian chancery and royal *mandata*, E. BOURNAZEL, *Le gouvernement Capétien au XIIe siècle, 1108-1180*, Limoges 1975.

60. Above, p. 22.

for the pleasure of punishing them (1300-1301). *B* distinguished the functions of the two swords on Christ's command to St Peter to sheathe his sword :

> What pertains to the cloth should be no concern of kings; neither should the bishop handle what pertains to the king. Peter, figuring the spiritual power, wielded the material sword in some sense when he cut off the servant's ear, and deserved that the Lord should rebuke him for doing so (1476).

B rejects by omission the papalist claim to hold both swords and to delegate the material sword to secular rulers to wield on his behalf. According to *B*, it seems, the secular ruler held his sword directly from God.

A sentence in one of the Laon collections supplies a background to *B*'s teaching and makes it explicit. Kings sometimes grant secular offices to prelates, whence they may support themselves in their business. The list of such offices surprisingly includes the right to take payments from subjects for absolution from excommunication, as well as the right to preside over judicial ordeals. But prelates owe powers belonging to the material sword to royal grants; they do not receive the material sword itself; nor should they deny it to kings, who alone have the right to kill evildoers, unless the prelate receives a special command from God to do so, as in Samson's case[61]. This sentence agrees with what we know of school doctrine of the early twelfth century on St Paul's command to obey the powers ordained by God (*Rom.* 13, 1-7)[62]. The heat of Gregorian polemic had died down. Masters, respectful to the papacy as they might be, did not care to belittle royal authority. *B* went beyond his exegetical sources in stating his position on the relations between *regnum* and *sacerdotium* more clearly and updating it.

On poverty texts he took pains to stress that poverty must be

---

61. O. LOTTIN, *Psychologie et morale aux XIIe et XIIIe siècles* V, Gembloux 1959, 324-325.

62. W. AFFELDT, *Die weltliche Gewalt in der Paulus-Exegese Rom. 13, 1-17 in Römerbriefkommentaren der lateinischen Kirche bis zum Ende des 13 Jahrhunderts*, Göttingen 1969, 161-166. See also L. J. DALY, *Political Implications of some Medieval Commentaries on I Peter II, 13-17*, in *Manuscripta, Science Medicine and the University: 1200-1500. Essays in Honour of Pearl Kibre*, ed. N. G. SIRAISI and L. DEMAITRE I, Missouri 1976, 137-149.

voluntary and not enforced, in order to qualify the poor man for blessedness; a rich man may qualify, provided that he be poor in spirit (1284-1285). *B*'s scale of rewards for virtue set poverty lower than meekness and sorrow (1289). He soft-pedalled texts on Christ's poverty. Though *Foxes have holes etc.* (*Mt.* 8, 19-20) meant that Christ had no house of his own, its main significance was that it rebuked simoniacs, who wanted to follow Christ for gain (1323). *Go sell what thou hast, etc.* (*Mt.* 19, 21) commanded contempt for wealth; renunciation did not suffice (1413). Christ's words in the parable identifying himself with the poor (*Mt.* 25, 40-43) applied only to the poor in spirit who did God's will, not to all poor men in general (1464). True, *B* followed *A* on the last three texts (foll. 125vb, 159rb, 178ra); but he did so from choice, since he differed from *A* where it suited him.

He made an original contribution on the mission of the apostles to preach without taking any provisions for the journey (*Mt.* 10, 9). His sources told him that the ban on provisions was absolute. It ensured that the apostles should be seen to practise what they preached, when they taught men to despise riches. All agreed that the ban applied only to preaching while Christ lived on earth; later, the apostles were allowed to accept money or to earn it by working for their bread[63]. *B* held to the absolute nature of the ban, and illustrated it in detail. The apostles were forbidden to carry a bag, 'because wayfarers put their provisions, such as cheeses, loaves, pepper and candles and the like into bags', a *vignette* of medieval travel (1339)[64]. *B* went on to give his own reasons why the ban expired after Christ's Passion. Christ acted as the apostles' steward, while he lived in this world, and had money to feed them. He did not want them to worry about expenses for as long as they were under his stewardship. He used to send them out without provisions because he would see to their needs. But after he had withdrawn from their sight he allowed them to have money in his stead, just as he himself had had, even though they might wish to live on their subjects' goods, as did St Paul, though Paul often worked for his living too (1339-1340). *B* saw Christ as a wise

63. *A*, fol. 31va; Bede, *ed. cit.* on *Lc.* 9, 2, 105; Raban Maur, PL 107, 893.
64. MS *Laud. misc. 87*, fol. 26rb, omits 'piper, candela'; but if they were interpolated it must have been early, since they already appear in MS *Lyell 66*, fol. 58ra.

steward (*procurator*) administering property for his apostles, as an abbot might do for his monks. It is a far cry to the Franciscan view of Christ and his disciples.

When not original, *B* excels at putting content into generalisations. The ban on divorce (*Mt.* 5, 32) led him to specify conditions for a valid dissolution of marriage. Husband and wife may separate on religious grounds by mutual consent, so that one may become a monk and the other a nun. But suppose that a freeman marries a bondwoman (*ancilla*) in ignorance of her servile state? *B* answers that the freeman must try to persuade her lord to free her; if the lord refuses, then the freeman may repudiate her; God's law does not injure earthly lords by robbing them of their slaves, male or female: 'Non enim lex Dei facit iniuriam dominis mundi ut eis servos auferat vel ancillas' (1299). The question was actual in a serf economy; a lord would lose the bondwoman's children as well as the bondwoman herself, if she escaped. *B* safeguarded the lord's rights. Zachary of Besançon and Peter Lombard followed him on this point. Serfdom belonged to the established order of property relationships and must not cede to gospel precepts[65].

B found another topical illustration for the precept not to care for the morrow (*Mt.* 6, 34). The stock explanation was that 'today' included the whole agricultural year and 'tomorrow' the years afterwards. *B* enlarged on it: an abbot who stored food for himself and his monks for the current year would be 'provident'. He would be guilty of undue anxiety only if he despaired of God's goodness and stored up for several years ahead (1313). The present problems of the Church take shape before our eyes when *B* specifies the *dogs* and *swine* of *Mt.* 7, 6, traditionally 'heretics and despisers of God's word', as 'snappy heretics, whores, drunkards, certain scornful laymen, and even clerks, who belittle the mystery of the Eucharist'. Preachers must not throw the pearls of mystery before such as these (1314).

Our commentator, like the Fathers before him, scented danger in the extremes of poverty and renunciation. Hence he brought readers face to face with the difficulties of applying gospel teaching to their own milieu. At the same time he improved on exegetical

---

65. PL 186, 321; *Sent.* IV, d. 36, c. 1.

technique and reached out to new sources, while avoiding apocrypha. These merits were his gift to the schools.

III

Comestor's commentaries on all four gospels have survived in *reportationes* of lectures given at Paris, going through the gospels consecutively 1159-1178[66]. Faced with large numbers of manuscripts, I have made an arbitrary selection, dictated mainly by convenience of access. Here is a list.

For *St Matthew and St Mark* I used (1) MS *Oxford, Bodl. Laud. misc. 291 (L)*, written at the abbey of Bury St Edmund in the second quarter of the thirteenth century. The incipits, *Fecit Deus duo luminaria* and *Vidi, et ecce quatuor quadrige*, with other means of identification are given in RB 6575-6[67]. (2) MS *Oxford, Bodl. 494*, Summary catalogue 2108 *(B)*, for St Mark. This copy of St Mark forms item II in a set of four manuscripts bound together. The first three items, written in England in the early thirteenth century, were given to Exeter cathedral for the use of poor scholars by Hugh of Wilton, archdeacon of Taunton sometime after 1230[68]. There is a fragment of Comestor on St Mark in MS *Cambridge, Pembroke College 7*, late twelfth or early thirteenth century from Bury St Edmund (RB 6576)[69], which I have checked for identification.

The lectures on *St Luke* exist in an incomplete copy in MS *Cambridge, Pembroke College 75 (P)*, early thirteenth century from Bury St Edmund[70]. It omits the master's prologue, *Pedes eorum pedes recti* (RB 6577) and begins in the middle of his exposition of the Gloss prologue. I supplemented it from a complete copy

66. See above, p. 4.

67. H.O. COXE, *Bodleian Library Quarto Catalogue* II, reprinted from the 1858-1885 edition with corrections and additions by R.W. HUNT, Oxford 1973; O. PÄCHT and J.J.G. ALEXANDER, *Illuminated MSS in the Bodleian Library* III, Oxford 1973, 36.

68. K. EDWARDS, *The English Secular Cathedrals in the Middle Ages* (2nd ed.) Manchester 1967, 187.

69. M.R. JAMES, *Catalogue of MSS in the Library of Pembroke College, Cambridge*, Cambridge 1905, 7.

70. *Ibid.* 65.

in MS *Durham Cathedral Library A.I. 9 (D)*[71]. The contents of
this manuscript have given rise to such confusion that a description
of them will be in order. The whole is written in two columns
in English or north French hands of the mid thirteenth century.
From fol. 8[r] to the end, fol. 179[v], many leaves are stained by damp
and torn off at the top. The wide margins contain many notes
in various hands, some in English by fourteenth and fifteenth
century hands. The commentaries have no capitulation. Modern
chapters have been added in the margins by a later hand. There
are many insertions in the margins to rectify omissions. The scribes
did not systematically underline the text of the Bible and the
Gloss in red, but sometimes left dots as a guide to the rubricator.
There are many gaps where the exemplar had gaps or was illegible.
Spaces are left for initials. The contents are (a) an extract from
Justinian's *Code* IV with marginal notes, flyleaves foll. 1-2. (b) List
of contents : « Postilla super IV evangelia et epistolas canonicas,
actus apostolorum, cantica canticorum, apocalipsim et super librum
exodi », fol. 3[r], followed by a commentary on St Matthew,
foll. 3ra-65ra. Stegmüller listed it as a variant of Comestor on
St Matthew (RB 6575, 1). It is, in fact, merely a defective copy,
lacking Comestor's prologue and omitting many passages found in
L. (c) A commentary on St Mark, *Cum omnibus legitime certantibus*,
foll. 65va-80ra. Stegmüller listed it as a variant of Comestor on
St Mark (RB 6576, 1). Collation with *L* and *B* shows that it is
quite another commentary, not even derived from Comestor's.
Hauréau lists an anonymous copy of it in MS *Paris, Bibl. nat.
nouv. acq. lat. 217*, fol. 96, a thirteenth century miscellany from
Savigny (?)[72]. (d) Notes on St Mark, fol. 80[ra-vb] : « Notularum
Marci congrua additio hec est : *Et baptizabantur a Johanne confi-
tentes peccata sua*, quod homines baptizandi debeant confiteri
peccata. Ibi habetur confessio et pulchritudo in conspectu eius,
scilicet sponsi ... incepit narrando illud quod per Iohannem factum

---

71. T. RUD, *Cat. Codicum manuscriptorum Ecclesiae Cathedralis Dunelmensis*,
Durham 1825, 5, summarises the contents as 'Postillae sive (ut vocantur in fine
libri) Glossae satis prolixae super 4 Evangelia, Epistolas Canonicas, Cantica
Canticorum, Apocalypsim, Exodum'.
72. *Initia operum scriptorum latinorum medii potissimi aevi* I, Turnhout n.d.,
fol. 287.

est. Expliciunt». (e) Comestor on St Luke (RB 6577), foll. 81ra-142vb. This copy supplements *P*, which lacks Comestor's prologue; but *P* has a better text. Here we have some omissions and many mistakes. (f) An incomplete commentary on St John, foll. 143ra-178vb: «Huic evangelio prescribit Ieronimus prologum in quo ostendit... filium mundo manifestetur. *In principio erat verbum*. Principium pluribus modis dicitur... Glosa Augustini: *Non dicit spatio non posse capi, sed a captivitate* [*sic*] *legentium*...» [73] A marginal note, fol. 162va, reads: 'Nota deficiunt hic tria capitula', where the commentary on 7, 28-11, 1 is missing. This fragmentary commentary, lacking the author's prologue and three chapters, is not the same as Comestor's. It appears again in an even more fragmentary form in *P*, following Comestor's, foll. 138vb-154vb, breaking off at 5, 22. (g) Notes on St John, foll. 178vb-179ra: «Item ex semine verborum huius libri evidenter colligitur quod Petrus plus diligebat Christum quam Iohannes... in tranquilitate». The piece consists of a *quaestio*, where the two apostles Peter and John are taken to signify the active and contemplative life respectively. (h) «Sententia sancti Ieronimi de essentia et de invisibilitate et de immensitate Dei. Omnipotens... et brachio excelso», fol. 179^{ra-va}. This is an excerpt from Pseudo-Jerome, *De essentia divinitatis* (PL 45, 1199-1200) [74]. (i) A commentary on the Canonical Epistles, not listed in RB, foll. 180ra-198va, «Iuxta numerum evangelistarum... resistit et hoc ante omnia secula etc.» Hauréau lists another anonymous commentary with the same incipit on the same books from a thirteenth century miscellany in MS *Bibl. Apost. Vat. Palat. 287* [75]. (j) A commentary on Acts, foll. 198va-202ra, listed under *anonymi* RB 9075. (k) A fragmentary commentary on the Canticle, foll. 202va-218ra. The top of the leaf has been torn off: «Deus ergo pater *osculum* (1, 1), id est delectationis et certificat... *montes aromatum* (8, 14), id est super illos qui sunt montes altitudine virtutum, quorum conversatio in celis est, et sunt aromata fama bone vite. Hic vide illam glosam *Ita fuge etc et illa*

73. The gloss here ascribed to Augustine is neither in the printed edition of the Gloss nor in Augustine's commentary on St John.

74. E. DEKKERS, *Clavis Patrum Latinorum*, in *Sacris erudiri* 3 (2nd ed.), Bruges 1961, 144, no. 633.

75. *Initia, op. cit.* 3, fol. 245^v.

cum in montibus etc.» (l) A commentary on the Apocalypse, foll. 219ra-233rb, listed under *anonymi* RB 9076. (m) A commentary on Exodus 1, 1-10, 1, lacking prologue, foll. 233va-242rb; a marginal note, fol. 242^r, reads 'Hic deficiunt 16 capitula'. Listed under *anonymi* RB 9077; fol. 242^v is blank.

For our purposes *D* contains a defective copy of Comestor on St Matthew and a complete copy of him on St Luke. The other commentaries in the volume are not his. Judging from the commentator's procedures, I should date them to the late twelfth or early thirteenth century and classify them as Paris lectures. The fragmentary commentary on St John, found also in *P*, has a reference to academic processions in the prologue to illustrate the order of the evangelists: 'Unde in processionibus maiores et digniores, quasi magistri et rectores extremi sequuntur cunctos' (*P*, fol. 138va). A study of these anonyma might be informative.

For *St. John, Omnia poma, nova et vetera* (RB 6578), I consulted three copies (1) that in *P*, described above. (2) In microfilm MS *Paris, Nat. lat. 15269*, foll. 1ra-28va, from the Sorbonne, written in French hands of about the second quarter of the thirteenth century (*S*). *P* and *S* agree closely, though *P* has fewer scribal mistakes. (3) *B*, already mentioned, has another copy, immediately preceding that on St Mark. At first sight it seems to be identical with *P* and *S* and is so listed by Stegmüller. Collation showed up a number of omissions, scattered throughout. The discussion on the baptism of St John Baptist in *B*, fol. 8^{ra-va} differs from *P*, foll. 94va-95rb and *S*, foll. 4va-5ra. There is some repetition as well as omission, as though the scribe had broken off and then started again at the wrong place, and some difference of substance. *P* and *S* seem more reliable witnesses to the original than *B*. It is not a question of two *reportationes*, since there is far too much textual identity. I quote from *B*, as being ready to hand, but have checked my quotations from *P* and *S*.

The reporters of all Comestor's lectures normally wrote *inquit* when recording the master's personal views, but occasionally preferred *magister dicit*. In one case the reporter gave the lecturer's name. On the question of what Christ meant by his frequent answer *tu dicis* to interrogation (*Mt.* 27, 11), we read :

Non enim videtur dici quod interrogando queritur. Secundum magistrum P.M. credendum est ydioma hebreum fuisse in hoc verbo, ut sit sensus : quod tu dicis interrogando dicere potes vere asserendo... (*L*, fol. 88vb).

One problem arising from these *reportationes* is that many passages are inset in the columns, as they are also in copies of Comestor's *School History*. The editors of the latter present them as footnotes to the chapters. Do they stand for the master's afterthoughts or did his pupils add them on their own initiative? One 'footnote' has the words : *Dicit Magister* (PL 198, 1626). An inset on *Mt.* 1, 2 is headed *Magistralis adiectio* (*L*, fol. 6vb). The insets vary from copy to copy, some being inserted in the text in one and not in another. A comparison of those in *B*, *P* and *S*, for instance, shows that *B* lacks the insets of the other two and has many of its own. *S* has only six insets in all, foll. 6va-7vb. *P* has all six and one extra, not found in *S*, foll. 98ra-100va. Only a critical edition would clear up the problem of the insets. I incline to accept them as magisterial, or as emanating from the master via his pupils, as a working hypothesis.

Much of the lecture material reappears, either verbatim or nearly so in the *School History* (PL 198, 1557-1644)[76]. I have therefore included it in my study of Comestor on the gospels.

IV

A study of Comestor's technique must begin with his prologues. It became customary in the later twelfth century to open one's prologue with a text from Scripture, which would then be applied to the contents of the book in hand, just as preachers quoted a text as their introduction to a sermon[77]. Hence the prologue to a lecture course on *sacra pagina* would resemble a sermon in its beginning, and in its end as well : the lecturer would conclude

---

76. I shall quote from the *School History* by the column, taking PL 198 as read.

77. J. LONGÈRE, *Œuvres oratoires des maîtres Parisiens au XIIe siècle* (*Études Augustiniennes*) Paris, 1975, I, 52-55. It is not certain precisely when the opening text became a stereotype. Most of Geoffrey Babion's sermons, but not all, show this technique; Peter Lombard's all do. See J. B. SCHNEYER, *Repertorium des lateinischen Sermones des Mittelalters für die Zeit von 1150-1350* (*Beitr. Gesch. Philos. Theol. Mittelalters* 43, 2) Münster 1970, 150-159; 3, 1972, 700-704.

his prologue with a prayer for a blessing on himself and his hearers. This was a departure from earlier practice. Commentators had opened their prologues by plunging straight into their subject matter : *Liber evangelii grece, bonum nuntium latine, Cum post ascensionem Domini, Dominus et redemptor noster* are examples. Comestor is the first lecturer on record to have opened his prologue with a biblical text. His master Peter Lombard had not done so; but Comestor hints at predecessors in his prologue to St Mark. Comparing the four rings of the ark (*Exod.* 25, 12) to the four evangelists, he raises the question : which two are signified by the right and left hand rings respectively? He cites two opinions. They do not come from Bede's *De tabernaculo*[78]. The tabernacle and its furniture lent themselves so well to the sermon-type prologue, as we know from many later examples[79], that Comestor may well have had an earlier prologue in mind when he discussed the correspondence between the evangelists and the rings.

Whoever invented the practice, whether Comestor or a predecessor, fashioned a model which would last all through the middle ages. The choice of an opening text for one's prologue led to misplaced ingenuity and repetition, as the number of suitable and hitherto unused texts sank to zero. In its origins it gave solemnity and perhaps excitement to the first lecture of the series. Comestor does not yet introduce the final prayer of the prologue, though perhaps his reporters have omitted it.

Another innovation was to adapt the Introduction used in the arts course with its headings : *auctor, intentio, utilitas, modus tractandi, finis* or some combination of these terms. Lecturers on Scripture went on to transfer the terms *ars extrinsecus, ars intrinsecus* to the literal and spiritual exposition. It has been argued that Peter Abelard was the first to introduce the arts course Introduction headings into prologues to biblical books[80]. Comest-

78. CCSL 119 A, 16. PETER OF POITIERS discusses the problem, elaborating on Bede, in his *Allegoriae super Tabernaculum Moysi*, ed. P. S. MOORE and J. A. CORBETT, Notre Dame (Indiana) 1938, 90-91. He does not give the exact equivalent of COMESTOR's two opinions, and was anyway writing later; see LONGÈRE, *op. cit.* 1, 22.

79. B. SMALLEY and G. LACOMBE, *The Lombard's Commentary on Isaias and Other Fragments*, in *The New Scholasticism* 5 (1931) 127-129, 156; RB 6455-6; 6489; 7744; 7744, 2; 7745; 7767; 7783; 7811; 7819; 7830; 7837.

80. R. W. HUNT, *Introductions to the "Artes" in the Twelfth Century*, in *Studia Mediaevalia in honorem R. J. Martin O.P.*, Bruges, s.d., 85-112; N. M. HÄRING,

or's practice was not standardised: he has *materia, intentio, finis, modus agendi* in his prologue to St Matthew, but omits *finis* on St Mark (*L*, foll. 1^{va-b}, 92vb); he has *causa, materia, intentio, modus agendi* on St Luke (*D*, fol. 81rb), but only *materia, intentio, modus agendi* on St John (*B*, fol. 1vb). He does not use the later headings *ars extrinsecus, ars intrinsecus*.

The second lecture of the course dealt with the Gloss prologues. Comestor's reporter shows how his master tailored his introductory matter on the fourth gospel to the timing of his lectures. The Gloss began with a prologue ascribed to St Jerome, *Hic est Iohannes* (RB 624). St Augustine's prologue *Omnibus divinae Scripturae paginis* (RB 628) was written in the margins besides the former, and so would normally be read first. Comestor decided to reverse the order, beginning with *Hic est Iohannes* and going on to *Omnibus divinae Scripturae paginis*, because the second would be too short for a lecture and the two together too long. He therefore took Augustine's into his next lecture, which included the first words of his text. The reporter gives a vivid description of these first efforts to organise a sequence:

> Nota quod Augustinus, qui precipue exposuit Iohannem, fecit introitum, qui sic incipit: *Omnibus divine scripture paginis*, sed magister ad introitum Augustini quodammodo preparavit ingressum, ut commodior esset introitus vel accessus, et inde quia introitus Augustini legendus est ante prologum, facimus tamen ordinem preposterum, quod non propter aliud introductum est nisi quia nimis modica esset lectio, si quis legeret introitum solum, et nimis prolixa, si quis in introitu legeret prologum. Primo ergo legimus prologum *Hic est Iohannes etc.* Premittit Ieronimus huic operi prologum ad sequentis operis commendationem... id est auctoritatis.
>
> *Omnibus etc.* Hec glosa est introitus ad Iohannem facta ab Augustino, et hec continentia glose (*B*, foll. 1vb-3ra).

Comestor's tailoring of his prologues to St Matthew has already been noted[81]. His sequence became standard in the schools[82].

The Lectures of Thierry of Chartres on Boethius de Trinitate, in *Arch. Hist. doctr. litt. Moyen Age* 25 (1959) 120-121.

81. B. SMALLEY, *The Study of the Bible in the Middle Ages* (3rd ed.) Oxford 1983, 217.

82. HUGH OF ST CHER follows it in his postills on the gospels 1130-1136. On Hugh see T. KAEPPELI, *Scriptores Ordinis Praedicatorum Medii Aevi* II, Rome 1975, 269-281.

Passing from the prologue to the commentary, the reader comes up against Comestor's obsessive care to 'order' the glosses in relation to the text. He handles his glossed text as any conscientious teacher will handle a new apparatus. Comestor distinguishes between the *glosator*, the individual glosses, and the *expositor*, that is the earlier commentator from whose work the *glosator* made excerpts : 'Ut ergo secundum mentem Rabani, [glosa] interlinearis exponatur, intelliges originale peccatum non reatum sed fomitem ...' (*L*, fol. 17ra). Rabanus was the *expositor* here. Again Comestor refers to *expositor* on the text : *oculos suos clauserunt, ne quando videant oculis* (*Mt.* 13, 15). The Gloss on the passage offers two alternative explanations of *ne quando* : *either* the spiritually blind would never see *or* they might sometime open their eyes and be converted. The question is left open. Comestor comments :

> Utrum accipiendum sit *ne quando* pro 'nunquam', vel *ne* pro 'ut' in ambiguo relinquit expositor (*L*, fol. 63va).

The *expositor* was again Rabanus (PL 107, 943). Comestor will praise, but also criticise the *glosator*, as on his comparison of the seven petitions of the Lord's Prayer to the seven gifts of the Holy Spirit; Comestor warns his pupils not to misinterpret the comparison, an allusion to the Lombard's teaching on the inseparability of the virtues (*Sent.* III, xxxvi, 1) :

> ... Quantum ad expositionem littere a diversis tamen auctoritatibus multa collegit [glosator], et, ut fieret elegantior lectio, introducta est hic satis elegans adaptatio... Cave tamen ne in huiusmodi adaptatione vim facias, ut intelligas singulis petitionibus singula peti dona, per singula dona singulas impetiri virtutes et non omnes (*L*, fol. 22va).

Above all, he distinguishes between the senses of Scripture adduced in the glosses :

> Moraliter, et vide quod non est allegoria, sed moralitas (*L*, fol. 58vb).
> Hucusque est glosa metaphorica, et ab hoc loco allegorica (*L*, fol. 96vb).
> Partim morale est [quod infra subditur], partim allegoricum, et hoc est *non solum etc.*, quasi non solum moraliter sed et allegorice ... (*L*, fol. 76va).

He took care to establish the literal sense, following *B*, and avoided the patristic notion that apparent 'absurdity' signified 'mystery'.

Comestor's main exegetical source, apart from the Gloss, was *B*, whom he refers to occasionally as 'Master Geoffrey Babion' (mistakenly as it seems)[83]. Even when he fails to mention the name, *B* underlies his commentary. I have taken care to check my quotations from Comestor against *B*, to make sure that Comestor's remarks were personal to him. He quotes or alludes to Peter Lombard sometimes as *alii* and sometimes as 'our master': 'secundum magistrum nostrum' (*S*, fol. 5ra)[84]. Otherwise he does not specify what near-contemporary sources he had to hand.

Comparison with his favourite source, *B*, shows that Comestor expanded his original in a thoughtful way. *B* took up the traditional interpretation of the five talents of the parable (*Mt.* 25, 14-30) as signifying the skill of managing external business according to man's five senses (1460). Comestor explains that such skill applies to political or domestic or private office, that is, to civic rule or governance of a household or personal morals. God gives to each man according to his capacity, since he has not willed to choke nature's good in us by undue generosity or meanness:

> Quibusdam dat Christus quinque talenta, id est scientiam administrationis rerum exteriorum in ministerio quinque sensuum comparatam, scilicet politicam vel domesticam vel privatam, scilicet de regimine civium vel de gubernatione familie vel in seipso de comparatione morum... *Secundum propriam virtutem* (cf. Gloss *ad loc.*), non plus quam possit sustineret, quia non vult [Deus] bonum nature in nobis suffocare, nec ex largitate vel ex avaritia aliis dat plus, aliis minus, sed cuique det pro modulo facultatis sue (*L*, fol. 83rb).

The distinction between public and private in the skill of governance recalls Hugh of St Victor's division of 'practical knowledge' in his *Didascalicon*[85]. It shows Comestor looking to wider horizons, from the starting point of his sources; he appreciated the skill required for administration.

---

83. See above, pp. 24-29.

84. See above *ibid.* 154. LANDGRAF has pointed to passages where Comestor mentions the Lombard as *alii*, *Dogmengeschichte der Frühscholastik* 3 (1), Regensburg 1954, quoting *S*; see 177-179, 289. He did not notice that in discussing St John Baptist's knowledge of Christ and of Christian baptism, Comestor actually wrote 'secundum magistrum nostrum' in support of his chosen opinion (*S*, fol. 5ra).

85. ii, 19, ed. C. H. BUTTIMER, Washington 1939, 37-38: 'Practica subdividitur in solitariam, privatam et publicam; vel aliter, in ethicam œconomicam et politicam; vel aliter in moralem et dispensativam et civilem... Eademque publica, politica, et civilis...'

The *reportatio* technique takes us away from his sources and into his classroom. He spoke to a student audience, appealing to his pupils' experience. Jesus fasted forty days and forty *nights* (*Mt.* 4, 2). The *nights* were added 'in case you might think that he lived like students, who fast by day and eat at night' (*L*, fol, 18[rb]). On *scandals* (*Lc.* 17, 1) he illustrates again from experience : the disciple feels shocked and disillusioned when a master, whom he has admired, is mocked at and belittled by others, so that his teaching falls into disrepute :

> Cum enim audivimus nobis aliqua dogmatizantem et videmus doctores quos arbitramur peritos doctrinam eius irridere et parvipendere, statim doctrina eius in negligentiam cadit (*D*, fol. 126[va]).

Changing academic fashions and impressionable students! Comestor kept in touch with the world outside the schools. Bede noted on *Haec descriptio prima facta est a praeside Syriue Cyrino* (*Lc.* 2, 2) that Cyrinus was *censor patrimoniorum*. Comestor compared the imperial *patrimonia* to allods, that is estates held directly from the ruler, unlike fiefs, which were held mediately through a lord. He explained that Caesar could tax his allods directly, whereas the holder of a fief or an estate held for some definite rent was responsible to the person from whom he held it :

> *censor patrimoniorum*, id est allodiorum. Nichil enim exigebat nisi de allodiis, ut si quis haberet terram in feodo vel sub censu definito responderet ei a quo haberet. Si autem haberet in allodio, cogebatur respondere presidi romano, et sic dicitur *censor patrimoniorum*, id est allodiorum (*P*, fol. 8[va]).

Allods were disappearing fast in northern France during the twelfth century; lords interposed themselves between the allod-holder and the central government, though allods survived in some quantity south of the Loire, where social bonds were looser; their holders clung to their status tenaciously[86]. Comestor pointed to an actual and clearly observable process, when he distinguished between allods and lands held in fee. His comparison contrasts with the literary allusion made by *B* to the functions of scribes

---

86. R. BOUTRUCHE, *Seigneurie et Féodalité. L'apogée, XI*e*-XII*e* siècles*, Paris 1970, 276-289, 294; *Une Société provinciale en lutte contre le régime féodal. L'alleu en Bordelais et en Bazadais du XI*e* au XVIII*e* siècle*, Paris 1947.

as 'chancellors'[87]; Comestor took his comparison from real life and not from a book.

V

The *School History* on the Old Testament shows the author's interest in the literal historical sense. Like other twelfth-century scholars, he looked to rabbinic tradition for new sources of information. He quoted Andrew of St Victor's commentaries, where Andrew had transmitted Jewish lore, and he may have made independent enquiries[88]. Jewish exegesis as a source supplementing the biblical text dried up when he came to the New Testament. The chosen people of the Old Testament rejected their Messiah in the New. One would not ask a contemporary rabbi what the Jews thought of the gospel story, except for purposes of anti-Jewish polemic[89]. Hence a western scholar of the twelfth century had no extra-biblical material at his disposal apart from Josephus, Eusebius, and his knowledge of pagan history; he did not know Greek. Yet Comestor's hunger for information sharpened when he passed to the gospels. What new sources, if any, could he find?

A tempting library of Christian apocrypha lay ready to hand to cover the all too bare bones of the text before him. *B* had ignored apocrypha. Comestor failed to resist the temptation so sternly. Apocryphal legends, such as the names of the Magi, found their way into his *School History*; he mentions others in his lectures[90]. Yet he warned his hearers in most cases that such stories were not authentic and would not vouch for their truth, sometimes preferring the plain words of the New Testament, as on the apocryphal tale that the apostles fasted from the Ascension to Pentecost; we are told only that they prayed during this period

87. See above, p. 53.

88. B. SMALLEY, *The School of Andrew of St Victor*, in *Rech. Théol. anc. méd.* 11 (1939) 146-151. For recent discussion of the rabbinic sources of the *School History* see *Bull. Théol. anc. méd.* 11 (1974) 621.

89. The only references to Jewish traditions on the New Testament come from the Gloss and Jerome; see PL 198, 1607, *L*, foll. 79rb, 132ra; JEROME on *Mt.* 12, 44, *ed. cit.* 208.

90. M. MCNAMARA, *op. cit.*, n. 54, 39-40, 55, 76, 98 (PL 198, 128-131, 136), for the *School History*. Other allusions to apocrypha in the lectures occur in *D*, fol. 109vb, *L*, fol. 14ra.

(1569). Odd as it may seem, Comestor showed rather more reserve on Christian apocrypha, for all their colour and piety, than he did on rabbinic traditions on the Old Testament.

'Where there's a will, there's a way' : Comestor proved the truth of this saying by reaching out to what was available to him in his aim to bring the story to life for his pupils and to supplement the evangelists' tale. He had recourse to the liturgy, iconography, relics, and the archaeology and topography of Palestine.

His predecessors had invoked the liturgy occasionally. Comestor incorporates it into the narrative. The gospel lived on in the sacred drama of divine service. His account of the entry into Jerusalem, the Last Supper, the Crucifixion and Resurrection read like a commentary on the liturgy for Holy Week and Easter, both in the *School History* and in the lectures. Ritual practice recalls Christ's teaching. The Church commemorates the mission of the apostles when the deacon carries the gospel to read to the people. He goes as one sent to preach it by God. A server carries its covering, as though to say to the deacon : 'You ought not to carry life's necessaries with you, because others should provide them for you' (1563, *L*, fol. 53[ra], *D*, fol. 109[rb]). The text *Ioan.* 1, 5 explains why candles are carried in church services (*B*, fol. 6[rb]). It would take a liturgiologist to do justice to Comestor's sources. He does not name them. Possibly he used the *Rationale* of his contemporary John Beleth (1160-1164)[91]. Certainly he did some research on his subject, referring to rubrics *in antiquis gradualibus* (1598). He contrasts practices in religious Orders and in churches (1601, 1632, 1598, *L*, fol. 95[ra]), and the usages of the Latin and Greek churches on baptism (*B*, fol. 8[vb]). Differences between the

---

91. An inset on *Ioan.* 1, 29 (*B*, fol. 7[va], but not in *P* or *S*) : 'Alia ratio, que est in Amalario, sicut habetur in Iohel : Filii Israel, timentes captivari, cum fletu dicebant : Parce Domine, parce populo tuo; et si cum illi timentes captivitatem temporalem, dicebant hoc, verbis scilicet Parce etc, ita nos timentes eternam, dicimus : Agnus Dei miserere nobis, et hoc bis. Tertio dicimus : Dona nobis pacem, quia illi dicebant : et ne des hereditatem tuam gentibus'.

This quotation of *Ioel* 2, 17 as the precedent for the words of the canon is not to be found in the liturgical works of Amalarius, ed. I. M. HANSSENS (*Studi e testi* 139-140) 1948-50; but John Beleth gives it, *ed. cit.* 2, 84-85. On patristic use of the liturgy as an authority see B. CAPELLE, *Autorité de la liturgie chez les Pères*, in *Rech. ·Théol. anc. méd.* 21 (1954) 5-22. Comestor may have been aware of such precedents.

customs of the early and contemporary Church interested him.
In the early Church all the faithful present went to communion
at Mass. Today they do not, since not all can partake worthily;
but the priest gives the kiss of peace, so that all can be joined
in the sacrament of union at least (1618). He enlarges on the
change in custom in his lecture on *Lc.* 22, 16. In the early Church
all present either communicated or else withdrew after the offertory,
that is after the Mass of the catechumens. Then it was ruled that
all should communicate on Sundays. Later still, communion was
restricted to Christmas, Easter and Pentecost. Now it is restricted
to Easter. The origin of this custom puzzled Comestor; he could
find no authority for it:

> Quis autem restrinxerit [eam] ad unam solam festivitatem, sicut fit in
> temporibus nostris, non legi (*D*, fol. 142ra).

John Beleth mentioned the restriction of lay communion to three
festivals, but not the further restriction to Easter (communion at
Easter was made compulsory at the Lateran Council of 1215)[92].
Comestor had searched in vain for earlier authority. The restriction
arose by custom and changing attitudes; he probably could not
have found it in writing. The interesting point is that he looked.

The liturgy served also as evidence for events left obscure in
the gospels. The Fathers disputed the exact hour of the Resurrection.
Jerome fixed it at midnight, Augustine at dawn. Comestor cited
the Church's practice of celebrating two Masses between the third
and sixth hour of the night on Easter Eve and a third on the
morning of Easter Day to confirm Augustine's view (1627, *L*,
foll. 90vb-91ra). Similarly the use of the Church witnesses to the
number of holy women who visited the empty tomb; she represents
three, whereas some put the number at two (1635).

Medieval writers on the liturgy delighted in its allegorical interpretation. Typical of his outlook is Comestor's preference for its
historical meaning: the liturgy in his view re-enacted, recalled and
even offered evidence for the gospel story.

Landgraf has already pointed to the function of pictures in
theological exposition in a chapter of his *Dogmengeschichte* called

---

92. BELETH, *ed. cit.* 84-85; see also *Sent.* IV, xii, 6.

'Kunst und Glaubenslehre'. A commentator on Hebrews of the first half of the twelfth century, a disciple of Abelard, explains that St Peter with his keys and other saints were painted on church walls to replace pagan idols in temples. Another commentator on St Paul of about 1170 describes the iconography of the Jesse tree, stemming from the root of Jesse, showing David as the trunk, the Virgin among the leaves, and Christ as the flower (*et ita solet depingi*). Landgraf quotes two examples from Comestor, which I shall describe presently, on the Transfiguration and the positions of St Peter and St Paul on either side of Jesus. It is significant that Comestor supplies two of his few examples[93]. A study of their context shows that Comestor used pictures not only as illustration, but as evidence, and I have found two more passages where he mentions them.

First the Nativity : the tradition that an ox and an ass stood by the manger puzzled commentators, since the two animals derived from Old Testament prophecies and had no warrant in the gospels. Comestor admitted to doubts on the subject in his lecture on *Lc.* 2, 7. It was probable that Joseph had brought an ass for Mary to ride, but improbable that he had an ox as well, unless he intended to put it up for sale : 'Quod autem dicitur fuisse repositus inter bovem et asinum non multum, inquit, de auctoritate habetur ...' (*D*, fol. 86vb). In the *School History*, however, Comestor found some authority for the two animals 'in pictures in churches, which are as the books of the laity', where they are represented to us (1340). The ox and ass by the manger do in fact go back to very early Christian iconography.

Pictures of Christ and the apostles with flowing locks of hair raised the question whether Christ was a Nazarene; we know that Nazarenes did not shave their heads (*I Reg.* 1, 11). Comestor explained that Christ was called *Nazaraeus* from his birthplace (*Mt.* 2, 33); it means 'holy'; he was not a Nazarene. Comestor decided that the hair in the picture was symbolic, denoting sanctity :

> Unde Christus et apostoli depinguntur criniti, non in re, sed in sanctitate (1609).

93. A. M. Landgraf, *Dogmengeschichte der Frühscholastik* 2 (1), Regensburg 1953, 24-26.

Twelfth century moralists disapproved of long hair styles for men as effeminate; hence Comestor's proviso that the flowing locks were symbolic.

The Transfiguration suggested pictures to support an argument in theological discussion. Many divergent views were held in the schools on the nature of Christ's body when transfigured (*Mt.* 17, 2, *Lc.* 9, 29). Among the various opinions put forward, Comestor cites the following : no mortal body could have shone with such splendour, not even the Lord's. Therefore, the holders of this opinion argue, the splendour revealed to the disciples was not in the Lord's body, but in the air surrounding him. Wall paintings in churches, where the Transfiguration is depicted, support their opinion : rays of splendid light are shown *around* the Lord's body and *distinct* from it :

> Ideoque tradunt splendorem illum non fuisse in corpore dominico, sed in aere circumfuso, cui opinioni consonant picture in parietibus ecclesiarum, ubi depingitur transfiguratio. Solent depingi quidam radioli splendoris circa corpus dominicum seorsum distincti a corpore dominico (*L*, fol. 69va on *Mt.* 17, 2, and *D*, fol. 106vb on *Lc.* 9, 29).

We have no surviving wall paintings or mosaics of the Transfiguration for the twelfth century in the West; but miniatures showed rays of light issuing from Christ's body[94]. If Comestor saw the convention transferred to wall paintings, he could well have interpreted the rays as belonging to the surrounding air. The pictorial evidence did not convince him, however. He would not determine in favour of any opinion, on the grounds that it would be rash 'to seek nature in the miraculous', a caution which he expressed in the *School History* too (1582).

Again, in discussing the symbolism of the rings of the tabernacle, he adduced pictures to support the view that the rings on the left signified Matthew and John, because they knew Jesus in his mortal state, and the rings on the right Mark and Luke, who knew him only as immortal after the Resurrection; the left signified mortality and the right immortality. Pictures showing St Peter and St Paul one on each side of Christ place St Peter on the

---

94. G. SCHILLER, *Iconography of Christian Art*, transl. J. SELIGMAN, London 1971, 565-578.

left and St Paul on the right. St Paul knew Christ only in his immortal state, as did St Mark and St Luke :

> ... quia per sinistram mortalitas, per dextram immortalitas solet intelligi, quibus videntur consonare picture ecclesiarum. Ubi enim depinguntur Petrus et Paulus Domino collaterales, Paulus depingitur a dextris, Petrus a sinistris. Unde a simili per duos anulos a dextris significari videntur duo evangeliste qui Dominum in carne non viderunt, sicut nec vidit Paulus (*L*, fol. 92[va]).

The position of St Peter on the left and St Paul on the right of the Saviour was current from the early middle ages, though we cannot know what pictures Comestor saw[95]. Hugh of St Cher substituted the seal on a papal bull for 'pictures', when borrowing from Comestor's prologue to St Luke[96]. Paschal II's chancery (1089-1118) introduced the heads of the two apostles in the same position on papal seals, and the type persisted[97].

Pictorial evidence had been a hitherto untapped source for commentators. The only earlier parallel known to me comes from Adhémar of Chabannes, *Epistola de apostolatu Sancti Martialis*. According to Adhémar, a doubter of St Martial's apostolicity was confuted on being shown faded pictures in an old ruined church, where St Martial was portrayed serving the Lord, with other scenes from his life. Adhémar may have invented the pictures as part of his forgery[98]. In any case, Comestor probably had not read the *Epistola* and he seems to have observed real pictures for his researches.

---

95. G. LADNER, *I ritratti dei papi nell'Antichità e nel Medioevo* I, Città di Vaticano 1941, 16-37, 168-170; *Die Papstbildnisse des Altertums und des Mittelalters* II, Città di Vaticano 1970, 56-57, 80-90.

96. *Post. in Bibl.*, Paris 1530-1545, *ad loc.* : '... secundum quod Paulus, qui post ascensionem Domino adhaesit, ponitur a dextris in bulla papae, et Petrus, qui mortali adhaesit, ponitur a sinistris'.
STEPHEN LANGTON had described the papal bull in his commentary on the Pauline Epistles, perhaps borrowing from COMESTOR; see LANDGRAF, *op. cit.* 26.

97. R. L. POOLE, *Lectures on the History of the Papal Chancery down to the Time of Innocent III*, Cambridge 1915, 25, 120, 220; A. DE BOÜARD, *Manuel de diplomatique française et pontificale*, Paris 1929, planche xli, fig. 1-2.

98. PL 141, 101-102: 'Mox ibi ei ostendit picturas multa antiquitate vix parentes et ait : Unde sint istae picturae? Ille videns Martialem ministrantem Domino ad mandatum, et caeteras picturas, sicut legitur in eius Vita, rubore confusus non sine omnium qui aderant derisu confessus est mendacium suum'.
The *Vita* was forged by Adhémar, see above, p. 16.

Relics threw another bridge to the past. It came naturally to
Comestor to describe the history and location of relics as a
prolongation of the New Testament. Bede and others had done
so occasionally[99]; Comestor incorporates relics into his *School
History* and lectures. Here is just one example, interesting because
it suggests that Comestor had made a personal inspection, and
shows how he used relics as evidence, just as he used the liturgy
and pictures. On the date of Herod's slaughter of the Innocents
and their age at the time, Comestor says that some of their bones
are too big for children of two years old, though it could be said
that men were larger in stature then than they are now (1544).
The idea that once there were 'giants in the land', and that men
had lessened in size as time went on, was traditional : St Ambrose
estimated the antiquity of two recently discovered bodies of
martyrs by their size. Comestor may have seen or heard of relics
of the Holy Innocents at the abbey of St Victor at Marseilles,
brought there by Cassian from Bethlehem[100].

His interest in the history, topography and antiquities of Palestine
is already well known. A glance at the pages of his *School
History* and of his lectures will bear it out. A 'spot check' on his
statements shows that they were accurate, as far as he could have
told. The 'column of the flagellation', still bloodstained (it had
veins of red marble), was displayed to pilgrims to Jerusalem, as
was also the supposed site of the Temple altar, where the Saracens
had set up a clock, still to be seen (1628, 1608)[101]. He says that
a big marble stone, on which Jesus sat when talking to the
Canaanite woman (*Mt.* 15, 21-28) was preserved intact in heathen
hands, but that the Franks and Venetians damaged it. Later, he
adds, a church in honour of the Saviour was built over its remains
(1578). The Venetians indeed helped the Frankish king of Jerusalem
to take and sack the city of Tyre in 1124, and a cathedral was
built there[102].

99. BEDE on St Mark, *ed. cit.* 509-510.

100. *Dict. d'archéologie et de liturgie*, ed. F. CABROL 6 (1925) 610-613; H. FICH-
TENAU, *Zum Reliquienwesen im früheren Mittelalter*, in *Mitteilungen der Instituts
für Österreichische Forschungen* 60 (1952) 89.

101. H. VINCENT and F. M. ABEL, *Jérusalem. Recherches de topographie, d'archéologie et d'histoire* II, Paris 1914, 274, 278, 971.

102. T. S.R. BOASE, *Kingdoms and Strongholds of the Crusaders*, London 1971,
37, 120.

The Gloss prologue to St Mark (RB 607) states that this evangelist wrote in Italy. Comestor accepted the statement as authoritative, but stressed that St Mark wrote his gospel in Greek, not Latin. Some men falsely claimed to have it in both tongues, believing that St Mark provided it with a Latin translation. Comestor dismissed the claims as legendary (*L*, fol. 94[ra]). The reporter added that then, just as the master said so, there was a certain master of great repute in the schools, called John Beleth, who used to claim to have seen the chair of Mark, where he wrote the gospel in Latin (*ibid.*). Master John Beleth could well have been teaching in the Paris schools at the same time as Comestor[103]. His claim to have seen the chair of St Mark (where is not stated) witnesses both to current interest in New Testament monuments and to varying degrees of credulity. Comestor was more critical than his colleague.

Whence did he draw his exceptional concern and power of criticism on monuments and topography? He had a lead from Bede, who described the Holy Sepulchre according to the account of those who came to Britain from Jerusalem[104]; but Bede was untypical. Comestor's own master, Peter Lombard, gives no inkling of anything of the sort in his published works and recorded oral teaching. Perhaps the historian, William, later archbishop of Tyre, gives us the answer. William, born in the Holy Land, went abroad to study 1145/6-1165. He prided himself on having studied under Peter Lombard for six years[105], in which case he must have had Comestor as his fellow pupil. His *Historia rerum in partibus transmarinis gestarum* shows his absorption in the history, topography and monuments of Outremer. Comestor may have tapped his brains, though the *Historia* itself was written after Comestor's death. He could also have consulted guide books for pilgrims and visitors to the Holy Land on their return.

The modern biblical scholar with all the resources at his command may see Comestor's efforts in Balzac's words as 'les

---

103. See above p. 52, n. 53. Beleth wrote his book on the liturgy 1160-1164 and died about 1182.

104. In *Mc.* 15, 46, *ed. cit.* 638.

105. R. B. C. HUYGENS, *Guillaume de Tyr étudiant. Un chapitre de son "Histoire" retrouvée*, in *Latomus* 21 (1962) 823.

ignominies justifiables des petits ménages parisiens'. That would be unfair. Comestor took the only way open to a scholar of his time, moving from the known to the unknown and thereby giving his pupils a better understanding of the gospel story. The liturgy, pictures, relics and monuments, which they could see, hear or touch, supplemented the scanty literary sources available, to freshen often-read lessons, and even to provide new evidence. Comestor saw the possibilities and explored them.

VI

On doctrine Comestor followed in the footsteps of *B*, treading deeper and developing the argument. He had a natural sympathy with *B*'s outlook. Like *B*, he called the pope 'Christ's vicar' (*L*, fol. 37vb), who had no superior to correct him, as had other prelates. Unrepentant heretics must be cast out of the Church; but hirelings, that is bad prelates, must be tolerated, provided that they do not teach heresy (*L*, foll. 27vb-28ra). A private person is forbidden to avenge himself. He must leave it to the secular authority to keep order (*L*, fol. 86va). Christ rebuked St Peter for wielding the material sword (*Mt.* 26, 51-52); Peter's zeal had misled him to imitate Phineas, who slew evildoers (*Num.* 25, 7). The material sword has less force in the New than in the Old Testament :

> Nota Petrum deceptum. Putat enim meritorium esse quod extendat gladium in servum, exemplo Fineas; sed fallitur, quia modo non habet tantas vires gladius materialis quantas habebat tunc. Non enim habet locum in novo sicut in veteri testamento (*L*, fol. 141vb).

Comestor's reserve on the 'two swords' text (*Lc.* 22, 38) suggests that he did not subscribe to the opinion that the pope held two swords and delegated the material to secular princes to wield on his behalf. Comestor merely says that the Church wields the spiritual sword of excommunication. Even that should be used sparingly against princes. Excommunicate princes wreak their wrath on the many, causing much trouble to the Church thereby, he comments on Mt. 13, 30 (*L*, fol. 64va).

Comestor took the whole apparatus of secular judicial procedure for granted. He did not question the validity of the ordeal by fire and water, although this mode of trial was already coming under attack by reformers : Peter the Chanter would condemn it as blasphemous[106]. Comestor notes in passing that the first verses of St John's gospel confute heresies; hence it is credible that they would ward off sorcery also. Persons who have to undergo the ordeal of hot water or hot iron carry these words of the gospel on scraps of parchment, lest the truth should be tampered with by the witchcraft of men or devils :

> Nota quia sicut hoc principium valuit ad hereses repellendas, ita credibile est ut reppellat fantasmata. Ideo qui habent facere iudicia in aqua calida et in ferro calido, ne veritas rei impediatur maleficiis hominum vel demonum, portant super se descriptum hoc evangelium in quibusdam cartulis (*B*, fol. 4[ra]).

White magic combatted black magic! Comestor had no word of disapproval for the practice.

He treats poverty texts in the same spirit as *B*. If someone objected that labour and prudence were forbidden to a man in religion, who should rely solely on God (on *Mt*. 6, 31-34), Comestor answered that the Lord himself provided necessaries for his disciples and had money (*L*, fol. 40[rb]). The command to sell all one's possessions as a condition of perfection (*Lc*. 18, 22) struck him as 'hard'. Some did so when they entered religion and gave their goods to the poor (*D*, fol. 115[va]). Even that did not exempt them from the ordinary rules of society. They might take steps to regain the bare necessaries of life, in spite of the precept *ne repetas* (*Lc*. 6, 30), though not mere superfluities (*D*, fol. 99[ra]).

Comestor brought his own common sense to bear on such problems as 'sickness cause of sin'. Should the patient consult a doctor? The answer is a compromise : a wise physician should urge the sick man to confess his sins before undergoing medical treatment, which would be useless if sin had caused his disease; this accorded with current medical etiquette[107] :

> Unde prudens medicus, accedens ad egrotum, statim debet ei persuadere : Frater, prius confitere peccata tua, quia si forte pro peccato tuo contingit

---

106. COLIN MORRIS, *Judicium Dei : the Social a.d Political Significance of the Ordeal in the Eleventh Century*, in *Studies in Church History* ed. DEREK BAKER 12 (1975) 95-111; J. W. BALDWIN, *op. cit.* I, 326-330.

107. L. C. MACKINNEY, *op. cit.*, n. 12, 25-26.

tibi morbus iste, quicquid medicine impenderetur cederet irritum (1567, L, foll. 47vb-48ra).

Again he explains in his matter-of-fact way that the ban on advertising almsgiving (*Mt.* 6, 2) does not preclude proclamation, if it serves a charitable purpose; then it is not hypocrisy. A rich man giving alms in time of famine quite rightly has a bell rung before him or sends a crier through the town to gather poor folk together to receive his bounty (*L*, foll. 34vb-35ra). This was common medieval practice, as we know from Matthew Paris's *Chronica maiora*; he describes it in detail[108]. The victims of famine had to know where to go and at what time to get poor relief.

We shall now watch Comestor confronting the precepts of the Sermon on the Mount with a crusading, litigious Christendom. To begin with crusades : the pope called them and blessed crusaders. Comestor had qualms; but he was not squeamish. He made two distinctions to justify the crusades as against the command to love one's enemies and turn the other cheek. Some precepts applied to would-be perfect Christians only, not to the imperfect. The would-be perfect fall into two classes, divided in time, those of the early Church and those of today. The martyrs obeyed the precept by showing patience. Their patience made converts then; it would be misplaced nowadays. What would happen now if the ban on vengeance were to be applied to vengeance on heathen : 'Quid enim si non vindicetur in paganos?' (*L*, fol. 86va). The heathen would abuse our patience and would not yield land to Christians. The virtue which laid the Church's first foundation would harm her now. Christ spoke to the apostles *pro tempore* when he sent them to preach to all the world :

> *Diligite inimicos.* Hoc enim tam perfectis quam imperfectis congruit. Quod autem hic subdit de prebenda maxilla congruit solis perfectis, et solis perfectis illius temporis. Dominus enim pro tempore loquebatur, quia in universum mundum missurus erat apostolos... Non ergo congruit modernis perfectis huiusmodi patientia in lesione corporum, quia non habet hodie locum. Immo, si ita sustinerent afflictiones corporum, abuterentur pagani patientia eorum nec dimitterent terram, et ita quod primo valuit ad ecclesie fundamentum sic esset nunc in ecclesie detrimentum (*L*, fol. 33ra).

108. Sub anno 1258, *Opera* ed. H. R. LUARD (Rolls Series) 5, 693-694.

The Church approved the military religious Orders of the Temple and Hospital, thus permitting vengeance on heathen even to would-be perfect :

> Perfectis igitur huius temporis licita est ultio iniuriarum proprii corporis, alioquin minime permitteret hec ecclesia templaribus et hospitalaribus, qui sunt viri religiosi (*D*, fol. 99[ra]).

Comestor made the same point on Jesus' rebuke to the disciples for asking that fire from heaven should destroy their enemies (*Lc.* 9, 55). The early Church was founded on patient bearing of torments; the Church today must either resist the heathen or perish :

> In primitiva ecclesia non erat vindicandum, quia per patientiam tormentorum fundata erat ecclesia. Modo autem in paganos vindicandum est. Sicut enim per patientiam tunc ecclesia dilateretur, ita modo submergeretur (*D*, fol. 108[rb]).

Litigation among Christians roused the type of animosity illustrated by Hemming[109]. It was universal : every landholder, lay or ecclesiastical, had lawsuits on his hands. Comestor used much the same argument to justify it as he used on the crusades. The Church allowed it. Both the imperfect and the would-be perfect might go to law to defend their rights; otherwise the promulgators of canons and decretals would have deceived them. He had some scruples : litigation was inexpedient, though licit, since it distracted the mind from prayer and reading. Hence contemplative religious should not go to law. Even here, he inserts an escape clause : contemplatives might ask, as distinct from claiming at law, for restitution, either themselves or through their friends. He was expanding the Gloss on *Mt.* 5, 44 that litigation by lawful means was permitted, if it were not contentious :

> Solet tamen fieri circa hoc satis elegans distinctio magistralis. Imperfectis licet et expedit sua repetere sub iudice, sed non cum contentione; ... ergo nec perfecto nec imperfecto licet contendere, id est rixas et iurgia prorumpere. Perfectis autem coniugatis et prelatis licet quidem sua repetere sub iudice, alioquin decepissent eos qui promulgaverunt canones et decreta. Licet utique, sed non expedit, quia impedimentum est eis tumultus causarum, nec libere possint vacare orationi et lectioni. Perfectis autem speculativis, qui omnibus postpositis nudi nudum

---

109. See above p. 47.

sequuntur Christum, non licet nec expedit sua repetere sub iudice aliquo pacto. Possunt tamen repetere per se vel per amicos suos (*L*, fol. 33^{ra-b}).

The command not to judge applied to 'rash' judgements only and to those made by an equal. Prelates had a right to judge their subjects with discretion and mercy (*L*, fol. 40va). Again, the Church's authority supports changes in marriage laws. Comestor invoked it on *Mt*. 5, 32. Remarriage was forbidden in apostolic times; now it is permitted twice or thrice *pro incontinentia* (*L*, fol. 31vb). Canon law, like secular law, belonged to his scheme of things.

Masters put forward various opinions on the obligation to forgive one's enemy, a fellow-Christian (*Lc*. 6, 35). All agreed that the Christian must drive hatred from his heart; but must he do more than that? Some held that he was bound to provide his enemy with the necessaries of life, if he seemed to be in want. Others distinguished, arguing that only the would-be perfect need do so. The Christian was more obliged to help an offender who begged pardon. If he did not apologise, then even the would-be perfect were not obliged to greet or converse with him; indeed they might even excommunicate or have him excommunicated. Comestor cited his master Peter Lombard's stricter opinion that contemplative religious were a special case: they ought not to have their enemies excommunicated for any reason (*D*, fol. 126vb)[110]. Comestor does not commit himself to any one opinion.

Just occasionally he puts his foot down and condemns current practice. On *Mt*. 6, 33, *Primum quaerite regnum Dei*, he makes the familiar distinction between perfect and imperfect. The former are told not to pray for earthly blessings. The Church concedes to weaklings by praying for harvests, health and so on; but there are limits. It is blameworthy to have Masses celebrated for a lost horse and suchlike (*L*, fol. 53ra).

Comestor has never been included in the now fashionable group of writers who put forward theories of historical development: Hugh of St Victor, Rupert of Deutz, Anselm of Havelberg and later Joachim of Fiore. He contented himself with the old pattern of seven ages of the world, speculating only on the precise year

110. Above, p. 9.

when the sixth age, 'the time of grace', began, and citing various opinions (1540, 1552, *L*, foll. 16[vb]-17[ra]). Yet he had an implicit theory of historical change. Christ founded the Church with the pope as her head. The Church must move with the times and adapt to changing circumstances, as when she approves the military Orders and provides canon law procedures : *autres temps, autres mœurs*. Gerald of Wales puts this very maxim into Comestor's mouth. Gerald claimed to have heard him say in the hearing of all his school, attended by many learned men, that the rules of clerical celibacy should be relaxed to suit the times :

> Ideoque nunc aliud tempus, alii pro tempore mores. Hoc autem magistrum Petrum Manducatorem in audientia totius scholae suae, quae tot et tantis viris literatissimis referta fuit, dicentem audivi, quia nunquam hostis ille antiquus in aliquo articulo adeo ecclesiam Dei circumvenit, sicut in voti illius emissione[111].

The same suggestion on clerical celibacy was later put forward by Peter the Chanter. There is nothing improbable in Gerald's statement[112]. The maxim expresses Comestor's attitude well. He accepted established institutions, though not abuses, as necessary adjustments to promote the well-being of Christendom. Both *B* and Comestor agreed with the twelfth century canonists, who realised that many rules and customs departed from early Christian practices, but regarded changes as necessary and beneficial[113]. Nostalgia for the *ecclesia primitiva* did not infect either of our two commentators. They registered facts, without making value judgements, and relied on divine guidance of the Church.

---

111. *Gemma ecclesiastica* 26, in *Opera*, ed. BREWER (*Rolls Series*) 2, 187-188. It was compiled c. 1197; see A. A. GODDU and R. H. ROUSE, *Gerald of Wales and the « Florilegium Angelicum »*, in *Speculum* 52 (1977) 492.

112. BALDWIN, *op. cit.* (above n. 58) I, 42, 341. Other quotations from Comestor in *Gemma ecclesiastica* probably also derive from his oral teaching; see R. M. MARTIN, *Notes sur l'œuvre littéraire de Pierre le Mangeur*, in *Rech. Théol. anc. méd.* 3 (1931) 65. The proverb was current in various forms both in the vernacular and in Latin in the twelfth century; see S. SINGER, *Sprichwörter des Mittelalters* I, Bern 1944, 166-167; H. WALTHER, *Lateinische Sprichwörter und Sentenzen des Mittelalters*, Göttingen 1963-1967, nos. 19331 and 31206. 'Nunc aliud tempus ...' is first found in HILDEBERT, *Carmina minora* no. 17, ed A. B. SCOTT, Teubner 1969, 6.

113. G. OLSEN, *The Idea of the « Ecclesia Primitiva » in the Writings of the Twelfth-Century Canonists*, in *Traditio* 25 (1969) 61-86; B. SMALLEY, *Ecclesiastical Attitudes to Novelty c. 1100-c. 1250*, in *Studies in Church History*, *op. cit.*, n. 32, 113-133.

VII

Comestor and his source, the mysterious *B*, made a lasting impact on gospel exegesis. An account of their influence must wait for a later study. Comestor's achievement may be summarised as follows. He commented on the text and its glosses, unlike *B*, who quoted the Gloss anonymously. Comestor made an effort to 'order' the glosses both in relation to the text and to the literal and spiritual senses, assigning each gloss to its proper text and to the sense of Scripture it referred to. He tidied up at least some of the muddle inherited from the Fathers and their successors on distinction between the senses. His awareness of the problem marks him out as an innovator. His search for new ways of tackling the literal exposition of the gospels led him to exploit the resources of contemporary usage, plus the liturgy, relics, iconography and the antiquities of Palestine. He faced the challenge of applying gospel teaching on meekness and poverty to present conditions, as he found them. The previous use of *quaestiones* helped him to formulate his ideas. He met the challenge by putting forward an implicit theory of historical development. Changes were necessary; the Church had reason to authorise departures from a strict adherence to the Sermon on the Mount, in order to survive. A *via media* on the relations between *regnum* and *sacerdotium* seemed to him to offer the best solution to the need to keep order in society. It had always been customary to denounce abuses. Comestor followed tradition in doing so; he was less original in this respect than in others.

His originality in devising classroom techniques of lecturing on *sacra pagina* is open to question, because we know so little of what went on in the early twelfth century schools. However, if we take him as the first master actually recorded to have practised techniques later to become standard, we have, as well as lecturing on a glossed text, the first use of a sermon-type prologue and a division of the Gloss prologues as subject for lectures; this enabled the master to allot his time evenly between them, before starting on the first words of his text. 'The Master of the Histories' was also 'the Master of school exegesis'.

ADDITIONAL NOTES

p.43, n.25: H. Silvestre notes that St Jerome invented the formula *Nudum Christum nudus sequi, Epist. ad Rusticum* 20, CSEL 56, 142, though it did not become common until the eleventh century; See *Bull. Théol. anc. méd.* 13 (1981) 95.

p.59, n.71: See RB no. 10728, 7928-7934, 7808 for other items in the Durham MS.

p.70: Augustine, *De consensu evangelistarum* iii, 24, CSEL 43, 357-8, put the Resurrection at dawn. Dr. H. Silvestre kindly gave me this reference and told me that the reference to Jerome had not been traced, in a letter dated 20.2.81.

p.73, n.95: Peter Damian discusses the reasons why St. Peter is shown on the left and St. Paul on the right 'in pictures of the chief apostles throughout all provinces adjacent to Rome'; *Opusculum* xxxv, PL 145, 589-596.

p.79, n.108a: Dom Jean Leclercq has edited from a MS at Troyes Comestor's reply to a question put to him by the patriarch of Jerusalem on whether it was permissible for Christians to fight and kill pagans. Comestor urges the need to make war on Christ's enemies, cites earlier popes' approval and contrasts, as he does in his commentary, the duty of the early martyrs to suffer patiently to the present Christian duty to defend the Holy Land, by bloodshed; see 'Gratien, Pierre de Troyes et la seconde croisade', *Studia Gratiana* 2 (1954) 585-593.

3

An Early Paris Lecture Course
on St. Luke

On June 1, 1977 the Bodleian Library bought a manuscript, now shelf-marked as Lat.d.th.45, at Christie's sale (lot 159). It belonged originally to the Cistercian abbey of Morimondo in the diocese of Milan, and passed through the hands of the humanist scholar Paolo Giovio (1483-1552), who is known to have acquired some MSS from this abbey. It contains an unidentified commentary on the Gospel of St Luke. Dom Jean Leclercq has edited two catalogues of Morimondo MSS, one of the turn of the twelfth century, the other of the seventeenth. Neither of them lists the Bodleian commentary; but Dom Leclercq has shown that the monks continued to enlarge their library after the first catalogue was made, though their books were dispersed later; the second lists only a residue[1].

Since MS Oxford Bodl.lat.d.th.45 has not yet been described in the accessions to the Department of Western MSS, I shall give a provisional account of it here.

I. Foll. 1ra-54va, commentary on St Luke. 'In Lucam evangelium' is written in the top margin in a hand later than the text, fol. 1ra. *Prol.inc.*: In archa Domini erant iv anuli [*sic*] aurei, quibus inmissis duobus vectibus portabatur de loco ad locum. Erant autem duo anuli a dextris, duo a sinistris [from Exod. 15, 12-14]. Per archam intelligitur ecclesia, que sicut archa Domini secreta continebat, vas, scilicet in quo erant manna et virga Aaron que fronduerat. Ita ecclesia verba Domini secreta et sacramenta continet. Per iv anulos iv designantur evangeliste, qui bene et anuli et aurei dicuntur... *expl.* fol. 1va, ... ipse sedit ad dexteram, interpellans pro nobis sacerdos in eternum secundum ordinem Melchisdech.

Titulus idem est qui in aliis: *Incipit evangelium* Luce. Evangelium bonum, angelus nuntius. In evangelio quasi bona adnuntiatio, et vere que hic de Christo dicuntur vel ab ipso dicta recitantur bona sunt, quoniam ad salutem edificamur. *Prol. of St Jerome inc.*: Sicut in ceteris evangeliis, ita in evangelio Luce premittit Ieronimus prologum, in quo iv principaliter facere intendit, scilicet commendat personam et eius negotium; ostendit causam agendi et modum... *expl.* fol. 2va: ...quam prodesse fastidientibus.

1. *Textes et manuscrits cisterciens dans les bibliothèques des États-Unis*, in *Traditio* 17 (1961) 173-182. The staff of the Bodleian Library have been helpful in giving me information on this MS.

Comment on text inc.: *Quoniam quidem*: Facturus Lucas sermonem de omnibus que dixit et fecit Iesus usque ad ascensionem, premittit prologum, in quo primo redarguit temeritatem eorum... *expl.* fol. 54va [on *Lc*.24,53] ...ita quod occidant victimas, sed in laude Dei et benedictione, et ita celebratur novum sacerdotium, celebrando corpus et sanguinem Christi, qui laudabunt et benedicent Deum.

In same hand in darker ink: Expliciunt glose super Lucam.

II.   Excerpts from St Ambrose and other authors on various texts of St Luke: *inc.*fol.54va: Lucas, *qualis esset ista salutatio* [1,9]. Ambrosius: Maria ex verecundia pudet, ex prudentia novam benedictionis formulam mirans... *expl.* ...se iudicat idoneum qui poscit etc.[2]

III.   A discussion on penance and confession of heresy and sin: *inc.*fol.54va: Item Lucas ibi *occurrerunt ei x viri leprosi etc.* [17, 12]. Ambrosius, glosa: *Quisque heretica pravitate vel gentili superstitione etc, necesse est ut ad ecclesiam veniat...corrigit et sanat*[3]. Fere omnes divini [*sic*] hac occasione istius auctoritatis beati Ambrosii tenebant et dicebant quod quamvis hereticus veraciter in corde penituit, heresim suam detestando...*expl.* fol.54vb: ...id est secrete et occulte absque cognitione multorum corrigit et sanat.

IV.   A Christological discussion *inc.* fol.54vb: Quidam dicunt quod maius et excellentius est quod verbum caro factum est et Filius Dei est factus homo quam Filius Dei est genitus a Patre, et sic maius et excellentius est misterium generationis temporalis quam misterium eterne generationis, et hoc volunt probare per hac ratione...*expl.* fol.55ra: ...hoc est opus maius et excellentius opus quod Deus fecit.

In same hand in darker ink: Expliciunt glose super Lucam.

V.   A commentary on St Jerome's prologue to St Luke *inc.*fol.55ra: Hic incipit prologus. Huic autem operi vel libro Ieronimus prologum premittit, ubi ostendit unde oriundus fuerit Lucas evangelista, scilicet de Siria... *expl.*fol.55va: ...ad exponere scripturas nauseantibus.

VI.   Notes (?) for a sermon, fol.55vb: 'In ramis palmarum' is written on the top margin; *inc.*: *Noli timere filia Syon...asine etc* [*Ioan*.12,15]. Si coram nobis, fratres, Christus positus est mortuus...et pullum filium eius etc.

VII.   Fragments of sermons (?), fol. 55rb: Alibi legitur: *Sumite in vasis vestris...reportare* [*Gen*.43,11].
Si quis est Domini, iungatur michi...et detur vobis benedictio [Exod.32,26-29]. Verba hec sunt Moysi et filiorum Levi post fractum ab eis vitulum conflatilem. Moyses est Christus, filii Levi doctores sunt ecclesiarum...levate signum ad populos.
Dignus est agnus [*Apoc*. 5,12]. Flebat Ioannes in Apocalipsi quia non

---

2. The excerpts come partly from the original commentary of St Ambrose on Luke, ed. M. ADRIAEN, CCSL 14 (1957) 34, 288, and partly from the excerpts from it in the *Glossa Ordinaria*. I quote the Gloss *ad. loc.* from the Lyons 1589 ed. with the Postills of Nicholas of Lyre, the Additions of Paul of Burgos and other matter. One quotation ascribed to Ambrose comes from the Gloss and is not found in the original.

3. This passage is in the Gloss, but not in the original of St Ambrose.

inveniabatur...prima spiritualis anima, secunda corporis. Legi in libro Numerorum quod Dominus locutus est Moysi dicens: *Fac tibi duas tubas ductiles...castra* [*Num.*10,2]. Istoria patet; sed quoniam Moyses gerit in multis figuram Christi...ipsa potestate qui vivit et regnat etc Amen.

This represents a sermon on the feast of St Peter and St Paul.

Audi Israel, Dominus Deus tuus unus est... [*Deut.*6,4]. Sub tegmine idoli occultum est misterium iniquitatis...traditiones hominum relinquimus.

VIII.   Opening words of a letter (?), fol.57[rb]: Venerabili in Christo patri et domine.

The rest of the column is blank.

On fol.57[vb] in a sixteenth century hand: 'Liber sancte Marie de Morimundo N° XL'.

On fol.58[ra] is a list of words and their meanings in no discernible sequence. The top of the column has been rubbed and is illegible.

inc.: Librarii et notarii idem sunt.

expl.: ...remissus a fide vel a sancto proposito.

The rest of the folio and fol.59[r-v] are blank.

Written on parchment in two columns in light brown ink by various Italian hands of the early thirteenth century. No colour or decoration. A contemporary hand has made interlinear corrections; otherwise there is no annotation. The text of St Luke has no capitulation either in the text or in the margins. 10 × 7 cm. Italian binding of the seventeenth century; pale brown sheepskin over pasteboards, simply tooled with a triple fillet in blind.

I have not succeeded in identifying any of the miscellanea following the commentary proper (foll.54[va]-58[ra]). The theological pieces comprising items III and IV seem to be pre-scholastic. They are not set out in *quaestio* form; the discussion on penance refers to confession and abjuration either in public or in private 'before several priests'.

Turning to the commentary on St Luke, we have one other known copy in MS Montecassino 240, foll. 107-183 (RB 9851)[4]. Here, too, it is anonymous. This MS is written in thirteenth century gothic hands with coloured initials. It forms part of a collection of biblical commentaries: Peter Comestor on St Matthew and anonymous

---

4. F. STEGMÜLLER, *Repertorium Biblicum Medii Aevi* (Madrid, 1950-1977) in progress. Vols 8 and 9 were prepared by N. REINHARDT, who very kindly identified the Montecassino copy from the *Initia*, now in press. I refer to the *Repertorium* as RB, giving the number.

commentaries on St Luke and Genesis (RB 9852-3)[5]. I have not seen this MS; but the incipits are verbally identical with those in the Morimondo MS; the explicits differ only in that the Montecassino copy breaks off incomplete at *Lc.*24,50, whereas the Morimondo, which includes the same comment (fol. 54ra), goes on to the last words of the Gospel, *Lc.*24,53.

The provenance of our two copies might lead to the supposition that the commentary came from an Italian monastic author. Its presence in the company of Peter Comestor on St Matthew and of commentaries whose incipits suggest a scholastic milieu in the Montecassino MS should make us think twice. A reading of the Morimondo copy justifies our doubts. I shall call our anonymous *L*, since he cannot be identified at present. Folio references will be to MS Oxford, Bodl.lat.th.d.45, unless otherwise noted.

The place was the Paris schools. *L* refers to the liturgical use of 'the Paris church', evidently meaning Notre-Dame:

Unde et in ecclesia Parisiensi, eo die quo cantatur hoc evangelium *Missus est angelus etc*, ministrant sacerdotes in omnibus... (fol. 5^{ra-b}).

He alludes to academic rivalries, supposing that a number of masters will be teaching simultaneously. When the Baptist's disciples tell him of Jesus (*Lc.*7, 18), the Gloss says that their motive was to make their master envious. *L* comments:

Quod adhuc fit sepe, cum discipuli alicuius magistri aliquem novum vident consurgere et suo preferri (fol.24rb).

He was a secular clerk or priest, jealous of religious claims to superiority. Thus he managed to deduce from number symbolism on *Lc.*19,4 that monks ranked lower than seculars:

Unde constat indigniores monachos [esse] clericis (fol.27ra).

He had a low opinion of bishops who retired from office to end their days in religion. Those who have led bad lives leave office in order to make a good end in the desert, whereas good bishops, such as Martin and Augustine, remain in office to the last; indeed they persist in preaching and governing all the more ardently (fol.18va).

We have a *terminus post quem* for the date, since *L* quotes an

5. M. INGUANEZ, *Codicum Casiniensis Manuscriptorum Catalogus* 2 (Montecassino, 1928-1934) 52-53.

opinion of Peter Lombard, to be found in his *Sentences*. The Gloss on *solvite eum* (*Lc.*19,30) links Christ's command to the disciples to loose the foal of the ass to his promise that they should have power to loose from sin on earth and in heaven (*Mt.*18,18). The second text raised the problem of the priest's part in remission of sin in his penitent. *L* cites two opinions without deciding between them:

Solvite hac pena, secundum magistrum Hugonem, vel *solvite*, id est ostendere solutum in culpa, secundum magistrum Petrum, quia *quecumque solveritis* hac pena, secundum magistrum Hugonem, vel *solveritis*, id est ostendens, secundum magistrum Petrum, *erunt soluta et in celo* (fol.46ra).

Master Hugh may be either Hugh of St Victor in *De Sacramentis* or the author of the Victorine *Summa Sententiarum*. Both explain that the priest releases his penitent from the penalty due to his sin in the future[6]. Peter Lombard, on the contrary, argues that priests show their penitents to be absolved in God's sight:

Hi ergo peccata dimittunt vel retinent, dum dimissa a Deo vel retenta iudicant et ostendunt... Et notandum, quia quos satisfactione poenitentiae ligant, eo ipso a peccatis solutos ostendunt (*Sent.*IV, xiii, 6).

L would have had the *Sentences* in mind when he quoted *quidam* on the question of the efficacy of the baptism of St John Baptist (*Lc.* 3,30):

Quidam sic exponunt hoc, ut refertur remissio peccatorum non ad baptismum, sed ad penitentiam. Baptismus enim Iohannis non conferebat remissionem peccatorum, quia fiebat tantum in aqua, non in spiritu. Hic tamen sic exponitur, ut quod dictum est *in remissionem peccatorum* referatur ad baptismum, non tamen ad baptismum Iohannis, sed ad baptismum Christi, quem scilicet Iohannes predicabat, id est futurum prenuntiabat (fol.12ra).

This gives the gist of the Lombard's teaching: remission of sin in this context meant penance, not deletion of sin, as conferred by the baptism of Christ (*Sent.* IV, iii, 2-3).

According to recent dating, the Lombard composed his *Sentences* 1155-1156, gave copies to his pupils 1156-1157, and read them in the Paris schools 1157-1158[7]. It follows that *L* was lecturing after 1158,

---

6. PL 176, 566 and 148-149. On the *Summa sententiarum* see D.E. LUSCOMBE, *The School of Peter Abelard* (Cambridge, 1969) 198-213. It is now held to be anterior to the *Sentences*.

7. *Magistri Petri Lombardi Sententiae in IV Libris Distinctae, Prolegomena*, in *Spicilegium Bonaventurianum* 4, I, 1 (Grottaferrata, Rome, 1971) 128*-129*.

or perhaps, if he had an advance copy of the *Sentences*, a few years earlier.

L mentions no other masters by name. His very silence gives us a *terminus ante quem*. He shows no acquaintance with Peter Comestor's lectures on the Gospels, Paris 1159-1178[8], or with his *Historia scholastica*, c.1170. The latter quickly took its place as a set text on sacred history: Comestor was known as 'Magister historiarum' and quoted as 'Magister in historiis'. Fol.21 of our manuscript is an inset, a quarter the size of the other leaves. It has a passage written in two columns in a different and possibly later hand; the verso is blank. Here is a commentary on *Lc*.6,1-2:

Et factum est in sabbato secundo…per sata. Hoc capitulum a magistro sic exponitur in istoriis. Primo sic: *secundo primo*, adverbium, id est adverbialiter positum…*non licet in sabbatis*? Excusabat eos Dominus multis modis etc.

The passage corresponds with only slight verbal variants to the *Historia scholastica* (PL 198, 1572). Our inset represents an insertion to the original text; it is not an omitted piece of *L*'s commentary, which continues without any break on the leaves before and after fol.21. This seems to prove that *L* lectured without benefit of the *Historia scholastica*; some other scholar, or perhaps *L* himself, sought to improve the original by quoting 'Magister in historiis' on *Lc*.6,1-2. That would put *L* before 1178 at least, and we can be sure that he was not a pupil of Peter Comestor.

Was he a pupil of Peter Lombard? A date c.1156-c.1178 for his lectures suggests that he might have heard the Lombard before teaching as a 'master of the sacred page': the Lombard became bishop of Paris 1159. The question is easily answered by a comparison of *L* with Peter Comestor's quotations from Peter Lombard's lost lectures on St Luke; Comestor was the Lombard's pupil and a faithful recorder of his teaching[9]. I checked Comestor's three quotations of the Lombard on St Luke in *L*, and drew a blank on two of them (*Lc*. 17,4 and 20,47). A third yielded something more positive. Comestor says that his master prided himself on finding the right interpretation of the word *donavit* (*Lc*.7,43); he took it to

8. See above, chapter 1, p. 4.
9. Ibid., pp. 7-11.

include the meaning *condonavit*, that is to *forgive* as well as to *give*. *L* does mention the meaning *condonavit*:

Sed hic plus debenti plus condonatur et est plus diligens et dilectus (fol.25ʳᵇ).

We catch an echo of the Lombard's lecture, suggesting that *L* knew how he interpreted *donavit*; but it will not suffice to make him the · Lombard's pupil. If he had been, he would surely have made more use of his master's work.

Pending the discovery of the Lombard on St Luke, if that ever happens, we have in *L* the earliest known Paris lecture course on a Gospel; it antedates Comestor's, which hitherto has been taken for the first to survive, though one suspected that he had predecessors other than the Lombard[10]. Comestor's have come down to us in *reportationes*, whereas *L*'s represent the master's own notes, as far as I can tell. Their early date will repay scrutiny of technique and content.

L begins with a prologue, quoting a text from the Old Testament and applying it in its spiritual sense to the Christian dispensation. He states his author's *materia*, *intentio*, *causa scribendi* and *modus agendi*; then he expounds St Jerome's prologue as found in the Gloss (RB 615), a form of introduction which became the stereotype. He lectured on a glossed text of St Luke, as did Peter Lombard and later Peter Comestor. Like Comestor, he read out the glosses ('Lege textum cum omnibus glosis usque illuc.') and distinguished between their literal and spiritual references ('Lege tèxtum ad litteram usque illuc... alie glose mistice sunt.'). Like Comestor, he notes the disposition of his glosses on the page, dividing the marginal from the interlinear ('Hec glosa hic dividit[ur] ab interlineari.'). Like Comestor, he points to differences in the glosses 'in certain books'. One gloss may be found 'in quibusdam libris', but apparently not in others. For instance, he mentions a gloss 'Hoc expirante Domino gestum est' on *Lc.*23,44. This, like the great majority of glosses which he quotes, comes from the *Glossa Ordinaria*, used by Peter Lombard and Peter Comestor, but it must have been lacking in some copies: complete standardisation of the Gloss had not yet been reached.

Thus *L* anticipated Comestor's technique; he may not have been

10. On Comestor's Gospel commentaries see above, chapter 2, pp. 37-82.

the first to do so. But he was teaching at a lower level than Comestor. The Gloss has a quotation from St John Chrysostom via Bede on *Lc*.1,26[11]. *L* felt obliged to explain to his pupils that Chrysostom meant 'Golden-mouth' (fol.4[vb]), supposing that the name would be unfamiliar to them. He did not venture far from his apparatus of glosses, though complaining of its shortcomings. The text *Lc*.5,19, where the friends of the paralytic let him down through the roof to reach Jesus, suggested a mystical interpretation; to climb up to the roof meant to understand Christ's divinity, hidden in the house of his flesh. But *L* had no note on this exegesis, apart from a few words in the Gloss:

Cuius expositionis nulla notula hic habetur, nisi quod super *tegulas* suprapositum est *Per divinitatem* [i.e. an interlinear gloss] (fol.19[rb]).

He remembered his study of grammar in the arts course. Christ's words when healing the paralytic are put first in the plural: *ut sciatis*, and then in the singular: *Tibi dico, surge* (*Lc*.5,24). *L* explains the transition as an exemple of aposiopesis and illustrates its meaning:

Huiusmodi genus locutionis satis est usitatum, velut si sunt duo modo presentes, et velim aliquid probare uni, per hoc quod facturus vel dicturus sum alteri, possum dicere: ut tu, Socrates, credas hoc quod dixi; dico tibi, Cato, hoc aliud vel facio. Volunt auctoritates quedam hoc esse aposiopesis, ut subintelligatur aliquid hoc modo: *ut sciatis etc*, *dico* hoc paralytico; [ad] quod subintelligendum interponit evangelista aliis verbis: *Tolle grabatum* (fol.19[rb])[12].

A quotation from Juvenal *Sat*. X, 249 on the numbers present at the feeding of the multitude (*Lc*.19,14) does not come from *L*'s sources, but was fairly banal:

Unde Iuvenalis: Iam dextra computat annos (fol.27[ra])[13].

Otherwise we find in embryonic form the kind of matter which appears in the homiletical commentaries of Peter Comestor and Peter the Chanter and his circle. There is one *exemplum*: a philosopher told

---

11. Ed. D. HURST, CCSL 120 (1960) 28. BEDE refers to 'Iohannes Constantinopolis urbis antistes'; but the Gloss has 'Chrysostomus'.

12. *L*'s source was probably verbal teaching on a grammatical text.

13. Juvenal was used as a school text and commented on in the twelfth century; see *Classical Influences on European Culture A.D. 500-1500*, ed. R. R. BOLGAR (Cambridge, 1971) 55, 89, 208.

a thief to take his treasure and let him sleep in peace (fol.27[rb])[14]. Satire greets us in the usual gibes against greedy bishops and archdeacons and against promotion for favour or simony (foll. 26[vb], 46[rb]). Monks spend too much money on their fine cloisters and meadows (fol.10[ra]). The Carthusians, on the other hand, receive praise for their unworldliness: if a thief steals their cattle, they send him yokes and carts and ask whether he wants anything else, saying that he would have stolen only what he really needed; so nobody dares to steal from them (foll.22[vb]-23[ra]). *L* fits into pattern, too, by making contemporary allusions to clarify his text. Caesar's collection of tribute recalls a mode of assessment 'still used in certain towns'. Unfortunately the description is too unspecific to be located:

…quomodo fit adhuc in quibusdam civitatibus. Computatur enim quantam pecuniam quisque habeat et quantum valeat et quantas habeat possessiones, et cognita summa per singulas urbes persolvit duos nummos vel plures iuxta consuetudinem civitatis (fol.8[ra]).

The current practice of division of labour in monasteries is suggested by *Lc.*5,33: monks incapable of higher things are sent off on business, such as gathering the harvest, since they will just be idle and entertain worldly thoughts if they are shut in and set to books and search for divine secrets (fol.20[rb]). ·

The historian of early scholastic thought will find little here to interest him. The famous texts on buying a sword and on the two swords (*Lc.*22,36-38) are passed over without a hint at their place in disputes on the relation between *regnum* and *sacerdotium* (foll.49[vb]-50[ra]). The only flicker of concern with theology, apart from the two allusions to the *Sentences* already mentioned, comes in a *quaestio* on the Jews' responsibility for the Crucifixion. Christ prayed that they might be forgiven, because they acted in ignorance (*Lc.*23,34). It seems, therefore, that some Jews sinned from ignorance rather than from malice, killing Christ in the belief that he was bad. These committed a much lesser sin than those who recognised him for what he was, and killed him from envy. Christ's prayer for the ignorant

---

14. F.C. TUBACH, *Index Exemplorum. A Handbook of Medieval Tales* (Helsinki, 1969) no.3746, lists a variant which became popular, though he is wrong in deriving it from Valerius Maximus. The source is *De nugis philosophorum*, ascribed to CAECILIUS BALBUS, ed. E. WOEHFFLIN (Bâle, 1855) 34. Dr R.W. Hunt kindly pointed this out to me.

saved them; but they sinned all the same in not believing when they might have done so. There follows a sentence which is cryptic as it stands in our text: *L* seems to have switched from the question of the Jews who killed Christ to the Jews and pagans of his own time:

Illi vero iudei, quomodo sunt, et pagani, non sunt dicendi nescientes, sed contemptores, cum veritas palam sit (fol. 34[va-b]).

L shows awareness of two problems: (1) the effect of intention on action, raised controversially by Abelard, who argued that the Jews' ignorance excused them from the guilt of crucifying Christ[15]; (2) the problem, raised acutely by the crusades, of the salvation of contemporary Jews and infidels. On this it was generally held that the truth of the Christian faith was sufficiently widespread to be known to all; hence neither Jews nor pagans evaded guilt when they persisted in their unbelief[16]. *L* seems to have compromised on the first problem: the Jews who crucified Christ in ignorance sinned, but might still be saved. He shared the common view on the second problem: Jews and pagans were not ignorant, but despisers of the Christian faith.

This brings us to the adaptation of Christ's teaching to the contemporary Church. Earlier and later commentators noted the contrasts, which some justified, as did Peter Comestor, or deplored, as did Peter the Chanter. *L* knew what was at stake. On *Lc.*3,11, *Qui habet duas tunicas, det non habenti*, he explains that the command does not apply to a man who needs his two coats; a monk may have several without sin; indeed, many call this a counsel, not a precept (fol. 13[ra]). On *Lc.*6,27, *Nolite iudicare*, he distinguishes between actions and persons. Some *actions* are patently bad; we may rightly judge them to be so. Others, such as fasting, are uncertain, depending on intention; these should always be given the benefit of the doubt; *persons* should never be judged, since a bad man may change for the better (fol. 23[ra]). *Qui aufert quae tua sunt, ne repetas* (*Lc.* 6,30) seemed to forbid litigation. *L* modifies the ban: one should not ask for anything which one ought not to have, as though a monk were to ask permission to take vengeance or to get married (ibid.). As far as can

15. *Peter Abelard's Ethics*, ed. and transl. by D.E. Luscombe (Oxford, 1971) 58-62; on later discussion see Luscombe, *The School of Peter Abelard*, op.cit. 256-257.
16. L. Capéran, *Le problème du salut des infidèles*, 2nd ed. (Toulouse, 1934), passim.

be seen, *L* would have subscribed to the moderate views put forward by Peter Comestor, accepting the Church's institutions as they were, and condemning only abuses in their working. But *L* is less forthcoming than Comestor on the subject.

His most personal and individual trait is his interest in the liturgy: liturgical use and ritual crop up at every turn [17]. Before reading *L*, I surmised that Comestor was an innovator in this respect. Now I realise that *L* may have suggested interest in the liturgy to Comestor. Some of their allusions are similar; but there is no evidence that Comestor borrowed from *L* directly, and they use the common matter in different ways. Perhaps Comestor took the idea from *L* or perhaps it was 'in the air' at Paris. One of *L*'s rare *quaestiones* turns on a liturgical point (*Lc.*2,32) and may be transcribed as an illustration. Why, he asks, do we set up the paschal candle, signifying Christ, at Eastertide only, when Christ is always present to us in the Eucharist? He answers that Christ appeared visibly at Easter, and afterwards only in the species of bread and wine. The passage begins with a comparison of the paschal candle to the two lights of the Old and New Testaments, the pillar of fire going before the Israelites in the wilderness, and Christ as the light of the world. It continues:

Utramque lucem representat lux cerea paschalis, unde et eius benedictio nocte dicitur, quia sicut dies illuminabatur, et quia lux ista a pascha usque ad pentecosten conversata est cum apostolis, ad significandam hanc presentiam eius debet in hoc tempore in ecclesia esse erectus cereus paschalis. Ab ascensione usque ad pentecosten non fuit Christus presens apostolis in carne, [sed] quia promisit se in proximo daturum Spiritum sanctum gaudebant expectatione Paracleti et recordatione primi ascensionis Christi, tanquam presens carne eis adesset. Sed oppones quia adhuc presens est nobis in carne Christus, cum singulis diebus communicamus eius carne et sanguine, quare non est viduata a sponso ecclesia, cum et corporaliter sit semper cum ea; ad quod respondetur: non apparet Christus nobis in specie humana, immo quasi latet nobis sub alia figura, ideoque cum non ostendat se nobis in propria specie, qua apparuit apostolis, non letatur ab eius visione ecclesia hac, et tamquam non habeat eum presentem dicitur a Deo viduata (foll.10vb-11ra).

Another comment shows interest in the history of liturgical usage, again anticipating Comestor. On *Lc.*1,9 *L* explains the Jewish arrangements for ensuring continuity in the high priesthood; a new

17. V. PERI, *Nichil in Ecclesia sine causa. Note di vita liturgica romana nel XII secolo*, in *Rivista di Archeologia Cristiana* 50 (1974) 249-74.

high priest replaced his predecessor immediately after his death and before his burial. That used to be the custom in the papacy too:

Unde traditum est ut olim, mortuo papa, antequam sepeliretur, alius substitueretur (fol. 3vb).

L implies the contrast with his own times, when the new pope was not enthroned until after his predecessor's burial. The canonist Rufinus, commenting on Gratian's *Decretum* on papal elections, where it is said that the new pope must be elected three days after his predecessor has died, explained that the old custom was intended to prevent indecent neglect of the papal funeral[18]. Rufinus finished and published his *Summa decretorum* 1157-1159, either while still a master at Bologna or after he became bishop of Assisi[19]. If *L* was teaching at Paris in the 1160s, as seems probable, he could have read the *Summa decretorum* or at least known something of its content on the change from old to new customs.

He was not only interested in ritual, but a stickler for correctness. The priest at the altar should stretch out his arms straight, to make the form of a cross; but some sin by negligence, bending their arms as though they were warming themselves at the fire (fol. 22ra). Commenting on the Presentation in the Temple (*Lc.*2,28), *L* says that every newly baptized infant should be brought to the altar for communion; this custom should be observed throughout the Church (fol. 10ra). The admission of newly baptized infants to communion was general in many churches until the thirteenth century[20]. *L*'s insistence on it suggests that it was already falling out of use.

Can we identify *L* from internal evidence? His passion for the liturgy points to Master John Beleth, who produced his popular *Summa de divinis officiis* 1160-1164, probably while he was teaching

---

18. *Die Summa Decretorum des Magister Rufinus*, ed. H. SINGER (Paderborn, 1902) 169: *Quando? ... Quia tertio die depositionis prioris pape ... Quod quidem*, scilicet ut non ante eligeretur alius, ex causa olim constitutum fuit, quia maxime solliciti ad aliud eligendum non curabant de mortuo sepeliendo, sicut decebat. Hodie vero ex consuetudine Romane ecclesie econtraria hoc abolitum est; prius namque alius eligitur quam mortuus sepeliatur.
  Dr. S. KUTTNER kindly put me on the track of this reference.
19. *Dict. de Droit Canonique* 7 (1965) 779-784.
20. *Dict. d'archéologie chrétienne et de liturgie* 3 (1914) 2444.

at Paris[21]. Comparison gave a negative result at least. Not only is there no significant similarity between *L*'s lectures and Beleth's *Summa*; there is one important difference. Beleth says nothing in his section on baptism of the communion of newly baptized infants, on which *L* insisted[22]. From the point of view of dates, Master Odo, teaching theology at Notre-Dame from c. 1145 and chancellor there 1160-1166/7, would be a possibility; but he resigned from office and entered the Cistercian abbay of Ourscamp[23]. *L*'s pro-secular bias makes the identification with Odo of Ourscamp unlikely, unless he experienced a sudden conversion. Other masters were teaching at Paris in the 1160s and '70s[24]. We must leave *L* unidentified among these lesser fry of the schools.

It is no wonder that his lectures survive only in two copies in Italian monasteries. Presumably the monks of Morimondo and Montecassino obtained their exemplars from Paris in an attempt to keep up with school learning. The pace of development at Paris was so fast that *L* would have 'dated' in a matter of years, as new masters came on the scene. Comestor had a better mind, as well as an improved technique. New sources for exegesis opened up, and its mode became more sophisticated. *L*'s value for us, apart from the charm of freshness, is his witness to an early stage of lecturing on *sacra pagina* and its glosses, and to subsequent progress. Comestor appears less original and yet more advanced than had been thought. He inherited a framework of teaching the Gospels, if not directly from *L*, at least from his milieu; but Comestor put new content into it. Our homely little book from Morimondo looks like a stepping stone to higher things.

---

21. N. HÄRING, *Chartres and Paris revisited*, in *Essays in Honour of Anton Charles Pegis*, ed. J. R. O'DONNELL (Toronto, 1974) 306. H. DUTEIL has edited the *Summa* (CC Contin.med. 41, 42, 1976) with an account of Beleth's career and writings.

22. Ibid., 42, 208-209.

23. I. BRADY, *Peter Lombard: Canon of Notre Dame*, in *Rech.Théol.anc.méd.* 32 (1965) 288-289. Odo left theological *Quaestiones*, whereas *L* took little interest in theology, making the identification even more implausible.

24. Ibid., 287-291.

4

The Gospels in the Paris Schools
in the Late Twelfth and
Early Thirteenth Centuries

Peter the Chanter, Hugh of St. Cher,
Alexander of Hales, John of La Rochelle

Concepts of the *vita evangelica vel apostolica* form a central theme in medieval studies today. We now know more about the background to the rise of the Mendicant Orders; we can watch the development of various aspirations to live according to the Gospels among both orthodox and heretical groups in Christendom. We have a better, though by no means complete understanding of the friars' efforts to carry out the plans of their founders, St. Dominic and St. Francis. Here I want to quarry in an area of information which is still largely unexplored: lectures on the Gospels given in the Paris schools c. 1173–1245. The conflict between secular masters and Mendicants from the 1250s onward has high–lighted polemical exegesis of biblical texts. The commentaries of the great schoolmen are available in print. But there is a gap in our knowledge of Bible teaching in the schools in precisely the period when Mendicants took over from seculars. Earlier neglect of this subject need cause no surprise: of the four scholars named in my title only Hugh of St. Cher on the whole Bible can be read in print, and that in early uncritical editions. The others' commentaries are still in manuscript and bristle with difficulties. They raise problems of authenticity, inter–relationships and variants, sometimes stemming from several *reportationes* of the same lecture course. And yet Gospel commentaries in particular suggest crucial questions: how did masters, secular or religious, interpret the Sermon on the Mount, apostolic poverty and preaching to their pupils? Disputations and commentaries on the *Sentences* or *Summas* would provide a framework for such interpretation; the Gospels focused attention on it. No lecturer could evade problems posed by the contrasts between the life and teaching of Jesus on the one hand and the practice and theory of the contemporary Church on the other. A master could blame or justify, with varying shades of emphasis; he could not avoid expressing his opinions; his students would expect it of him. His teaching, moreover, would stretch out to wider circles than his immediate audience which included future prelates and preachers, members of religious Orders or potential recruits to Orders. His commentaries would be read as well as heard. How far did the friars bring a new approach to lectures on the Gospels? How far, if at all, did they differ from their secular predecessors?

Teased by these questions, indeed gadfly–driven, I set out on a voyage of discovery. It entailed much technical prospecting and the amount of material made it impossible to map out the territory at all thoroughly. My findings are subject to future research. This paper follows on two others, which prepare the way for it. The first dealt with early twelfth–century Gospel commentaries, originating mainly in the schools of Laon and Paris, the second with Peter Comestor on the Gospels and his sources.[1] Only the second need be summarised here. Peter Comestor or Manducator, best known as 'the Master of the Histories,' the classic medieval textbook on Bible history, left lectures on the Gospels, given at Paris 1159–1178. They have come down to us as *reportationes*. Comestor lectured on a glossed text of the Gospels; his gloss was what became standard as the *Ordinaria*. His main source, apart from the Gloss with its patristic excerpts, was a commentary on St. Matthew printed under the name of Master Anselm of Laon (PL 162, 1227–1500). The true author, it is now agreed, was not Anselm but another scholar, writing c. 1140–1150. Master Geoffrey Babion has some claims to authorship. They are so insubstantial, it seems to me, that we have to treat the writer as anonymous. I call him '*B*' without prejudice to the attribution.

To describe Comestor's attitude briefly: he was 'Establishment–minded,' like his preferred source *B*. He accepted the differences between the early and the present–day Church as right and proper, given correct behaviour in all ranks of society. He upheld uses and denounced only abuses. He was not an extreme papalist. The question of poverty as a condition of Christian life, except for strict religious

---

1 See above, chapters 1 and 2.

Orders, did not enter into his scheme of things. Even the strictest Order might hold property, though its members should avoid protecting it by personal litigation. Christ and his apostles had money. *B* saw Jesus as a steward, administering the apostles' belongings, so as to free them from worry while he lived with them on earth. The friars' ideals were foreign to the thought world of *B* and of Comestor. In this the two latter masters contrasted with their successor, Peter the Chanter.

My excursion into Gospel teaching will necessarily involve considerations of changes in technique and use of sources, since they belong to the master's mode of expressing himself and affect his outlook. I shall begin with Peter the Chanter, who fills the gap between Comestor and the first friar doctors at Paris.

II

Peter the Chanter acted as St. John Baptist to the friars, though his wilderness was the Paris schools and he was no hermit, but a professor and ecclesiastical dignitary. His career and connexions are well documented.[2] To summarise: he had his first schooling at Rheims, followed by a lifelong association with the cathedral. He held the office of Chanter at Notre Dame from 1183. The dates of his studies and of his regency in theology at Paris are not certain. Late evidence suggests that he was already a master in 1173. The circle of pupils surrounding him formed a galaxy of talent; many of them went on to promotion to high office in the Church. Meanwhile he doubled his teaching duties with ecclesiastical business, being much in demand as a judge delegate. The chapter of Rheims elected him dean in 1196; but he retired to the Cistercian abbey of Longpont and died there in 1197 before he could take up his duties as dean. The last documentary reference to him is a papal mandate of January 29, 1197, appointing him judge delegate in a dispute in the diocese of Beauvais.[3]

His Gospel commentary belongs to a series of lectures on books of the Old and New Testaments. It makes a focal point in his pro-

---

[2] J. W. Baldwin, *Masters, Princes and Merchants: The Social Views of Peter the Chanter and his Circle* (Princeton, 1970). I shall refer to this book as 'Baldwin.'

[3] D. Lohrman, *Papsturkunden in Frankreich*, 7 (Abhandlungen der Akademie der Wissenschaften in Göttingen, 3F, 95, 1976), no. 344, p. 650.

gramme for the reform of the Church, as outlined in his *Verbum Abbreviatum*[4] and in his *Summa de Sacramentis et Animae Consiliis*. The *Verbum abbreviatum* in its longer version may be dated 1191/1192. It is a *Summa* on moral behaviour and misbehaviour (mainly the latter) illustrated by *exempla*. Later scholars used it as a quarry for sermons and homiletics. The title comes from the text: "Verbum abbreviatum faciet Dominus super terram" (Romans 9.28). Its author gives us a classic example of the longwinded speaker who begins: 'I shall be brief.' The Chanter lashed out at his colleagues for their superfluous glossing of Scripture. It wasted time. Far worse, it obscured the revealed truth of the New Testament by concentration on irrelevant details, such as 'places, dates, genealogies and descriptions of buildings such as the tabernacle and the temple image. Scripture was given to us that we should seek out not the vain and superfluous, but faith and moral doctrine and counsels and answers to the countless matters arising in Church affairs' (PL 205, 27–28).

The purpose of *De Sacramentis* was precisely to consider these 'countless questions.' It takes the form of a series of *quaestiones* on casuistry, probably representing discussions in the schools ranging over many years. It is a composite work, where one can distinguish the Chanter's contribution from additions by his pupils. The compilation and editing was begun after 1191/1192 and perhaps interrupted by his death in 1197.[5] Here he touches again on his predecessors' neglect of essential matters when they commented on the Bible. Even the *sancti expositores* come in for criticism: why did they busy themselves so much with numbers, places, [descriptions of] tabernacles and allegories, and so much less with the moral teaching of the Old Testament and judgments or decisions or infliction of punishment? Perhaps because they meant us to understand that no exposition was needed, but all was to be understood literally:

---

[4] Baldwin, I, 14–15. He found three versions of *Verbum Abbreviatum* in the MSS, a long version, which he takes as the original, a shorter, abridged from the longer, printed in PL 205, 23–370, and 'finally occasional marginal additions to the short version which echo the long version... some of the omitted material was restored in the marginal notations.' These are added as an appendix, PL 205, 370–528. I shall refer to the PL edition throughout.

[5] *Summa de Sacramentis et Animae Consiliis*, ed. J. A. Dugauquier, *Analecta Mediaevalia Namurcensia*, 4, 7, 11, 16, 21 (1954–1967). I shall refer to this edition by volume and page numbers. I abbreviate it as AMN. On its date and composition see 4, ix–cxiii; 7, v–xvi; 11, 17–32.

Et mirum quod sancti expositores ita diligentes fuerunt in numeris, in sitibus locorum, in tabernaculis, in allegoriis, quare non fuerunt ita diligentes in moralibus veteris testamenti et iudiciis vel decisoriis vel inflictoriis pene. Forte ideo ut darent intelligi ibi nullam esse expositionem, sed omnia etiam ad litteram intelligenda (AMN, 16, 163).

There lay the hub of his problem. The Chanter blames, though he does not name, his older colleague Peter Comestor, 'the master of the *Histories*.' Comestor was influenced by the movement, starting mainly from Hugh of St. Victor and his pupil Andrew, to deepen understanding of the literal historical sense of Scripture by exploiting new sources. For Old Testament study they turned to Jewish tradition, mediated by contemporary rabbis. Comestor succeeded in finding hitherto untapped sources for the literal historical exposition of the Gospels. The two Peters were colleagues in the Paris schools in the 1170s; Comestor died in 1178, soon after retiring to spend his last days at the abbey of St. Victor. The Chanter knew both the *Historia Scholastica* and the Gospel commentaries, as we shall see.[6] They embodied his *bête noire*; Comestor paid too much attention to irrelevant detail. The Chanter perhaps had another colleague in mind when he attacked concentration on descriptions of buildings. Peter of Poitiers, who taught at Paris 1169–1193, produced just such a work in his *Allegoriae super Tabernaculum Moysi*.[7] While distracting their pupils' minds by *trivia*, these masters diluted Gospel teaching. They made excuses for disobeying Christ's precepts in favour of 'new traditions,' on the plea that 'times had changed' (PL 205, 233–242). Comestor had done exactly that. Such masters evaded what the Chanter saw as the essential question: how can we reconcile Gospel teaching, taken literally, with current practice? He faced it squarely.

The Chanter's discussions on those 'countless matters arising in Church affairs,' in his *Verbum Abbreviatum* and in his *Summa*, hinge mainly on his interpretations of Gospel texts. It seems logical, there-

---

[6] Below, p. 108. He quotes the *Historia Scholastica* in his *Summa*, 16, 317 as 'Comestor dicebat...' See PL 198, 1575.

[7] P. S. Moore, *The Works of Peter of Poitiers Master in Theology and Chancellor of Paris (1193–1205)*, (Washington, 1936), 6–7, 50–77; *Petri Pictaviensis Allegoriae super Tabernaculum Moysi*, ed. P. S. Moore and J. A. Corbett (Publications in Mediaeval Studies, University of Notre Dame, Notre Dame, Indiana, 1938).

fore, to survey his approach to the Gospels in these two books before
going on to his lectures on the Gospels themselves, by way of preparation.

Of course all moralists denounced abuses. Greedy, negligent prelates, lax monks etc. were standard targets. The Chanter joined in
this mud–slinging with gusto. What differentiated him from most
satirists was his doubt where to draw a dividing line between use and
abuse. Many uses sanctioned by the Church struck him as abuses.
Hence he called for reform in theory as well as in practice; bad rules
and customs must be suppressed, not only offences against existing
norms of behaviour. Professor Baldwin portrays him as a sensible
reformer, pointing out that some of his suggestions passed into canon
law at the Lateran Council of 1215:

> Although disinclined to discuss reform on an abstract level, Peter
> crammed his writings with concrete proposals for resolving existing
> evils. To him reform consisted of eliminating human traditions
> to return to the simple and purified commands of Scripture.[8]

The statement is true enough as it stands, but it points to an ambivalence in the Chanter's mind, which we must probe more deeply.

On the one hand, he was a pillar of orthodoxy, a Paris master
and precentor of Notre Dame. He was also a high churchman (more
so than Comestor). He upheld papal authority over the Church, since
he looked to the pope for reform: we should have recourse to the pope
in doubtful cases; fullness of knowledge and power reside in him
(AMN, 21, 732). The Chanter venerated St. Thomas Becket (never
mentioned by Comestor) as a model archbishop and as a martyr in
the cause of ecclesiastical liberties.[9] On the other hand, he saw a
yawning gap between the Church of the present, which he supported,
and the early Church of Christ and his apostles. Modern churchmen
resembled the Pharisees in burdening men's consciences with new
rules (PL 205, 232–239). They also 'allegorised' the New Law of the
Gospel so as to explain it away. A learned Jew at Rheims objected
to attempts to convert him:

---

[8] Baldwin, 1, 315.

[9] PL 205, 81, 132, 231, 547; Baldwin, passim; see also his review of my
The Becket Conflict and the Schools, Speculum, 51 (1976), 358–359, for links between
the Chanter and two of Becket's close friends at Rheims: Ralph of Sarre and
Philip of Caune.

> You Christians say that everything in the Old Law must be understood allegorically... but you yourselves burden the simplicity of the Gospel with manifold allegorical exposition; so you dishonour your law, given to you by the divine mouth... And since none of you observe your own law, I don't want to be a Christian (PL 205, 553).

The casuistry of the *Summa* is so complicated that only a careful reading will bring out its revolutionary import. In at least sixteen cases the Chanter advises a man to follow Gospel teaching against secular and canon law. Eleven concern marriage and fornication, especially marriages between serfs or between a bondman or bondwoman and a spouse of free status. The Chanter inclined to think that a marriage should stand, in accordance with Christ's teaching against divorce, even though secular and canon law forbade the withdrawal of serfs from their masters by reason of marriage. On fornication, he considers the case of a noblewoman who wishes to seduce one of her serfs. The serf fears that he will be unable to resist. Ought he to escape if he can? The texts Matt. 28.9 on scandal and 1 Cor. 6.18 are quoted. The reporter of the *quaestio* writes:

> It seems to the master [the Chanter] that he ought to flee [from temptation] although the decrees [*decreta*] say the contrary (AMN, 16, 159–161).

Again, if a serf's master prevents him from serving God as freely as he thinks he should, and he cannot do the penance imposed on him, does he sin if he flees to a cloister, when the canons say that his master has the right to reclaim him? 'I think,' the Chanter answers, 'that he does not sin, because he is more obliged to God than to his master.' While not condemning slavery or serfdom, sanctioned from apostolic times, the Chanter readily weakened the bond, if it led to mortal sin (ibid., 295–296).[10]

Other questions deal with dispensation from oaths. The Chanter accepted the current interpretation of the ban on swearing (Matt. 5.34) as applying only to oaths taken with ill intent, but asked whether a man who swore for a good purpose could be absolved from his vow. Suppose the canons of a church swear not to admit an unsuitable candidate as prelate, but have to give way to force. Does absolution

---

[10] For other cases where the Chanter sets conscience above canon law see AMN, 16, 247; 21, 453–455.

from their oath by the authority of higher prelates suffice to dispense them? 'Our counsel is that those canons who swore should move to another canonical church until the unsuitable prelate is taken from their midst' (AMN, 21, 459). Even the pope cannot grant dispensations except in necessary cases. A man absolved by the pope in any other case is held to be excused by the Church; but he is not excused in God's sight. The pope may be misled when he grants dispensations; then the Church approves his action, but God does not (AMN, 21, 731–732). The Chanter goes so far as to call 'ridiculous' canons which forbid a marriage to be celebrated at forbidden times even in cases of necessity (AMN, 21, 739). Disobedience may be justified: a priest need not obey an order to excommunicate a man neither convicted nor confessed and whom he thinks to be innocent (AMN, 7, 384).

The Chanter was stricter than most of his contemporaries in condemning current practices as simoniacal, and adamant in his opposition to any churchman's being a party to judgments involving bloodshed. Even a legal right to jurisdiction did not excuse it (AMN, 16, 390–393), nor did the duty to suppress heresy. The Cathars (and he takes the most dangerous heretical sect of his time for illustration) should be 'separated,' but not killed: 'Recludendi ergo sunt, non occidendi' (PL 205, 231). Repression might lead to abuses and punishment of the innocent with the guilty (PL 205, 547).[11]

Piecemeal reforms, which he realised could not be enforced anyway, failed to reach the heart of the problem. Here are three revealing texts from his *Summa*. (1) On property rights: the earth was common to all by natural law: 'mine' and 'thine' are a consequence of sin. 'The elements are still common to all, earth to tread, air to breathe, water to drink or bath in. Why then are fishing, hunting and fowling forbidden? Do not princes sin when they mutilate men for the sake of wild beasts [according to forest laws]? Almost all churches have appropriated water rights and have fishponds, of which I'm not speaking. It is difficult to advise princes on this matter, for it is difficult to condemn the universal Church' (AMN, 6, 132).

(2) Churches should not offer prayers in exchange for a gift nor differentiate between rich and poor in their prayers. 'If it is objected that no church today would refrain from this, we may seem to be

---

[11] Baldwin, 1, 320–322.

condemning all churches; it is answered: we do not teach what is done, but what ought to be done' (AMN, 21, 767).

(3) Preachers collect money by carrying around the relics of saints who despised money in their lives; is this simoniacal? 'Since almost the whole Church sends preachers to collect money by this means, I dare not state that there's simony in it, lest I may seem to condemn the Church thereby. Yet I daren't altogether deny it, since spiritual things are administered for temporal, for this kind of preaching would stop, I think, if it held no prospect of gain' (AMN, 21, 770).

To set up the Gospel as a rule was to condemn the Church! The Chanter could only state the dilemma; he saw no solution. It became sharper when he lectured on the Gospels.

These lectures can be dated between autumn or winter 1187 and his retirement in 1197. The *Verbum Abbreviatum* and *Summa* are composite works, prepared over a long period; the Gospel commentary belongs to the same time span.[12] He lectured on a conflated text of the Gospels, hence the title *Super Unum ex Quatuor*, 'four in one.' Stegmüller lists twenty extant manuscript copies, some incomplete (RB, 6504-7).[13] There are also derivatives; one may have been prepared by the Chanter's pupil, the English William de Montibus.[14] The commentary has not been printed. To discover the original version would be a daunting task. As is the case in his other works, marginal annotations vary from copy to copy; some are omitted in one copy, but form part of the text in another. The interim solution is to take the text and its varying annotations as a whole, ascribing it to 'the Chanter and his pupils.'

I have used mainly MS Oxford Merton College 212 (M), written in the second quarter of the thirteenth century, probably in France.

---

[12] See above, p. 7.

[13] F. Stegmüller, *Repertorium Biblicum Medii Aevi* (Madrid, 1950-1977). Vols 8 and 9 were prepared by N. Reinhardt. I refer to the *Repertorium* as 'RB,' giving the number.

[14] William de Montibus was probably a pupil of the Chanter and was certainly influenced by him; see H. Mackinnon, *William de Montibus a Medieval Teacher*, in *Essays in Medieval History presented to Bertie Wilkinson*, ed. T. A. Sanquist and M. R. Powicke (Toronto, 1969), 32-45. Dr. R. W. Hunt tells me that an *Unum ex Quatuor* derived from the Chanter's exists in at least five MSS; some are listed by Stegmüller under *Anonymi* (RB 10109). Dr. Hunt suggests that William de Montibus may be the author.

A number of Oxford masters owned it in the late fourteenth and early fifteenth centuries.[15] MS London, British Library, Royal 2.C.IX, written in a thirteenth–century English hand,[16] has served as a check on occasion.

The structure of *Unum ex Quatuor* is based on the Diatesseron in its Latin translation, which precedes the commentary in some copies. The Chanter made some modifications, disagreeing with Zachary of Besançon, whose *Unum ex Quatuor* followed much the same pattern, and preferring the sequence of Comestor's *School History*.[17] His main exegetical sources, apart from the Gloss, were *B*, quoted sometimes independently of Comestor, under the name of Master Geoffrey Babion, and Comestor himself, normally quoted anonymously.

The exercise of *lectio* at Paris in the late twelfth century supposed an established technique. The Chanter followed it, differing little from Comestor in his method. He lectured on a glossed text (from the Gloss later called *Ordinaria*) as Comestor had done and Peter Lombard before him. He borrowed Comestor's custom of referring to the liturgy as a source, adding observations of his own on the uses of different churches, especially of his own church of Rheims (M, fol. 26ra). The development of technique at Paris, as well as personal inclination, explains why he was anecdotal and gave space to casuistry.

One anecdote will offer a sample. It describes an otherwise unrecorded dispute between St. Bernard and Abelard on the interpretation of Christ's saying: 'there hath not arisen among them that are born of women a greater than John the Baptist' (Matthew 11.11). St. Bernard and Master Peter Abelard disputed on this pre–eminence and superiority of the Baptist among the saints. Master Peter preferred St. Paul to Christ's forerunner, because Paul toiled more than any other saint on the Church's behalf, and therefore deserved the greater reward. St. Bernard stuck up for the Baptist (M, fol. 60ra). The tale is apt, even if untrue: the ascetic preferred the Baptist, the philosopher St. Paul.

---

[15] For its Oxford history see F. M. Powicke, *The Medieval Books of Merton College* (Oxford, 1931), 202–203.

[16] G. F. Warner and J. P. Gilson, *British Museum Catalogue of Western MSS in the Old Royal and King's Collections*, I (London, 1921), 52–53.

[17] See above, p. 32.

The Chanter's comment on the parable of the tares growing in the wheat (Matthew 13.24–30) is an example of his casuistry. It interests us here for two reasons. First, it shows a motion picture of the passage from the general to the particular and from principle to application in school exegesis: we can follow the exposition of the parable from *B*, through Comestor to the Chanter. The developing technique in dealing with cases will prepare us to understand the Chanter's successors, Alexander of Hales, Hugh of St. Cher and John of La Rochelle. Second, the Chanter's comments throw more light on his personal views on proceedings against heretics than we find elsewhere in his writings.

According to patristic tradition the tares signified heresies growing in the field of the Church. The lord in the parable forbade his servants to root out the tares, telling them to let the tares and wheat grow together until harvest time. That raised the question: how should heretics be dealt with? The organisation of the Inquisition as an institution in the early thirteenth century followed a long period of uncertainty, during which heretics were sometimes tolerated and sometimes repressed by rough and ready methods.[18] Yet the lord's instructions to his servants seemed to prescribe patience. Bishop Wazo of Liège had invoked the parable when asked for advice in dealing with a group of heretics 1043–1048. He had heard that heretics had been identified by their paleness, 'as though anybody who was pale was undoubtedly a heretic'; many Catholics had been killed as a result of this hysterical mistake. Wazo interpreted the parable to mean that heretics must be excommunicated, but left to God's judgement at the final harvest.[19]

B too drew the lesson that patience and discretion were in order when dealing with heretics. He ruled that bishops might not kill heretics, but only separate them from the Church by excommunication, not from the world by death (PL 162, 1273). Comestor added details: proceedings against heretics must be neither hasty, irreversible nor based on mere hearsay, lest the heretic be given no time to

---

[18] H. Maisonneuve, *Etudes sur les origines de l'Inquisition* (2nd ed., Louvain, 1960), 93–126.

[19] *Gesta Episcoporum Leodensis Aecclesiae*, ed. *Monumenta Germaniae Historica*, Scriptores, 7, 21–24. For translation and commentary see R. I. Moore, *The Birth of Popular Heresy* (London, 1975), 21–24. The heretics were killed, but Wazo would have interceded for them, had he been present.

repent, or lest the good should be rooted out with the bad. A man must be proved guilty and confess before he may be convicted (MS Oxford, Bodl. Laud. misc. 291, fol. 64va). Both B and Comestor took a final death penalty, inflicted by the secular power, for granted. The Chanter did not exclude it, but was much more worried than they were at possible miscarriage of justice. Prelates, signified by the servants of the parable, had a duty to teach and to advise the secular prince to punish evildoers by the material sword. Then the Chanter distinguished: 'rooting out' is of two kinds, the one by excommunication, the other by beheading. Both were used at the present time, and the process was threefold. In no case should it be 'hasty, irreversible or on mere suspicion' (here he repeats Comestor). His threefold distinction is 'general or sub–general, particular or special.' The Lord had forbidden the 'general': a general excommunication would endanger the Church's very existence. *Sub–generalis* is also forbidden as too sweeping. The multitude should be treated less severely than the few. The sins of a prince must not be visited on the people at large, though the Chanter granted that a city might be laid under interdict, if the citizens consented to the prince's wickedness after his excommunication. 'Special or particular' rooting out was actually commanded in the case of one or several infected members of the flock, in order to save the others from disease. But the Chanter entered a *caveat*, repeating his stricture on hasty procedure, which was wholly forbidden, since it might imperil the innocent and prevent the guilty from repenting. Descending to the particular, he named the Cathars and pointed to the danger of hasty procedure. A heretic might repent and work for the Church, given time. A holy Catholic woman, pale and wan from fasting, might be accused of heresy by those who took devilish greediness as a sign of godly orthodoxy! Characteristically, the Chanter was more afraid of injustice than of the spread of heresy.[20]

---

[20] M, fol. 65ra: "Quomodo ergo multitudo catharorum auctoritate ecclesie perempta est, cum aliquis bonus esset inter eos vel qui defacili penitet, etsi expectaretur ad penitentiam, vel qui ad exercitium ecclesie potuit superesse?... Cum viderunt quandam sanctam mulierem, pallidam, ieiunantem, macilentam, et signa christiane religionis habentem, statim clamitant eam esse catharam, signa gastrimargi et diaboli dicentes esse Dei."

This seems to echo Wazo's letter of advice and the comments of the author of the *Gesta;* but it is unlikely that the Chanter knew them directly. The cathar *perfecti* were noted for their pale and wan appearance.

The secular power's role in suppressing heresy brings us to his views on the relations between *regnum* and *sacerdotium*. They illustrate the paradox of his position as a high churchman and as a critic of the contemporary Church. The text from the Sermon on the Mount, 'Blessed are they that suffer persecution for justice's sake: for theirs is the kingdom of heaven' (Matthew 5.10), raises a question not considered by Comestor: 'Am I to expose myself to death for the sake of ecclesiastical liberties?' The Chanter answers 'yes.' One should do so for the sake of spiritual things, but not for temporal things such as fields and rents. We often defend temporal things for motives of greed rather than justice (M, fol. 29va). He must have had Becket in mind as a defender of clerical privilege, regarded as a spiritual cause. Admiration for Becket comes out in his comparison of the saint with Christ, who showed himself to his captors, saying 'Ego sum' (John 18.5), and did not hide from them. This, says the Chanter, is an argument against those who counselled Blessed Thomas to hide from his slayers; he took up the burden of martyrdom notwithstanding their advice (M, fol. 139rb).

The two swords text with its glosses (Luke 22.38) led the Chanter to consider the relations between the temporal and spiritual powers.[21] Did the pope, 'Christ's vicar' as the Chanter calls him, following contemporary usage (M, fol. 27va), receive both swords directly from God, and delegate the temporal to the secular ruler to wield on his behalf, or did the latter receive his sword from God directly? Christ told St. Peter to sheath his sword when he cut off Malchus' ear (John 18.10–11). That was meant to show that Christ suffered his capture willingly, but that the apostles might have defended him, had he allowed them to. The Chanter deduced that the pope had two swords; he sheathed the material, as Christ had commanded the apostles, but not the spiritual. The emperor drew the material sword by papal authority and killed evildoers. Hence the pope wielded the material sword also, but indirectly through the emperor. The Chanter saw no crack in the argument; he must have weighed the *pro* and *contra* carefully.[22] It carried him further than *B* and Comestor, and anticipated the friar doctors' regard for the papacy as a fount of reform in

---

[21] For school debates on this problem see Baldwin, 1, 164–170. He does not mention the Chanter's lecture on the 'two swords' text, where the Chanter is more explicit than elsewhere.

general and of theirs in particular. As the Chanter saw it, theologians put forward plans for reform, which the pope would realise.

That was consistent. It was inconsistent to condemn canon law on the same text, as the Chanter did. How could the pope reform the Church otherwise than by promulgating canons and employing canonists? A gloss on the two swords text interpreted the two swords as signifying the Old and New Testaments; together they sufficed Christians as arms in spiritual warfare. Therefore, said the Chanter, it contradicted Christ's saying, that two swords were enough, to deny that the two Testaments sufficed without the addition of decretals or any other writings (M, fol. 132va), a slap in the face to canon lawyers. It accorded with his dislike of 'new and burdensome' additions to Scripture, expressed in his *Verbum Abbreviatum*, and marked a growing estrangement between theologians and canon lawyers. Hugh of St. Victor had seen the canons as an extension of the New Testament.[23] Comestor invoked them in order to justify departures from the literal observance of the Sermon on the Mount.[24] The Chanter found a sad discrepancy between canon law and Scripture. Presumably he hoped that masters of the Sacred Page might oust canon lawyers in the papal Curia.

Of all problems posed by the Gospels, poverty was the most agonising. The Chanter, like his predecessors, accepted the fact that Christ handled and possessed money; but he registered the simple life style of Christ and his disciples. The sisters Martha and Mary had no servant, cook or porter in their home to help them entertain visitors (M, fol. 58va). A teacher of Scripture ought to recall churchmen to that modest way of life. Yet 'people would think us mad, if we advised them to take no thought for the morrow' (Matthew 6.31). Well, let them think so! We should be adulterating, lying expositors,

---

[22] M, fol. 132va: "Ad litteram autem alter gladius est extractus super Malcum ad ostendendum quod quidem possent [apostoli] se defendisse si vellant [*sic*], ut dictum est in glosa. Alter [gladius] est absconditus, ut ostenderetur Dominum sponte subiisse passionem. Propter hoc exemplum abscondit dominus papa gladium materialem, non spiritualem. Imperator suum evaginat, qui auctoritate pape interficit, et ita papa. Huic enim rationi non video quomodo refragari possit quis."

I have paraphrased rather than translated this condensed argument.

[23] *Didascalicon*, IV, ii, ed. C. H. Buttimer (Washington, 1937), 72: "In tertio ordine primum locum habent Decretalia, quos canones, id est regulares appellamus, deinde sanctorum patrum et doctorum ecclesiae scripta."

[24] See above, p. 79.

if we loosened the reins, tempering and softening the rigorous truth of Christ's counsels and precepts. Better and safer that scandal should arise than that truth be set at nought.[25]

The apostles were sent to preach without taking provisions for their journey (Matthew 10.9–10):

> What shall we say, when the Church's use and custom in head and members are contrary? It's unsafe to preach that the Church errs both in head and members, but dangerous to expound the Lord's words, and especially his precepts, otherwise than he would wish them to be expounded... One thing I do say: both text and glosses are repugnant to the custom of the Church (M, fol. 42ra).

Suppose that this passage on the mission of the Apostles is read out in synod. If it is not to be observed literally, but only figuratively, then the ceremonial precepts of the Old Law might just as well be read out instead: 'But how can it be understood literally, when churchmen today possess more worldly goods than laymen?' To illustrate this discordance, he adds: 'a certain great prelate said that the Gospel command applied to ragged fishermen only,' not to him (M, fol. 42rb).

The Chanter traced the decline in standards back to the Donation of Constantine and the enrichment of the Church under Pope Sylvester. Then the devil sowed tares in the good seed in the field, as signified in the parable of the wheat and tares (Matthew 13.24). He comments on the words *good seed*:

> that is, of faith and good works, that is of the holy martyrs, up to the time of Sylvester, when the Church became greater in dignity and riches, but lesser in religion for few have received the martyr's crown since then.

A tag on the corrupting effect of riches clinches his point:

> Nam turpe fregerunt secula luxu divitie molles[26] (M, fol. 65ra).

---

[25] M, fol. 38ra: "Hoc capitulum facile est quoad littere seriem et superficiem, quoad etiam sanctorum expositionem; sed difficilissimum quoad presentis moderne ecclesie usum, quia si curare velimus, non dico ad hanc consiliorum, sed preceptorum Domini, que hic traduntur observationem, videbimur insaniri. Si autem ei frena relaxaverimus, preceptorum temperantes et mollientes rigorem, immo veritatis tenorem caupones et mendaces erimus expositores. Sed melius et tutius est ut scandalum oriatur quam [ut] veritas relinquatur."

Caupones alludes to Isa. 1. 22; see also PL 205, 210.

[26] H. Walther, *Lateinischen Sprichwörter und Sentenzen des Mittelalters*, 5 (Göttingen, 1967), 408, 55a.

The Chanter's sources on this text make his outburst all the more surprising. *B* (PL 162, 1273) and Comestor elaborating him (MS Oxford, Bodl. Laud. misc. 291, fol. 64ᵛᵃ) had explained that the devil sowed tares, that is heresies, when prelates grew lazy and began to nod after the end of persecution. But their neglect was remedied by the holy doctors of the church; Ambrose, Jerome and Augustine understood how to discern heresies from their study of Scripture. The Chanter was more pessimistic. He did not mention the healing effects of the holy doctors. Heretics were known by their evil works, he said, and still are (M, fol. 65ʳᵇ).

The forged Donation of Constantine to Pope Sylvester was generally accepted as authentic in the West; it could be interpreted in various ways by political theorists.[27] Critics of the Church's wealth blamed Pope Sylvester's acceptance of the Donation for decline from primitive standards, reinforcing it by a story that the devil or an angel's voice from heaven cried out: 'Today poison has been poured into God's Church.' The Chanter does not mention this legend, but would have had it in mind if it circulated so early. Gerald of Wales, an admirer of the Chanter, whose *Verbum Abbreviatum* he pillaged,[28] repeats it in a number of his books; his *Gemma Ecclesiastica* seems to be the first to mention it, 1196–1199. Gerald always puts the words into the mouth of the devil, *antiquus hostis*. The alternative, that the voice came from heaven, has been traced back to the German minstrel Walter von der Vogelweide in the early thirteenth century. Both Catholics and heretics quoted it in protest against ecclesiastical wealth and corruption thereafter.[29] The Chanter anticipated the feelings which evoked the legend and made it so popular.

---

[27] A. Linder, "The Myth of Constantine the Great in the West: Sources and Hagiographic Commemoration," *Studi Medievali*, 3rd series, 16 (1975), 43–95.

[28] Baldwin, 1, 42.

[29] For references to Gerald's and later versions of the Sylvester story, see A. Linder, "Ecclesia and Synagoga in the Medieval Myth of Constantine the Great," *Revue Belge de Philologie et d'Histoire*, 54 (1976), 1058–1059. Gerald's works are difficult to date, but his *Gemma Ecclesiastica*, perhaps in an early draft, belongs to 1196–1199; see R. W. Hunt, "The Preface to the *Speculum Ecclesiae* of Giraldus Cambrensis," *Viator*, 8 (1977), 197; *Giraldus Cambrensis Speculum Duorum*, ed. M. Richter and others (Cardiff, 1974), xx–xxi 102n., 172. Dom Jean Leclercq noted the angel version in a Canticle commentary by Odo of Cheriton, 'Pétulance et spiritualité dans le commentaire d'Hélinand sur le Cantique des Cantiques,' *Archives d'Histoire Doctrinale et Littéraire du Moyen Age*, 31 (1965), 49; "Hélinand ou Odon de Chériton?" ibid. 32 (1966), 61–69.

His anguish and pessimism in his commitment to the Gospel does not seem to have infected his circle. Robert of Courson, Stephen Langton and others saw reform as 'the art of the possible,' a 'possible' which was limited, but not hopeless. All the same, we happen to know of one student who returned from the schools taking one of the Chanter's more extreme ideas seriously. Our student appears in a letter collection of Alan, prior of Christ Church Canterbury and then abbot of Tewkesbury, 1186–1202.[30] Since Alan wrote the letter as abbot it must belong to this period. He addresses it to a friend, newly returned from the schools. The scholar has picked up the idea that a religious disobeys the command not to take thought for the morrow (Matthew 5.31) if he makes provision for more than one year ahead:

> My friend, you have lately returned, a new man, from the new schools, putting new life into learning which had grown outdated, drawing from it that learning which you have been taught anew. You strive indeed to stick less closely in the footsteps of the Fathers, [following them] according to the words, but not according to the general sense of what they say, when you judge that the fruits [of the earth], granted to meet human needs, cannot, without incurring grave blame, be stored up to help out the coming year[s]. And while your discerning mind was eagerly focused on this point, and yet did not seem altogether to avoid the broad highway of sounder judgement, it turned its vehemence into a narrower path [or byeway] so that you have now asserted that what you had previously said was universally forbidden, is forbidden only to those who renounce the world, as if they were not allowed to stretch the vision of their forethought beyond the bounds of a year; such men are forbidden even to think about tomorrow. My friend, you are formulating this view without making a proper distinction, as if all who, whatever their motives, have done what you so clearly state should not be done, were included in one and the same error.[31]

---

[30] M. A. Harris, "Alan of Tewkesbury and his Letters," *Studia Monastica*, 18 (1976), 77–108.

[31] Ibid., 6 (1977), no. 33, 321–322. The Latin is involved and difficult. I am grateful to Miss Harris for sending me offprints and photographs of the two MSS used for her edition. Dr. A. B. Scott kindly gave me a translation as close to the text as possible.

"A novis, amice, renovatus scolis nuper rediisti, ex ea quam de novo edoctus es scientia doctrinam innovans antiquatam, nisus [MSS visus?] quidem verbotenus non tamen ex sententia antiquorum patrum vestigiis minus inherere, dum esti-

The new schools with their new teaching and revival of old learning must surely refer to Paris. The exegesis of the text as described by Alan had a long history. The Gloss from Augustine permitted forethought for present needs, but condemned undue anxiety for the future: the 'present' covered harvest for the following year. *B* applied the text to an abbot, who might provide for his monks for a year ahead without incurring blame (PL 162, 1313). Comestor elaborated on this in his gospel commentary and gave it a general application. He replied to a possible objection:

> Someone might say that such toil and forethought are in no way allowed to a religious; indeed he should commit himself to God wholly. No [is the answer], because the Lord himself provided for himself in necessaries and had money...[32]

Peter the Chanter stated categorically in his *Summa* that he believed it to be altogether forbidden to hermits to make provision for necessaries for more than a year.[33] Abbot Alan's friend, returning fresh from the schools in the years between 1186 and 1202, could easily have heard the Chanter. In his enthusiasm he stretched the Chanter's 'hermits' (perhaps hermits living in groups) to include all religious.

The abbot, himself a master, pointed out that such a ban on forethought would be impossible to observe. What would happen in

---

mas fructus humane deputatos necessitati in futuri anni subsidium sine graviori culpa reponi non posse. Cumque ad id tua instaret Discretio, nec videretur sanioris sententia publicam stratam penitus declinare, suam instantiam in semitam declinavit artiorem, ut quod prius omnibus asseruit inhibitum, id tantum seculum [MSS seculo] renuntiantibus firmaret illicitum, quasi hiis non liceat oculos providentie ultra anni terminos extendere, quibus videtur inhiberi etiam de crastino cogitare. Hanc promulgas, amice, indistincte sententiam, quasi unus error omnes habeat involutos, qui quacumque de causa id egerint, quod sic palam predicas non agendum."

[32] MS Laud. misc. 291, fol. 40rb: "...Conceditur ergo nobis a Domino providentia de presentibus, ut nomine presentis intelligas annum, sed de futuris, id est ultra annum... In presentibus ergo nobis prohibet sollicitudinem superfluam, sed concedit laborem et providentiam... Poterat enim dici ab aliquo: talis labor et providentia nulli conceditur religioso, immo se totum committere debet Deo. Non, quia Dominus ipse sibi providet [*sic*] in necessariis; loculos habuit..."

[33] AMN, 21, 596: "Sed heremite omnes aliquid reseruant. Possunt ne reseruare quod sufficit usque ad annum? Quod uidetur. Quia seminant et plantant et fructus colligunt unde uiuant. Cum ergo fructus non redeant nisi de anno in annum uidetur quod possunt reseruare sibi necessaria ad annum, plus autem nullatenus credo eis licere obseruare."

a season of bad harvest? He brought forward many texts from both Testaments where long–term forethought is recommended. His friend should not take the precepts literally, but have regard to their spirit:

> Attende, amice, et e latebris littere mortificantis elice latentem spiritum vitae.

He ends his lecture on forethought by writing that it suffices for an interpreter of good will, who does not twist the understanding of sayings to his own sense.[34]

We hear no more of the unnamed enthusiast; but he helps to explain why reforming scholars welcomed the Mendicant Orders to Paris. The movements for poverty and wandering preachers, which marked the first half of the twelfth century, had slowed down. Their members settled into communities, endowed with lands and rents, however much vowed to austerity. The ecclesiastical authorities suspected the more popular movements of the later twelfth century, witness the fate of Valdès and his followers.[35] St. Dominic and St. Francis, despite the differences between them, represented attempts to follow the Gospel *ad litteram*. Alan of Tewkesbury's rebuke to his friend and his plea for a more 'spiritual,' here meaning 'adulterated,' understanding of Scripture exemplified the Chanter's complaints against his colleagues' softening of Christ's teaching. The Chanter did not live to see the Mendicants' arrival in Paris; but he would surely have approved of both their way of life and their studies. If the laity and secular clergy could not be reformed easily, at least religious could live the Gospel *ad litteram*. The friars at first lived simply on alms of the faithful, just as Alan's young friend thought that religious ought to do, taking no thought for the morrow. The Mendicant programme of study, leading through reading to disputation to preaching would have appealed to the Chanter, as a realisation of his famous statement on *lectio, disputatio, praedicatio*: school

---

The Chanter does not discuss this question in his gospel commentary.

[34] Ed. cit. 325: "Sed benigno interpreti, et qui ad suum non distorquet dictorum intelligentiam, hactenus ista sufficiunt."

Either 'suum' (clearly written in the MSS) is a mistake for 'suam' or 'sensum' may have dropped out.

[35] For a survey, see M. L. Lambert, *Medieval Heresy: Popular Movements from Bogomil to Hus* (London, 1977), 43–47, 67–91.

learning culminates in preaching.[36] A true understanding of what Scripture teaches necessitates rational discussion.[37] It must issue in a call for reform.

The Chanter as master of *sacra pagina* and Alan's correspondent, as his possible pupil, help to explain why the Mendicants received a warm welcome at Paris, before jealousy endangered their status. We can see why they made so many recruits in the schools. The Chanter points to the springs of their welcome and of vocations to their Orders. His trust in the papacy as a fount of reform seemed to be justified by papal support for the friar doctors of theology.

III

The Mendicants came to Paris. Did they fulfil the Chanter's hopes as lecturers on the Gospels? What new insights did they bring as religious, vowed both to poverty and to study?

The first pair of friars to leave commentaries on all four Gospels was the Dominican Hugh of St. Cher and the Franciscan Alexander of Hales, though Alexander's postills may perhaps belong to his teaching period as a secular master of theology, *antequam esset frater*. I shall examine first Hugh's and secondly Alexander's and thirdly those of Alexander's pupil, John of La Rochelle. Hugh's Dominican colleague, Guerric of St. Quentin must be omitted here, since only one of his postills survives, that on St. John.[38]

To begin with our data on Hugh of St. Cher: he joined the Dominican Order in 1225, already a doctor of canon law and a bachelor of theology; he taught at the Paris *studium* first as lector of the *Sentences* and then as master of theology 1229–1233. His *Sentence* commentary belongs to the years c. 1231–1232. Hugh had held the

---

[36] PL 205, 25. Baldwin edits, translates and comments on the longer version of the text, 1, 90–91; 2, 63–64.

[37] The Chanter considers further the importance of discussion in his *Summa*, under the heading "De Fideli Expositione Diuine Scripture" (AMN, 16, 288–289). He summarises: "Unde diuina scriptura nichil commendat nisi querendum ratione quod consentiat ueritati fiatque ipsa ueritas auctoritas, sine qua nec esset, nec ualet auctoritas."

[38] F. M. Henquinet, 'Notes additionelles sur les écrits de Guerric de Saint-Quentin,' RTAM, 8 (1936), 373; H.–F. Dondaine, 'L'Object et le medium de la vision béatifique chez les théologiens du XIIIᵉ siècle,' ibid., 19 (1952), 120; T. Kaeppeli, *Scriptores Ordinis Praedicatorum Medii Aevi*, 2 (Rome, 1975), 61–70.

office of prior provincial of France 1227–1230, and was prior of the
Paris convent 1233–1236. The second office did not prevent him from
teaching at the same time. He left the schools in 1236 to act as provincial of France again until 1244, when Pope Innocent IV made him
a cardinal. He died in 1264.[39] His *Postilla super Totam Bibliam* survives in two versions, a longer and a shorter. The longer is printed in
early editions. I have used the Paris edition of 1545, fully aware of
the risks involved: there may well be mistakes, omissions and additions.[40] But Hugh's readers have to make do with what lies ready to
hand. A modern critical edition would entail a lifetime's labour. The
date of the postills can be fixed roughly in his teaching period before
1236. If he went through the whole Bible from beginning to end, as
seems probable, he would have reached the Gospels towards 1234–
1235. He certainly postillated them in order, since he referred back
to his exposition of the first two Gospels in his prologue to St. Luke:
'De Mathaeo et Marco iam vidimus; nunc de Luca breviter videamus.'
A reference to his own *Sentence* commentary on John, 13.1 at least
gives us a firm *terminus post quem*, c. 1231–1232. Discussing and
reproving the Greek use of leavened bread for the Eucharist he
brings forward among other arguments:

> Item Romana ecclesia, quae omnium ecclesiarum mater est et ma-
> gistra, conficit de azymo, quia hoc habuit ab apostolis, qui fuerunt
> cum Domino quando fecit pascha; ergo conficiendum est de azymo.
> Istae rationes sunt contra Grecos, qui in tantam insaniam versi
> sunt, quod non erubescunt dicere evangelistas esse mentitos qui
> dicunt Dominum communiter cum aliis comedisse... Quorum opi-
> niones habentur in historiis et super quartum sententiarum, et
> ideo hic praetermitti possunt.

'The histories' refer to Peter Comestor's *Historia Scholastica* (PL 198,
1615–1616) and 'super quartum sententiarum' to Hugh's commentary on *Sent*. IV d. viii, c. 1. At the beginning of his commentary on
IV, viii, Hugh states that he will treat sixthly 'de erroribus heretico-
rum contra hoc sacramentum et controversia grecorum et latinorum'
(MS Vat. lat. 1098, fol. 143vb).[41] He might well excuse himself for not

---

[39] T. Kaeppeli, op. cit. 269–281. On the Mendicant chairs at Paris before
the conflict with the seculars in the 1250s, see M.–M. Dufeil, *Guillaume de Saint-
amour et la polémique universitaire Parisienne* (Paris, 1972), 1–34.
[40] I shall refer to Hugh's postill on the gospel text *ad loc.*, since the foliation
of the edition is too erratic to serve for reference purposes.
[41] Fr. Kaeppeli kindly sent me photographs of the Vatican MS.

treating the subject more fully in his postill, seeing that some five columns of small text are allotted to it on the *Sentences* (fols. 149vb–151ra). His arguments here correspond in part to those sketched in the postill, including:

> Item ecclesia romana, que domina et magistra est omnium, conficit de azimo, que hoc habuit ab ipsis apostolis, qui tunc fuerunt cum Domino, quando fecit pascha. Ergo conficiendum est cum azimo, quod concedimus (fol. 150^{ra-b}).

Hugh was quoting himself verbally.

The date is certainly after c. 1231–1232 and before 1236, probably closer to 1236; but the actual composition of the postills presents an insoluble problem. How much is Hugh's? No master could have completed so daunting a task as postillating the whole Bible, especially when he acted as conventual prior for three years of his regency. All parts of the *postilla* which I have examined, not only those on the Gospels, form a mosaic of quotations, with occasional comments probably original to Hugh. It seems that he must have had a team of friars to help him, as Fr. H. Dondaine has deduced.[42] This kind of team work, where younger or less gifted friars were drafted by their superiors to act as amanuenses or research assistants in a project organised by seniors was a speciality of the mendicant Orders; their *studia* made it possible on a large scale.[43] Hence we cannot know the extent of Hugh's responsibility for the scissors–and–paste business of compilation. This proviso must remain in mind in any study of his postills.

Alexander of Hales was an Englishman, educated at Paris. He became master of arts before 1210 and bachelor of theology in 1215 and then master of theology 1220–1227, probably 1223–1227. He joined the Franciscan Order in 1236 and taught in the Franciscan *studium* at Paris until his death at the Council of Lyons, 1245. He had John of La Rochelle as his pupil among many others.[44] Alexander

---

[42] Op. cit. (above n. 38), 83.

[43] M. B. Parkes, "The Influence of the Concept of *Ordinatio* and *Compilatio* on the Development of the Book," *Medieval Learning and Literature: Essays presented to Richard William Hunt*, ed. J. J. G. Alexander and M. T. Gibson (Oxford, 1976), 137–138.

[44] The Quaracchi editors of the *Glossa in Quatuor Libros Sententiarum* (*Bibl. Franc. Schol.* 12, 1951) 110*–116* give the most recent notice on Alexander's career.

took the habit after many years of teaching theology as a secular master. His *Quaestiones Disputatae* 1220–1236 and his *Glossa in Quatuor Libros Sententiarum*, probably 1222–1229, have been edited.[45] Both belong to his teaching period *antequam esset frater*. He left the beginnings of a theological *Summa*, completed by John of La Rochelle and others. Alexander's postills on the Gospels have been identified, but never printed or studied.[46] The MSS are corrupt and defective. They raise two problems. First comes their date: do they belong to the period *antequam* or *postquam*? The fact that his postills on the Gospels are ascribed to 'Master Alexander' in those manuscripts which have an ascription to an author suggests that they circulated before he joined the Order; after joining it he would normally have been referred to as 'Frater.' Fr. I. Brady argues for *antequam* on other grounds: 'As the *Quaestiones Antequam* clearly indicate, Alexander followed the practice of Stephen Langton and others and thus separated disputations on the Scripture (or cognate questions) from the *lectura* of the books themselves. A study of the *Quaestiones* will show what parts of Scripture Hales postillated between 1220 and 1236 (even if a more precise chronology is impossible at present). At least thirteen *Quaestiones* grow directly out of lectures on Scripture; and from them we may reasonably conclude that in this first period Master Alexander had commented on the Pentateuch or parts of it, Matthew, Mark, Luke, Romans, II Cor., I Col., and Hebrews.'[47] I think the argument is over–confident. We know too little of school practice in the early thirteenth century to assume that a *quaestio disputata* on a scriptural text necessarily 'grew out' of a lecture on the scriptural book where that text occurred. An argument for *postquam* as against *antequam* would be that the practice of lecturing on large numbers of biblical books, and circulating the lecture course, went out of fashion in the secular schools after Langton's departure in 1206. True, John Halgrin of Abbeville, teaching at Paris in the years around 1216, commented on Genesis to I Kings and the Canticle, as well as leaving sermons on the Psalter (RB 4532–42);

---

[45] *Bibl. Franc. Schol.* 19–21 (Quaracchi, 1960); ibid. 14–17 (1951–1957).

[46] RB 1, 1151–4; 6, 9960; 8 (Supplementum), 1151–4; I. Brady, "Sacred Scripture in the Early Franciscan School,' *La sacra scrittura e i francescani* (Pontificium Athenaeum Antonianum: Studium Biblicum Franciscanum, Rome/Jerusalem, 1973), 72–74.

[47] Ibid. 71.

but that makes a poor score compared with the Chanter's and Langton's. The Mendicants revived the practice of lecturing on *sacra pagina* extensively and 'publishing' their lectures. They came to hold a monopoly in this field. Alexander would fit into pattern better if he lectured on Scripture *postquam*. A third possibility would be that he lectured on Scripture first as a secular and then brought his notes with him to the Franciscan *studium*, when he took the habit, to use again for his lectures there. The mere fact of their survival supports this hypothesis. Friars had more facilities for 'publishing' their lectures than had seculars. The 'published' lecture course had more chance of survival in a Mendicant house of study than if it had circulated among individual readers.

To anticipate: I have found no evidence to support any of these three surmises. Nor have I discovered any connecting link between the relevant parts of the *Quaestiones Disputatae* and the *Glossa in Sententias*, on the one hand, and the postills on texts cited in the two former on the other. There are more positive reasons for *antequam* than for *postquam*; but they are not quite conclusive.

The second problem concerns the relationship between his postills and Hugh's. Collation showed that there was a relationship, but who borrowed from whom? The editors of Alexander's *Glossa in Sententias* found that Hugh and Alexander, both lecturing on the *Sentences*, seemed to ignore each other, but that Hugh knew Alexander's commentary and occasionally depended on it.[48] Hugh's postills on the Gospels contain two references to Alexander by name. Alas! Neither settles the question of priority. On Matthew 5.34 "Nolite iurare omnino" Hugh's postill reads:

> Alexander: istud praeceptum est apostolis solis, cum primitivam aedificarent ecclesiam. Si enim tunc iurassent, tunc scandalum oriretur, quia reputarentur apostoli non tam perfecti.

I have not found this reason for the ban on swearing given to the apostles in Alexander's postills or in his *Quaestiones Disputatae Antequam* or in his *Glossa in Sententias*. The section *De Mandatis* in the *Summa* ascribed to Alexander is now known to be the work of John of La Rochelle and does not give this reason anyway. We can only suppose that Hugh was referring to some unrecorded teaching by Alexander, perhaps to lectures given in the schools *antequam*. The

---

[48] *Gloss. in Sent.* ed. cit. 1, 110*–112*.

second quotation is on Mark. 1.7 'solvere corrigiam calciamentorum. The Gloss on the text reads: '"corrigiam calciamentorum," mysterium scilicet incarnationis, quomodo verbum caro factum est.' Hugh also quotes an *auctoritas* deriving from St. Gregory's homilies:

> 'Venit ad nos calciata deitas' dicit auctoritas, ex qua videtur quod deitas incarnata sit, et ita, si filius Dei incarnatus fuit, videtur quod in quantum est homo non sit quid, ergo nec aliquid, quod est contra Alexandrum.[49]

Again, I found no parallel in Alexander, either on Mark 1.7 or on Matthew 3.11. However, this time Hugh's quotation seems to refer to an addition to the E codex of his *Glossa in Sent.*: 'Item Christus, secundum quod homo, est aliquid; quaeratur ergo Quid?'[50] It follows that when Hugh quoted Alexander on Christology he was not using Alexander's postills but his teaching in other contexts.

It remained to collate Hugh's and Alexander's postills to settle the question of priority. After weeks of wrestling with the problem and subtracting known sources common to both, I came to the tentative conclusion that either Alexander borrowed from Hugh or else that they drew on a common source unknown to us, although Alexander is basically independent in his comments and in his choice of authorities. An attractive hypothesis would be that Alexander revised his postills given as a secular, with the help of Hugh's, when Alexander taught as a Franciscan. After all, Hugh left the schools, with his postills completed, in 1236, the very year when Alexander began his regency as a friar. Hence they would have been available to him as an aid to teaching.

There is no proof either way; but it will be convenient to begin with Hugh's postills. I shall review his sources briefly, describe his technique and outlook, and then pass to Alexander's, discussing their relationship to Hugh's and their original contribution to lecturing on the Gospels. John of LaRochelle comes after Hugh and Alexander; there is no doubt here; hence he will be discussed last of the trio of friars.

---

[49] Lib. I, Hom. vii, PL 76, 1101: "quasi calceata ad nos divinitas venit."
[50] Ed. cit. 14, 118, no. 15, *Sent.* iii, d. 10.

ADDITIONAL NOTE

Dr. J.H.A. van Banning has made a meticulous comparison of quotations from the *Opus imperfectum* of Pseudo-Chrysostom on St. Matthew in Hugh of St. Cher on the one hand and in Alexander of Hales' postill on the other. He found 317 quotations in Hugh of St. Cher, mostly ascribed to Chrysostom or else anonymous. Alexander has some 39 quotations, from the same textual family as Hugh's. All but 6 of the 39 seem to have been lifted from Hugh. The 6 exceptions, where Alexander's quotations cannot be found in Hugh, keep closer to the text of the original. This very much strengthens the argument for placing the postill on St. Matthew by Alexander to *postquam esset frater* and some time after Hugh completed his postill on St. Matthew, c. 1234-1235. It does not rule out the possibility that Alexander revised lectures given as a secular when he came to teach at the Franciscan *studium*. Dr. van Banning kindly allows me to take his data from his unpublished D.Phil. thesis, *The Opus Imperfectum in Matthaeum*, deposited in the Bodleian Library (1983) 2, 496-501.

(PART TWO)

IV. Hugh of St. Cher

Hugh's postills, as we have them, represent the fruit of team work. It is easy to imagine a team of assistants supplying the master with suitable excerpts for each text of the Bible. But whatever their final form may be, they originated as lectures. There are references to *lectio* and to *lectura*: "sicut videbitur in lectione" (Matt. 5.1); "ut in prima lectura dictum est" (Matt. 5.22). The master's statements are put sometimes in the singular: "Et haec opinio magis placet mihi" (Luke 22.19), and sometimes in the imperative: "Nunc lege litteram" (Luke 22.42). The possibility that the original derived from a *reportatio* appears when Hugh is referred to as 'the master.' One passage seems to represent a reporter's note on Hugh's discussion of Matt. 12.25. Jesus' answer to the Pharisees, who accused him of casting out devils in the name of Beelzebub, raised a grammatical point. He refuted them by an analogy: *Omne regnum divisum contra se desolabitur; et omnis civitas vel domus divisa contra se non stabit.* According to the postill, the Lord here refuted the Pharisees indirectly by synaeresis (drawing together or contraction) and/or by hypozeugma (combination of several subjects with a single word or predicate); but 'the master' in the postills altered the text so as to make it a major proposition:

> Infirmat Dominus quod de eo dixerant pharisaei, primo indirecte dupliciter per synaeresim vel hypozeuxim sumpto quod dixerant, et ex hoc deducens eos ad inconveniens, et secundum ordinem

litterae, licet magister in postillis hoc modo permutet textum,
ut sit propositio maior: *Et si Suthanas*, assumptio, *omne regnum*,
omnis civitas, assumptionis probatio vel probationis supprobatio·

'The master' cannot mean Comestor or the Chanter; they discuss the
text in different terms. Hence it must refer to Hugh himself.

The only safe hypothesis must be that the postills were given as
lectures and in some places reported, either before or after the *travail
d'équipe* of Hugh and his assistants. A study of the shorter version,
which has not been printed, and a comparison with the longer version
available in print, might clear up the problem.

A mere glance at the postills suffices to show that we have a mosaic of quotations. Hugh's purpose, it follows, was to provide masters
and students of the sacred page with a vast *instrument de travail*,
incorporating traditional and more nearly contemporary sources into
its framework. This intention did not permit that fresh approach to
the Gospels which we might expect from a Friar Preacher. Hugh
wanted instead to equip his colleagues with the best means to continue and enlarge the work of his secular predecessors. That need not
discourage us from looking for flashes of personal opinions, reflecting
the new *milieu* of the friars' *studia*. It does mean that a study of
his postills must proceed like an archaeological dig, beginning with the
top layer of twelfth–century sources and moving downwards to earlier
commentaries. Only after sorting out and identifying these pieces
can we hope to discover what Hugh thought for himself and what
he contributed to Gospel exegesis. The tedious process of excavation
will have its reward in showing us what sources Hugh preferred and
how he differed from Alexander of Hales and John of La Rochelle
in his choices.

Peter the Chanter is quoted by name on Matt. 13.19 on the
various kinds of seed in the parable. Hugh suggests three meanings
for *seed*, adding that the Chanter gave a fourth: 'Quartum scilicet
apponit Cantor, scilicet bonum propositum, quod dicit bonam voluntatem." This corresponds roughly to the Chanter: "*Semen*... vo-
luntas bona, cui collaborat liberum arbitrium" (M. fol. 63va). Hugh
sometimes also quotes from *Unum ex quatuor* anonymously. He
ascribes to the Chanter an *exemplum* on Matt. 8.3: "sicut narrat
Cantor Parisiensis...": a priest who shunned lepers contracted leprosy
himself. I have not found this in *Unum ex quatuor* or elsewhere in
the Chanter's works; but his oral teaching was remembered at Paris
after his death.

Comestor supplied Hugh with his major modern source. He quoted him by name on Matt. 7.4, Matt. 9.5, Matt. 17.23.[1] The *School History*, quoted as 'Magister in historiis,' frequently appears.[2] More often Hugh borrowed from Comestor anonymously. It is unsafe to ascribe any comment to Hugh without verifying that he did not take it from Comestor's lectures or from the *School History*. Hugh also copied Comestor's techniques. He lectured on a glossed text as Comestor did, though he quoted the Gloss less systematically. Like Comestor, he felt free to criticise it. On John 5.25, he declared that he preferred his own to the Gloss interpretation:

> Licet glosae aliquantulum videantur aliter exponere, tamen mihi videtur quod respiciunt magis mysterium quam litteram. Unde dico...

He seems to have remembered that the Gloss on St. John had been compiled by Anselm of Laon. On John 11.39 he quoted it as 'Anselmus':

> *Iam foetet*. Anselmus: Timebat remoto lapide potius foetorem excitare quam fratrem resuscitare.

Some copies of the Gloss on St. John had this ascription to Anselm: Hugh may have used one.[3]

Comestor's commentaries may have suggested to Hugh the use of topical allusions to the schools, to contemporary institutions and to local custom. The following examples, which may be original to Hugh, have parallels in Comestor. Hugh warns pupils not to be jealous for their own and detract from the renown of another master (on John 3.27). An educated man prides himself on his books, "quia sunt

---

[1] "Manducator dicit quod prelatus qui est in peccato mortali non debet corripere, quia si corripit, peccat mortaliter." "Secundum Manducatorem: utrum facilius videtur vobis vel solo verbo dimittere peccata vel opere efficere ut infirmus surgat."

Both quotations correspond to Comestor's postills, MS Oxford Bodl. Laud. Misc. 291, fols. 40vb, 48ra, also the two quotations of Comestor on the *didrachma* (Matt. 17.23), as "Manducator in postillis," ibid., fol. 71rb.

[2] On John 4.20, John 13.1, John 13.23, and on the signs of Domesday, Luke 21.17. The quotations can be verified from *Historia Scholastica* (PL 198, 1568; 1614; 1617; 1611).

[3] See above, pp. 3-4.

bene postillati et emendati" (Luke 9.7). The merchants in the Temple (Luke 19.45) resemble burgess usurers, "sicut alibi parati sunt burgenses, quia mutuant ad usuras." He contrasts the *praedium* (John 4.5), that is land held by purchase or conquest, with the *feodum*, the fief held by service, which may be lawfully withdrawn in default of service. The sea throws up corpses, and the frying pan of the abbey of St. Germain des Près throws out bad eggs (on Matt. 5.22); this local wonder perhaps echoes a current joke. Comestor made constant use of the liturgy as a supplement to the Gospel text. Hugh follows him: *the light to lighten the gentiles* (Luke 2.32) leads him to expound the properties of the candle in church as "a book for the laity." On the other hand, he was selective in his choice of techniques. Comestor, intent on historical research, relied on the liturgy for evidence as well as for edification; Hugh used it for the latter purpose only, nor did he share Comestor's interest in topography and iconography as aids to understanding. Hugh quotes Comestor on these subjects, but adds nothing personal. There is even some backsliding on the relations between the literal and spiritual senses. Comestor and Hugh both took the 'four senses' for granted and furnished their text with allegories and/or moralities. But, whereas Comestor had shown a concern for establishing what was the literal and what a spiritual interpretation, Hugh was less precise in doing so.

Turning back to Comestor's sources, we find that Hugh used Comestor's main source, known to the latter as 'Geoffrey Babion' (mistakenly, as it seems), directly, and quoted him independently of Comestor (PL 162, 1227–1500). Hugh quoted on Mark 1.9:

> *In Iordane*. Gaufredus: Iordanus interpretatur descensus. Descendit Christus, ut non descendamus... Nec simulata nec indevota nec tristis humilitas habet gratiam apud Deum.

B (as I call the anonymous) explained *descensus* as referring to the humility required in baptism (PL 162, 1267). Hugh borrowed from him anonymously too, independently of Comestor or the Chanter: his story that Herod burned the Magi's ships at Tarsus on Matt. 2.12 (PL 162, 1257) is a verbal quotation. Thus Hugh drew on Comestor for comment and technique and as a guide to sources. It will be all the more significant, therefore, if we find that he differed from Comestor in his attitudes.

He enlarged on Comestor in his use of patristic sources. So far as I know, he was the first Paris commentator on the fourth gospel to draw upon Burgundio of Pisa's translation of St. John Chryso-stom's homilies on St. John. The Pisan judge had translated them from Greek into Latin by 1174,[4] too late for Comestor or the Chanter to have used them. The most striking instance turns on the story of the woman taken in adultery, John 8.3–11 in the Latin Vulgate. Hugh noted in his preliminary 'division' of this chapter that Chryso-stom omitted the story and said nothing about it. Hugh went on to say that Burgundio, who translated Chrystostom's book, gave the reason in his prologue to his translation: the story is not found in the old books in Greece, nor is it read in the Greek Church, because the Greeks think that it was added to the original Gospel by certain per-sons, just as the fable of the dragon and Susanna was added to the book of Daniel. Hence the Greeks regard it as apocryphal.[5] Hugh leaped to the defence of the Latin Church, answering the Greeks that the story could have been added by St. John himself after he had finished his Gospel; hence it is not found in all copies universally: "Can it be believed that somebody would have been rash enough to dare to add anything to so great an evangelist?" It was an ingenious suggestion to explain the addition, while taking Chrysostom's rea-sons for omitting it into consideration. Apart from this disagreement, Hugh valued Chrysostom highly. In some instances he gives an exact reference for his quotations, as *Hom.* 4 (on John 1.1) and *Hom.* 38 (on John 5.14).[6] He expresses approval: 'as Chrysostom says, and it is true' (on 5.9). He calls him 'maximus inter magistris graecorum' (on. 13.1). He will even prefer him to Jerome and Augustine (on. 1.31): "Expositio Chrysostomi magis tangit veritatem litterae, et ideo ipsum sequimur per totum." The literal interpretation, so pro-nounced in the Greek Father, appealed to the schoolman in Hugh, as it had appealed to his secular translator, the judge and diplomat Burgundio. Although Hugh is the first known commentator to quote Chrysostom's *Homilies* on St. John, he may already have had select extracts at his disposal. He refers twice to Chrysostom 'in originali' (on 5.18 on the chapter division of 8) as though he had excerpts to

---

[4] P. Classen, *Burgundio von Pisa Richter–Gesandter–Übersetzer* (Sitzungs-berichte des Heidelberger Akademie der Wissenschaften. Philos.–hist. Kl. 4, 1974), 52.

[5] Classen edits Burgundio's prologue, where he gives this explanation, ibid., pp. 98–100.

[6] PG 59, 43, 49, 211.

hand and used them as a guide when he wanted to look up the original. Lecturers on Scripture were accustomed to do so when using authorities quoted in excerpts in the Gloss.[7] Perhaps the *fratres adiutores* at the Paris *studium* had performed this service for him.

Naturally he quoted abundantly from Burgundio's translation of Chrysostom's *Homilies* on St. Matthew. Burgundio had undertaken his translation at the pope's request in 1151; hence it was available in the late twelfth–century schools,[8] joining Pseudo–Chrysostom's *Opus imperfectum*, already well known. A comparison of Hugh's quotations of Chrysostom on St. Matthew with the originals shows that he referred to the authentic homilies and to the *Opus imperfectum* indiscriminately as 'Chrysostomus.' His quotations from both are often verbal; but occasionally he had to rely on his memory, as on Matt. 24.15:

> Christus plenus gratiae et veritatis, antichristus cupiditatis et falsitatis. Credo quod haec sunt verba Chrysostomi.

His memory misled him here; neither the genuine nor the Pseudo–Chrysostom has the quoted words on this text.

His Latin patristic sources are unremarkable and need not concern us. I shall focus on the more remarkable pieces in the mosaic which come from medieval writers.

The *Periphyseon* of John Scot Erigena makes an unexpected and unique entry into Hugh's discussion of Moses and Helias at the Transfiguration (Luke 9.30). He quotes various opinions on the question how a soul could appear in its own body or another's:

> De Moysi et Helia varie sunt opiniones, quomodo apparuit anima in suo corpore vel alieno. Rabanus... Ioannes Scotus: Helias non in suo corpore, non in aliqua sensibili materia aliunde assumpta apparuit, sed quadam ineffabili virtute, soli Deo cognita, invisibilis spiritus visibilis factus est. Aliter Ambrosius in glosa...

The quotation corresponds almost verbally to *Periphyseon* iii, 13 (PL 122, 662). Hugh may have taken it from some intermediate source, such as glosses on John Scot's translation of the Pseudo–

---

[7] B. Smalley, *Study of the Bible in the Middle Ages*, 3rd ed. (Oxford, 1983), pp. 226–228.

[8] P. Classen, op. cit., p. 34.

Dionysian *corpus*.[9] In any case it witnesses both to the industry of Hugh and his team of assistants, and to the continuing interest in *Periphyseon* even after its condemnation as heretical in 1210 and 1225.[10]

There are two quotations from a 'Gilbert,' one of which Fr. N. M. Häring has kindly identified for me as probably Gilbert of La Porrée:

> *Hic est filius meus* (Matt. 17.5): Gilleb.: Certe, si Filius aliud esset, quam Pater esset, non posset Pater in Filio sibi complacere. Quid est dicere *complacui mihi* nisi: sicut placui mihi in meipso, ita placui in Filio?

Fr. Häring wrote to me: "Gilbert and his school advocated a subtle distinction in the doctrine of the Trinity. They interpreted John 10.38 in the sense that with regard to the divine essence the Father is in the Son and the Son in the Father. But they denied that this could be said of the divine persons or hypostates. The text in Matt. 17.5 was held to be in agreement with this view by distinguishing *in meipso* and *in Filio*... The doctrine is expounded very briefly in Gilbert, *De Trin.* II, 1, 27 and more thoroughly in the *Summa Zwettlensis* II, 81–84." Hugh's quotation does not correspond verbally with either passage in Gilbert, who does not quote Matt. 17.5;[11] but as Fr. Häring pointed out, others cited it in discussions on the Trinity, so that Hugh may well have been referring vaguely to the teaching of the *Porretani*. The other quotation of Gilbert is more doubtful; it comes on Luke 13.29:

> Gilb.: Ab occidente portae tres, per quas intrant furantes regnum, scilicet occultae afflictiones, humiles confessiones.

Fr. Häring comments that an unprinted *Sententiae collectae ex dictis magistri Gisleberti, episcopi pictaviensis*, which does not include this

---

[9] I have to thank Monsieur l'abbé E. Jeauneau for this reference and for suggesting various intermediaries between Hugh and the original. Even if one could be discovered, it would be hard to prove that he had not borrowed from the original.

[10] M. Cappuyns, *Jean Scot Érigène* (Louvain/Paris, 1933), pp. 245–250; H.-F. Dondaine, 'L'objet et le "medium" de la vision béatifique chez les théologiens du XIIIe siècle,' *R.T.A.M.* 19 (1952), 73.

[11] See Fr. Häring's editions of *The Commentary on Boethius by Gilbert of Poitiers* (Pontifical Institute of Mediaeval Studies, Studies and Texts, 13, Toronto, 1966), p. 168; *Sententie M. Petri Pictaviensis*, in *Die Zwettler Summe* (Beitr. zur Gesch. der Philos. und Theol. des Mittelalters, N. F. 15, 1977), 92–93.

saying, proves at least that *"dicta* of Master Gilbert were afloat."
On the other hand, we shall see that Alexander of Hales quoted a
'Gilbert' who was probably a Cistercian commentator on the Canticle.
Whatever their provenance, neither of Hugh's 'Gilbert' quotations
comes *via* Comestor or the Chanter.

Bernard and Pseudo–Bernard supplied a large proportion of the
pieces in Hugh's mosaic. He quoted the *Vita Prima* of St. Bernard
on John 5.35, on the simplicity and humility of 'the poor of Christ'
at Clairvaux (PL 185, 247–248). I made a rough count of quotations
ascribed to Bernard in Hugh's postill on St. Luke; the number of
surviving sermons on the first two chapters of this gospel dictated
my choice.[12] The approximate score of quotations (sometimes repeated) is: *De Laudibus Beatae Virginis* 17; *Sermones in Cantica* 10;
Sermones in Epiphania 9; *De Consideratione* 6; *Sermones in Nativitate Beatae Virginis* 5; *Sermones in Purificatione Beatae Virginis* 5;
Sermo in Nativitate 5; *Sermones in Annuntiatione* 3; *Sermones de Diversis* 3; *Sermones in Circumcisione* 3; *Sermo in Vigilia Nativitatis* 2;
Sermo ad Clericos 2; finally 1 each from the sermons *In Octava Assumptionis, In Festivitate Omnium Sanctorum, In Resurrectione, In
Nativitate Sancti Iohannis Baptista, Per Annum*; 1 each also from
De Praecepto, De Gradibus Humilitatis, Epistola ad Guilelmum. There
are at least three quotations from the Pseudo–Bernard *Flores*.[13] A
number have not been identified and may have come from other
Pseudo–Bernardine writings. One comes from Geoffrey of Auxerre's
report of Bernard's teaching on Luke 14.33: *Recte, Petre, fecisti,...*'[13a]

Hugh used St. Bernard in two ways: partly as an exegetical
source, as when he quoted from sermons on the infancy Gospel in
St. Luke, and partly to sugar his comments on the text with pious
thoughts and rhetorical exclamations. Bernardine spirituality appealed to our Dominican. Although his secular predecessors at Paris,
such as Stephen Langton, had sometimes praised or quoted from St.
Bernard, this massive infiltration was new. Bernard's writings cir-

---

[12] The quotations listed have been identified from *Sancti Bernardi Opera,*
ed. J. Leclercq, C. H. Talbot, H. M. Rochais, 1–7 (Rome, 1957–1974). Fr. A. H.
Martens has taken great pains to help me to trace them from the index to the
Opera, now in preparation. It was hard labour, since Hugh seldom gives the
title of the work quoted: "ut dicit beatus Bernardus" is the sole guidance. I
am most grateful to Fr. Martens for his help.

[13] *Opera S. Bernardi* (Paris, 1586), pp. 938, 991, 927.

[13a] From Geoffrey's *Declamationes*, PL 184, 438; see J. Leclercq, *Receuil
d'études sur S. Bernard et ses écrits*, 1 (Rome, 1962), 17, 19.

culated widely in the originals and in excerpts; now they found a
new channel to a large public in school lectures, which would themselves circulate both within and without the classroom. It is note-
worthy that Jordan of Saxony, Master General of the Order, quoted
St. Bernard in sermons preached in 1229.[14]

St. Anselm of Canterbury, though he lived earlier than St. Bernard, was a later comer to the schools. His doctrinal works made
little impact on theological teaching until Alexander of Hales took
them up in his *Glossae in Sententias* and his *Quaestiones Disputatae
Antequam Esset Frater*. Alexander "guaranteed Anselm's position in
the Parisian schools and transmitted him to posterity as an *auctoritas*
on the Redemption." Dr. McGuire proved his statement by showing
that Alexander quoted *Cur Deus Homo* and other books frequently,
often by chapter; the quotations are accurate according to the texts
published in Anselm's *Opera Omnia* by F. S. Schmitt (Edinburgh,
1946).[15]

Hugh seems to have been aware of the current fashion and tried
to keep up with it, without having made a close study of the Anselmian *corpus*. His longest and most verbally accurate quotation is
decorative rather than doctrinal: "O angustiae... istud execrabor"
on the pains of Hell (Luke 21.23) from Anselm's *Meditationes*.[16] His
one quotation from *Cur Deus Homo* suggests a glance at the original,
misleading even so (on John 1.9):

> Sicut enim dicit Anselmus in libro Cur Deus homo : Non est cre-
> dendum quod ex quo Deus hominem fecit ad participandum
> beatitudinis unquam fuisse tempus in quo mundo isto non fuerint
> aliqui praeparati ad quod homo creatus est.

Anselm argued only that God made man capable of partaking in
blessedness.[17] Hugh quotes 'Anselmus in libro de concordia et prae-
scientia et libero arbitrio' on John 1.1. Again the so-called excerpt
suggests a mere glance at *De Concordia*.[18] He invokes Anselm against
the Greeks on John 1.3:

---

[14] A. G. Little and D. L. Douie, "Three Sermons of Friar Jordan of Saxony,
the Successor of St. Dominic, Preached in England A.D. 1229," *English Historical
Review*, 54 (1939), 14–19.

[15] B. P. McGuire, *The History of St. Anselm's Theology of the Redemption
in the Twelfth and Thirteenth Centuries* (Oxford D. Phil. thesis, 1970), pp. 215–216.

[16] *Opera*, ed. cit., 3, 78–79.

[17] Ibid., 2, 67–95.

[18] Ibid., 2, 247–253.

> Et hoc aperte dicit Anselmus in libro de Spiritu Sancto contra
> Graecos, ubi aperte dicit : Pater fecit omnia per Verbum licet sit
> eiusdem substantiae cum Patre, quia fecit omnia sua potentia
> quae est idem Filio.

Again, this is not verbally exact.[19] "Sicut dicit Anselmus in libro de
veritate..." (on John 1.16) is followed by another rough summary of
a passage of *De Veritate*.[20] Hugh realised that St. Anselm was now an
authority, but had not quite mastered him.

Pagan writers do not figure largely in the ensemble. One finds
the expected tags from Seneca and a few allusions to Aristotle. Of
these the most apt is from the *Topics* i,10 on the nature of questioning
(on John 4.31):

> *Et interrogaverunt*: Interrogatio ista non est per modum dubita-
> tionis, nisi sicut dicitur in *Topicis* quod dialectica propositio est
> interrogatio probabilis, non quod sub dubio proponatur quantum
> ad inhaerentiam praedicati sub subiecto, sed quia quaerit con-
> sensum a respondente.

The saying that men are friends because they have an enemy in
common from *Posterior Analytics* i,34 was probably a cliché. A reference to *Historia Animalium* (?) is inaccurate (on John 3.4):

> Dicit enim Aristoteles quod animalia habentia dentes acutos
> similes sunt foetui ursus, in quo non apparet nisi ungues.

Aristotle does not say this in *Historia Animalium*. Hugh also quotes
from Pseudo–Aristotle, *Liber de Causis Primis et Secundis*, showing
some knowledge of its content (on John 5.17):

> Philosophus in libro de causis: Causae secundae sunt et quae
> causae sunt habent a causa prima, et nisi ipsa esset in eis conti-
> nendo et movendo ad causationem nec essent nec causae essent.

But this is not a verbal quotation.[21]

We shall get a closer insight into Hugh's mind if we look for the
influences at work on him, showing themselves in parallels rather than

---

[19] Ibid., 1, 10.

[20] Ibid., 1, 176–177.

[21] Ed. R. de Vaux, *Notes et textes de l'Avicennisme latin aux confins des
XIIe–XIIIe siècles*, (Bibliothèque Thomiste 20, Paris, 1934), 88–140.

borrowings. He stood in the tradition of what has been called 'the biblical moral school,' whose most outstanding members were Peter the Chanter and Stephen Langton. Hugh resembled Langton more than he did the Chanter. He felt little or nothing of the latter's pessimism on the state of the Church. What he did was to echo the call of both scholars to preaching and active reform work. They taught that the study of Scripture should issue in preaching; the student should leave the schools as a reformer and never allow himself to be corrupted or intimidated. He should preach to the laity as well as to the clergy; a lay congregation might prove the more receptive, provided that the preacher fitted his sermons to their understanding.[22] Hugh knew Langton's lectures on Old Testament books and sometimes quoted them on relevant texts. He could not do the same on the Gospels, since Langton left no commentaries on them. Instead, he took up and developed Langton's message from the Old Testament commentaries. A few examples picked consecutively from Hugh's postill on St. Luke will show his adherence to Langton's teaching. Christ's return to Galilee from the desert (4.4) signifies return from contemplation to action, that is from the schools to preaching. Christ teaches clerks that they should sometimes return to the places where they were nurtured, that is to the churches which nourished them [paid their expenses?] in the schools. The widow and lepers (4.26–27) signify sinful laymen, who often receive God's word more devoutly than clerks or even religious. Many scholars in the desert of poverty (7.20) that is, in the schools with their fellows, confess the truth openly by word and deed; but when they get rich and are promoted to high offices they change their opinion and begin to doubt or deny altogether what they knew and asserted before. The disciples' offer to buy bread for the multitude (9.13) signifies that men should go to the Paris schools in order to learn what they will feed back later on to those who come to hear their sermons.

The mission of the apostles to preach (Matt. 10.12) suggests the prophecy that "swords shall be turned into ploughshares" (Isa. 2.4); this means that scholars shall turn disputations and lectures into preaching (the Chanter's famous *lectio, disputatio, praedicatio*). If a doctor preached to peasants as much as to clerks, the former would do penance for their sins and do better than clerks. Scholars must not stay idle in Paris instead of preaching (Matt. 28.8). Finally, we

---

[22] B. Smalley, *Study of the Bible*, op. cit., pp. 242–257.

hear an audible echo of Langton's moralisation of Micah. 4.3 and Judg. 3.31. Langton interpreted the swords in these texts as subtle dialectic and knowledge gained in the arts course, which doctors turned into ploughshares, that is plain theological teaching; Samgar killed six hundred men, signifying vices, with a ploughshare, whereas Aod slew only one with his sharp sword.[23] Hugh quotes these same Old Testament texts with identical moralisations on Matt. 31.1 and Mark 4.5. Langton's teaching is brought up to date when Hugh specifies what was *not* suitable to popular preaching. The Baptist's preaching of penance (Matt. 3.1–2) rebukes 'curious' preachers, who set their mouth against heaven (Ps. 72.9), speaking with the tongues of angels about various hierarchies and suchlike. This crack refers to quotations from Pseudo–Dionysius on the hierarchies. Peter Comestor had quoted the *Ecclesiastical Hierarchy* in his sermons; but he was addressing an audience of clerks.[24] Hugh himself quoted the *Celestial Hierarchy* and *On the Divine Names* in his postills on John 5.18 and 1.1. Ironically enough, his postill on St. John was corrected for its bias to Greek thought after the condemnation of 1241. He also quoted a series of definitions of hierarchy current in the early thirteenth century schools in his Sentence commentary.[25] The contrast brings out his distinction between preaching and school exercises. The professor could quote learned works; the preacher must not pander to those who come to sermons for wrong reasons, such as to get book-learning rather than instruction on good living, to keep up appearances or as a social custom (Luke 9.13). On the other hand, Hugh followed Langton's lead in sprinkling his postills with verses, jokes, proverbs

---

[23] MS Oxford, Oriel College 53, fol. 153[rb]: "Hoc impletum est in Paulo et Dionisio et Augustino et aliis multis et cotidie adimpletur in litteratis, cum gladio subtilitatis dialectice et ab eliminatione rethorice et studio quadrivialis scientie transeunt ad rudia verba theologie, quibus verbis tamquam vomere terram conscientie excolunt et exercent et faciunt bonorum operum fructum. In huius falce reprehensionis divine resecant vitia et extirpant, sicut Samgar vomere uno sexcentos viros occidit..."
MS Oxford, Trinity College 65, fol. 92va: "Per gladios enim subtiles sententie philosophorum intelliguntur, quos ipsi [doctores] convertebant in vomeres et sententias grossas, per quas convertebant ad fidem alios."

[24] J. Longère, *Oeuvres oratoires des Maîtres Parisiens au XIIe siècle* (Études Augustiniennes, Paris, 1975, 1), 111.

[25] H.–F. Dondaine, "L'objet et le 'medium," op. cit., pp. 83, 119; "Cinq citations de Jean Scot chez Simon de Tournai," *R.T.A.M.*, 17 (1950), 304; M.–T. d'Alverny, *Alain de Lille: Textes inédits* (Paris, 1965), pp. 94–99.

and *exempla*, which would be suitable for use in sermons *ad populum*.

It was traditional to stress that contemplation fertilised action. Hugh makes the theme explicit on John 2.12:

> Those preachers conquer the devil who not only sally forth to preaching, but sometimes stay quiet in their order (*in ordine suo*) to care for their own souls (*custodia sui*) and for discussion. Such a soul is Christ's bride truly, being both Rachel and Lia, Martha and Mary together. She has chosen the better part, since action is good, but contemplation better. The best part is that which includes them both, having a mother's fruitfulness in preaching without loss of a virgin's purity, which she keeps in contemplation.

Hugh's *lectio* included the function of religious *lectio divina*, leading to prayer and mystic contemplation. He describes the ascetic stages to be passed through before rapture into ecstasy on Luke 2.46. The three days' search by Mary and Joseph for the boy Jesus signifies three types of cognition, of the senses, of the imagination and of the intelligence, preparatory to the ecstasy of finding Jesus, raising the soul above sensible, imaginable and intelligible. Another threefold cognition leads to the finding of Jesus in the Temple, that is in one's own heart. The first shows that the world is nothing, the second that one is nothing oneself, the third that man must acknowledge himself to be nothing while he is a slave to sin. He who seeks Jesus according to these three days will find him certainly. This threefold type of cognition recalls Richard of St. Victor's *Benjamin Minor*, a treatise on preparation for contemplation: he insisted on the role of imagination as a medium between the senses and the intelligence in the ascent to mystic union.[26] Hugh's elaboration (which I have omitted) on acknowledgement of the nothingness of the world and of oneself, if subject to it, draws on the *contemptus mundi* and *scito teipsum* themes, both dear to Richard of St. Victor and to St. Bernard.[27]

---

[26] PL 196, 4–5: "...inde manifeste colligitur quia ad invisibilium cognitionem nunquam ratio assurgeret, nisi ei ancilla sua, imaginatio videlicet, rerum visibilium formam repraesentaret... sed constat quia sine imaginatione corporalia nesciret, sine quorum cognitione ad coelestium contemplationem non ascenderet..." 12: "Imaginatio ergo, quando instrumentum significat, est vis illa animae qua cum voluerit quodlibet imaginari valet." 16: "Sciendum autem quia illud contemplationis genus, quod in pura intelligentia versatur, huiusmodi speculatione... quanto subtilius, tanto nimirum excellentius esse cognoscitur."

[27] Ibid., p. 56. See P. Courcelle, *Connais–toi toi–même de Socrate à Saint Bernard* (Paris, 1974), pp. 242–243, 258.

Hugh's reader expects him to join all these threads together and to draw the logical conclusion. Contemplation, study, preaching and pastoral care: the Friars Preachers devoted themselves to these activities as an integrated whole. The Dominican Order with its *studia* and ministry was carefully organised to forward the realisation of these functions in the collective and individual life of its members. But Hugh never mentions either his Order or its founder. The only religious Orders to be named are the Cistercians, Carthusians and Grandmontines, cited as examples of men living literally *in the fields of the woods* (Ps. 131.6) on Luke 2.39. When Hugh defines grades in the Church he uses traditional terms: *prelati, claustrales, clerici, scholares*. An abbot should join together monks and lay brothers, active and contemplative religious, together in peace and love; a bishop should associate clerks, laymen, secular clerks and scholars in the bond of peace (John 10.16). The Mendicants have no place in this scheme. Was Hugh being modest about his Order, unwilling to annoy the older religious and the seculars by cracking up the friars? He blamed religious who boasted that their Order excelled all others and had more saints (John 4.22). Perhaps he wished to set them an example of humility. Or was he just conservative, afraid to introduce novelties into his postills? His predecessors in the 'biblical moral' school had taught before the Mendicants came to Paris; did Hugh deliberately refrain from bringing his models up to date? I do not know what his reasons were; I can only record his reticence.

The question then posed itself: does Hugh show any specifically Mendicant traits in his lectures? First, was he interested in that eschatological speculation which we associate with the friars?

Certain it is that Joachimite types of speculation had no appeal for him, although he knew and quoted Joachim in his postill on the Apocalypse on the seven seals (Apoc. 5). Far from predicting a future age of the Holy Spirit, he was anxious 'to counter rash and dangerous speculations' on the Last Things.[28] His postills on the Gospels merely record the traditional view that Antichrist would reign for three and

---

[28] D. M. Solomon, "The Sentence Commentary of Richard Fishacre and the Apocalypse Commentary of Hugh of St. Cher," *Archivum Fratrum Praedicatorum*, 46 (1976), 372; R. E. Lerner, "Refreshment of the Saints: The Time after Antichrist as a Station for Earthly Progress in Medieval Thought," *Traditio*, 32 (1976), 121.

a half years (Matt. 24.22).[29] The furthest he goes is to mention a prophecy that the Jews would live in Jerusalem and rebuild a Temple there at the time of Antichrist, 'as some say' (Luke 21.24). Hugh's *quidam* go back to the *Catechisms* of St. Cyril of Jerusalem, 348; the legend that the Jews would rebuild the Temple as a seat for Antichrist gained currency during the middle ages.[30] Nothing adventurous here!

Secondly, was he stricter than the seculars on Gospel precepts? His teaching on the Sermon on the Mount falls midway between Comestor's and the Chanter's and is therefore not wholly consistent. On Luke 6.30, he follows Comestor in allowing that the Military Orders make legitimate war on the heathen. On the ban on litigation (Matt. 5.40) he allows that the 'imperfect' and prelates may go to law, though it is not expedient. Religious and anchorites ought not to do so, except indirectly through a friend or protector. Then he goes more fully into the vexed question of litigation, by religious, admitting with sorrow that it has become customary and that religious themselves justify it. Some of them claim that they may bring their suit before a church court, but not a secular court. They say that all religious Orders (*omnis religio*) would lose everything and perish if litigation were not allowed to them. Yet who can dispense them from Christ's precepts? It is better to forfeit all one's goods than to lose truth and obedience. Hugh lists the evils of litigation and praises the virtue of patient suffering of spoliation of one's earthly goods. The Chanter's nostalgia for the early Church finds an echo in Hugh's reluctant admission that bad customs have come to stay. His comment on scandal, including again the problem of litigation in self–defence (Matt. 18.7–9), goes back to Comestor's support for the status quo. If it were forbidden, then the bad would rob the good of all their belongings and get worse themselves in the process. Hugh makes a new proviso, not found in Comestor or the Chanter, that such litigation should not prejudice a person in authority or the commonwealth (*respublica*). The concept of the common good as a criterion for action had a brilliant future; but Hugh merely touches on it in passing. It is striking again that he never mentioned the early Mendicants' abstention from litigation.

The Chanter's dislike of legalism comes out on Mark 7.2, where

---

[29] Ibid., p. 100.

[30] A. Linder, "Ecclesia and Synagoga in the Medieval Myth of Constantine the Great," *Revue Belge de philologie et d'histoire*, 54 (1976), 1033.

Hugh complains of preference for human traditions to divine commandments: many are more moved today if someone breaks human traditions than God's commands. Again on Matt. 15.3: *propter traditionem vestram*, archdeacons on their inspections make enquiries as though they were washerwomen, asking only whether the church linen and altarcloths are clean and so forth; they punish disobedience to synodal decrees rather than disobedience to God. It seems that Hugh tempered the Chanter's pessimism with Comestor's cheerful acceptance of the need for modification of early rigour. Departure from primitive practice was a pity and to be lamented, but one could not put the clock back. It may be that Hugh's experience of the friars' mission to set an example and to evangelise made him more optimistic for the future than the Chanter had been.

Much the same applies to Hugh's teaching on the relations between *regnum* and *sacerdotium* and to the pope's position in the Church. The Chanter had been more of a high churchman than Comestor. Hugh follows the Chanter, but hesitantly. Like the Chanter, he admired St. Thomas of Canterbury as a martyr for ecclesiastical freedom, listing this as one of the causes qualifying a man for martyrdom (Matt. 2.16), and as a type of the good shepherd, who gave up his life for his sheep (John 18.8). The second comment was prompted by the Chanter's allusion to St. Thomas on the same text (M, fol. 139[rb]). But Hugh's pronouncements on the Church's control over secular rulers are ambiguous: St. Peter's sword (Matt. 26.51) is interpreted as 'the sword of excommunication,' which must not be wielded rashly. The two swords of Luke 22.38 suggest, Hugh says, that the Church holds both the material and the spiritual swords. Perhaps this furnishes her with occasion to fight with the material sword; otherwise one would have been superfluous; Christ said that *two* were enough:

> Materialis et spiritualis [gladius] est in ecclesia... [here follows a *distinctio* on the spiritual sword, 'of the word, of the spirit etc.'] Hic forte sumit ecclesia materiam et occasionem pugnandi gladio materiali, nam aliter superflueret unus gladius.

Hugh may have been thinking of Pope Gregory IX's invasion of the kingdom of Southern Italy and Sicily during Frederick II's absence on a crusade; Frederick had been banned by the pope, although a crusader. The 'soldiers of the Keys,' recruited by Gregory, fought the 'soldiers of the Cross' on Frederick's return from Palestine (1228–1230).

The pope had wielded the material sword of an invading army as well as the spiritual sword of excommunication in this case. If Hugh felt obliged to justify Gregory, he did so lamely; the *forte* and the phrasing of the sentence suggest an unwillingness to commit himself to approval of papal armies. *Perhaps* the pope held two swords and might wield both if necessary. It should follow that he delegated the secular sword to the lay ruler, to wield on his behalf; consequently the secular ruler did not receive his sword directly from God, but from the papacy. Hugh broke off without drawing this conclusion. Moreover, he was the first lecturer to my knowledge to extend the customary strictures on prelates to include the pope and cardinals. He moralised the text from the psalmist on "going down to the sea in ships" (Ps. 106.23) apropos Christ's command to the apostles to "keep watch" (Mark 13.13): the sea signifies the world, a ship the Church universal and ships in the plural particular churches. The lord pope is captain of the one, and prelates captains of the others. But alas! the proverb *thou shalt be as one sleeping in the midst of the sea* (Prov. 23.34) applies to many of them. The empty tomb (Mark 16.7) signifies the outward show of religion, empty of its inner presence: "the angel bade the women to go and tell the disciples and Peter, that is the pope and cardinals, to take counsel." Criticism brushes lightly on the pope and Curia; but Hugh hints at least that they ought to bestir themselves on behalf of the Church.

Finally, after describing his omissions and ambiguities, I can end on a more positive note. A new vision of poverty and the apostolate does come through. "He who preaches poverty lies, unless he be poorly clad" (Mark 1.6). Christ's sojourn in the wilderness among beasts rebukes those who scorn to dwell among crowds and evildoers (Mark 1.13). Men who teach others to despise riches should be poor themselves (Matt. 10.9). Hugh is tenderer to involuntary poverty, as distinct from voluntary, than his predecessors. Poor men are forced by necessity to enter the kingdom of heaven; the fire of poverty tests them by divine dispensation; God will not punish them by damnation to the fire of judgment to come (Matt. 11.12). The five talents of the parable signify poverty, infirmity, insults, wrongs and death; their fruits are purity, security, peace, humility and haste towards salvation; the true pauper has nothing to grieve him (Luke 6.24). Poverty drives out the devil of greed by the withdrawal of earthly goods (Luke 9.1). The moat defending a castle signifies poverty; the devil tries to fill it up again, since he could find no entry otherwise (Luke

10.38). Christ hungers and thirsts in his poor (John 4.6). Hugh dwelt on the poverty of the bridegroom whose wine ran out (John 2.3) in an original way. He believed in the friars' mission to preach to the heathen. Comestor had asked why miracles were more frequent in the primitive Church than subsequently, answering that then they were needed to convert the heathen, whereas today many more have been converted to the faith. Hugh quotes him and adds: "If the faithful preached to the Saracens today, I believe that the faithful would work miracles, since signs are given to infidels, not to believers" (Mark 11.23).

Best of all, the postills can be linked to Hugh's *Quaestio Disputata* of 1235.[31] He presided as regent master over an official university debate at Paris on the lawfulness of holding benefices in plurality. It was a burning question, where principle clashed with expediency and theologians disagreed with canonists. Pluralism oiled the wheels of the ecclesiastical machine; dispensations were granted freely. Canon lawyers accepted them as a fact, holding that they were necessary and useful to the Church, and differing among themselves only on the question: who had the right to grant them, bishops or the pope alone?[32] Theologians, on the contrary, objected to pluralism on the grounds that it led to neglect of souls, if the benefices in question carried cure of souls, and to neglect of other duties, if they did not. A canon holding prebends in several cathedrals would perforce be non–resident in all but one. Hugh defended the thesis that no man could hold two benefices without committing mortal sin, if one of them sufficed to provide him with food and clothing. The majority of masters, secular as well as religious, agreed with Hugh. Three years later the bishop of Paris again asked for a decision and obtained it unanimously: two benefices could not be held together with safety to one's soul, if one of them were worth fifteen Paris pounds.

The hub of Hugh's argument in the *Quaestio* was that a man who undertook charge of several flocks at once acted wrongly and foolishly. Just so a physician would be foolish, if he undertook to care for patients living on opposite sides of the sea; he could not

---

[31] Edition and historical introduction by F. Stegmüller, "Die neugefundene Pariser Benefizien–Disputation des Kardinals Hugo von St. Cher. O.P.," *Historisches Jahrbuch*, 72 (1935), 176–204.

[32] K. Pennington, "The Canonists and Pluralism in the Thirteenth Century," *Traditio*, 51 (1976), 35–48.

attend to them properly.[33] Hugh's comment in his postill on Luke 9.38, where the widow pleads for her only son, encapsulates this argument:

[handwritten marginal note: meaning his epileptic son]

> [The text] is against those who hold several churches, for they have as many peoples [in their charge] as they have churches, and hence as many weaklings. If a man be insufficient to cure one weakling [in this flock] how will he cure so many?

Christ's cleansing of the Temple (John 2.15–16) was traditionally interpreted as signifying blame of simony. Hugh enlarged on the theme to blame trafficking in prebends and pluralism as well.

The Gospel postills help to explain why Innocent IV raised their author to the cardinalate in 1244. Hugh's was one of a number of 'crisis promotions.' Pope Innocent had decided to renew the struggle with the emperor Frederick II, which had lapsed during the vacancy after Gregory IX had died. The new pope needed to gain support for his policies by filling the depleted ranks of the Sacred College with able churchmen, who would act as his agents in the coming struggle. He also needed to reassure Christendom as to the righteousness of his cause and on his pastoral concern; he must appear as supreme pastor, not only as war leader. Three doctors of theology figure among his promotions: two seculars, Odo of Chateauroux and Peter of Bar–sur–Aube, and the Dominican Hugh of St. Cher.[34] The Order of Preachers in general supported the papacy; Hugh might be expected to rally his Order behind Innocent. His Gospel postills and his *Quaestio Disputata* testified to his zeal as a reformer.

To sum up: there are two aspects to Hugh on the Gospels. He was a compiler, working in the tradition of the 'biblical moral' school and especially in Stephen Langton's version of it. This is immediately obvious. Less obvious, indeed elusive, is the Friar Preacher, devoted not only to preaching, but to preaching in poverty. Will his successors be more explicit?

---

[33] Stegmüller, op. cit., p. 187.

[34] A. Paravicini Bagliani, *Cardinali di Curia e 'Familiae' Cardinalizie dal 1227 al 1254* (Italia Sacra, 18, 1972), 163–167, 198–209, 211–220, 256–265.

V. ALEXANDER OF HALES

Alexander's postills on the Gospels have been listed by Stegmüller (RB 1151–1154 and Suppl. 1151–1154,1) and authenticated by Fr. I. Brady.[1] I have consulted the following manuscripts:

1) *on Matthew, Mark and Luke*

MS Bibl. Com. Assisi 355, to be referred to as 'Ass.' I have seen it in microfilm. It is written in two columns in various hands of about the mid–thirteenth century in northern France, possibly Paris. The text of the commentary has many gaps, where the exemplar must have been illegible. There is no decoration. Modern chapter numbers have been added in the margins by a later hand. There are many marginal notes, including corrections and insertions, guides to content, such as *divisio* and *moraliter*, and names of authors quoted in the commentary. Some notes show that the commentary was used for sermons, as 'In ramis palmarum' (fol. 55va), 'In festo sancti Stefani' (fol. 60rb). A hand contemporary with the text has written prayers and invocations in the top margins: 'Benedictus sit Iesus Christus filius Dei vivi' (fols. 1^r, 17^r, 25^r, 57^r, 59^r, 65^r and *passim*). The quires are numbered; the invocations or prayers often mark the beginning of a new quire, but not consistently. The exemplar was incomplete, since the quires go straight from VIII (fol. 65^v) to IX (fol. 66^r) although the scribe noted that the end of the commentary on St. Matthew and the beginning on St. Mark were missing. The volume belonged to the Franciscans of Assisi.

I. St. Matthew

Fol. 1ra Prologue inc.: *Implete ydrias aque et fundite super holocaustum et super ligna* [1 King 18.34]. Legitur enim hoc cum conveniret Helyas cum prophetis Baal. Premittitur autem quod edificavit altare de xii lapidibus secundum numerum filiorum Israeli Nota quod altare illud est passio Christi... Expl.: ...Finis est ut nati spiritualiter per Christum in baptismo et edocti de regno celorum et contra tentationes per opera et patientiam conformiter patientie Christi perveniamus ad gloriosam resurrectionem.

---

[1] "Sacred Scripture in the Early Franciscan School," *La Sacra Scrittura e i Francescani* (Pontificium Athenaeum Antonianum. Studium Biblicum Franciscanum, Rome, 1973), pp. 69–74.

Fol. 1rb Commentary on Gloss prologue (RB 590) inc.: *Matheus ex Iudea*. In hoc prologo dicitur quis scripsit evangelium et ubi, et determinatur materia et finis. *Ex publicanis actibus*, quia accipiebat tributum... Fol. 1va Expl.: ...quasi dicat: hec fuit intentio nostra ut ostenderemus hec. Commentary inc.: *Liber generationis... filii Habraam*. Sicut dicit Ambrosius: *Quemadmodum* corruptio generis humani principio [*sic*] scilicet Adam vetus, primus liber veteris testamenti dicebatur liber generationis veteris Ade, ita eodem reparato per novum Adam primus liber novi testamenti dicitur liber generationis novi Adam, scilicet Christi...

Fol. 65va Expl. on Matt. 26.26: ...*fregit*. In hac fractione significatur multiplicitas passionis. Nichilominus ipse mansit constans et infractus. The rest of the leaf is blank except for a note in the lower margin in a contemporary hand: Explicit postilla super evangelium Mathei. Deficiunt tamen in fine tria capitula. Hic incipit postilla super evangelium Marci. Deficiunt tamen in principio tria capitula et modicum de quarto.

II. Fragment on St. Mark[2]

Fol. 66ra: IVum capitulum evangelii Marci.
Inc.: Penitentes significantur, qui sunt in amaritudine peccati... *Ascendens in navim* [Mark 4.1] ut exemplo amoris doceret eos ascendere... Fol. 109vb Expl.: *sequentibus signis* [Mark 16.20] ...compunctio auditorum, conversio peccatorum, confirmatio iustorum.

III. St Luke

Fol. 110ra The scribe of the invocations has written in the top margin: Incipit Lucas evangelista. Quo lucet Lucas nos, Christe, passione ducas. Prologue inc.: xxi Iosue: Date sunt levitis de tribu Ephraim iv civitates [cf. Josh. 21.21]. Ephraim fructificans interpretatur et significat arbores in ecclesia, que nobis fructum generant doctrine [1 ½ lines blank]. Iste iv civitates comparantur quadripartite evangelice doctrine... Expl.: multiplex ostensio ipsius Christi.
Fol. 110ra Commentary inc.: *Quoniam quidem*. In hoc proemio tangit Lucas rationem quare scripsit evangelium, ad confutationem scilicet aliorum... verbo enim et signis fides nostra firmatur.
Fol. 110rb in a different but contemporary hand: Hic incipit Lucas secundum magistrum Alexandrum. *Fuit in diebus* [Luke 1.5]. In prima parte huius capituli agitur de adventu Christi et de hiis que acta sunt usque ad predicationem ipsius, sed prius agitur de generatione Ioannis baptiste tamquam lucerna...
Fol. 153rb Expl.: ...*non credentibus* [Luke 24.41] ...in meipsum, i ad Col.: *Adimplebo que desunt passionum* [Col. 1.24]. Mel in cera, divinitas in humanitate, xxxiii Deut.: *inundationem* [cf. Deut. 33.19]. Nine lines at end of column left blank. At the bottom: In isto libro omnes quaterni sunt XVII. The rest of the leaf is blank.

---

[2] On the fragmentary nature of this commentary see RB 1152, 1.

Ass gives us defective copies of all three commentaries: St. Matthew breaks off and St. Mark begins incomplete, St. Luke ends incomplete. The commentary on St. Matthew includes the gloss prologue, that on St. Luke does not.

2) On all four Gospels

MS Durham, Cathedral Chapter Library A II 22, to be referred to as 'D.' In folio; outer 40 × 16 cm, inner 31 × 12 cm. Written on parchment in two columns in a number of hands towards the mid thirteenth century. Red and blue initials. Annotated by many hands, some probably English and not much later than the text. The text has been corrected. Many spaces have been left where the exemplar was illegible. The chapters of the biblical text have been marked spasmodically, sometimes in the text and sometimes in the margins only. Bound in Durham, perhaps in the late thirteenth century. Binding wooden under leather with metal clasps. Flyleaves from a late seventh–century Northumbrian Gospel book were restored to the original, MS A II 17, in the nineteenth century. The new fly-leaves are blank.[3]

A thirteenth century inscription on fol. 4ᵛ reads: "Liber sancti Cuthberti de Dunelmo ex dono magistri Gilberti Aristotelis cuius anime propitietur Deus." Mr. Alan Piper of Durham University has kindly sent me a dossier on Master Gilbert Aristotle.[4] The Durham Cathedral archives contain "a copy of his undertaking not to seek means to impugn the Prior and Convent's right to the church of Branxton, which they had granted to him."[5] The history of Branxton church (Northumberland) places Master Gilbert Aristotle's tenure of

---

[3] T. Rud, *Codicum Manuscriptorum Ecclesiae Cathedralis Dunelmensis* (Durham, 1825), 21. On the medieval Durham books see A. J. Piper, "The Libraries of the Monks of Durham," *Medieval Scribes, Manuscripts and Libraries. Essays Presented to N. R. Ker*, ed. M. B. Parkes and A. G. Watson (London, 1978), 213–249. The Dean and Chapter of Durham kindly allowed me to have the MS deposited in the Bodleian Library for study.

[4] In a letter dated May 17, 1975. More data is given than I have space for here. 'Aristotle,' though unusual, was not unknown in England. For other masters of the same name, see C. Clay, "Master Aristotle," *English Historical Review*, 76 (1961), 303–308.

[5] Printed by J. Raine, *The History and Antiquities of North Durham* (London, 1852), Appendix, p. 140, no. DCCLXXXVIII. Mr. Piper kindly sent me a photo of the original.

the rectorship before 1252, since the church became a vicarage after the last known rector, Master Richard de Bervil, named in that year. One parson of Branxton is notified between 1200 and 1252, a Master Alan de Wakerfeld, in a document dated Feb. 14, 1235. Master Gilbert Aristotle therefore was parson of Branxton before or after 1235. The script of his undertaking is impossible to date with certainty before or after. We do not know where he studied or when he died. Presumably he acquired this manuscript from Paris directly or indirectly. He was one of a number of masters associated with Durham in the first half of the thirteenth century who helped the monks to continue building up their library. The postill on St. Matthew has no contemporary ascription; the others have.

I. Fol. 5ra (following blank fly leaves) Prologue to commentary on St. Matthew, inc.: *Implete iv ydrias aqua* etc. Hoc habetur Reg. XVIII [1 Kings 18.34], et premittitur ibi quod fecit altare...
Expl. fol. 5va: ...edocti ad gloriosam eius perveniamus resurrectionem.
Commentary on text inc.: *Liber generationis Iesus Christi* etc. Secundum Ieronimum cui totum illud prohemiale est usque ad illud: *cum esset desponsata...*
Fol. 73va Expl. on Matt. 28.20: consummationem seculi... quod delicie sue sunt esse cum filiis hominum. Expliciunt postille super Matheum.
Fol. 73 blank apart from partially erased notes by one of the annotators.
II. Fol. 74ra rubric in same hand as the text: Incipiunt postille M. Alexandri super Marchum. Prologue inc.: Exod. xxvii legitur [quod] fecit altare holocausti de lignis sethim vi cubitorum. Sequitur cuius cornua... receptacula [cf. Exod. 27.1–2]. Altare Christus, ultimo Hebr.: *Habemus altare* (Heb. 13.10).
Fol. 74rb Expl.: ...Expositores sunt Ieronimus et Beda continui, sed alii plerique incidentur.
Commentary on text inc.: *Initium evangelii.* In prima parte determinat de initio vocationis et sic primo de baptismo...
Fol. 108vb Expl. on Mark 16.20: *sequentibus signis,* que sunt compunctio auditorum, conversio peccatorum, confirmatio iustorum. Amen.
A piece headed 'Beda de temporum ratione Domino adiuvante dicturi...,' a passage from Bede *De temporum Ratione* has been squeezed into the rest of the column (see *Bedae Opera de Temporibus,* ed. C. W. Jones, Cambridge, Mass., 1943, pp. 179–180).
III. Fol. 109ra rubric in contemporary hand: Incipiunt postille M. Alexandri super Lucam. Prologue inc.: Ut habetur xxi Iosue, date sunt levitis de tribu Ephraym iv civitates refugii [cf. Iosh. 21.21]. Effraim fertilitas...
Fol. 109rb Expl. ...secundum omni credenti.
Commentary on text inc.: *Quoniam* Hic ostenditur quare scripsit et ad cuius petitionem et ratio petentis...

Fol. 155va Expl. on Luke 24.53: ...patebit veritas, implebit caritas, ful-
gebit glorificata humanitas. Hic explicit.
IV. Fol. 155va Prologue inc.: v. Mich: *In Bethlehem Ephrata parvulus
es... parturiens pariet* [Micah. 5.2–3]. In hac auctoritate tangitur materia
huius libri. Tangitur etiam forma, scilicet modus procedendi... Fol. 156rb
Expl. ...patet ergo ex iam dictis que causa materialis et formalis et finalis.
Ordo vero patet in aliis.
     Four lines left blank.
Rubric in same hand as text: Incipit tractatus magistri Alexandri de
Hal⁻ super Iohannem evangelistam. Commentary inc.: Cum novum
testamentum dividatur a veteri secundum umbram et veritatem, x Hebr.:
Lex est umbra futurorum, non habens ipsam ymaginem rerum [cf. Heb.
10.1]. Veritas autem per Iesum Christum facta est, sicut habetur i Ioan.
Lex per Moysen data est [John. 1.17]... Expl. ...Unde due sunt partes in
hoc libro. Prima est processio eterna. Hec processio notatur ibi *In principio erat verbum*.
Fol. 156va commentary inc.: *In principio*: duplex est expositio vel ut
notetur ordo qui est temporis...
Fol. 238va Expl.: ...*que si scribantur etc.* [John. 21.25] vel intellectus ex-
cederet, vel aliter: Spiritus sancti gratia illuminet sensus et corpora nostra.
     A red line has been drawn to the end of the line. The rest of the leaf
is blank except for some partially erased notes.

3) *On St. John*

MS Paris, Bibl. nat. lat. 14438, to be referred to as 'P.' I have
seen this manuscript in microfilm. It is written in two columns in a
Paris hand of the mid–thirteenth century or rather later. The text
has many gaps where the exemplar was illegible. The volume belonged to the abbey of St. Victor. The incipits and explicits correspond
to those of D on St. John. The commentary has no ascription of
authorship.

4) *On all four Gospels*

MS Rheims, Bibl. munic. 162,[6] to be referred to as 'R.' I have
seen this manuscript in microfilm. It is written in two columns in a
mid–thirteenth century north French hand. There are corrections
and some marginal notes in contemporary hands. All four postills
are ascribed to 'Magister Alexander de Halis' in different but contemporary hands. The volume was gives to the chapter of Rheims by

---

[6] *Catalogue géneral des bibliothèques publiques de la France. Départements*
38 (Paris, 1904), 147–148. This description is so detailed that I have not added
to it except to note the essentials.

Guy de Roye, archbishop of Rouen (d. 1409). The incipits and explicits correspond to those of D, and also to those of P for the postill on St. John. The text of the commentary has fewer blank spaces than any of the others, though it has some; but the scribe seems to have made more mistakes than is common in D and P. e.g. 'Bissacenus' for 'Nazianzenus' (fol. 1va).

These manuscripts all represent working copies used by scholars. The text of the postills is incomplete and defective. Some parts were lost before our copies were made. It was customary for the lecturer on Scripture to expound the Gloss prologues, after his own prologue to the book in hand, and before he began his commentary on the text. Yet the only trace of commentary on a Gloss prologue occurs in the Assisi copy on St. Matthew. It would be surprising if Alexander had broken with custom, making only one exception for one postill. There is also an addition to the original. The prologue to St. John, '*In Bethlehem Ephrata...*' lists 'the causes' of the book, whereas Alexander observes the earlier terms, *materia, finis* etc. The piece beginning "Cum novum testamentum dividatur... x Hebr..." represents a prologue, complete in itself and conforming to Alexander's normal pattern. The scribe of D differentiated the two prologues, ascribing only the second to Alexander: "Incipit tractatus magistri Alexandri de Hal⁻ super Johannem evangelistam." Of course Alexander himself may have supplied the first prologue as an afterthought: we cannot tell.

The copies which I have consulted give two *reportationes* for the postills on the first three Gospels: Ass on one side *versus* D and R on the other. D, P and R have the same version of the postill on St. John, which is missing in Ass. A comparison of Ass with D and R shows the classic signs of two *reportationes* of the same lecture course. I have not found the phrases 'magister dicit' or the use of the third person for the lecturer; otherwise there is no reason to put the two versions into any category other than *reportationes*. Ass is fuller than D and R; it could therefore perhaps represent the version authorised by Alexander, perhaps as revised by him. On the other hand D and R have some details not in Ass. We have the witness of John of La Rochelle to the use of the fuller *reportatio* found in Ass. He borrows from Alexander anonymously; but his reliance on the Ass version will appear in the following extracts, put in inverted commas. I put Ass and D on the text Matt. 5.22 in parallel columns; the content of the *quaestio* itself will be discussed later.[7]

---

[7] See below, p. 166.

D, fol. 21va

Qui irascitur fratri suo : numquid qui irascitur infideli, ut publicano et saraceno peccat mortaliter?

Respondeo: aliud est respicere naturam et aliud peccatum, quia [frater] est filius Dei per creationem, item per fidei religionem. Qui autem infideli irascitur non quantum ad naturam et creationem irascitur, sed quantum ad fidei religionem, quam, si vellet habere, posset.

Hoc notari videtur in Ecclesiastico: *Da bono et non receperis peccatorem* [Ecclus. 12.5].

Ass, fol. 14^{rb–va}

Frater est qui in religione fidei communicat. Frater enim est qui eundem habet patrem. Sed numquid qui irascitur alicui, qui non est frater suus in religione fidei, ut pagano, numquid erit *reus in iudicio*? Respondeo: aliud est respicere naturam et aliud respicere peccatum. Unusquisque est filius Dei per creationem; item filius dicitur per fidei unitatem. Quod ergo dicitur hic *fratri suo* hoc intelligengendum [est] propter duo, scilicet quod frater est per nature concreationem, et in eo est possibilitas ad fedare fraternitatem, id est ad unitatem fidei. Omnis ergo qui irascatur *fratri*, quicumque fuerit, si respiciat ad nature communionem et possibilitatem unitatis fidei, *reus erit iudicio*. Item aliud est irasci *fratri*, aliud peccato. Unde per hoc quod dicit *irascitur fratris* excludit illud. Numquid est peccatori debitum? Sed hoc dicitur xii Ecclesiastico: *Da bono et non receperis peccatorem*.

John of La Rochelle, MS Oxford, New College 48, fol. 44vb

Ergo cum sancti viri irascuntur malis causa iustitie peccant, cum hic nullum excipiat. Item cum hic mentionem faciat solum de fratre, per quem intelligitur "frater in religione fidei", ergo qui irascitur iudeo vel "pagano" non peccat. Respondeo: ad primum, "aliud est irasci *fratri*, aliud irasci peccato." Irasci peccato provenit ex amore iustitie et est virtutis ire, scilicet per zelum, et hoc non prohibetur. Ad secundum dicendum quod est frater per creationem ; quilibet enim est frater per fidei unitatem, et hoc dupliciter, vel secundum potentiam, ut gentiles et iudei, vel secundum actum, ut christiani. Frater ergo accipitur hic per "nature communionem et per possibilitatem ad fidei unitatem." Item nota quod "aliud est irasci *fratri*, aliud vitio," sicut dictum est. "Omnis ergo qui *irascitur fratri*, quicumque fuerit, si respiciat ad communionem nature vel possibilitatem ad fidei unitatem, *reus erit iudicio*."

John worked out the question for himself; but in doing so he quoted verbally from the fuller *reportatio* of the Assisi manuscript. He could not have taken his quotations from the shorter *reportatio* found in D and R.

Unfortunately Ass is fragmentary, as we have seen. I have used both Ass and D, with a preference for Ass on the first three Gospels, where it exists (it is incomplete at the end of St. Matthew and fragmentary on St. Mark). Fortunately both *reportationes* quote the same sources or very nearly. His sources are the starting point and clue to Alexander's performance.

Alexander's postills resemble Hugh's in consisting of a mosaic of quotations. His personality comes through the mosaic much less than Hugh's, which makes us all the more dependent on his choice of authorities to grasp, or rather to guess at, his aims as a postillator.

The basic patristic sources are the same in both: Ambrose, Jerome, Augustine, Chrysostom, Hilary, Bede, Rabanus and the Gloss. Some quotations from them occur in both on the same text; many more do not, showing separate recourse to the *originalia*. A scrutiny of proximate sources brings out a clear difference. Alexander turned his back on the commentator on St. Matthew, whom I call *B*, known to Comestor and the Chanter as 'Master Geoffrey Babion,' and to Hugh as 'Gaufredus,' Nor did he care very much for Comestor himself, who was one of Hugh's main sources. Alexander refers occasionally to 'Magister in historiis,' independently of Hugh, as on the bones of the Holy Innocents (Ass. fol. 5ra; PL 198, 1514); but he does not seem to have used Comestor's Gospel commentaries or the Chanter on *Unum ex Quatuor*, although, if Hugh had them, they must have been available to Alexander at Paris. Instead, he returned to an earlier commentator on St. Matthew, whom he calls 'Anselmus.' This is the commentary, drawn mainly from patristic and earlier medieval sources, ascribed to Anselm of Laon in MS Alençon 26, but now thought to be a post–Anselmian product of the Laon milieu. *B* had used it extensively;[8] but Alexander did not use *B* as his intermediary. He probably took 'Anselm' to mean Anselm of Laon; had he confused him with St. Anselm of Canterbury, he would have

---

[8] See above, pp. 15-21.

described him as 'beatus' at least once; St. Anselm had been cano-
nised between 1163 and 1171.[9]

A few illustrations will serve to show Alexander's fidelity to
'Anselm.' He sometimes abridges, but generally keeps to the original closely. MS Alençon 26 will be referred to as A.

D, fol. 8ra, Matt. 1.20: Anselmus: *in sompniis* apparuit, ut sopitis
sensibus exterioribus liberius perciperet divinitus annuntiatum.
A, fol. 97vb: *in sompniis* apparuit angelus, ut sopitis sensibus
exterioribus liberius perciperet quod annuntiabatur.
D, fol. 16vb, Matt. 4.19: Anselmus: Sic ponit gratiam, ut non tolleret liberum arbitrium, quia hominis est preparare animam, Dei
dirigere gressum.
A, fol. 108ra: Et nota quia sic ponit gratiam, ut liberum non
tolleret arbitrium.
D, fol. 19va, Matt. 5.10: Anselmus; Si quis non pro iustitia, sed
pro culpis patitur, non beatitudo, sed ultio iudicatur.
A, fol. 111ra verbally identical.
D, fol. 20ra, Matt. 5.13: Querit Anselmus; hic dicit evangelista
ad nichilum valet, quasi diceret: Ita in cathedra *Moysi sederunt
scribi et pharisei*. Que dicunt facite, que autem faciunt, nolite
facere. Respondet: magistris tantum ita dicatur ne moribus impugnent que verbis docent. Periculose docere presumit qui sibi
insulsus alios fetore vite sue corrumpit [cf. Matt. 23.2–3].
A, fol. 111va: Sed si de vita doctorum et doctrina dicatur, quomodo
ergo dicitur: *super cathedram Moysi sederunt scribe et pharisei*;
que dicunt facite, que autem faciunt, nolite facere? Sed magistris
novi testamenti sicut et de iustitia phariseorum sensum et quasi
latentem ista erant innuenda, ne moribus impugnent que verbis
docent, quia etsi sana est doctrina, periculose tamen presumit
docere qui sibi insulsus alios fetore vite sue corrumpit.
D, fol. 58ra, Matt. 21.10: Anselmus: Propter Lazarum noviter
suscitatum turba ei obvenerat et mirabantur, dicentes: magnus
est et mirabilis.
A, fol. 163vb: Et nota quia propter Lazarum noviter suscitatum
multa turba ei obviam venit ut eum miraretur et dicebant:
Magnus est, potens est, mirabilis est.
D, fol. 68va, Matt. 26.51–52: Anselmus; recondi gladium precipitur,
quia non humano eos verbo, sed eterno erat reprehensurus.
A, fol. 181va: Recondi gladium precipit, quia eos non humano,
sed oris sui gladio esset perempturus.

---

[9] R. W. Southern, *Saint Anselm and his Biographer* (Cambridge, 1963),
338–341.

Alexander went to the trouble of comparing 'Anselm' with the Gloss. The latter on Matt. 2.3 reads, on Herod's fear:

> *Turbatus est* vel quia exitum regni sui timet vel propter iram Romanorum, si hoc pateretur, qui decreverant ne quis rex vel dominus sine eorum consilio diceretur. Nato rege coeli, rex terrae turbatus est, quia nunc terrena altitudo confunditur, cum coelestis celsitudo praedicatur.
>
> Ass, fol. 4[rb]: Tres erant cause turbationis sue, una causa ne incurrent odium romanorum, quia statuerunt ne aliquis diceretur rex sine assensu eorum, item quia timuit propter astantem multitudinem committantem magos. Alia autem fuit quia timebat destructionem regni sui. Hec ultima ratio est Anselmi, prime due Rabani in glosa.
>
> A, fol. 99[rb]: Et propter se, quia timet exitum regni sui et propter iram romanorum, quam pateretur si consentiretur... Turbatus est etiam propter astantem multitudinem magos committantem, quasi erubescens alium queri quam se regem.

Alexander's choice of 'Anselm' as a favourite source on St. Matthew suggests that he hoped to find in him an earlier and purer authority than was offered by *B*, Comestor or the Chanter.

'Anselm' (*A*) quoted copiously from Claudius of Turin on St. Matthew. Claudius (d. *circa* 827; RB 1949-1975) was less in evidence in other twelfth–century commentaries than here. Hence *A* may have guided Alexander to Claudius. However, Alexander used him directly, without the mediation of *A* or of Rabanus, who had quoted Claudius, though less often. A cross–check proved that *A*'s references to Claudius on the texts Matt. 2.5; 3.7; 5.22 (fols. 99[vb]; 103[rb]; 112[va–b]) are not taken up by Alexander. On the other hand he quoted Claudius where *A* did not, as on Matt. 5.1; 5.34; 13.1; 13.13 (D, fols. 15[rb]; 33[rb]; 46[ra]; 46[vb]). Claudius on St. Matthew has been printed only in part; I therefore checked Alexander's quotations from MS London, British Library, Royal 4. C. viii, a twelfth–century copy (RB 1958). The result was positive. I note one illustration, omitting verbal identity, on Matt. 5.34:

> D, fol. 23[rb]: Claudius: *nolite iurare*, quia periurare grave peccatum est... appropinquare.
>
> Ms Royal 4. C. viii, fol. 32[ra–b]: *nolite iurare*, quia periurare grave peccatum est... propinquare periurio.

Alexander even took the trouble to quote Claudius on St. Matthew on a parallel text in St. Mark (3.31):

D, fol. 79vb: *mater et fratres...* fratres secundum cognitionem, non, ut dicebat Claudius, [iuxta] hereticos, secundum carnem.
MS Royal 4.C.viii, fol. 72^{rb–va}: Fratres Domini non filii beate semper virginis Marie iuxta Helvidium, nec filii Ioseph ex alia uxore secundum quosdam putandi, sed potius intelligendi sunt eius cognati.

Alexander also quotes an *expositor* on all four gospels, unknown to Comestor, the Chanter or Hugh of St. Cher. The term *expositor* had been used to denote some collection of excerpts made before the Gloss became standard.[10] An *expositor* had more authority than a *magister*.[11] Was Alexander quoting from a compilation of this kind or was his *expositor* a single author? It was hard to think of any earlier commentator on all four gospels who would not have been referred to by name. One quotation supplied a clue; the *expositor* is called 'Peter' and the source is St. Peter Chrysologus, bishop of Ravenna *circa* 425–450, *sermo* ix:

Ass, fol. 17va, Matt. 6.3; Petrus expositor: sicut in dextera virtutes, ita in leva pars vitiorum significatur. Fugiamus ergo que a sinistris sunt, si in futurum a dexteris desideramus assistere.
Sancti Petri Chrysologi Collectio a Felice Episcopo Parata Sermonibus Extravagantibus Adiectis, ed. A. Olivar (C.C. ser. lat. 24, 1975) 67 : Sicut sunt nobis in dextera parte virtutes, ita nobis pars vitiorum in sinistra... Fratres, in hoc saeculo fugiamus quae a sinistris sunt, si in futurum ad dexteram desideramus adstare.

Alexander's *quidam expositor*, anonymous this time, comes from St. Peter Chrysologus, *sermo* xxviii:

Ass, fol. 11va, Matt. 5.1: Quidam expositor: Quoniam gratia sit in virtutibus et beatitudini cognata, paupertas et terrena et celestis comprobat disciplinam;. ..confligit cum fluctibus nauta nudus; miles in acie non nisi expeditus astat.
ibid. 161, a verbal quotation.

We find Chrysologus referred to by name as 'Ravennatensis' the title generally given to him by medieval writers. Such quotations can be verified from the original, for instance:

---

[10] B. Smalley, *Study of the Bible*, op. cit., 63.
[11] Peter Comestor, quoting a twofold opinion on chronological sequence concerning the wedding feast of Cana (John. 2.1), contrasts them: "De serie autem historie duplex opinio est, et utraque catholicorum doctorum, non dico magistrorum, sed expositorum" (MS Paris, nat. lat. 15269, fol. 6ra).

D, fol. 48va on Matt. 13.55: Ravennatensis: *fabri filium*, ut arte vili ars lateret auctoris.
Sermo xlviii, PL 52, 334, verbally identical.

Other examples are found: D, fol. 35^{ra-b} on Matt. 8.29 and 32, from *Sermo* xvi (C.C. ser. lat. 24), 100–101. 'Ravennatensis' was a favourite with Hugh of St. Cher, but Hugh's quotations do not correspond to Alexander's. Moreover, Hugh's tend to be bunched together, whereas Alexander's *expositor* and 'Ravennatensis' are spread out over all four Gospels. The new edition of the Chrysologus sermons has not yet been completed and the textual tradition includes many *spuria*. In the absence of adequate indexes it would be a time–consuming labour to decide how often Alexander's *expositor* was Chrysologus.[12] It seems probable that he had some collection of excerpts based on Chrysologus, whom he also read in the original and quoted as 'Ravennatensis.' The compilation of an *expositor* of this kind would have meant hard work, since Chrysologus left sermons on various texts, not arranged as a consecutive commentary. A compiler would have had to re–arrange his excerpts according to the Gospel text to make an *instrument de travail* for a postillator. The notable point is that Alexander supplemented the Gloss with another aid to study. This suggests another effort to make a new approach to the *originalia*.

The most elusive of his more frequently quoted authors is 'Victorinus': who was he? The most likely candidate is Victorinus, bishop of Pettau, martyred in 304. The hunt for him began as long ago as 1911, when Wilmart noted a homily *De Decem Virginibus* in a manuscript containing works of St. Jerome. He suggested that it represented an excerpt from an early Latin commentary on the Gospels, set into a framework of *morceaux choisis d'exégèse*, compiled by Victorinus of Pettau. Wilmart cited two later Latin exegetes, who claimed to have read 'Victorinus': St. Jerome in the prologue to his com-

---

[12] I have failed to find the 'expositor' on Matt. 6.9: "Quatuor affectionum causas, letitie, timoris, tristitie et spei hic designat. Dum recolimus patrem, spei conceptione gaudemus, sed nichilominus ad reverentiam timor sollicitat, ne tantus pater inveniat nos degeneres, indignos et ingratos. Dum dicimus *Qui es in celis*, licet admodum mordet tristitia quod longe a Domino peregrinamur, nichilominus cum letitia concupimus cives celi fieri, immo celi, ut sit pax in nobis" (Ass, fol. 18rb). It is certainly an excerpt from some commentary on the Lord's Prayer.

mentary on St. Matthew and Cassiodorus in his *Institutiones*.[13] Stegmüller listed a number of fragments of commentaries ascribed to Victorinus of Pettau (RB 8297–8302 and Suppl. 8299–8301). Rabanus
stated that he had used 'Victorinus' on St. Matthew for his own
exposition (PL 107, 729): but his name is absent from the authors
cited explicitly in Rabanus' text. This need not mean that Rabanus made an idle boast: copyists neglected his plea that the names
of his authorities should be written besides the quotations; the printed
editions of his commentary on St. Matthew are a sorry muddle.
However, Paschasius Radbertus, following Rabanus' example in
giving a list of his authorities on St. Matthew, noted Victorinus with
Fortuniatus as those said to have written on this Gospel, whose books
he had not been able to find: "...licet Fortuniatum et Victorinum in
eo opuscula edidisse dicantur, quos necdum invenire potuimus"
(PL 120, 34). Victor of Capua is another suggestion: Dr. F. Brunhölzl
found that Smaragdus (d. *circa* 830) quoted a 'Victor' in his homilies
on the Gospels and thought that it might mean Victor of Capua
(d. 534).[14] It is just possible that our quotations and mentions of
'Victorinus' represent a mistake for 'Victor'; but it seems unlikely,
seeing that no work on the New Testament is ascribed to Victor of
Capua (RB, Suppl. 8286, 2–5), as against a number to Victorinus of
Pettau. I have not found 'Victorinus' in medieval library catalogues.
The latest editors of St. Jerome on Matthew content themselves
with a reference to Stegmüller's entry on Victorinus of Capua, where
Jerome lists Victorinus among his authors.[15]

Alexander copied Rabanus' catalogue of earlier commentators
on St. Matthew, including 'Victorinus' (Ass. fol. 1rb) and went on to
quote him on a number of texts of both Matthew and Luke. Unfortunately the texts on which Alexander quotes 'Victorinus' do not
occur in any of the fragments ascribed to Victorinus of Pettau nor
vice versa: these fragments correspond to nothing in Alexander's

---

[13] A. Wilmart, "Un Anonyme ancien *De Decem Virginibus*," *Bulletin
d'Ancienne Littérature et d'Archéologie Chrétienne*, I (1911), 102.
    [14] *Geschichte der lateinische Literatur des Mittelalters* (München, 1975),
p. 446.
    [15] D. Hurst and M. Adriaen, C.C.S.L., 77 (1969), 4–5. For Alcuin's references
to 'St. Victorinus,' see J. D. A. Ogilvy, *Books Known to Anglo-Latin Writers from
Aldhelm to Alcuin (670–804)*, (Cambridge, Mass., 1936), p. 87.

postills. It occurred to me that Alexander might have found his quotations from 'Victorinus' in a copy of Rabanus on Matthew where the names of authors were given correctly, supposing that such a good copy existed and was available to Alexander. I collated five of his quotations, picked at random, with the corresponding passages in Rabanus. The result was as follows:

(1) Ass, fol. 55ra, Matt. 21.1: Victorinus: *Bethphage* [erat] viculum sacerdotis in Iudea, in cuius latere erat Bethania civitas.
Rabanus, PL 107, 1035: verbally identical.
(2) Ass, fol. 60va, Matt. 23.36: *generationem hanc*: Victorinus: Mos est scripture duas generationes texere ; una est ibi: *qui non ex sanguinibus etc* [John 1.13], altera que ibi dicitur: *vos ex patre diabolo estis* viii Ioan. [John 8.44]. Omnium iniquorum a Chaym usque ad finem una est generatio. Omnis enim ad unam civitatem Babilonis pertinet.
No equivalent in Rabanus on the text.
(3) D, fol. 71ra, Matt. 27.32: *invenerunt hominem Cyreneum*: Allegorice Victorinus: misticum fuit ut iudeis in Christum sevientibus ad compatiendum peregrinus occurrit, dicente apostolo II. Cor. [*sic*] ii : *si sustinebimus...* [2 Tim. 2.12].
Rabanus, PL 107, 1135: roughly equivalent and quotes the same Pauline text.
(4) D, fol. 71va, Matt. 27.44: *et latrones*: Victorinus: quod unus blasphemat, alter non, homine [sic] in ecclesia geritur. Sunt enim qui ficta mente dominica passionis sacramente venerantur; sunt alii qui cum apostolo non gloriantur nisi in cruce.
Some words have dropped out after 'non': 'typum hominis' (?).
Rabanus, PL 107, 1137, has the same content but quite different wording.
(5) Ass, fol. 150rb, Luke 22.62: *Et egressus foras Petrus flevit amare*: Victorinus: Egreditur Petrus foras ut ab impiorum consilio seclusus sordes negationum liberis fletibus alluat.
Rabanus, PL 107, 1125, Matt. 26.75: Egreditur foras ut ab iniquorum consilio secretus pavidae negationis sordes liberis fletibus abluat.

Quotations of Victorinus (1), (3), (4), (5) might have come from Rabanus, allowing for difference of wording in (4). (2) has no equivalent in Rabanus. Finally, the one quotation of 'Victorinus' in Hugh of St. Cher that I have found is on Luke 22.62; the content is similar; but the wording differs from Rabanus' and Alexander's: 'Victorinus: ut haberet locum liberum flendi.' The evidence from these five quotations would be consistent with Alexander's having used a fuller and different text of Rabanus on St. Matthew, citing his authors correctly, than we have in print. Neither does it exclude Alexander's use of some other *catena* including excerpts from 'Victorinus.' Hugh of St. Cher must have picked up his one quotation from some intermediate source, perhaps from Alexander, if he used Alexander's postills, which is uncertain. A glance at these five quotations will bear out my impression from many others: 'Victorinus' brought no startling originality of approach to bear on the Gospels. Alexander's use of him interests us in offering further proof of his thirst for the Fathers and his quest for ancient sources. He may not have known who Victorinus was, but supposed him to be early, since Rabanus counted him as an authority.

Turning to homiletic and devotional and doctrinal writers of the late eleventh and early twelfth centuries, we find that Alexander had some acquaintance with their spiritual teaching. I have found no quotations from St. Anselm, which is surprising in view of the value set on him in Alexander's theological works.[16] He quoted St. Bernard as often or more so than did Hugh of St. Cher. On a rough count, 9 of 46 quotations by Hugh from St. Bernard or the *Flores Bernardi* in his postill on St. Luke appear on the same texts in Alexander's. They may have drawn on a common source; but even so the proportion of quotations not in common shows that they also drew on Bernardine literature independently of each other.

I noted the names of three devotional writers, only one of whom can be identified. None appears in Hugh *ad loc.*:

(1) D, fol. 48[vb], Matt. 14.11, a morality on the beheading of St. John Baptist ascribed to 'Hugo' comes from the *De Claustro Animae* II, xvii, of Hugh of Fouilloy, often confused with Hugh of St. Victor (PL 176, 1069.[17]

(2) 'Gilbertus' quoted twice:
Ass, fol. 61[va], Matt. 24.28: Gillebertus: Esto tu aquila et acutis in spiritualibus spiritualis assuesce contemplationis mane[re?] in petris; immo singularis illius petre, que Christus est, cavernas ingrede.
Ass, fol. 62[ra], Matt. 24.41, recalling Luke 17.34: *duo erunt in lecto uno*, quotes 'Gilbert's' *distinctio* on 'bed': Gillebertus: Lectus qui quietis opportunitatem in delectationem convertit visionis eterne... Gillebertus: otiosa vita est lectus eorum qui libertatem temporis ducunt in occasionem voluptatis.

I drew a blank on the Canticle commentaries of the Cistercians Gilbert of Hoyland and Gilbert of Stanford on Cant. 1,15. Is Alexander's

---

[16] See above, p. 133.
[17] Hugh of Fouilloy died 1172–4; see *Dict. de la spiritualité*, 7 (1969), 880–886.

'Gilbert' the same writer as Hugh quoted, who might perhaps be Gilbert of La Porrée in some unidentified work?[18]

(3) Galfredus

Ass, fol. 5rb, Matt. 2.14: Unde dicit quidam Galfredus: si versaris in tenebris tuis et peccata tua iugi conscientie meditatione consideras, moritur in te Herodes, id est elatio extinguetur.

This is not *B*, the commentator on St. Matthew quoted by Comestor, the Chanter and Hugh of St. Cher as 'Master Geoffrey Babion' or 'Gaufredus.'[19] Is he perhaps the prolific Geoffrey of Auxerre, St. Bernard's secretary, later abbot first of Clairvaux and then of Fossanuova and of Hautecombe, who died at Clairvaux sometime after 1196?[20] His commentaries on the Canticle and the Apocalypse are so voluminous that to find this one quotation would be like looking for a needle in a haystack. His editor, Dr. Ferruccio Gastadelli, kindly told me by letter that he could not lay hands on it, but that it "sounded like Geoffrey of Auxerre."

Alexander's quotations from Hugh of Fouilloy, 'Gilbert' and 'Galfredus' show the same kind of eclectic dipping into twelfth–century homiletics as we found in Hugh. It goes without saying that both postillators quoted from Hugh and Richard of St. Victor. That was to be expected.

There is one quotation from the Lombard's *Sentences* on *periurium* (Matt. 5.33):

> Periurium fit tribus modis xxxix d. tertii libri sententiarum, capitulum *sed melius* (Ass, fol. 15[vb]).

The reference is to *Sent.* III, d. xxxix, c. 3. Alexander seems to have been the first to divide the books of the *Sentences* into *distinctiones*, a division not found in the Lombard's original work. Alexander used *distinctiones* in his Sentences commentary, 1223–1237; he would sometimes also refer to *capitula*.[21] In this reference in the postill he refers to the chapter by its opening words *Sed melius*.

---

[18] Above, p. 131.

[19] Above, p. 128.

[20] The Apocalypse commentary is edited by F. Gastadelli, *Tempi e testi* (Storia e Letteratura), 17, 1970, and the Canticle commentary ibid. 19 and 20, 1974, with data on Geoffrey's career and writings.

[21] *Magistri Petri Lombardi Sententiae in IV libris distinctae. Prolegomena* (Spicilegium Bonaventurianum, Grottaferrata, Rome, 1971), pp. 143*–144*.

It is time to face the question whether Hugh of St. Cher borrowed from Alexander or *vice versa* or whether they worked independently on common sources. Neither quoted the other verbally. It is sometimes easier to detect priority if one compares two writers with a common original, which they both name. If X and Y both quote Z, it may be clear that X or Y quoted Z intermediately. Alas! my comparisons produced no conclusive answer.

I compared the two postills on Mark 5.25, Christ's healing of the woman with the issue of blood. Both postillators started from Comestor's *Historia Scholastica*. I shall begin by transcribing Comestor's account of the healing and of its subsequent commemoration, as recorded in post–biblical sources; then I transcribe Comestor's sources; then we shall see what Alexander and Hugh did with them.

> PL 198, 1569–1570
> Ambrosius in sermone *De Salomone*[22] dicit hanc fuisse Martham. Ennumerans enim beneficia Christi circa genus humanum, post aliqua praemissa subdit: "Dum languidum sanguinis fluxum siccat in Martha, dum corpus redivivi spiritus calore constringit in Lazaro"... *Addit*. 1: In Ecclesiastica Historia legitur quod quidam fecit statuam aeream in honore Salvatoris, et propius statuam Marthae ubi sanata est, et quedam herba nascebatur ibi, quae quandoque crescebat, ita, quod tangebat fimbriam vestimenti, et erat tantae fortitudinis, quod quicumque sumeret ex ea ab omni languore sanabatur.

Comestor's sources are (1) Pseudo–Ambrose, PL 17, 698:

> Quae itinera virtutum duxerit, in quas vias beneficiorum circa humanum genus fuerit ingressus... dum largum in sanguine fluxum siccat in Martha.

(2) The *Historia Tripartita* vi, 41 (ed. W. Jacob and R. Hauslik, C.S.E.L. 71, 1972) 363:

> Fuit enim signum quidem virtutis Christi et indicium contra principem iracundiae Dei. Cum enim agnovisset [Iulianus] in Caesarea Philippi, civitate Phoeniciae... insigne Christi esse simulacrum, quod sanguinis liberata profluvio constituerat, eo deposito suam ibi statuam collocavit. Quae violente igne de caelo

---

[22] The printed text has *De Salvatore*, which can be corrected from MSS, e.g. Oxford, Bodl. Rawl. C.46, fol. 224[vb], and Oxford, University College 190, fol. 90[va].

cadente circa eius pectus divisa est et caput cum cervice una parte
deiectum atque in terra fixum; reliqua vero pars hactenus restitit
et fulminis indicium reservavit. Statuam vero Christi tunc quidam
pagani trahentes confregerunt, postea vero Christiani colligentes
in ecclesiam recondiderunt, quo hactenus reservatur.
Ibid. 42, 363: Hoc itaque simulacrum, sicut refert Eusebius, omnium passionum et aegritudinum noscitur esse medicamentum.
Iuxta quod quaedam herba germinavit, cuius species nullus nostrae
terrae medicus licet expertus agnovit.

Comestor found his identification of the woman with the issue
of blood with Martha in Pseudo–Ambrose, and the story of the statue
of Christ and the healing properties of the herb growing beside it
in the *Historia Ecclesiastica Tripartita*. The latter does not identify
the woman healed by Jesus as Martha. The *Historia Tripartita* tells
us that she set up a statue of Christ to commemorate her cure, and
what happened to it, adding the detail about the medicinal herb.
Eusebius in his *Historia Ecclesiastica* vii, 18 mentions *two* statues, of
Christ and of Martha, again without identifying the woman. What
fragment from Eusebius' Greek *History* reached Comestor and how,
I do not know. He omits the subsequent story of the fate of Christ's
statue.

Alexander moralises the issue of blood as 'sin added to sin,'
quoting Hos. 4.2: *Maledictum et mendacium... et sanguis sanguinem
tetigit.* This moralisation is not found in the Gloss. He then quotes the
same passage from Pseudo–Ambrose *De Salomone* as Comestor does,
going on to quote Eusebius and Jerome, to whom he ascribes the
Historia Tripartita. The gist of his quotation corresponds to Comestor's, but is longer and closer to the originals. He tells the story of
what happened to Christ's statue, omitted by Comestor, and inverts
the order followed in the *Historia Tripartita*, describing the miraculous herb before, instead of after, the tale of the statue. It is notable
that Alexander cuts out the *School History* on the *two* statues; he
keeps to the record of the *Historia Tripartita* that there was *one* statue,
of Christ, set up by· the woman whom he healed.

Tunc est peccatum in profluvio quando peccatum peccato super-
ponitur, unde iv Os. *Maledictum... tetigit.* De hac muliere dicit
Ambrosius in tractatu de Salamone: Dominus largum... Martha.
Eusebius dicit in ystoria ecclesiastica quod ista mulier sanata
fecit quandam ymaginem salvatoris, que omnium egritudinem
erat in medicamentum, iuxta quam ymaginem herba germinavit,
omnibus medicinalis. Ieronimus vero refert in ystoria tripartita

> quod cum Iulianus apostata cognovisset in Cesarea Philippi,
> deposuit ipsam ymaginem et loco illi suam ymaginem collocavit,
> que postea ictu fulminis [MS fluminis] est confracta. Statuam
> vero Christi quidam paganorum trahentes confregerunt. Post-
> modum vero christiani collegerunt et in ecclesia collocaverunt
> (Ass, fol. 72va-b):

Hugh's comment is verbally identical to Alexander's, beginning
with the same moralisation and text from Hosea. He quotes both
passages from the *Historia Tripartita*, but reverts to its original
sequence, mentioning the miraculous herb after, instead of before,
the story of Christ's statue; his chapter and verse may have been
added later:

> Hieronymus in Historia Tripartita lib. 6, cap. 4, dicit quod cum
> Iulianus... collegerunt et in ecclesia condiderunt, quod simula-
> crum, ut refert Eusebius, omnium aegritudinum noscitur esse
> medicamentum, iuxta quod quedam herba germinavit omnibus
> medicinalis.

In this case both postillators begin with the same moralisation
of the issue of blood, which is not in the Gloss. Then they both have
recourse to the *School History*, but adapt and enlarge it by going to
Comestor's sources. They both repeat his excerpt from Pseudo–
Ambrose; then they quote from the *Historia Tripartita* verbally.
Both omit Comestor's statement that there were two statues, one
of Christ and one of the woman whom he cured; neither identify her
with Martha in this context. Both postillators quote the subsequent
history of Christ's statue verbally from the *Historia Tripartita*. Their
quotations correspond verbally, apart from Alexander's inversion of
order. Clearly one was borrowing from the other here. They were not
working independently on the same source. But who borrowed from
whom remains unclear. Hugh's *penchant* for post–biblical stories,
derived from his familiarity with Comestor, rather suggests that his
postill was the original; it certainly does not constitute proof.

Comparison with another source, Richard of St. Victor's *De
Spiritu Blasphemiae* on Matt. 12.31–32, shows on the other hand
that the dependence was not constant. In this case they start from
the same original and use it independently; each will invert the order
and modify in his own way. Four excerpts from Richard of St. Victor
are relevant. (1) Richard distinguishes blasphemy from other types
of sin, as being directed not against oneself or one's neighbour, but

against God. There are also two kinds of blasphemy, the first due to compulsion or ignorance, the second due to deliberate ill will. The second is much worse, and indeed the worst of all sins (PL 196, 1187–1188). (2) Richard defines blasphemy as the inclination and wish to vituperate against God; 'affectio et desiderium vituperationis divinae (ibid.). (3) The devil's sin of blasphemy can never be remitted, but the human sin sometimes can be. Richard repeats and refines what he said above: a man may blaspheme against God either under compulsion or through ignorance or through ill will only. All three are blameworthy as to the action; but the first two have some excuse, whereas the third has none and is therefore irremissable. The first is a sin against the Father, the second against the Son, the third, irremissable, against the Holy Spirit (ibid. 1189). (4) Richard distinguishes sins which can be committed in this life only, such as adultery and theft, and those which can be committed both now and hereafter. He who dies while hating God sins for all eternity and merits eternal punishment. He who is guilty of hating God is guilty of sinning eternally (ibid. 1190).

Alexander inverts the order of Richard's definitions, (2), (1), (3) and omits (4) altogether (Ass, fol. 35rb). Hugh keeps to Richard's order, dividing (3) into two separate parts, but omits (2). Each one abridges, selects and develops Richard's work independently. Hugh of St. Cher copies his excerpts in a mechanical way; Alexander's version of them is more thoughtful. He adds to Richard's words on (1) that blasphemy, the height of wickedness, has no ceiling: "quia malitia semper non habet summum." He also adds to Richard's excuses for blasphemy anger or bad company; this kind of blasphemy, derived from human weakness, may be pardoned. In this case it cannot be excluded that neither Alexander nor Hugh had knowledge one of the other; but it is certain that whichever knew the other did not copy him slavishly.

The plot thickens when we compare topical allusions, *exempla* and *moralitates*. Hugh was more prone to comic touches than Alexander. I drew up a long list of such pieces peculiar to Hugh; I did not find any peculiar to Alexander. A few are common to both. ...re is one example: the disciples' answer to Jesus' question: *Whom do men say that I am?* and their answer (Mark 8.28) is moralised by Alexander as referring to false gods worshipped by the heathen, supposing them to be rulers of the cosmos. He quotes Wisd. 13.2: *But have imagined either... the sun or the moon to be the gods that rule the world.* Such worshippers are again moralised as various types of sinner. Worshippers of the moon signify hypocrites. Alexander recalls the folk story of the man in the moon, banished there to punish him for gathering sticks on a Sunday.[23] The sticks in turn suggest thorns: hypocrites' thorns resemble a hedgehog's spikes in pricking only on the outside; they shall all be plucked out like thorns, according to the text: *transgressors shall all of them be plucked up as thorns* (2 Sam. 23.6):

> Lunam faciunt deum ypocrite, qui portant fasciculum spinarum, sicut rusticus qui est in luna, sed non pingit, sicut hericus, qui habet spinas exterius, interius nullas, II. Reg. xxii [*sic*]: *Prevaricatores quasi spine evellentur* (Ass, fol. 82[va]).

Hugh on the same text has the same extravagant, far–fetched morality, almost word for word. This is typical of Hugh, but untypical of Alexander: therefore it might be supposed that Alexander borrowed it from Hugh.

The problem of their relationship may be solved in one of three ways, none of them conclusive. It is possible, but improbable, that Hugh borrowed from Alexander. It is conceivable that Alexander borrowed from Hugh. In that case his postills, as we have them, belong to the period of his regency as a Friar Minor, *postquam esset frater.* Perhaps he updated lectures given as a secular by adding passages borrowed from the newest source available, when he lectured on the Gospels to his new audience. The third possibility is that Hugh and Alexander drew on a common source, which supplied them with those parts of their postills where they correspond. The third suggestion seems to be a cowardly way out, since I have no idea what the common source may have been. It must have come from a scholastic milieu. The author knew his *School History* and Richard of St. Victor's *De Spiritu Blasphemiae.* His ,*moralitates* prove that he was familiar with the techniques of the biblical moral school. Anonymous scholastic gospel commentaries of the late twelfth or early thirteenth centuries survive, though I know of none covering all four gospels. Further research might dig out a common source or sources for Hugh and Alexander. So I leave the problem open at present. Meanwhile comparison has yielded one positive result at least. The differences between

---

[23] H. Bachtold–Hoffmann–Krayer, *Handwörterbuch des deutschen Aberglaubens,* 6 (Berlin, 1934–5), 512.

Hugh and Alexander outweigh their resemblances. Whatever the nature and extent of borrowing, they were basically independent of each other. Even where they start from the same passages found in an earlier writer, they are capable of treating them in different styles.

That sharpens the curiosity raised by the question whether they agree or differ on fundamentals concerning the observance of Gospel precepts 'here and now.' Alexander's *Quaestiones Disputatae Antequam* whets the appetite, since he introduces a new concept, the priority of the common good in decision making. Is it permissible to reclaim one's belongings in a law suit (on Luke 6.30)? Alexander makes the usual distinction between the imperfect and the would–be perfect, but allows reclamation to the latter if it is for the common good, which must be preferred to one's own or one's neighbours':

> Respicere ergo debet perfectus non tantum quod suum est, sed bonum proximorum et etiam bonum commune. Si ergo repetit propter bonum proximorum vel propter bonum commune non dicitur repetere sub prohibitione. Et nota quod bonum commune preponderet bono proximi, bonum proximi bono proprio. Si ergo tantum sit ibi bonum proximum, non licet repetere ; si vero salus proximi concurrat, repetere (ed. cit. 20).

The same criterion applies to the question whether a slave may be reclaimed in the same way as land or money. A slave serves two purposes, his master's and that of the common good; therefore he must not be treated in the same way as other property:

> Postea quaeritur de rationali, utrum si servum habes, sic est de servo sicut de fundo vel pecunia. Dico quod non, quia servus in se duplex habet bonum: et quod tuum est, et quod bonum commune: unde sic non est repetendus servus sicut alia (ed. cit. 624–630).

Alexander's application of the common good as the overriding factor in obedience to the Gospel precept opened up wider horizons. No longer would decision rest with the individual Christian conscience and his obligation to love his neighbour. The community to which they belonged had claims superior by its very nature. Hugh of St. Cher had stipulated that litigation should not prejudice a person in authority or the commonweal (*respublica*).[24] Alexander carried Hugh's timid suggestion much further.

---

[24] Above, p. 139.

No such new vistas open up in Alexander's postills. He kept to the old paths, showing no particular interest in poverty and condemning mendicancy.   On the parable where the unjust steward says that he is ashamed to beg (Luke 16.3), Alexander explains that begging is shameful, because men ought to work:

> Mendicat qui in se non habet, sed aliunde petit, xxv Mat., de virginibus fatuis ; et nichil recipit qui laborare noluit, xx Prov.: *Propter frigus piger arare noluit; mendicabit ergo estate, et non dabitus illi* (D, fol. 140vb).

Ironically, the seculars would rely on Prov. 20.4 as a key text in their attack on the Mendicants. There is no apocalyptic speculation either. If Alexander knew of Joachim, he ignored him to the point of not even warning against him. Alexander accepted the Augustinian time scheme of the six ages of the world (D, fol. 110va on Luke 1.26). The friars are never mentioned.

On the Sermon on the Mount and the mission of the apostles Alexander seems closer to Comestor (though he does not quote him) than to the Chanter or to Hugh of St. Cher. He repeats the usual interpretations: poverty must be voluntary to be meritorious; Christ did not forbid the apostles to carry necessary supplies on a normal journey. Alexander had thought out for himself the current modifications of the precepts. The question, 'does the command not to be angry with one's brother (Matt. 5.22) apply to infidels such as a Saracen or a heretic?' suggests a more subtle distinction than he could have found in his sources on this text. Alexander says that sin is one thing and nature another. We must not be angry with one who shares in our human nature as God's creature and in the bond of faith; but we may be angered by his lack of faith, which he could have if he would:

> Numquid qui irascitur infideli, ut publicano[25] et saraceno, peccat mortaliter? Respondeo: aliud est respicere naturam et aliud peccatum, quia est filius Dei per creationem, item per fidei religionem. Qui autem infideli irascitur, non quantum ad naturam et crea-

---

[25] The *Publicani* were heretics, named as such with variant spellings, from the 1160s; see R. I. Moore, *The Origins of European Dissent* (London, 1977). pp. 182–185.

On the fuller *reportatio* of this question see above, p. 149.

tionem irascitur, sed quantum ad fidei religionem, quam si vellet habere potest. Hoc notari videtur in Ecclesiastico: *Da bono, et non receperis peccatorem* [Ecclus. 12.5] (D, fol. 21ᵛᵃ).

The use of the Old Testament to modify the Gospel precept speaks for itself.

The mention of heretics, *publicani*, leads on to his attitude to contemporary heresies. He was aware of them, as his predecessors had been. Dualist heresies may be referred to when Alexander says that the miracle of the water turned to wine (John 2.9) exposes the falsehood of those who hold that all bodily things were created by the devil, the prince of darkness; Christ blessed God's creatures manifestly by his miracle (D, fol. 165ʳᵃ). Alexander echoes the Chanter and Hugh of St. Cher (or Hugh echoes Alexander) on Matt. 13.20: should heretics be persecuted? He answers that they must not be cast out of the Church on mere suspicion, lest the faithful suffer with them (D, fol. 47ᵛᵃ).

Alexander is even less forthcoming than Hugh on the relations between *regnum* and *sacerdotium*. We find the usual commonplaces: it is right that a good priest should quell a king's wickedness (Luke 1.5, D, fol. 109ʳᵇ); Jesus told Peter to sheathe his sword to teach us patience (Matt. 26.52, D, fol. 67ᵛᵇ). The two swords (Luke 22.38) signify the material sword used in battle (*materialis in militia*) and the spiritual, which resides in the Church. Alexander quotes St. Paul on obedience to the secular power (Rom. 13.4) and goes on to exhort knights to be more vigorous in defence of the Church. He adds that some adduce a third type of sword, namely that wielded by abuse of power, as when Saul killed himself (1 Sam. 31.4). Alexander drops the subject here (D, fol. 150ᵛᵇ). Evidently he did not care to define papal power in the Church or *vis à vis* the *regnum* precisely.

We may now compare Alexander with Hugh as a commentator. His *Quaestiones Disputatae Antequam* show that he accepted the superiority of the mystical to the literal sense of Scripture. In a question on the office of preaching he distinguishes three kinds: anyone whether clerk or lay may teach the young to recite the Creed and the Lord's Prayer; the exposition of the literal sense in doctrine pertaining to piety is attached to the order of priests or deacons, and belongs to them; the third kind of exposition, that is of the tropological, allegorical or anagogical meaning, belongs to those who have both the office and the learning required:

> Est alia praedicatio, scilicet expositio intellectus tropologici, allegorici vel anagogici, et haec pertinet ad eos qui habent officium cum scientia (ed. cit. 19, 518–519).

The postills bear out his depreciation of the literal or 'carnal' sense, as he sometimes calls it, in favour of the spiritual senses. He took less interest in the literal sense than Hugh, to the extent of stating that St. Mark wrote his Gospel in Italy (the current tradition) *in Latin* (Ass, fol. 1ra); Comestor had corrected this mistake and Hugh followed him. Alexander was even less concerned to distinguish between the senses than Hugh was, often passing over the literal with a cursory 'littera patet' or omitting it altogether. His allegories and moralities tend to be of a traditional kind, except for those brighter passages which he has in common with Hugh.

On the positive side, Alexander was more analytical in expounding his text: the theologian speaks. A good short example is his introduction to the beatitudes (Matt. 5.1), where he defines beatitude as the final end, moving the reason to what other things conduce to it. The two *reportationes* between them clarify his meaning:

> A beatitudine sermonem incipit, quia sicut finis est principium in ratione movendi ad alia que sunt ad finem, sic beatitudo (D, fol. 18rb).
> Incipit predicationem suam a beatitudinem, quia beatitudo est sicut finis. Prius est in ratione et movet ad alia que sunt ad finem (Ass, fol. 11va).

The best long example is his opening division of John 2. He knits the miracle of Cana into its context; it follows on the sacrament of baptism described in the preceding chapter. Alexander gives a *précis* of what is required for the ministry of baptism: function, intention and form must be correct. Baptism draws its efficacy from Christ's passion. Hence the account of baptism is followed by the miracle of the transformation of water into wine, by which his passion was signified. Alexander then refers to the subsequent cleansing of the Temple as an example of ministry. He passes on to the wedding feast itself. The three days of the feast signify the three kinds of illumination: first, recognition of the divine essence, shown in the Baptist's witness to Christ's divinity; second, illumination leading to virtue, which enabled him to perceive Jesus as divine; third, illumination leading to action, as manifested by Jesus in the miracle at the wedding feast. Alexander quotes *The Celestial Hierarchy* on the threefold division: substance or essence, virtue, action. His approach to John 2 is an impressive attempt to bring out the theological content of two episodes taken as a unity. We have an account of the institution of the sacrament of baptism, first by St. John Baptist, then by Jesus in prefiguring his passion at Cana. One admires Alexander's skill in linking his teaching on baptism with the cleansing of the Temple; he sets the wedding feast between them. The connexion is thoughtful and neat.

This bears out Alexander's reputation as a skilful innovator in the technique of dividing one's text so as to draw out its *sententia:*

Nam ante eum nec erat littera trita nec sententia litterae elicita.[26]
D, fol. 164^{va-b}, collated with P, fol. 9rb:
Die tertia etc In hoc capitulo post ostensionem virtutis in eo qui baptizat interius et invitat alios ad baptizandum exterius, sicut supra habitum est: *Hic est qui baptizat in spiritu* [1.33], subditur de officio et de intentione ministrorum. Ista enim requiruntur ut sint debitum officium et debita intentio. De forma enim satis expressum est superius, officium ubi exprimit misterium in ipsa aqua mutata in vinum. Intentio vero notatur in ipsa eiectione illorum qui vendebant oves et columbas, quos omnes proiecit Dominus de templo. Quia vero baptismum [MSS baptistal] habet virtutem a passione, ideo subditur tertio [MSS tertium] de ipsa passione Christi, cum dicitur *Responderunt iudei etc* [2.18].

Primo ergo de officio, ubi notatur de mutatione aque in vinum, usque ad illud: *Post hoc autem* etc [2.12]. Secundo vero est de eiectione ministrorum non habentium debitam intentionem usque ad illud: *Responderunt* etc. Tertio est de virtute passionis Christi. Dicitur autem primum in figura nuptiarum, ubi primo manifestantur nuptie, secundo vero defectus vini ibi: *et deficiente vino* [2.3]. Tertio notatur conversio aque in vinum, cum dicitur: *erant autem ibi etc* [2.6]. Quarto notatur effectus mutationis, cum dicitur: *Ut autem* [2.9]. Quinto notatur usus indebitus vel debitus, cum dicitur *vocat sponsum* [2.9]. Sexto notatur finis, cum dicitur: *Hoc fecit* [2.11].

Dicitur ergo *Et die tertio* etc, in quo notatur tempus, cum dicitur *die tertia*, locus cum dicitur *in Chana Galilee*, convive, cum dicitur: *Et erat mater Iesu*, ipse nuptie cum dicitur *ad nuptias*. Dicitur ergo *die tertia*. Nota quod triplex est illuminatio, prima quantum ad cognitionem essentie, unde dicitur sine determina-

---

[26] Quoted by Fr. I. Brady from *Chronicon de Lanercost*, ed. J. Stevens (Edinburgh, 1859), *Magistri Petri Lombardi Sententiae*, ed. cit. *Prolegomena*, p. 144*. See his account of Alexander's technique as a commentator on the *Sentences*, ibid.

tione: *Iohannes testimonium perhibet etc* [1.15], secunda quantum
ad illuminationem virtutis, unde dicitur *Altera die vidit* [1.29],
et hec germinatur propter illuminationem ad virtutem dupliciter.
Tertia fit per hec illuminatio ad operationem, unde sequitur *Die
tertia*. Ostenditur enim hec illuminatio per mirabile factum.
Dicitur ergo *Die tertia etc*. Tamen propter tertiam illuminationem,
sicut dictum est, omnes supermundani intellectus dividuntur,
sicut dicit Dionysius, in essentiam, virtutem et operatione,.[27]

Compare Hugh's mechanical division of John 2:

Hic incipit sexta pars huius libri, quae continet xii capitula.
Et dividitur communiter in duas partes, in miracula et verba
Christi. Sed istae partes non separantur, quia in quolibet capite
simul reperiuntur. Hoc autem caput dividitur in tres partes.
In prima parte agitur de mutatione aque in vinum, in secunda
de descensu et mansione ipsius in Capharnaum, ibi: *Post haec
descendit*, in tertia de ascensione ipsius in Hierusalem et eiectione
ementium et vendentium de templo, ibi: *Et prope erat*.

A comparison of their allegories and moralities shows that Alexander's are more sustained than Hugh's. Alexander shows less
inclination to jump from one to another. Where the content is the
same, Alexander will expound at greater length and attach it to a
longer text. Examples are his fuller exposition of the wedding feast
as signifying the marriage between Christ, the bridegroom, and the
Church, his bride (D, fol. 164[vb]), and the treatment of the types of
sin signified by the unclean spirits and their entry into the swine
(Mark 5.1–13). Three types of pig correspond to three kinds of sinner
(Ass, fols. 69[vb]–71[rb]). Alexander uses the same morality for the pigs,
tame, wild and spiky; but he develops it.

In judging him as a postillator we should remember that he
was the first Paris master to lecture on the *Sentences*. This was to
take a decisive step towards separating creative thought on doctrine
from the task of lecturing on Scripture. Alexander seems to have kept
the best part of himself as a teacher for theology. His theological

---

[27] Pseudo–Dionysius, *Celestial Hierarchy*, II, 2, in John Sarracen's translation, *Dionysiaca*, ed. P. Chevallier, 2 (Paris, 1936), 930: "...ea quae secundum
ipsas est supermundana ratione omnes divinae mentes in substantiam et virtutem
et operationem." Hugh of St. Cher quoted the same division from *The Celestial
Hierarchy* on the Baptist's confession: "*Quia non sum Christus*" (John. 1.20).
One may have borrowed from the other, but they use the passage differently.

works show originality; his postills on the Gospels show less, though his analytical approach to his text suggests the theologian's mentality. Such originality as he had comes out in his choice of sources: he reached back behind Hugh's favourites, Comestor, the Chanter and Stephen Langton, to what he supposed to be earlier and therefore more authentic. That would account for his recourse to 'Anselm,' 'Victorinus,' Claudius and his mysterious 'expositor.'

Altogether he was less personal than Hugh. Given goodwill and hindsight, one can catch something of the ethos of a Friar Preacher in Hugh's compilation. Nothing in Alexander's gives an inkling that he was a potential or actual recruit to the Order of Friars Minor.

VI. John of La Rochelle

John of La Rochelle entered the Order of Friars Minor at an unknown date, probably before he became a master of theology. He taught as a master in their Paris *studium* from 1236, at latest, until his death, Feb. 8, 1245. John was one of the four masters who expounded the Rule, 1241–1242. He seems to have taught concurrently with Alexander of Hales. They collaborated in preparing the *Summa* ascribed to Alexander. John's *Tractatus de Legibus et Praeceptis* was composed before the *Summa Alexandri* and was incorporated into the last part of it. Parallels between John's postills on Scripture and earlier parts of the *Summa* point to his collaboration there too. It used to be thought that John was Alexander's pupil; but the contrasts between John's teaching on law and Alexander's has cast doubt on that. However, a pupil need not agree with his master on all counts. We may find that John borrowed from Alexander as a postillator, if not as a theologian.[1]

---

[1] The notice in P. Glorieux, *Répertoire des maîtres en théologie de Paris*, 2 (Paris, 1933), no. 302, needs some correction; see I. Brady, op. cit. (above p. 317, n. 1), pp. 74–78; *Jean de la Rochelle Tractatus de Divisione Multiplici Potentiarum Animae*, ed. P. Michaud–Quantin (Textes philosophiques du Moyen Âge, 11, Paris, 1964), 7–8. On his *Tractatus de Legibus* see W. H. Steinmüller, "Die Naturrechtslehre des Joannes de Rupella und des Alexander von Hales," *Franz. Studien*, 41 (1959), 310–422; B. Smalley, "William of Auvergne, John of la Rochelle and St. Thomas Aquinas on the Old Law," *St. Thomas Aquinas 1274–1974 Commemorative Studies*, 2 (Toronto, 1974), 47–71. On his *Generalis Introitus ad Sacram Doctrinam*, see F. M. Delorme, "Deux leçons d'ouverture de cours

He left lectures on all four Gospels. They have come down to us in his official text, not in *reportationes*, as have Alexander's.[1] C. Nappo has made a thorough study of John on St. Mark;[3] so I shall deal only with his postills on the other three Gospels. My choice of manuscripts has been dictated by easiness of access; they are as follows:

I) *on Matthew (RB 4898), Anonymous.*

MS Oxford, New College 48, to be referred to as 'NC.'[4]

In folio: 30 × 20 cm. Written on parchment in two columns in a hand, probably French, of the second half of the fourteenth century. Dr. R. W. Hunt tells me that an erased inscription on the bottom margin of fols. 2 reads: Liber collegii beate Marie de Wintone in Oxon. donatus eidem collegio per magistrum Robertum Pawnton quondam socium eiusdem collegii. Orate pro eo et pro benefactoribus eius." Master Robert Pawnton was a fellow of New College 1386–1392. He was M.A. of Oxford by 1386 and died as rector of St. Edmund's, Lombard Street, London, 1426.[5] A letter, dated 1861, kept inside the cover of the volume states that the abbé Cholet, canon of La Rochelle, identified the author as John of La Rochelle. Many marginal corrections, additions and notes in various hands. The commentary is divided into modern chapters.

The contents are as follows:

I. Fol. 1ᵛ (the writing on fol. 1ʳ is so rubbed as to be illegible) in a fourteenth–century English hand, a treatise on preaching (?): Inc.: Reverendi magistri et domini mei [*sic*]. Tria inter cetera sunt predicatori valde utilia. Primum est suavitas in vivendo... Expl.: ...et michi ad aliquod proponendum.

---

bibliques données par Jean de la Rochelle," *La France Franciscaine*, 16 (1933), 345–360. On parallels between the postills and the *Summa*, see C. Nappo, "La Postilla in Marcum di Giovanni de Rupella e sui reflessi nella Summa Halesiana," A.F.H., 50 (1957), 332–347; E. Lio, "Alcune 'Postillae' sui Vangeli nei rapporti con Alessandrio di Hales, Giovanni de la Rochelle e la "Summa" Fratris Alexandri," *Antonianum*, 30 (1955), 257–313.

  [2] This was Fr. Brady's judgment, op. cit. p. 74. It seems to me to be well founded.

  [3] op. cit., above, n. 1.

  [4] H. O. Coxe, *Cat. Cod. MSS qui in Collegiis Aulisque Oxoniensis Hodie Adservantur* (Oxford, 1852), *Cat. Cod. MSS Collegii novi*, 66.

  [5] A. B. Emden, *A Biographical Register of the University of Oxford*, 3 (Oxford, 1959), 1439.

II. Fol. 2ra 'Postille super M.', written in the same hand as the commentary. A different hand has added 'secundum doctorem'.

Fols. 2ra–3va Inc.: Introitus to all four Gospels: [S]*imilitudo vultus animalium...* [Ezech. 1.10] *...ad laudem et gloriam Salvatoris.*

Fols. 3va–4rb Exposition of the Gloss prologue (RB 591). Inc.: *Matheus ex Iudea. Istud prohemium Ieronimi continet quatuor partes...* Expl.: *quinta pars, ubi notatur que intentio.*

Fol. 4^{rb-va} Introitus to St. Matthew[6]: Inc.: *Ysa xxiii Dominus iudex noster... ipse salvabit nos* [Isa. 33.22]. *In hoc verbo comprehenditur tota intentio evangelii Mathei...* Expl.: *...In tertia quod iudex noster, infra xxiii: Et egressus Iesus de templo ibat* [Matt. 24.1].

Commentary on text Fols. 4va–302rb. Inc.: *Liber generationis... Posuerunt super caput eius...* Expl.: *...magnam in Israel et de hoc dicit interlinearis: cum finitis laboribus mecum regnabitis. Quod nobis concedat etc. Amen. Explicit.*[7]

III. Fol. 302^{va-b} in a different but contemporary hand a table of Epistles and Gospel for the year.

IV. Fol. 303^{r-v} Miscellanea written in a hand resembling, but not idenrical with, that of the first flyleaf: biblical *quaestiones* headed 'Postille super Matheum'. Most of the writing is so rubbed as to be illegible: "Dubitatur quare Moyses potius eduxit..." is legible on fol. 303^v. A caution mark 'in cista antiqua' (names of borrowers illegible) is written at the bottom. Fol. 304^r is blank; fol. 304^v is filled with a writing exercise.

2) on *Luke* (*RB 4900 and supplement*), *Anonymous.*

MS Oxford, Bodl. 412, to be referred to as 'B.' The *Summary Catalogue* (2308) describes it as "written on parchment late in the thirteenth century in England." It belonged to the abbey of Bury St. Edmund.[8] There are many marginal corrections, notes and headings in various hands. The contents are:

I. Fol. 1^{ra-vb} Prologue to St. Luke inc.: *Habentes pontificem magnum...* [Hebr. 4.14]. *Notantur in hoc verbo cause introductorie...* Expl.: *Quia igitur ex presenti evangelio habemus pontificem magnum, speramus quia filii Dei credimus quia Iesum, id est salvatorem amore teneamus, quem credimus et in quem speramus Christum Dominum, qui est benedictus in secula. Amen.*

---

[6] See I. Brady, op. cit. p. 76. NC has a shortened version of the prologue; the explicit does not correspond to that cited by Brady.

[7] The explicit corresponds to RB 4898 except that the citation of the interlinear gloss to Matt. 28.20 has been added here. The incipit of the commentary on Matt. 10.1 (fol. 91rb) also corresponds.

[8] F. Madan and H. H. E. Craster, *Summary Catalogue of Western MSS in the Bodleian Library at Oxford* 2, i (Oxford, 1922), 301.

Fols. 1ᵛᵇ–3ʳᵇ Exposition of the Gloss prologue (RB 620). Inc.: *Lucas Syrus Nota quod huic libro duplex proponitur prohemium*... Expl. incomplete on *volentibus Deum*... omittere.

Commentary fols. 3ʳᵇ–251ʳᵇ, inc.: *Quoniam quidem*... istud prohemium proponit Lucas... Expl.: *In templo*, loco sancto... *laudantes* etc, ut in loco orationis inter laudum devotiones expectent promissum spiritus sancti adventum.

This is identical with the explicit given in RB 4900, with an addition here, which is probably from the original: Et hoc concludit Beda in originali: Pulchre hoc in templo complevit, cum apostolis verbi ministris, scilicet novi sacerdotis futuris, non in victimarum sanguine, sed in laude Dei et benedictione concludit, ad quam benedictionem nos perducat etc. Amen.

II. Fol. 251ʳᵇ⁻ᵛᵃ, a note in the same hand on Christ's satisfaction for Adam's sin: Inc.: Item ut per iustitie equitatem satisfaceret pro peccato Adam in transgressione... Expl.: ...vilissimum genus mortis sustinuit, ut nullum genus mortis timeamus etc.

III. Fol. 252ʳ Table of contents of commentary, in a different but contemporary hand, a rubric: Quere subscripto capitulo Luce xiii. A division of chapters of St. Luke according to letters of the alphabet A–Z, starting afresh Ab–Ao. Each division has a summary of content and authors, e.g. Josephus and Ambrose. 5 columns have been ruled, but the piece breaks off in the middle of col. 4 with the rubric: Capitulum xiv: *Et factum est cum intraret.*[9]

The rest of fol. 252 and fols. 253–256ʳ are blank.

There are some scribbles on fols. 256ᵛ–257ʳ.

IV. Fol. 257ᵛᵇ Table of Gospel for Sunday and the year from St. Luke.

V. Fol. 258ʳ Scribbled notes for sermons.

3) *On John*

Fr. Brady has restored this postill to John of La Rochelle after its mistaken attribution to Alexander of Alexandria, RB 1111.[10]

MS Oxford, Merton College 80, to be referred to as 'Merton.' Written in several English hands of the early fifteenth century. The college acquired it between 1466 and 1468.[11] The text of the commentary has been corrected by the scribe. There are *quaestio* signs in the margins but no other annotation.

---

[9] On late medieval preparation of books with guides to content, see M. B. Parkes, "The Influence of the Concepts of *Ordinatio* and *Compilatio* on the Development of the Book," *Medieval Learning and Literature: Essays presented to R. W. Hunt*, ed. J. J. G. Alexander and M. T. Gibson (Oxford, 1976), pp. 115–141.

[10] op. cit., 76. It is still ascribed to Alexander of Alexandria in RB Supplement 1111.

[11] See F. M. Powicke, *The Medieval Books of Merton College* (Oxford, 1931), p. 202.

The contents are:

I. Fol. 1ra, exposition of the Gloss prologue (RB.624) inc.: *Hic est Iohannes...* Huic autem evangelio Ieronimus prologum premittit... Expl. fol. 2ra ...quo ordinatur in biblia (as in RB supplement 1111).
Commentary inc. fol. 2ra *In principio erat verbum.* Hoc evangelium dividitur in iv partes... (as RB 1111).
Expl. fol. 170ra ...sed capacitate legentium comprehendi fortasse non possent. Explicit (as RB 1111).
II. Fols. 170ra–171va List of chapters of St. John's Gospel with summary of contents taken from the commentary on each chapter division. Inc.: In primo capitulo huius libri inducitur persona mediatoris... Expl.: ...et quomodo specialiter se habuit ad duos, scilicet Petrum et Iohannem, ibi, *cum ergo prandasset* [John 21.15].

Discussion of the postills must begin with their relationship to John's other works. Unlike Alexander, who tended to keep the theologian and the biblicist in separate compartments, John used some of the same material in his postills and in his theological works, just as he did in his theological works themselves.[12] C. Nappo has already noted parallels between the postill on St. Mark and the *Summa* ascribed to Alexander. There are more in his other postills, though a much closer study of his whole output would be needed to establish a chronological order of priority.

The postillator of St. Matthew identifies himself with the author of *De Legibus et Praeceptis*, incorporated into the *Summa Alexandri*.[13] The salient points in both are an interest in the classification of law and in its promulgation, and insistence on the spiritual senses of the Old Testament *caeremonialia*. John defended the latter against William of Auvergne, who took over from Maimonides the opinion that the ceremonial observances prescribed in the Old Law had a literal meaning, grounded in reason.[14] The postillator offers a general introduction to the New Law, before broaching the Sermon on the Mount, and a particular introduction to the first words of the Sermon. He describes how the New Law was promulgated and how it was

---

[12] P. Michaud–Quantin, op. cit., pp. 25, 33.

[13] I shall refer to the Quaracchi edition of 1924–1948 by volumes and pages.

[14] See B. Smalley, op. cit. (above, n. 1). John expressed the same idea in his *Generalis Introitus in Sacram Doctrinam*, where he contrasted the Old and New Testaments; see Delorme, op. cit. (above, n. 1), pp. 348–349.

divided into first the general, a law for right living which applied to all men, and the special, which applied to the few, the would–be perfect. Law, to be perfectly established, must be declared and confirmed, as Christ first declared the New Law and then confirmed it by miracles. The promulgation had its 'narration' and 'exordium,' *Beati pauperes* (Matt. 5.3) and its conclusion: *Omnis qui audit verba mea* etc (7.26). John uses the technical terms of rhetoric:

> In exordio excitatur attentio, in narratione ostenditur legis conditio, in conclusione consummatio. Excitat ergo ad novam legem per convenientiam et differentiam nove legis et differentiam nove legis et veteris (NC, fol. 33va).

The similarity between the two Laws appears in that both were delivered from a mount. There were three **differences** between them: the Old was delivered *terribiliter*, the New Law *amicabiliter;* in the first the truth was hidden in riddles and figures; in the second it was set forth plainly, since it begins: *'Jesus opening his mouth;'* God descended from heaven to give the Old Law, whereas Jesus ascended the mount to give the New Law (NC, fol. 34ra). John ascribes spiritual as well as literal senses to both Laws. The spiritual sense of the New Law is indicated by the saying that Jesus 'opened his mouth':

> Non solum hac circumlocutione ostenditur sermo longior, ut dicit [glosa] interlinearis, sed etiam monstratur triformis intelligentia in doctrina Christi... allegoria, anagogica, moralis, vel litteralis, allegorica et moralis (NC, fol. 34vb).

The most striking correspondence with *De Legibus* comes where John classifies the various modes according to which Christ fulfilled the Old Law (Matt. 5.17). The Old Law had five parts: *moralia, iudicialia, caeremonialia, promissa, sacramentalia;* Christ fulfilled all five of them each in a different way:

> Moralia implevit perficiendo, iudicialia temperando, ceremonalia ad spiritualem intellectum referendo, promissa exhibendo et meliorem promittendo, sacramentalia rem figuratam exhibendo.

Special care is taken to stress that the Old Law *sacramentalia* were voided by the New Law and must now be understood according to their spiritual senses only (NC, fols. 40va–41rb). In *De Legibus* John distinguished three classes of precepts in the Old Law: *moralia, caeremonialia, iudicialia,* and explained how Christ fulfilled them:

Figuralia enim implevit, sed hoc tripliciter, scilicet per termina-
tionem, per manifestationem, per exhibitionem (4, 396, 400).

A single mind is at work on the same matter. John proposed five
divisions of the Old Law in his postill, as against three in *De Legibus;* but the idea is the same.

Not only resemblance in thought, but much verbal identity
appears in John's *quaestio* on the two swords text (Luke 22.38),
if we compare it with the *quaestiones* 'Utrum bellum sit licitum' and
'an habentibus spiritualem potestatem prohibeatur occidere' (4, 653,
683–688). Both questions are discussed in the postill (B, fols. 229ra–
230ra). The proof texts and the conclusions are all the same in the
postill and in the *De Legibus*, though arranged in rather different
sequence. They consist mainly of the *auctoritates* adduced by Gratian
in the *Decretum* (C. xxiii, q. 1, 4, 8). Theologians continued to use the
Decretum as a *florilegium*, when they discussed the conditions of a
just war and the question whether it was right for churchmen to
participate in warfare, even after subsequent canon law legislation
had supplemented Gratian.[15] Texts from St. Bernard's *De Consideratione* on papal power and the two swords form the main additions
to Gratian's *auctoritates* in both the postill and *De Legibus*. There
is also a strong family likeness between the postill, *De Legibus* and
John's unprinted *Summa de Vitiis*, where he poses questions concerning the conditions governing Christian participation in warfare
(the war must be just according to certain criteria) and the special
restraints on churchmen in fighting or giving orders to fight or to
kill (MS Oxford, Bodl. Laud. misc. 221, fols. 61ra–66vb). The Quaracchi editors of the *Summa Alexandri* mention an anonymous *Quaestio*
in MSS Assisi 138 and 182, *De Bello Iusto*, which has much the same
material in the same words as the corresponding sections of *De Legibus* and of the *Summa de Vitiis* (4, 678, n. 1, 683, n. 2). The problems
of the relationship between the *Quaestiones, De Legibus, Summa de
Vitiis* and the anonymous *De Bello Iusto* lie outside the scope of this
enquiry. They leave at least the certainty that John of La Rochelle's
postill of St. Luke belongs to his body of writings as otherwise known.

---

[15] See F. H. Russell, *The Just War in the Middle Ages* (Cambridge, 1975),
pp. 84–85. Professor Russell quotes both the *Summa de Vitiis* and the *De Legibus*
section of the *Summa Alexandri* in his chapter on 'The Medieval Theology of the
Just War,' pp. 213–257.

An earlier part of the *Summa Alexandri*, on Christology, is thought to have been compiled from previously existing writings by Alexander and John, sometimes verbally transcribed and sometimes elaborated (4, cccvi). John had this material to hand when he prepared his postill. He discussed the nature of Christ's glorified body after his Resurrection and at the Ascension. The text Luke 24.51 raises three questions on motion:

> (1) De hoc queritur an Christus glorificatus in corpore posset moveri de loco ad locum. Quod non, sic: omnis motus est actus imperfectus; sed corpus glorificatum est perfectum et nullus actus eius imperfectus, ergo nec motus (B, fol. 250vb).

This *quaestio* and the arguments *pro* and *contra* appear in the *Summa* under the heading: 'An sit ascensio' (4, 278); they are slightly abridged in the postill.

> (2) Secundo queritur an ille motus fuerit naturalis vel motus secundum quod videtur, quia fuit motus vectionis, *quia ferebatur in celum* (B, fol. 251ra).

The *Summa* poses the same question in different words; but the postill has the same substance and the same *auctoritates* as the *Summa*, somewhat abridged. They employ the same metaphor to illustrate the difference between the carrying needed to move an object which cannot be moved otherwise and carrying as a sign of honour. In the postill John cites the carriage of great men as an example of the second mode: "sicut modo subportantur magnates" (B, fol. 251ra); in the *Summa* the carriage of a king by his knights and of the pope by his bishops is cited (281).

> (3) Tertio an subito vel in tempore ascenderit (B, fol. 251ra).

The *Summa* sets out the same *quaestio* more fully and also the argument, followed by three solutions, one of which is the mean between the other two (283). Similarly *quaestiones* on the nature of Christ's glorified body and on how he could be seen and touched by unglorified bodies and eat food in a human manner occur in both postill and *Summa* and have much in common (B, fol. 247^{ra-b}; *Summa*, 271). In both the arguments turn on technical points concerning light, colour and dimension.

Both depend on the *Summa Aurea* of William of Auxerre[16] for some of their material and quotations. Both provide an unacknowledged borrowing from it of an example of naturally shining light in rotten wood and glow–worms (B, fol. 248va; *Summa*, 274; *Summa Aurea*, fol. 297ra). An unlocated quotation from Prepositinus comes from the *Summa Aurea* in the postill on John 11.49–50. Here the question is whether Caiphas sinned in prophesying that one man must die for the people:

> Ad oppositum, quia Cayphas hoc verbo intendebat dare consilium ut Christus occideretur. Ad hanc questionem dixit Prepositinus quod licet Cayphas peccaverit mala voluntate, tamen in proferendo non peccavit, quia Spiritus Sanctus est usus eo sicut instrumento, sicut etiam äsina Balaam... Alii dicunt quod... Cayphas protulit illud verbum ad malam intentionem, et non tantum protulit ut asina, sed ut homo perversus, et ideo peccavit. Per hoc patet ad argumentum quod sub alia intentione fuit a Spiritu Sancto et sub alia a Caypha, ubi non referebat verbum nisi ad malum finem (Merton, fol. 93vb).

The *Summa Aurea* has:

> Ad hoc dicebat magister Prepositinus quod Spiritus Sanctus usus est Caipha tamquam instrumento et illa locutio qua locutus est tamquam instrumento tantum non fuit fructus sue male voluntatis, quia illa non fuit nisi bona, voluntas vero eius non nisi mala... Sed obicitur contra quod... prolatio illius vocis processit ab eius mala intentione (fol. 49va).

John prefers William's opinion, without naming him, to Prepositinus.' This *quaestio* seems to have no parallel in the *Summa Alexandri*.

On the other hand, the postill sometimes differs from the *Summa Alexandri*, where they deal with the same subject, showing that there was no mechanical copying. John refers to 'the Philosopher' on the question of the wounds remaining in Christ's glorified body (Luke 24.39), a reference not found in the *Summa:*

> Item secundum philosophum, quod semper est accessit ei quod secundum maturam est; quod enim naturale est semper debet manere; sed huiusmodi cicatrices non fuerunt naturales; ergo non semper remanebunt (B, fol. 249ra).

---

[16] Paris, 1500. I shall refer to this edition. On quotations from it in the *Summa Alexandri* located by the editors, see 4, 268–270.

John may have had in mind *De Caelo* II, 3, 286a, 15–20: Aristotle argues that "nothing unnatural is eternal. The unnatural is subsequent to the natural, being a derangement of the natural." The reference to Aristotle is interesting in itself; John was not prone to quote the *Libri Naturales* in his postills. In this he followed in the footsteps of his predecessors, Alexander of Hales and Hugh of St. Cher; they seldom referred to the Philosopher.

We must pass now to a consideration of John's debts to these two masters as postillators. We should expect to find the Gloss and the *Historia Scholastica* underlying his postills. It is worth making a preliminary note that John drew on the *Historia Scholastica* independently. Two cases may be quoted to illustrate this. On Luke 21.25, *sonitus maris*, the postill has:

> Vel *sonitus* notat marinarum beluarum secundum magistrum in historiis (B, fol. 215vb; PL 198, 1611).

Again on Luke 21.26: "Require in historiis super evangelium" (B, fol. 218rb). Neither Hugh nor Alexander has these references. John brought his own critical judgment to bear on Comestor. On Matt. 16.1 Comestor mentions three Jewish sects, Pharisees, Saducees and Essenes, having taken the third from Josephus (PL 198, 1553). John dismissed the third as 'apocryphal,' because it was not named in the Gospels:

> Magister vero ponit in historiis tertiam sectam phariseorum, sed hii non leguntur in evangelio, sed in aliquo apocriforum (NC, fol. 169ra).

We have seen already that John quoted anonymously from the *reportatio* of Alexander on St. Matthew represented by MS Assisi 355.[17] His debt to Alexander comes out less in content than in his borrowing of Alexander's quotations. Collation shows that his quotations from 'Expositor,' Anselm and Victorinus all derive from Alexander's postills, with an exception to prove the rule. On the Lord's Prayer, *qui es in coelis* (Matt. 6.9), John quotes an 'Anselm' not to be found in Alexander:

> Anselmus: quod commune est omnibus nemo dicit meus, quod soli vero Christo convenit per naturam; aliis vero conceditur communis gratia adoptionis (NC, fol. 55va).

---

[17] Above, pp. 149ff.

I have not found the comment in Alexander's pseudo–Anselm, nor in St. Anselm of Canterbury; nor is it a mistake for St. Augustine on the Lord's Prayer. It seems certain that John knew 'Anselm' only *via* Alexander and that in this one case he had not consulted the original Pseudo–Anselm on St. Matthew, but found it elsewhere. Many other pieces from Hugh and Richard of St. Victor, for instance, and *unde versus* have been lifted from Alexander. Oddly enough, John did not quote from Claudius, one of Alexander's favourites. Perhaps John realised that Claudius had been accused of heresy.[18] The passage transcribed above to illustrate John's use of the Assisi *reportatio* shows him developing Alexander's thought by introducing the concepts of potency and act: non–Christians are potential Christians; Christians are Christians in action. What John says must always be compared with Alexander's postills to see how far he was original.

Hugh of St. Cher, also quoted anonymously, crops up in passages which have no counterpart in Alexander. Some of them come straight from Hugh. John's moralisation of the *sword* (Matt. 10.34) as God's word, which many scholars and preachers keep locked in their chests and note–books, just as Abimelech kept the sword of Goliath in a cover (1 Sam. 22.9), occurs verbally in Hugh *ad loc.;* it is a typically 'Hugh' morality (NC, fol. 101[va]). John probably took the statement that Simon Magus was the first Antichrist from Hugh on Matt. 24.5 (NC, fol. 237[vb]). He stresses Christ's poverty on Matt. 8.20 in words copied from Hugh (NC, fol. 77[rb]) and again on Luke 2.7 (B, fol. 13[vb]). Much of his discussion of Luke 21.5–6 comes from Hugh, with the same proof texts from Scripture (B, fol. 212[vb]). It is possible to watch him comparing Hugh with Alexander and tacitly preferring the latter where they differ on a specific point. Alexander, as we have seen, omitted Hugh's statement that the episode of the woman taken in adultery (John 8.3–11) did not appear in the Greek text of the Gospel.[19] John omitted it too, though he must have had Hugh's postill before him, and had St. John Chrysostom's commentary on St. John, Hugh's source for his statement, to hand as well (Merton, fol. 71[ra–vb]).

John differs from Hugh most strikingly in that he commented

---

[18] *Lexicon für Theologie und Kirche*, ed. J. Höfer and K. Rahner, 2 (Freiburg, 1958), 1220.

[19] See above, p. 129. John borrowed from Hugh of St. Cher in his postill on the Psalter, see A. Fries, 'Ein Psalmenkommentar des Johannes von La Rochelle O.F.M.,' *Franz. Stud.*, 34 (1952), 262–263.

self–consciously as a friar. Like Hugh, he never names his Order or his founder; but they lie just below the surface. Our postillator identifies himself as a Franciscan. First we see him as one of the four masters who expounded the Rule. He interprets the traditional ban on litigation by contemplatives or *perfecti* (Matt. 5.42) according to the distinction between property and use made in the *Expositio Regulae:*[20]

> Dicitur ergo quod viris perfectis non licet repetere sua... nec religiosis qui omnia renuntiaverunt in communi et in singulari. Cum non habeant rerum proprietatem, sed tantum usum, non possunt repetere nisi nomine illius fieret apud quem residet proprietas, ut eorum congregatio possit usum habere (NC, fol. 50rb).

The *Expositio* permitted friars to wear shoes in case of necessity instead of going barefoot.[21] John explains in his comment on the ban on sandals (Matt. 10.10) that it did not apply to the use of things needed for sustenance; the apostles wore shoes, as we know from the angel's telling St. Peter in prison to put his shoes on (Acts 12.8; NC, fols. 93vb–94ra). The Four Masters insisted on poverty in practice, as well as renunciation of property.[22] John recalls his Order when he teaches that religious must be bound together in the unbreakable bonds of love, since Christ's body is one. They must be naked in poverty, as Christ's body was naked on the Cross. Christ's body suffers scourging in his religious followers when wrong or violence is done to them (on Matt. 27.26, NC, fol. 287va). The special type of poverty practised by the friars, dissension in the Order and hostility from the secular clergy are all hinted at here.

Poverty was compatible with study in John's eyes. A sermon in honour of St. Antony of Padua shows him defending the study of philosophy and other secular sciences as a help to the understanding of Scripture: a doctor must read and teach Scripture, as Christ did.[23] John pointed out that Christ himself set an example by questioning the doctors in the Temple (Luke 2.46). Study goes together with

---

[20] L. Oliger, *Expositio Quatuor Magistrorum super Regulam Fratrum Minorum (1241–1242)* (Rome, 1950), pp. 152–153.

[21] Ibid. 134.

[22] Ibid. 148, 158.

[23] Balduinus of Amsterdam, 'Tres Sermones Inediti Ioannis de Rupella in Honorem S. Antonii Patavini,' *Coll. Franc.*, 28 (1958), 38, 50, 53–54.

worship; quiet concentration and questioning are both needful for learning:

> Sic ergo se habet exemplum in obsequio devotionis in cultu divinitatis. Deinde datur nobis exemplum studii veritatis... Duo sunt necessaria studio veritatis, vacatio et inquisitio. Vacatio requirit separationem a strepitu hominum, inquisitio ad auditum et interrogationem doctorum (B, fol. 35va).

A firm defence of study of the Franciscan type!

A second Franciscan trait in John is his eschatological speculation. The Friars Minor were more susceptible to Joachimism than the Preachers.[24] John normally kept clear of Joachimite speculation based on exegesis. There seems to be no trace of it in his theological works or in his postill on Daniel, a book which lent itself to prediction of the Church's future. But his postill on St. Matthew reveals a striking exception: the account of Christ's suffering (Matt. 27.28–31) tempted him to find a prophecy on the Church's fate 'at the end.' Christ's Passion prefigured that which the Church, his mystical body, was to endure. Christ submitted to being clad in a royal cloak in mockery, then to being stripped, reclad in his own garment, and led to execution. The royal cloak signified earthly power, which many churchmen sought; they had usurped the lordship of earthly power. Christ's reclothing in his own garment signified that the Church would return to poverty, her true garment. John quoted Isa. 4.1: *We will eat our own bread and wear our own apparel: only let us be called by thy name.* This will be the Church's last word. Then she will have to be satisfied with her own, whereas now even other men's goods do not satisfy her. Christ's being led to execution foretells the violent suffering which the Church will have to bear once more, just as Christ foretold in a figure to St. Peter, the head of the Church: *When thou shalt be old, another shall lead thee whither thou wouldst not* (John 21.18). It might be expected that John would imagine the Church's return to poverty as the work of reformers. But no! He ascribes it to the *ecclesia malignantium*, a handmaid who sets herself above her mistress, the Church, usurping her power and her temporal goods: Agar wanted to oust Sara [cf. Gen. 21.9–10]. Her usurpation is signified by an

---

[24] M. Reeves, *The Influence of Prophecy in the Later Middle Ages. A Study in Joachimism* (Oxford, 1969), pp. 161–190.

earthquake (the fourth following that which took place at the time of the Crucifixion, Matt. 27.51) to occur at the end of time, before the Last Judgment: *The earth shall be shaken... and shall be removed as the tent of one night. And the iniquity thereof shall be heavy upon it* (Isa. 24.20).

The passage deserves to be transcribed in full, condensed and difficult as it is, before we try to discern John's sources and his very personal interpretation of them:

> Hiis enim duobus modis robur corporale solet dimitti, scilicet in resistendo contra illa gravia et in portando onera.
>
> Impotens ergo [Christus] a perfidis estimatur, quia non cognoscunt Dei sacramenta, et hoc quia se permittit exui, indui et duci, quia tria in corpore mistico sunt figurativa passionis. Exutio clamidis est spoliatio terrene potestatis, quia spoliabitur ecclesie in fine; ideo in figura dicitur Cant. v [3]: *Expoliavi me tunica mea etc*; et hoc est pallium quod petit Ruth a Booz iii Ruth [9]: *Expande pallium tuum super ancillam tuam*, quod modo multi appetunt, usurpantes dominium terrene potestatis, similes Lucifero, Isa. xiv [12]: *Ascendam in celum etc*. Indutio proprii vestimenti est reversio paupertatis ad quam revertetur ecclesia in fine, iuxta illud Isa. iv [1]: *Panem nostrum comedimus et vestimentis nostris operiemur: tantummodo invocetur nomen tuum super nos*. Vox est finalis ecclesie. Tunc enim oportebit quod illi sufficiant propria, cui modo non sufficiunt etiam aliena. De hac veste Isa. xlix [18]: *Omnibus hiis velut ornamento vestieris*. Ductio vero significat violentiam passionis, quam iterum sustinebit ecclesia, in cuius figura dicit Dominus Petro, principi ecclesie, Ioan. ultimo [21.18]: *Cum autem senueris alius te cinget et ducet quo tu non vis*. Sic ergo legitur littera. Moraliter... (NC, fol. 286va-b).
>
> [The 'morality' is that Christ is still mocked and crucified when the poor and innocent are oppressed.]
>
> ...Ideo tertio in resurrectione movetur terra. Quartum non poterit sustinere terra cum heres domine fuerit ancilla ; et hoc erit ante iudicium in finali tempore, cum ancilla, id est malignantium ecclesia, erit heres domine sue, id est sancte ecclesie, usurpando sibi suam potestatem, et etiam temporalia; et ideo quarto in iudicio move[bi]tur terra; et sic commovebitur terra, *et aufer[e]tur sicut tabernaculum unius noctis, quoniam gravabit eam iniquitas sua* (Isa. 24.20] (NC, fol. 290ra).

What prophetic tradition in exegesis did John draw upon? The Gloss on Dan. 12.12 authorised the expectation of peace, *refrigerium sanctorum*, in the period to come after the death of Antichrist and before the Last Judgment.[25] Joachim and his followers took this authorised expectation of peace to mean an age of spiritual progress: the Church would be purified and would receive a fuller understanding of Scripture. To summarise crudely, as a background to John's prophecy: the followers of Joachim made his ideas more explicit. The Old Testament represented the age of the Father, the New that of the Son; a third age of the Holy Spirit would fulfil the promises of the first two. It was tempting to see the Mendicant Orders as heralding the third age. St. Francis led the way and his sons stood on the threshold of the new era.

John accepted the view that some interval would elapse between the defeat of Antichrist and the Last Judgment; but he did not **follow Joachim in looking forward to it as a time of spiritual** regeneration. Quite the contrary: he forecast a time of trouble and persecution of the Church by her enemies; she had deserved it on account of her greed for temporal power and earthly riches. Then, instead of seeing her spoliation as the prelude to the reign of a purified Church in an age of the Holy Spirit, he stops short there. The despoilers form a 'church of the wicked.' The closest parallel that I have found is in Pseudo–Joachim's commentary on Jeremias. Modern scholars have dated it to *c.* 1240 and probably soon before 1243 or 1248 at latest. Its authorship and *milieu* remain uncertain. The *milieu* may have been Franciscan or perhaps the circle of Joachim's Cistercian disciples in Southern Italy.[26]

Pseudo–Joachim states repeatedly that in the last age the Church will be robbed of her earthly wealth and humiliated by the sons of this world; he specifies the Roman empire as one of her chief persecutors.[27] Thus prelates will be forced to learn that they must seek out and know spiritual things only. He goes on to quote the same text as John does on Christ's prophecy to St. Peter (John 21.18).[28] The

---

[25] R. E. Lerner, 'Refreshment of the Saints: the Time after Antichrist as a Station for Earthly Progress in Medieval Thought,' *Traditio*, 32 (1976), 109 and *passim.*

[26] B. Töpfer, *Das kommende Reich des Friedens* (Berlin, 1964), pp. 53, 75, 98, 104–105, 108, 167, 351, 366. Töpfer argues for a Franciscan *milieu*; M. Reeves, more cogently to my mind, argues for a South Italian Cistercian, op. cit., pp. 56, 149–158.

[27] *Scriptum super Hieremiam Prophetam* (Venice, 1516), fols. 20va, 22ra, 27ra.

[28] Ibid., fols. 60va–61vb: "Tales [prelati] autem necessario patent necessitati a superveniente tempestate premendi, ut discant sola spiritualia querere vel

only difference is that John does not identify members of the *ecclesia malignantium*, who will despoil the Church; the Roman empire is not mentioned in his scheme of things to come. He could perhaps have read Pseudo–Joachim on Jeremias; the dates do not quite preclude it; or he could have picked up from other sources the ideas which inspired the writer. Whether observation of the contemporary scene or temperament inclined him to take a gloomy view cannot be known. What matters more than the content of his eschatology is the fact that he ventured into 'exegesis as prophecy.' We hear faint echoes of Joachim on his new mode of interpretation.[29] Joachim, who did not claim the gift of prophecy, but of exegetical charisma, believed that a true understanding of Scripture included discernment of prophecies contained in both Testaments. The historical sense of the Old Testament may be symbolic of the future, not only of the New Testament. The two combined may point beyond the New to the post–biblical period. The reader will have noticed how John of La Rochelle deploys Old Testament texts to reinforce the prophecies contained in the New. Joachim juggled with the traditional teaching on the four senses of Scripture, so as to enlarge the 'anagogical' sense. The literal sense, as distinct from the merely carnal, or from the words in themselves, extended to a spiritual understanding. John seems to think that his interpretation of Christ's Passion as referring to the future of his mystical body, the Church, belongs to an enlarged literal interpretation. He begins it as part of his literal exegesis and he ends it by saying: "Huc usque ad litteram"; he then distinguishes it from the 'morality' which follows. The figures of Agar and Sara, representing two peoples and two churches, whose history is projected into the future, play a key part in Joachim's exegesis.[30] They lie behind John's allusion to the handmaid and her mistress. Surely, then, he had taken a sip of the heady brew of Joachimism. Perhaps that one taste proved to be enough for him. Anyway, he drank no more, as far as we know.

---

sapere, et non in temporalibus abundare... Et quidem Petrus ducendus est quo non vult."

[29] M. Reeves, 'The Abbot Joachim's Sense of History,' *Colloques internationaux du Centre National de la Recherche Scientifique 1974*, no. 558 (Paris, 1977), 787–796; H. Mottu, *La Manifestation de l'Esprit selon Joachim de Fiore* (Paris, 1977).

[30] Mottu, 87–88; Reeves, 790.

A third Franciscan trait in his postills is John's papalism. Fr. Y. Congar has given a magisterial account of the ecclesiological aspects of the quarrel between Mendicants and seculars at Paris, which broke out in 1252.[31] It led to polemical arguments and to redefinitions of the pope's position in the Church. The friar doctors, relying as they did on papal protection for their mission, backed papal power and supremacy. The secular masters defended the status of the diocesan bishops in order to hold their own against the Mendicant 'intruders.' The Franciscans went further than the Dominicans in exalting the papacy. They had closer ties with the pope, who was their true father, temporally as well as spiritually: "L'Ordre des Mineurs était comme une grande famille d'enfants, jouissant de biens appartenant à leur parents. Le pape en était vraiment le père."[32] John of La Rochelle died about seven years before the quarrel broke out; but already he had taught that the pope wielded two swords and delegated the material sword to the secular power to wield on his behalf.

If we compare him with his predecessors on the 'two swords' and other controversial texts, we find that the closest resemblance is to Peter the Chanter.[33] The Chanter gave more power to the pope in the Church and over secular Christian rulers than did Hugh of St. Cher or Alexander of Hales. John supported the uncompromising view put forward by William of Auxerre; we have already noted his debt to William's *Summa Aurea*. William taught that the pope held two swords, one to wield and the other to delegate:

> Dicendum quod in veritate ecclesia duos habet gladios, unum quo utitur et quem habet in executione, alterum non sic, sed solum in conferendo.[34]

John upheld this opinion in his *De Legibus* in the *quaestio* already quoted; his treatment of the subject on Luke 22.38 in his postill need not be described here, since the gist of the arguments and the *auctoritates* are all to be found in *De Legibus*.[35] He made the same point in his *Summa de Vitiis:*

---

[31] 'Aspects ecclésiologiques de la querelle entre mendiants et séculiers dans la seconde moitiée du XIIIe siècle et le debut du XIVe,' *Archives d'Histoire Doctrinale et Littéraire du Moyen Age*, 28 (1962), 35–151.

[32] Ibid. p. 107.

[33] Above, p. 140.

[34] ed. cit., fol. 241va-b.

[35] Above, pp. 176-177.

> Numquid ecclesia non ordinat secularem potestatem, ut papa imperatorem; ergo tradit ei potestatem et auctoritatem. Sed ipse [imperator] interficit, ergo auctoritate pape? Respondeo: verum est quod papa ordinat auctoritate Dei secularem potestatem, id est, preficit gladium materialem... (MS Laud. misc. 221, fol. 65rb).

The pope, it is then explained, obeys God in commanding the emperor to wield his sword for the right reasons.

The postills on St. Matthew and St. John repeat the argument more sharply. That on Matt. 26.51–52 centres on the question of licit use of force by clerks and laymen, without touching on the papacy. John stresses, as he did also in *De Legibus* and *De Vitiis*, that a clerk must never use physical force. A layman may protect himself against attack and may go to war in a just cause; a clerk may not. Christ forbade St. Peter to use his sword because St. Peter was a prelate (NC, fols. 273rb–274rb). His intransigence on recourse to force by churchmen, here and elsewhere, underlines John's concept of their sacral character. His postill on St. John offers his most trenchant statement. He repeats his quotation of St. Bernard on the two swords[36] on John 18.10–11, and concludes without more ado:

> Uterque gladius est ecclesie, sed materialis est exercendus pro ecclesia, spiritualis autem exercendus ab ecclesia (Merton, fol. 141va).

Nothing could be more explicit. John anticipates more sophisticated arguments for papal authority, which would be put forward by the Franciscans later, under pressure from secular masters.

Now to compare John with Hugh of St. Cher: John was more obviously a Franciscan than Hugh was a Dominican, as they appear in their respective postills. But John was a Franciscan of the second generation. He was committed to the modification in the friars' way of life made necessary by their functions as teachers, confessors and preachers. He took less interest in poverty, as such, than Hugh did, to judge from his comments on the Gospels. The Franciscan

---

[36] This often quoted text comes from St. Bernard, *De Consideratione* iv, iii, 7, *Opera S. Bernardi*, ed. J. Leclercq and H. M. Rochais, 3 (Rome, 1963), 454: "Uterque ergo Ecclesiae, et spiritualis scilicet gladius, et materialis, sed is quidem pro Ecclesia, ille vero et ab Ecclesia exserendus: ille sacerdotis, is militis manu, sed sane ad nutum sacerdotis et iussum imperatoris."

ethos in John comes out in his justification of study and relaxation of the Rule within limits, as recommended in the *Expositio Regulae*, in his brief flirtation with eschatological prophecy and in his support of papal authority.

Did any link between the friar doctor and St. Francis' own personal feeling for the Gospel survive in the schools? St. Francis had an intensely personal and vivid sense of the literal meaning of the Gospel story; it entered into the experience of his heart and mind.[37] One single passage in John's lectures struck me as having an authentically early Franciscan note. In his commentary on the Magi's gifts to the Holy Child (Matt. 2.11) John first offers the traditional symbolic interpretation: gold was tribute to a king; incense was for sacrifice, and myrrh for burial; the first denoted Christ's royal power, the second his divine majesty, the third his human mortality. John goes on to say that according to the literal sense the gold was given to relieve the Mother's poverty, the incense to counter the stench of the stable, the myrrh to soothe the feeble infant's limbs:

> Nota ad litteram: aurum propter matrem, thus propter locum, mirram propter puerum. Aurum enim necessarium est ad sustentationem pauperis matris, thus contra fetorem stabuli, mirra propter confortanda debilia membra pueri (NC, fol. 18va).

But John had a literary source. He borrowed without acknowledgment from St. Bernard:

> Haec fortassis pro loco et tempore necessaria videbantur. Auri pretium ob paupertatem; myrrhae unguentum ob infantilis, ut assolet, corporis teneritatem; thuris adoramentum ob sordidam stabuli mansionem.[38]

The Franciscan turned to Cistercian piety when he wanted to depict the pathos of the Nativity. The phrasing differs; the thought is St. Bernard's.

---

[37] See especially A. von Rieden, 'Das Leiden Christi im Leben des hl. Franziskus von Assisi,' *Coll. Franc.*, 30 (1960), 5–30, 129–145, 241–263, 353–357; O. Schmucki, 'Das Geheimnis der Geburt Jesu in der Frommigkeit des hl. Franziskus von Assisi,' ibid., 41 (1971), 260–287.

[38] *Sententiae*, series prima, 15, *Opera*, ed. cit. 6(2), 11.

VII. Conclusions

My voyage of discovery has revealed the salient features of a little known landscape. The three postillators, Hugh of St. Cher, Alexander of Hales and John of La Rochelle, stand out like three peaks of a mountain range, joined together at the base. Hugh and Alexander drew on a common source, especially for their *moralitates*, unless we suppose that Alexander revised his postills, borrowing from Hugh, when he lectured at the Franciscan *studium*, *postquam esset frater*, having first lectured on the gospels as a secular master. Their common source, if they had one, is unknown at present. John of La Rochelle borrowed from both Hugh and Alexander. However, if we subtract their known sources, mainly the Gloss and Comestor's *Historia Scholastica*, we see three individual minds at work.

Hugh continued the tradition of the 'biblical moral' school of Peter the Chanter and Stephen Langton. He mixed grave and gay and devotional and homiletic matter with a standard interpretation of the literal, historical sense of Scripture. A reader of Hugh's postills will risk disturbing his neighbours in the library by chuckles of laughter. Not so the reader of Alexander's, except when his jokes occasionally correspond to Hugh's. Alexander is sober in comparison. He is more concerned to deploy the traditional allegories and moralities. They differ in their choice of *auctoritates*. Alexander made an effort to reach back to the earlier, or what he took to be earlier. Whereas Hugh drew on 'Geoffrey Babion' on St. Matthew, on Comestor and the Chanter on the Gospels, and on Stephen Langton's Old Testament commentaries, Alexander preferred others: 'Anselm,' that is the anonymous commentator on St. Matthew transmitted to us in MS Alençon 26, an unknown 'expositor,' probably based on St. Peter Chrysologus, Claudius of Turin, and a mysterious 'Victorinus.' All three *auctoritates*, quoted constantly by Alexander, point to a search for earlier and therefore, to his mind, more authoritative writers. My soundings on Gospel *auctoritates* used by Alexander reveal our ignorance about aids to study other than the Gloss, consisting of excerpts from the *originalia*, which circulated at Paris in the early thirteenth century. John of La Rochelle contented himself with *auctoritates* found in Hugh and Alexander, without seeking further.

All three postillators have a negative aspect in common: they share a lack of interest in research on the literal historical sense of the Gospels as evinced by Peter Comestor. The latter had brought the liturgy, relics, iconography and the monuments of Palestine to bear on his exegesis.[1] Peter the Chanter reacted self–consciously against Comestor's method, which he thought frivolous and irrelevant. Curiosity of Comestor's kind dried up after his death; it does not appear in our three postillators. They quote him, but do not add to him. It seems that they agreed with the Chanter.

If we compare their techniques as lecturers on the Gospels, then Alexander draws ahead of Hugh. Both used the method of division and subdivision of their text by chapters; but Alexander used it to better effect, so as to squeeze the last ounce of meaning from the chosen passages. The theologian inspired the analyst, although Alexander tended to keep theology proper distinct from his lectures on *sacra pagina*. He was more thoughtful and hence more heavy-going and difficult to read than the livelier Hugh. John of La Rochelle refined the techniques of division and distinction. He also brought back the custom of inserting theological *quaestiones* into his lectures on the Gospels; Alexander had partially abandoned it. The custom came down from the twelfth century and earlier. These biblical–lecture *quaestiones* were literary in the sense that the master dictated them; they do not represent actual debates in the classroom.[2] John transcribed and reorganised in his postills much material that he used also in his *De Legibus*, *Summa de Vitiis* and perhaps other theological works. The postills, as far as I can judge, add little or nothing to what is already known of him as a theologian. Their chronology in relation to his *opera* as a whole is uncertain; so perhaps the *quaestiones* in his postills were new to his pupils.

So far, so good! But the main object of my search had eluded me: how far, if at all, did the friars innovate as lecturers on the Gospels? Did they fulfill the Chanter's longing for a return to the principles of Christ's teaching? The friars themselves, the Franciscans in particular, gloried in the novelty of their Orders:

> Novus ordo, nova vita
> Mundo surgit inaudita.

---

[1] See above, chapter 2, pp. 69-76.

[2] O. Lottin, 'Quelques recueils d'écrits attribuées à Hugues de Saint–Victor,' *R.T.A.M.*, 25 (1958) 278, inclines to this hypothesis. No one as yet has demonstrated that *quaestiones* in biblical commentaries represent oral discussions in the course of the *lectio*.

So runs a sequence in honour of St. Francis.[3] A passage from a friars' sermon collection, written in the fourteenth century, dwells on the wonder of St. Francis' new religion:

> New things cause wonder, and new things cause men to ask questions. When blessed Francis began the new way of life [*religionem*] of his brothers, it was a very new thing to found so great an Order upon poverty — upon nothing; it was new and unprecedented. Blessed Benedict founded an Order of monks, but not upon nothing, indeed great revenues and possessions; in the same way Augustine founded his Order of regular canons... If you wonder and ask how an Order which has no foundation on earth endures, I reply: Christ placed the foundation there and rules it through his own self.[4]

The first friar doctors at Paris were by no means anxious to stress their novelty as postillators. They revitalized the teaching of *sacra pagina*, while quietly slipping into the tracks of their predecessors. Commentators on the Gospels had always distinguished the would–be perfect, religious who were expected to obey the precepts more strictly than others, from the 'imperfect.' The friar doctors fitted their Orders into the role of would–be perfect, without claiming any special status. The Chanter's anguish found no echo in their lectures. He had attacked contemporary uses, as well as abuses. The friars did not question the former, but contented themselves with traditional satire against misbehaviour. They seem to have accepted the Church as she was, her institutions included. Their passive attitude in the classroom contrasted with their missionary fervour outside it. Their classroom spirituality was Victorine and Bernardine. The Dominican Hugh of St. Cher shows more tenderness towards poverty as such than either John or Alexander. John identifies himself as a Franciscan, to be sure, but not in the sense that he strongly defended poverty or begging. One has to probe deeply to find Mendicant traits in any of them.

---

[3] *Analecta Franciscana*, 10, 402, ascribed to Thomas of Celano, who died soon after 1260; see B. Smalley, 'Ecclesiastical Attitudes to Novelty c. 1100–c. 1250,' *Studies in Church History*, ed. D. Baker, 12 (1975), 113–132.

[4] MS Paris, Bibl. nat. lat. 3736, fol. 247ʳ⁻ᵛ. See *Catalogue général des manuscripts latins* 6 (Paris, 1975), 666–684. Quoted by D. L. d'Avray, *The Transformation of the Medieval Sermon* (Oxford D. Phil. thesis, 1976), p. 317. I am grateful to him for drawing my attention to this passage.

Was their motive a modest desire to avoid self–advertisement or mere conservatism? Perhaps it was both. But the true reason lies in the very nature of their function as lecturers on the Gospels. They postillated the text with its Gloss. The meaning of these two terms 'gloss' and 'postill' gives a clue to their teaching in the schools.

'Gloss' and 'postill' could be used in a good and a bad sense in the early thirteenth century. To begin with 'gloss': it could mean to explain or clarify in a good sense or to gloss *over* or to explain *away*. St. Francis used it in the second sense when he asked that no glosses should be put upon his Rule and Testament, soon before he died on Oct. 30, 1226:

> And I absolutely order all my brothers, clerics and laymen, on obedience, that they should not put glosses on the Rule or on these words, saying: 'They want to be understood in this way': but, just as the Lord granted me to speak and write simply and purely both the Rule and these words, so simply and purely they shall be understood and put into practice until the last.[5]

The four masters who expounded the Rule, 1241–1242, included two experienced postillators, Alexander of Hales and John of La Rochelle. They disclaimed any intention to set forth a new *expositio* or *glosatura contra Regulam*, as some had accused them of doing.[6] They recognised the pejorative sense of 'glossing' and excused themselves on the grounds that their gloss was not *contra Regulam*.

The standard dictionaries of medieval Latin do not quote either of these two examples or any earlier of the pejorative sense of 'gloss'; but Ducange refers to it in a passage from the Bolognese municipal statutes of 1250–1267:

> We have decreed and ordered that no absolution, dispensation, interpretation, glosation (*glosatio*) or reformation of the statutes should be made upon any statute (*super aliquo statuto praeciso*).[7]

---

[5] ed. K. Esser, *Das Testamentum des heiligen Franziskus von Assisi* (Münster i–W., 1949), 102-103. The translation is by R. B. Brooke, *The Coming of the Friars* (London, 1975), p. 119.

[6] ed. L. Oliger, *Expositio Quatuor Magistrorum super Regulam Fratrum Minorum (1241-1242)* (Rome, 1950), p. 124.

[7] L. Frati, *Statuti di Bologna degli anni 1250-1267* (Monumenti pertinenti alla storia delle provincie di Romagna, ser. I, Bologna, 1863-1884), 1, 326, quoted by Ducange, *Glossarium Mediae et Infimae Latinitatis*, 4 (1885), 81.

Glosatio, as practised by the university jurists, is listed in a comprehensive ban on ways of getting round the plain words of the city statutes.

We catch sight of the word in a transitional sense in a letter written by a cardinal to Pope Innocent III as early as 1213. The pope had sent him as legate to England to raise the interdict laid on the country in consequence of King John's disobedience. The legate had instructions to raise the interdict only after the king had restored to the clergy, with damages, church property which he had seized from those who would not submit to his will. Restitution raised thorny problems. Cardinal Nicholas of Tusculum found that the pope's instructions were too vague and ambiguous. He begged for letters requiring no glosses nor admitting of any disputation, so that he could fulfil his mission to the honour of the Roman Church:

> ...tamen archiepiscopus et episcopi, interpretantes uestras litteras sicut uolunt, dicunt... Sed alii, contrarium sentientes, dicunt... de quibus omnibus [uestris litteris] diuersi diuersa sentiunt... [scribo] iterata supplicatione deposcens ut... ita plene et clare de omnibus mihi dignemini respondere quod littere uestre nec glosulis egeant nec aliquam disputationem admittant et ecclesia Romana... in omnibus debitum honorem consequatur.[8]

The legate viewed Innocent's letters as subject to glossing and disputation like a biblical text. *Glosulae* set on them by readers would twist the meaning in favour of each particular glossator. This would leave room for disputation, carried over from the process of glossing. The sinister meaning of 'gloss' has crept in already some fifteen years before St. Francis expressed his dread that glosses might be set upon his Rule.

Vernacular examples of both senses of 'gloss' occur in plenty in the continuation of the *Roman de la Rose* by the Paris clerk and poet Jean de Meung, 1269–1278. In one passage 'the gloss' means the authoritative *Glossa Ordinaria*, cited as proof for his interpretation of Matt. 23.2–4:

---

[8] A. Mercati, 'La prima Relazione del Cardinale Nicolò de Romanis sulla Legazione in Inghilterra (1213),' *Essays in History presented to R. L. Poole*, ed. H. W. C. Davis (Oxford, 1927), pp. 284–286; C. R. Cheney, *Innocent III and England* (Päpste und Papstum, 9, Stuttgart, 1976), pp. 348–351.

> Seur la chaiere de Moysi (car la glose l'espoint isi): / c'est le Te-
> stament Ancien / siderent scribes et pharisiens / (ce sunt les fausses
> gens maudites / que la lettre apele ypocrites).[9]

Again, he uses 'gloss' in the good sense of clarification when he
explains moonlight; his gloss will give his readers a better understanding of what he means 'por mieuz fere sclarcir la letre.'[10] More often
Jean says 'gloss' when he means 'to obscure' or 'to adulterate.'
Dame Reason says that God has taught her to 'call a spade a spade':
'de parler proprement des choses, / quant il me plest, sanz mettre
gloses.'[11] 'Reciter sans glose' means to speak plainly.[12] Jean refers
to a 'false gloss' on a dream, which ought to have been understood
literally.[13] The friars withdrew the banned *Eternal Gospel* because
even they could not explain away or gloss over its heresies:

> car ils ne savoient respondre / par espondre ne par gloser / a ce
> qu'em volait opposer / contre les paroles mal dites / qui en ce
> livre sunt escrites.[14]

The paradigm of this second sense of the term is in Chaucer's
Canterbury Tales: 'This is a verray sooth, withouten glose.'[15] By the
late fourteenth century in English idiom 'to gloss' meant to detract
from the truth of a statement.

'Postillation,' a less familiar term, had the same history as
'glossation.' *Postilla* seems to have been a word coined in the early
thirteenth century to denote a scholastic commentary on Scripture.
The lexicographers in their notices on *postilla* have failed to add
that it had an ambivalence similar to that of 'gloss.' Hugh of St.
Cher knew the derogatory sense of *postilla* and deploys it effectively
in his comment on Luke 21.36. Christ rebukes those who will not
listen to his teaching, but 'postillate' whatever they hear. They would

---

[9] I have used the edition by F. Lecoy, *Guillaume de Lorris et Jean de Meun.*
Le Roman de la Rose (Paris, 1965) and refer to the lines of the verses. This first
is vv. 11575–11580.

[10] vv. 16821–16824.

[11] vv. 7048–7053; see also vv. 6903–6905.

[12] v. 18432.

[13] vv. 6571–6589.

[14] vv. 11083–11089.

[15] Squire's Tale F, 166; see *The Canterbury Tales*, 2nd ed., F. N. Robinson
(London, 1957), p. 129.

quit their postills, Hugh says, if they heeded the mischief wrought
by the very first postill of all. That was Eve's postillation of God's
word, forbidding *the fruit of the tree of good and evil* (Gen. 2.17). The
devil tempted Eve to eat the forbidden fruit. She answered: *God
hath commanded us that we should not eat, and that we should not touch
it, lest perhaps we die* (Gen. 3.3). Thus she added her postill, 'perhaps,'
to God's caution. Hugh was blaming lazy prelates:

> Isti vero ad nullos sermones excitari possunt, quia nolunt, nec
> etiam auditis rumoribus de Christo et gloria eius, sed postillant
> quicquid audiunt. Sed certe si attenderent quantum malum fecit
> prima postilla, id est Evae postillantis verbum Domini, Gen. 3a,
> ipsi dimitterent postillas suas... Respondit Eva et addidit postil-
> lam suam: *Ne forte moriamur*. Dominus non dixit 'forte'.

Postillation brought about man's woe! Peter the Chanter disapproved
of 'superfluous glosses' as idle and useless. He also disapproved of
'adulteration' of the plain sense of the Gospels. Now his two *bêtes
noires* had come together. To gloss or postillate could mean to adulterate.

The friar doctors were caught up in a contradiction. They could
not help it. They could hardly have reversed a mode of exegesis
which they inherited and which had begun with the Fathers. Gospel
teaching, and the Franciscan Rule too, had to be adapted to current
needs. Moreover, as school teachers the friars had a duty to prepare
their pupils to pass examinations. No teacher could escape from the
tyranny of the syllabus. Spontaneity would have discredited him.

My study stops at the death of John of La Rochelle in 1245.
Their conflict with the seculars threw the friars' assumptions into
the melting pot. They had to rethink the interpretation of the Gospels.
Attack on their way of life, supported by arguments from Scripture
by the seculars provoked the friars and shook them out of their
conservatism. To defend themselves they had to scrutinise the 'plain
meaning' of the Gospels with new eyes. The landscape which I have
explored was basking in the calm before the storm.

ADDITIONAL NOTE

p. 143 at end: Addendum: Hugh turns the text John 1, 7 against those who preach
that pluralism is licit.

Christ in Majesty with the symbols of the four Evangelists.
(MS. Ashmole 1511, fol. 8ᵛ, Bodleian Library, Oxford)

5

The Gospels in the Schools
c.1250 – c.1280

Bonaventure, John of Wales,
John Pecham, Albert the Great,
Thomas Aquinas

I. BONAVENTURE

The storm broke out in the ten years between the death of John of La Rochelle, 1245, and Bonaventure's regency, 1254–1257.[1] The secular masters' jealousy of the mendicants, lowering for some years, flashed out in polemic, pamphlet-warfare and appeals to Rome.[2] Seen from the seculars' point of view, the friar doctors were brain-drainers, who enticed gifted students and hence withdrew both prestige and fees away from the seculars; some masters treacherously went over to the enemy camp. They were strike-breakers, continuing to teach during the Paris university dispersions of 1229–1231 and 1253. They were also sneaks, currying favour in high places and especially at Rome, the source of privileges and bulls of protection. The seculars had relied on papal support to establish the university as an independent corporation; now they felt the resentment of the elder child ousted from first place by its junior. They could act as spokesmen for wider circles, since the parish clergy increasingly disliked the pastoral role of the friars as interference with their own rights and duties.

The Franciscan *studium* at Paris came into the very heart of the storm, owing to the friars' attempt to gain a second chair in theology. The Dominicans already had two, dating from about 1230; the Franciscans had only one official chair; their second regent taught internally and they wanted him to be raised to university status. The secular masters of theology thought that three mendicant chairs were more than enough. They refused to recognise a fourth and even called in question the Dominicans' right to hold two at St. Jacques.

William of St. Amour stepped forward as the seculars' leading polemicist. His anti-mendicant tract, *De periculis novissimorum temporum* (first draft early 1256) attacked the university friars, never named, but referred to as false brethren, hypocrites and intruders, on a wide front, disputing their right to exist as religious Orders at all. He urged drastic measures: condemn begging and force the friars to earn their bread by manual work; that would put paid to their study and teaching at one blow; they would have no time for schools. William, a canonist and theologian, argued from a wide range of texts from the Old and New Testaments that mendicancy and what the friars attempted to practise as 'apostolic poverty' had no warrant in Scripture and indeed were blamed there. Even before the publication of *De periculis* William had confronted Bonaventure in *quaestiones disputatae* on the issues of poverty and mendicancy in the autumn of 1255. Even after *De periculis*

---

[1] For Bonaventure's life and writings see the table, *S. Bonaventura 1274–1974*, 2 (Grottaferrata, Rome, 1973), 11–16. I shall refer to this work as *Bon.*

[2] On the whole controversy see M.-M. Dufeil, *Guillaume de Saint-Amour et la polémique universitaire Parisienne 1250–1259* (Paris, 1972); J. D. Dawson, 'William of Saint-Amour and the Apostolic Tradition', *Mediaeval Studies*, 40 (1978), 223–238.

had been condemned at the Curia and William had left the schools in 1257, the bitterness of the controversy remained; the mendicants were still on the defensive. Bonaventure was involved in it both as a master, a claimant to a university chair, and as a member of an Order vowed to the *altitudo paupertatis*. His lectures on St. Luke and St. John belong roughly to his regency. We should therefore expect him to move away from the traditional, 'biblical moral' stance of his predecessors.

As well as defending his Order's ideals and means to achieve them from external attack, Bonaventure had to defend study within the Order. It had come to be accepted as necessary to the friars' preaching and ministry; but some members still felt disquiet and had scruples about the modification to their Rule which university life required. The way to dispel such doubts and scruples was to sanctify study, to make it seem a path to holiness and divine contemplation. A theologian-exegete, as Bonaventure was, would naturally turn towards the spiritual senses of Scripture, not understood as the mechanical allegories and tropologies of Hugh of St. Cher, Alexander of Hales and John of La Rochelle, but rather as 'anagogic', uplifting, signifying the heavenly things to be hoped for. Hugh of St. Victor and St. Bernard, both of whom he admired, had used the spiritual senses to this end. He would follow their example in mid-thirteenth-century idiom. A third problem posed itself concerning the doctrinal justification of the spiritual senses themselves. William of Auvergne, respected doctor of theology and then bishop of Paris, had argued against their use and had allowed comparisons only, not significations. John of La Rochelle had set out to demolish William's position in his treatise *De legibus*, incorporated into the *Summa* ascribed to Alexander of Hales.[3] Bonaventure must have known of the discussion, especially if, as seems probable, John of La Rochelle was one of his teachers.[4] The fourfold exposition needed further justification, before it could serve to integrate study into a life of holiness.

The scriptural works which concern us here belong to his regency, but must be read in the framework of his career. John of Fidanza, called Bonaventure, came to Paris from Italy and entered the Order of friars Minor as an M.A. in 1243. He qualified as doctor of theology in their *studium*, having Alexander of Hales, Odo Rigaud and probably John of La Rochelle as his masters. He lectured as a bachelor in theology 1248–1252 and disputed and preached as a *bachelarius formatus* 1252–1253. The secular masters' success in postponing the establishment of a second chair for the Franciscans prevented him from incepting officially as a doctor; hence his teaching as a

---

[3] B. Smalley, 'William of Auvergne, John of La Rochelle and St. Thomas Aquinas on the Old Law', *St. Thomas Aquinas 1274–1974* (Pontifical Institute of Mediaeval Studies, Toronto, 1974), 1, 10–71; reprinted in my *Studies in Mediaeval Thought and Learning from Abelard to Wyclif* (The Hambledon Press, London, 1981), 121–181.

[4] I. Brady, 'Sacred Scripture in the Early Franciscan School', *La Sacra Scrittura e i Francescani* (*Pontificium Athenaeum Antonianum. Studium Biblicum Franciscanum*, Rome/Jerusalem, 1973), 74–78.

doctor, 1254–1257, took place internally;[5] but his unrecognized status made no difference to the form of instruction given. This first teaching period ended with his election as minister general, Feb. 2, 1257; but he continued to write even while guiding his Order through a critical stage of its history, lectured as a guest professor at Paris 1267–1268 and gave his *Collationes in Hexaemeron* there in the spring of 1273. The pope insisted on making him a cardinal so that he might attend the council of Lyons, where he died on July 15, 1274.

A first mark of the effect of the mendicant versus secular conflict on Bonaventure's thought may perhaps be noted in a change of mind traced by Fr. Bérubé.[6] In his proemium to his lectures on the Sentences, given as bachelor about 1250 and retouched later, he departed from precedent and anticipated Aquinas by distinguishing between the study of Scripture and the study of doctrinal theology, based on both the revealed truth of Scripture and Catholic faith. Yet his prologue to his *Breviloquium*, a manual of theology for beginners, written between 1254 and 1257, really amounts to a programme for the study of Scripture, as though he equated it to that of theology. The trend towards concentration on Scripture with its authoritative commentators went on with the years, to culminate in the *Collationes in Hexaemeron*. These present Bonaventure's mystical exposition, a means towards disclosing his theology of world history and his eschatological speculations. Scripture came to absorb every other aspect of sacred doctrine into itself.

Much has been written on his theories about the nature of Scripture and on his principles of exegesis,[7] but very little on his actual surviving lectures on Ecclesiastes, St. Luke and St. John. Indeed it has been claimed that we should not look to them for his deeper thought; the school tradition hedged him into a narrow pathway.[8] If this were the case it would reflect unfavourably both on the school tradition and on the lecturer who let it trammel the free run of his ideas. On the contrary, what surprised me on reading his Gospel commentaries was their originality and his refusal to be obstructed by current classroom methods.

At first sight Bonaventure's teaching on the senses seems to reinforce the tradition of down-grading the literal-historical in favour of the spiritual senses. His early *Reductio artium ad theologiam* of 1254–1255 limits the literal sense to what the words sound outwardly. All the books of the Bible have in addition the allegorical, moral and anagogic senses. The allegorical teaches us what to believe of divinity and humanity, the moral how we ought

[5] Dufeil, op. cit. 103; 157–158.
[6] C. Bérubé, 'De la théologie à l'Écriture chez Saint Bonaventure', *Collectanea Franciscana*, 40 (1970), 5–70.
[7] H.-J. Klauck, 'Theorie der Exegese bei Bonaventure', *Bon.* 4 (1974), 71–128, and especially J. Ratzinger, *Die Geschichtstheologie des heiligen Bonaventura* (Munich/Zurich, 1959).
[8] H. Mercker, *Schriftauslegung als Weltauslegung. Untersuchungen zur Stellung der Schrift in der Theologie Bonaventuras* (Munich, 1971), 1–7.

to behave, the anagogic how to cleave to God. Hence the whole Bible teaches us three things: Christ's eternal generation and incarnation, the way to live and the union of the soul with God, prepared for by allegorical and moral understanding. A list of recommended authors for the study of Scripture omits any name for the literal-historical sense, no St. Jerome. Augustine is recommended especially for allegory, also Anselm (of Canterbury), Gregory for morality, Denis (Pseudo-Dionysius) for anagogy, and Hugh of St. Victor for all three. Anagogy closes the cycle of flux and reflux by linking study with divine contemplation.[9]

The prologue to *Breviloquium* contains the same teaching on the senses, though vastly elaborated. To pick out the essentials: Scripture represents knowledge moving to good and recalling from evil by means first of fear and then of love. Therefore it is divided into the Old and New Testaments, though the one is contained in the other by a *mira conformitas*, a wondrous correspondence. The legal, historical, sapiential and prophetical books of the Old Testament correspond respectively to the Gospels, Acts, Epistles and Apocalypse. The Gospels here count as legal rather than historical, because they contain the New Law. The whole prologue hinges on the dimensions of divine wisdom as revealed in Scripture: breadth, length, height and depth (see Eph. 3.14–19). When he reaches depth, Bonaventure repeats and justifies what he had said on the four senses, again with a preference for anagogy. It is right that Scripture should have a threefold sense, apart from the literal, since this agrees with its subject-matter, its hearer or student, its origin and its end. The subject-matter is God according to substance, Christ according to virtue, the works of reparation according to its operation; it is to be believed according to all four. Bonaventure develops his argument in detail. He goes on to modes of procedure: narrative, command, ban, exhortation, threat, promise, blame and praise. A man may be moved, if not by one, then by another. Narrative, that is the literal sense, provides *exempla*. Knowledge of the literal sense is needed as a preliminary, for the very reason that many senses are hidden under one. The exegete must have the whole Bible at his finger-tips, memorising it so as to compare passages in order to elicit their meaning. He who scorns the letter will never rise to possession of the spiritual senses.

Finally Bonaventure sets out rules for exposition, which he claims to have been drawn from the *De doctrina Christiana*, though St. Augustine never wrote anything so explicit. At least his main point comes through in the *Breviloquium*: the exegete must find some way to make every passage edifying, even if it means replacing an objectionable literal interpretation by a spiritual.

Nice distinctions between the senses which exercised contemporaries did not trouble Bonaventure. An absurd tale about a Jew reading or lecturing on Isaias at Paris, told in his *Collationes in Hexaemeron*, measures his distance

[9] I quote from the Quaracchi *Opera*, 5–7 (1891–1895), unless otherwise mentioned. For *Reductio artium* see 5, 319–325.

from current biblical scholarship. Here is the story as his two reporters took it down; they make better sense if read together. The text in question is the opening of the Suffering Servant passage (Is. 53.1).[10]

One must not read Scripture as the Jew does; he wishes for the outer shell only. Hence a certain Jew was once reading the chapter of Isaias beginning *Who hath believed our report etc.?* He read according to the letter and so he threw the book down, calling upon God to confound Isaias, because, as it seemed to him, what he said would not stand.

Note that a Jew, reading at Paris, held too much to the letter, which sometimes has a spiritual sense only. He wanted to expound the chapter of Isaias *Who hath believed our report?* to his hearers, Christian clerks. Being quite unable to expound according to the letter, he threw the book down.

Andrew of St. Victor in the twelfth century had made available the standard Jewish interpretation of the Suffering Servant since Rashi: the Suffering Servant signified the people of Israel; the gentiles would not believe the prophet's forecast of her redemptive role. Latin commentators henceforward discussed the problem of which or how many of the messianic prophecies should be taken as directly christological. They knew that 'the Jews' had their own interpretation of the Suffering Servant and that no Jewish reader of the passage would have been at a loss to expound it.[11] Bonaventure either did not know or deliberately ignored this development.

Passing to his Gospel commentaries themselves, we have two only, both from 1254–1257. That on St. Luke in its present form derives from lectures which he gave as *bachelarius biblicus*, 1248, revised while he was teaching as a master. It includes divisions, distinctions, allegories and moralities, but no separate *quaestiones*, the latter being the province of a master's lectures. Salimbene witnesses to its fame by describing it as *pulcra et optima*.[12] Bonaventure lectured on St. John as a master. Here we find in addition to the other matter short *quaestiones*, placed at the end of each section of a chapter. This commentary also was popular as the number of surviving manuscripts testifies. The collations on selected texts of St. John need not be

[10] 5, 421: 'Primum igitur est, quod homo habeat Scripturam non sicut Iudaeus, qui solum vult corticem. Unde quidam Iudaeus semel legebat illud capitulum Isaiae: *Domine, quis credidit auditui nostro* etc: et legebat ad litteram et non potuit habere concordantiam nec sensum, et ideo proiecit librum ad terram, imprecans, ut Deus confunderet Isaiam, quia, ut sibi videbatur, non potuit stare quod dicebat.'
Bonaventurae *Collationes in Hexaëmeron*, ed. F. Delorme (Bibliotheca Franciscana Scholastica Medii Aevi 8, 1934), 215: 'Nota de Iudaeo legente Parysius, qui, nimis tenendo litteram quae aliquando tantum spiritualis est, voluit exponere auditoribus suis clericis christianis capitulum hoc Isaiae: *Domine quis credidit auditui nostro?* et non valens omnino secundum litteram, proiecit librum ad terram.'
[11] B. Smalley, *The Study of the Bible in the Middle Ages*, 3rd ed. (Oxford, 1983), 164–165; 232–233; 391–392; G. A. C. Hadfield, *Andrew of St. Victor a twelfth-century Hebraist: an investigation of his works and sources* (Oxford D.Phil.thesis, 1971).
[12] *Cronica*, ed. O. Holder-Egger, *Monumenta Germaniae Historica, Scriptores*, 32 (1905–1913), 299.

considered, since they are in schematic form to serve as an aid to memory for evening addresses to the friars.

The first step towards spotting originality is to look for his sources. I could find no traces of Alexander of Hales or of John of La Rochelle. Perhaps he set them aside in order to make a fresh start. It is known that he took Hugh of St. Cher on Ecclesiastes as his principal source among the moderns;[13] so it seemed likely that the same might apply to his lectures on the Gospels. Collation showed that it does, as the following examples will show.

On St. John Baptist's answer to the crowd: . . .*there shall come one mightier than I, the latchet of whose shoes I am not worthy to loose* (Luke 3.16), Hugh gives first a literal and then three 'mystical' meanings as expounded by the *sancti*. According to the first, the Baptist expressed his humility. According to the first of the three mystical meanings, to loose the latchet means to explain the mystery of the incarnation; the latchet signifies Christ's humanity, the foot within, bearing the shoe, signifies his divinity. The latchet signifies the union of divinity and humanity, which no one suffices to explain. Secondly, the text would refer to the command of the Law: if a man died without leaving offspring, the next-of-kin should marry his widow. If he refused, the widow had the right to take off his shoes and to spit in his face before the elders (Deut. 25.5–9). The Baptist's answer signified, on this interpretation, that he was not the bridegroom, that is Christ, as the Jews thought, but rather the friend of the bridegroom; he was not worthy to receive the bride (the Church). Thirdly, the text would mean that the Baptist had not received the office of opening the Scriptures and carrying the message throughout the world; his mission was to baptize, not to preach. A supporting quotation from Bede argues that the apostles were shod with the nuptial shoe of preaching; the Baptist meant that he was not an apostle.

The alternative expositions all stem from the Fathers; but Hugh lists and clarifies them. Bonaventure prefers to count the alternative expositions as four, not one plus three, as Hugh had counted them. He reverses the order of the three mystical or spiritual, putting Hugh's third second and his second fourth. They quote some of the same texts but not all. Bonaventure shortens Hugh's exposition and ends by preferring the first sense (Hugh's literal) as stressing the Baptist's humility. The Franciscan's exegesis is so condensed and allusive that one could hardly understand it without first reading Hugh.

HUGH OF ST. CHER *ad loc.*

Cuius non sum dignus solvere corrigiam calceamentorum eius . . . Consueto quidem locutionis modo, Ioannes humilitatem suam exprimit. Mystice tamen a sanctis exponitur et tribus modis. Primo sic: *Non sum dignus*. . ., id est explicare mysterium incarnationis. Calceamentum enim est humanitas Christi. Psalmus: *In Idumeam extendam calceamentum meum* [59.10]. Pes intus latens, et calceamentum sustinens,

---

[13] C. Van den Borne, 'De fontibus Commentarii S. Bonaventurae in Ecclesiasten', *Archivum Franciscanum Historicum*, 10 (1917), 257–270.

est divinitas . . . Corrigia est unio divinitatis et humanitatis, quam explicare nemo sufficit . . . Secundo modo sic: *Non sum dignus* illum discalceare, et sponsam eius mihi usurpare. Et tangit hic legis consuetudinem, quae iubet quod si quis decederet, non relicto semine, propinquior eius suscitaret ei semen, quod si nollet, alius propinquior post illum discalcearet illum et duceret relictam mortui in uxorem. Deut. 25b[5]. Est ergo sensus secundum istam expositionem: Nolo sponsus credi, sed amicus sponsi. Ioan.3d[29] *Qui habet sponsam, sponsus est; amicus autem sponsi, qui stat et audit eum, gaudio gaudet propter vocem sponsi.* Tertio modo sic: *Non sum dignus . . .*, id est non habeo officium reserandi scripturam et portandi per mundum, quia non est mihi iniunctum officium praedicandi, sed baptizandi . . . Beda: Calceamentum nuptiale est evangelica praedicatio, qua calceati sunt apostoli. Unde Eph. 6c [14]: *State ergo succincti etc.* Est igitur sensus secundum tertiam expositionem: *Non sum dignus*, id est, non sum apostolus.

BONAVENTURE, 7, 79

Cuius non sum dignus . . . Ad litteram potest hoc esse, ut tantum se humiliet, quod non sit dignus servire ei in humillimo ministerio . . . Vel *spiritualiter* per *calceamentum* intelligitur humana natura assumta, secundum illud Psalmi: 'In Idumaeam extendam calceamentum meum'. Per *corrigiam* intelligo ipsam unionem. Est ergo sensus secundum Bedam: *Cuius non sum dignus* etc . . . id est evangelicam praedicationem per mundum portare; unde Beda: 'Calceamentum nuptiale est evangelica praedicatio, qua calceati fuerunt Apostoli'; ad Ephesios sexto: 'Calceati pedes in praeparatione Evangelii pacis'. – Aliter etiam exponitur quarto modo, ut sit sensus: *Non sum dignus solvere*, id est, ipsum secundum morem Legis discalceare et uxorem eius mihi copulare; unde Ioannis tertio: 'Qui habet sponsam sponsus est; amicus autem sponsi stat' etc – Sed secundum primum sensum maius videtur habere testimonium, in quo mira exprimitur beati Ioannis humilitas, ut, cum reputetur a Deo maximus, ipse reputet se minimum . . .

Another passage where Bonaventure must be read with Hugh to make him intelligible is the story of the woman taken in adultery (John 8.3–11). Hugh noted that Burgundio of Pisa, who translated Chrysostom's homilies on St. John, explained in his prologue that Chrysostom omitted it, since it neither appeared in the old Greek books nor was read in the Greek church, and was thought to have been added to the original Gospel, just as the fable of the dragon and Susanna was added to the book of Daniel. Hence the Greeks regard it as apocryphal. Hugh follows the Latins in accepting it as genuine. Perhaps, he suggests, St. John added it himself after finishing his book, for who else would be so rash as to dare to add anything to such a Gospel?

Bonaventure relegates the discrepancy between Greek and Latin texts of the Gospels to his answer to a question: why did the Pharisees put to Jesus a question (on punishment for adultery) which was already determined by the Law? He refers to the opinion of *quidam* that the whole passage was a human invention, like the story of Susanna, added to the book of Daniel; witness Chrysostom, they say, who makes no mention of it and passes it over. But Augustine and 'our expositors' expound it as part of the gospel. Why Chrysostom said nothing of it, Bonaventure did not know. Some [Hugh] say that it was not found in old Greek books, because John added it after finishing his gospel. Here again, Bonaventure has abridged Hugh, referring to him this time as *quidam*, and again his exegesis makes sense only in the light of Hugh's postill.

HUGH OF ST. CHER *ad loc.*

Nota quod historiam istam de adultera et a principio capitis usque ad finem ipsius dicunt quidam esse anticipationem . . . Alii coniungunt hoc ad praecedentia et sequentia, sicut etiam facit Augustinus et quaedam glosa et sicut textus etiam videtur sonare. Chrysostomus autem totum hoc quod dicitur de adultera praetermittit, nec aliquid tangit de hac historia in originali, et continuat id quod infra eodem, b, dicitur *Ego sum lux mundi* [8.12] ad finem praecedentis capitis. Causam autem huius praetermissionis assignat Burgundio iudex Pisanus, qui transtulit librum Chrysostomi in prologo eiusdem libri. Dicit enim quod ista historia in libris antiquis in Graecia non invenitur, sed nec in ecclesia Graecorum legitur, quia putatur a quibusdam apposita, sicut fabula draconis et Susannae ad Danielem. Unde Graeci iudicant historiam hanc apocrypham. Sed quia sancti Latini exponunt et quia in ecclesia Latinorum legitur, nos etiam exponemus, respondentes Graecis quod potuit esse post perfectionem libri a Ioanne evangelista addita. Et ideo non universaliter est in omnibus libris inventa. Quis enim tantae temeritatis esse credatur, ut tanto evangelistae aliquid audeat addere?

BONAVENTURE, 6, 355

Sed incidit hic dubitatio: cum quaestio ista faciliter esset determinata ex Lege, et qui tentat debeat dubia quaerere; unde est hoc, quod talem quaestionem Pharisaei dolosi Domino proposuerunt?

Respondent quidam, quod videtur totum industria humana factum; unde dixerunt quod hoc fuit immixtum Evangelio Ioannis, sicut historia Susannae Danieli. In cuius rei testimonium adduxerunt, quod Chrysostomus de hoc nullam mentionem facit; unde saltat ad illud: *Iterum locutus est Iesus* etc. Sed Augustinus et expositores nostri exponunt de serie Evangelii – Quod vero Chrysostomus nihil dicit, causam nescio. Quidam dicunt, quod in antiquis libris Graecis non inveniebatur, quia Ioannes addidit Evangelio completo.

The dependence on Hugh of St. Cher is less obvious on the Gospels than on Ecclesiastes, but no less real. Bonaventure chose or alluded to what appealed to him in the Dominican's vast mosaic. He omitted the jokes and topical allusions in the interest of sobriety and of his high religious purpose; evidently he disapproved of mixing grave and gay.

There are at least four quotations from the mysterious Victor(inus?) quoted more often by Alexander of Hales and only once (as far as I know) by Hugh of St. Cher. Bonaventure cites him on John 2.1 and on John 18. 10,11,15 and 26.[14] None of Bonaventure's quotations corresponds to his predecessors'; but it is interesting, in view of some future attempt to identify Victorinus, that almost all references to him come from a commentary on Christ's capture and trial, on whatever gospel text he is cited.

[14] 6, 272; 478; 480; 481; 484. For Alexander's and Hugh's quotations and John of La Rochelle's, copied from Alexander's, see above, pp. 155–158; 180. Bonaventure gives 'Victor' less authority than Augustine, 6, 272.

Like Alexander, Bonaventure had an *expositor*; his Quaracchi editors could not identify it; neither can I.[15] Alexander's had quotations from St. Peter Chrysologus,[16] which do not appear in Bonaventure's. The term *expositor* would be used for some patristic or supposedly patristic work; a contemporary or near contemporary would be more likely to be called simply *quidam*. Apart from 'Victor(inus?)' and his *expositor* Bonaventure had recourse to the expected sources duly noted by his editors: the Four Doctors, Chrysostom and Pseudo-Chrysostom's *Opus imperfectum* on St. Matthew, Pseudo-Dionysius, Bede, Hugh and Richard of St. Victor, St. Bernard, William of St. Thierry, the Gloss and the *Historia scholastica*,[17] with Hugh of St. Cher as his basis. In spite of his distaste for 'litigious Aristotelians', he alludes to Aristotle's books without naming them.[18]

The prologues to St. Luke and St. John conform to the school pattern: opening text, application to the book in hand; but Bonaventure bends it to his own purposes in a personal way. The prologue to Luke brings out with unction the themes nearest to his heart: the unity of the two Testaments, the centrality of Christ in both, the ideal qualities of teacher and hearer of Scripture. The *causa finalis tertia* of this Gospel is the 'disclosure of eternity' because it exhorts the reader to life eternal as its final end.[19] Here Bonaventure's preference for anagogy comes through. His comment on the evangelist's own prologue equally goes to the heart of his principles as a Franciscan doctor: he defends the scholastic method of scrutinising 'the order, distinction and sufficiency', meaning the divisions and subdivisions of the text; that was what St. Luke intended. Therefore it is not idle curiosity, but useful to describe its division, order and sufficiency; the same applies to the other Gospels too. A *divisio generalis* follows.[20] The prologue to St. John's dwells on the difference between his and the 'synoptic Gospels', as they are now called. Bonaventure explains why he uses narrative rather than 'demonstrative' form in order to generate faith and ends with the question whether man has the right to scrutinise things divine. Such scrutiny may be

[15] On Luke 3.22 and 5.1; 7, 84; 113: '. . . ut dicit expositor'; 'unde dicit quidam expositor'.

[16] Above, pp. 154–155.

[17] J. G. Bougerol, 'S. Bonaventure et la hiérarchie dionysienne', *Archives d'histoire doctrinale et littéraire du Moyen Âge*, 36 (1969), 131–167; 'S. Bonaventure et S. Bernard', *Antonianum*, 46 (1971), 3–79; 'S. Bonaventure et Guillaume de Saint-Thierry', ibid., 298–321; G. A. Zinn, 'Book and Word. The Victorine Backgound of Bonaventure's Use of Symbols', *Bon.* 2, 143–169.

[18] 7, 5; 6; 6, 243.

[19] 7, 3–6.

[20] 7, 12: 'Et sic patet, quod non est curiosum inquirere et perscrutari ordinem, distinctionem et sufficientiam in prosecutione eorum quae in hoc Evangelio conscribuntur; pari ratione nec in aliis. Si ordo attestatur sapientiae et bonitati, illi Scripturae potissime debet competere, quae procedit a fonte sapientiae et ducit ad finem bonitatis completae. Et haec est Scriptura evangelica; et ideo non est curiositas, sed utilitas, si describantur in sequentibus divisio, ordo et sufficientia, quia hoc intenditur ab Evangelista.'

diabolic, curious (as in the philosophers) or pious. St. John was inspired to do so: 'hence the Holy Spirit, not man, tells of Christ's eternal generation.'[21] Again, pious study of the divine is vindicated as God-inspired.

Lecturing on his text, Bonaventure broke with the custom of dividing his exposition neatly into 'literal' and 'spiritual'. The historical details and background of the gospel stories did not interest him; he thought them irrelevant. Hugh of St. Cher would not identify the bridegroom of the wedding feast with St. John the Evangelist and discussed at length the identity of Mary, sister of Martha and Lazarus: was she the same as the penitent of St. Luke's Gospel? Bonaventure backed tradition, stemming from Augustine, on St. John as the bridegroom[22] and on the identity of the penitent woman with Mary, making the revealing comment:

It is not unfitting that expositors should hold conflicting opinions on the subject of personal names, since there is no compelling force (*vis*) in them.[23]

He set aside his main source, Hugh's postill, when it displeased him.

Bonaventure got round the difficulty of nice discrimination between the senses by making the spiritual inhere in the literal. The historical event bears spiritual meaning: the Virgin's haste to visit Elizabeth (Luke 1.39) teaches us to hasten to perfection.[24] His method shows most clearly in the list of reasons he will give for certain actions, as when Christ and his disciples passed through cornfields and ate the ears on a Sabbath, for which some Pharisees blamed them (Luke 6.1–5). Christ's *passage* with his disciples shows that they were wayfarers and teaches us to pass through life without cleaving to worldly things. The second reason, why they picked the ears of corn, was their poverty and lack of supplies, which teaches us the virtue of austerity as against wishing for dainty dishes. That they did so on the Sabbath shows that the Sabbath is to be observed spiritually, not literally. The *spiritualis intelligentia* of the passage is that the Sabbath signifies the quiet of divine contemplation and the ears of corn the foretaste of its inner sweetness. Lastly the sweetness of Christ's word had so drawn them on that they had forgotten to eat.[25] When Christ told the healed leper to show himself to a priest (Luke 5.14) his command taught literally respect for the priesthood and the need for inner contrition and confession before absolution from sins.[26] Here the spiritual significance of the command is absorbed into 'the letter'. Christ fed the multitude (Luke 9. 17) to set an example to preachers to feed their hearers with spiritual food, and confirmed his example by a miracle.[27] He chose coarse barley bread instead

---

[21] 6, 239–244.
[22] 6, 272.
[23] 6, 397.
[24] 7, 28.
[25] 7, 135.
[26] 7, 121.
[27] 7, 224.

of wheaten loaves (John 6. 9) for two reasons: to enhance his miracle by transforming the best to the worst and to signify that the new Law of the Gospel was replacing the five books of the old Mosaic Law.[28] He chose spittle, clay and water to heal the blind man (John 9.6) for three reasons, literal, allegorical and moral, which Bonaventure sets down.[29] Thus deeper meanings belong to Christ's intention. We are far from the Gregorian metaphor of laying a literal-historical foundation, adding walls of allegory, and painting them with moralities. Bonaventure seems to have thought that the evangelist was in the secret too. St. Luke tells us the name of Zachaeus, his dwelling place, and even the kind of tree he climbed, in order to see Jesus (Luke 19.1–4), not because such details were significant in themselves, but because together they signified that Zachaeus the publican represented the gentiles in contrast to the Jews.[30]

The recurrence of school terms, *moraliter et ad litteram* (Christ's birth in a stable reproves soft bedding),[31] *allegorice, spiritualiter* and *figuraliter* (the Pharisees are prefigured by Joseph's brothers conspiring against him, that is Christ, Luke 6.11; Gen. 37.18),[32] and the allegories based on etymologies should not delude us into thinking that Bonaventure did not over-ride school tradition. On the contrary, his use of conventional terms and modes covers up a deeply personal approach to the senses; it harmonises with his theories in *De reductione artium* and in his prologue to *Breviloquium*. He put together things which had been separated. The spiritual meaning was one with the literal.

What differentiates him even more from his mendicant predecessors is his reading of Franciscan values into his lecture courses. He refers to the *Legenda* of St. Francis to make his points. St. Francis quoted the psalm *Cast thy care upon the Lord* (54.23) when he sent his disciples to preach; he was afraid to have a piece of skin to cover him when he was ill, lest he might appear to be a wolf in sheep's clothing; the word *daily* in the text *Let him . . . take up his cross daily and follow me* (Luke 9.23) suggests the dying words of St. Francis: 'Let us begin and progress . . .'; just so the penance of the cross must be renewed as a new beginning daily. Brother Giles is quoted in a passage on the seven grades of contemplation; he often experienced ecstasy, though a simpleton in speech.[33] Bonaventure dwells on the Franciscan ideal of humility, not only in commenting on the Nativity, an obvious place, but also on Christ's allowing himself to be baptized by a servant and on his inviting the disciples to follow him. In each case the master submits himself to his servants.[34] We have seen that Bonaventure prefers that one of many

---

[28] 6, 322.
[29] 6, 376.
[30] 7, 473–474.
[31] 7, 47.
[32] 7, 139.
[33] 7, 218; 219; 228; 231. The Quaracchi editors give the references.
[34] 7, 82; 129.

interpretations of Luke 3.16 which refers to the Baptist's humility.[35] Christ chose to heal especially the wretched, despicable and poor.[36] Poverty is stressed wherever the text gives occasion for it; the commentaries might be called 'treatises on gospel poverty in a lecture framework'.

A poor little Mother bore the poor Christ to invite us to poverty.[37] Jesus read from the book of Isaias that the Lord had anointed him *to preach the gospel to the poor* (Luke 4.18); indeed, the poor in especial have poverty preached to them by poor men. Christ was sent to preach to the poor (Luke 4.43).[38] On the first beatitude (Luke 6.20) Bonaventure comments that Christ called the poor *blessed* because they are prepared for blessedness. He said *theirs is the kingdom of heaven* in the present tense either to show the certainty of the promise or because the truly poor have begun to be kings already in some sense. Hence they are happy already, as it were; the evangelical and voluntary poor must not be counted as wretched.[39] Again his words *to the poor the gospel is preached* (Luke 7. 22) was a certain sign of his coming. He said *to the poor*, rather than to the virgins and obedient, because poverty is the basis and summit of gospel perfection. An excellent miracle it was that despised poor men should have the Gospel preached to them as though they were kings.[40] Neither humility nor austerity sufficed for the perfect imitation of Christ; that is why he added to the command to take up the cross *let him follow me* (Luke 9.23), that is, by poverty of the highest kind.[41] He wished his disciples not only to be poor, but to seem so; hence the ban on wearing shoes during their mission (Luke 10.4).[42] The shortage of provisions before the feeding of the multitude signified *mira inopia*, wondrous need (John 6.7–9).[43] Bonaventure deals with some disputed points in the secular versus mendicant conflict, as he did in his *Quaestiones de paupertate* of 1255. The words of the steward *to beg I am ashamed* (Luke 16.3) had been quoted against the friars. Bonaventure explained that the steward spoke as a weakling, who had not received grace to conform perfectly to Christ. Even so, he said *to beg I am ashamed*, not 'to beg I scorn', which would have been detestable blasphemy, not mere weakness. Manual labour, as practised by the Cistercians, and begging, as practised by the friars, are both hard to bear; but Christ makes them easy.[44] The command not to reclaim stolen goods (Luke 6.30) meant that religious who held no property might reclaim it only through those who held it for their use and

---

[35] Above, p. 206.
[36] 6, 373.
[37] 7, 47–48.
[38] 7, 98; 112.
[39] 7, 148.
[40] 7, 175.
[41] 7, 228.
[42] 7, 255.
[43] 6, 319.
[44] 7, 405.

were bound to defend it.[45] Innocent IV had vested property rights, formerly held by 'friends' of the Franciscans, in the papacy in his bull *Ordinem vestrum*, 1245. Bonaventure claimed apostolic authority for this type of poverty from St. Peter's words: *Behold we have left all to follow thee* (Luke 18.28). St. Peter invited others to imitate him; the prince of the apostles, upon whom the Church's authority is built, authorised perfect poverty by its apostolic observance.[46] These examples show Bonaventure's love for Franciscan poverty and his fierceness in its defence.

Special ties bound the friars to the papacy. Bonaventure recognised this when his text suggested it. St. Luke named Herod the king before Zachary the priest (1.5) in order to show that royal rule had precedence over priestly rule in the time of the Old Law; but the reverse is true now.[47] Christ said *it is enough* when shown two swords (Luke 22. 38) to show that the two swords signified the Old and New Testaments, a traditional interpretation, or else that they signified the spiritual and material swords, the latter to be wielded only on the Church's behalf. Bonaventure then quotes the passage from St. Bernard's *De consideratione* which was commonly accepted as subordinating the temporal power to the papacy.[48] He repeats this interpretation with the same quotation from St. Bernard on John 18. 11.[49] He went further than his predecessors had cared to go in standing up for the priority of priest-hood and papal primacy.

As a lecturer on the Gospels Bonaventure can truly be called 'second founder of his Order'. The title has been claimed for him on the grounds of his administration and spiritual guidance;[50] his lectures, when compared with earlier efforts, bring out his commitment to Franciscan values in the schools.

[45] 7, 155.
[46] 7, 465.
[47] 7, 13.
[48] 7, 555; S. Bernardi *Opera* (ed. cit.), 3, 454.
[49] 6, 481.
[50] H. Roggen, 'Saint Bonaventure second fondateur de l'Ordre des Frères Mineurs?', *Études franciscains*, 17 (1967), 66–79.

II. JOHN OF WALES

The Oxford Franciscan John of Wales was a camp-follower of Bonaventure, but original in his own way. John is best known for his preaching aids, the *Communiloquium* and others, with their amazing quantity of quotations, not least from pagan authors, John's admired 'philosophers'.[1] He also left a

[1] A. B. Emden, *A Biographical Register of the University of Oxford to A. D. 1500*, 3 (Oxford, 1959), 1960–1961. My pupil Mrs. Jenny Swanson has written a thesis on John of Wales, with special reference to his preaching aids, now deposited in the Bodleian Library. I am most grateful for the help she has given me.

commentary on St. John's Gospel and *collationes* or evening addresses on selected texts for younger and less learned friars on St. John and on St. Matthew.[2] In theory the collations on St. Matthew should have followed on from a commentary on the First Gospel; no such commentary has come down to us. Data on his career is scanty: he was lector at the Oxford Greyfriars c.1257–1262(?) and was at Paris in 1270 and in 1282, perhaps as regent. He died in 1285(?). He was certainly back in England in 1282, since his archbishop commissioned him to mediate with the Welsh prince Llewelyn on behalf of the English government in the autumn of that year. The fact that he came from Wales or the Welsh border would have made him suitable. Perhaps he interrupted his teaching at Paris for this business. The late '60s and '70s are virtually a blank in our knowledge of his life.

The commentary and collations on St. John have been printed mistakenly under the name of Bonaventure: *Opera* 2 (Rome, 1589), 313–466; 467–504 (*sic, recte* 510). I shall quote them from this edition as 'Bon.'. The collations on St. Matthew are preserved in MS Oxford, Magdalen College 27, fols. 1–90[v], and in MS Valentia Cathedral Library 186 (14th cent.). I have used the Magdalen College manuscript, to be referred to as 'M'. It consists of a number of items bound up together, of unknown provenance. The leaves which concern us are written in an English hand of the late thirteenth century[3] in single columns.

Incipit: *Liber generationis Iesu Christi etc*: tria insinuantur, dignationis filii Dei generandi, id est incarnandi immensitas . . .
Explicit: . . . ad quam perducat ipse qui est vita; qui cum Patre et Spiritu sancto vivit et regnat sublimiter, universaliter, ordinabiliter, perheniter sive eternaliter Amen. Amen.

The scribe was careless; he also left blank spaces where his exemplar was illegible or had gaps; the text is corrupt. A fourteenth-century hand divided it into 103 *Sermones*. The many marginal corrections and notes in different hands show that it was much studied.

The commentary and collations on St. John date from before the collations on St. Matthew, as cross-references indicate.[4] The sources quoted put all three into John's Oxford lectorship, 1257–1262(?). First, he quotes Clement (of Lanthony, died c.1190) on St. Matthew.[5] Clement's

---

[2] Balduinus ab Amsterdam, 'The Commentary on St. John's Gospel edited in 1589 under the name of St. Bonaventure, an authentic work of John of Wales, O. Min. (†ca. 1300)', *Collectanea Franciscana*, 40 (1970), 71–96; F. Stegmüller, *Repertorium Biblicum Medii Aevi* 3 (Madrid, 1951) no. 4514–6; 9, adiuvante N. Reinhardt (1977), pp. 194–195 (to be referred to as RB).
[3] Not 14th cent. as described by H. O. Coxe, *Cat. Cod. MSS qui in collegiis aulisque Oxoniensibus hodie adservantur* 2 (Oxford, 1852), *Coll. Magd.* 18–19.
[4] Balduinus ab Amsterdam, op.cit. 83–86.
[5] M, fol. 11: 'Et de hiis omnibus Clemens, parte 3, cap.xv°': Est corporale ieiunium, cum ex recordatione presentis miserie, ne deterius contingat, a vitiis abstinemus . . . labore reprimamus.'

vast commentary on a gospel harmony was used in England but did not reach the Continent.[6] John's reference cannot be checked since Part 3, which he quoted from, does not survive. Secondly, references to Robert Grosseteste's translation of the Pseudo-Dionysian corpus and his commentaries on it occur in all three of John's works, as I shall show later. The most recent estimate puts Grosseteste's work on Pseudo-Dionysius into four years of his rule as bishop of Lincoln, c.1239–1243. It 'took time to establish itself at Paris; Peter Olivi seems to have been the first prominent Scholastic to have used it,' whereas it was used earlier by John's English Franciscan contemporaries, Roger Bacon, William de la Mare and Thomas of York.[7] Negative evidence comes from the absence of Hugh of St. Cher's postill on St. John. He is quoted once only and that not on St. John, but on Isaias, a passage which John may have picked up from some intermediate source.[8] We have seen that Bonaventure used Hugh on St. John; the whole *postilla* became a standard reference-book in Paris, but was little read in Oxford until the fifteenth century.[9] Further, John expounds at much greater length than was the custom at Paris. Oxford lecturers spread themselves, witness Simon of Hinton and Thomas Docking.[10]

The commentary must have originated as a lecture course. Occasional use of the third person for the master suggests a *reportatio*.[11] John must have revised it himself, however: no student-reporter could have been trusted to take down all the references accurately and John may have made additions to the original.

Bonaventure on St. John was the Oxford friar's *vade mecum*. Their respective dates as lecturers, 1254–1257 and 1257–1262, make it possible that John could have got hold of Bonaventure's commentary in time to use it, given the close connexion between the Paris and Oxford *studia*. Beginning with John's prologue: the section on causes corresponds roughly to Bonaventure's. Both insert *quaestiunculae* into their prologues: John's fourth, sixth and seventh have been lifted from Bonaventure's. Passing to the lectures on the text, we find two consecutive passages with parallels from Bonaventure on John 1.7.[12] John's phrases 'ad hoc respondetur communiter', 'Et ad hoc respondetur magistraliter' introduce

[6] B. Smalley, 'Which William of Nottingham?', *Mediaeval and Renaissance Studies*, 3 (1954), 201–202; reprinted in my *Studies*, op. cit. 250–251.

[7] J. McEvoy, *The Philosophy of Robert Grosseteste* (Oxford, 1982), 69; 89n.

[8] Bon. 478 (*sic, recte* 476): 'De utroque: *Butyrum et mel comedet*, super quod Hugo exponens illud ait: Per butyrum restitutio boni operis, per mel dulcedo contemplationis.' See Hugh of St. Cher on Is. 7.15.

[9] N. R. Ker, 'Oxford College Libraries before 1500', *The Universities in the Late Middle Ages*, ed. J. I. Ijsewijn and J. Paquet (Louvain/The Hague, 1978), 309–311.

[10] B. Smalley, *The Study of the Bible in the Middle Ages*, 3rd ed. (Oxford, 1983), 319–323; J. I. Catto, 'New Light on Thomas Docking O. F. M.', *Mediaeval and Renaissance Studies*, 6 (1968), 135–149.

[11] 'ait ergo' (Bon. 329); 'respondet' (Bon. 330, 331).

[12] Bon. 322; Quaracchi ed. 6, 251

Bonaventure's opinions.[13] John repeats a verse 'Unde versus' quoted by Bonaventure on John 6.26, and the same one, quoted again by Bonaventure on John 7.24.[14] It is the old story: one cannot ascribe anything to John of Wales without first checking whether it comes from his magistral source. A trick of style, too, is common to both when quoting patristic authors: 'Et ideo exclamat Augustinus', 'qui exclamans ait', often repeated of Augustine, correspond to Bonaventure's 'Unde exclamat Chrysostomus', as expressions of empathy with the Fathers.[15]

John may well have been influenced by Bonaventure in his lack of interest in distinguishing between the senses, to be shown later, and in his abstention from attempts to amuse his hearers or readers. He also copied Bonaventure's strongly Franciscan stance. Bonaventure may have inspired him to compose collations as an adjunct to his lecture course, though a comparison with Bonaventure's schematic collations on St. John brought out no resemblance. Indeed, there is a contrast here: Bonaventure did not connect his collations with his commentary, John, writing much longer collations, took care to add cross-references. His commentary and collations correspond, when he refers to a *collatio praedicabilis* on a text, and so do a collation's references back to the commentary. He makes a specific promise to add *collationes* in his prologue to his commentary.

John seems to have been modest about his own contribution. He enumerates his two main patristic sources in his prologue and contrasts their methods. Augustine, principally in his *Tractate* on St. John, expounded some things literally and some allegorically, sometimes pointing to questions on the letter. Chrysostom, as Burgundio of Pisa (transcribed *verbatim*, though not named) wrote in his prologue, expounded the book in homilies to the people gathered together in church; each homily had a prologue and matter pertaining to morals culled from exposition of the text *ad litteram*; he refrained from allegorising throughout.[16] John proposes to bring the two saints together, as well as to add magisterial questions on the literal sense together with exposition of the letter. He does in fact compare and try to harmonise Augustine and Chrysostom or express a preference, as he proceeds through the text, and his explicit summarises what he must have seen as his basic project:

---

[13] Bon. 333; 344; 349; 352; 364; Quaracchi ed. 6, 264; 281; 289; 293; 316. Bon. 326: 'Unde dicunt magistri et bene quod Christus fuit plenus gratia triplici . . .' Quaracchi ed. 6, 255.

[14] Bon. 370; 380; Quaracchi ed. 6, 326; 346.

[15] Bon. 446; 451; 454; Quaracchi ed. 6, 258.

[16] On Burgundio's prologue see above, p. 129. John also alludes to it on John 8.3–11, omission of the episode of the woman taken in adultery (Bon. 384), and on John 6.12: St. John strove to tell the truth of Christ's doctrine rather than to enumerate miracles (Bon. 367).

Et ad praesens haec collecta ex dictis sancti Augustini et ex dictis sancti Chrysostomi super sacrum Evangelium . . . sufficiant.[17]

If John presents himself here as a mere compiler, he was one on a gigantic scale. Not only that, he put much of himself into his commentary and collations.

Two of his aids to study have defeated me. He adds an 'Anselm' to Augustine and Chrysostom as standard commentators in his prologue: 'Anselm expounded the Gospel in places (*alicubi*), as though to abbreviate the words of St. Augustine.' At first I supposed that he meant the Gloss on St. John, compiled by Anselm of Laon and ascribed to him in some copies of the Gloss; but no: John's quotations from Anselm do not come from the Gloss.[18] On the contrary he will sometimes contrast the Gloss to Anselm:

Jesus perrexit in montem Oliveti (John 8.1), ut ait Glossa, et Anselmus planius: Dominus maxime circa passionem suam hanc sibi effecerat consuetudinem, ut in diebus in templo praedicaret et signa ostenderet, sero reverteretur in Bethaniam ubi apud sorores Lazari hospitabatur et mane iterum ad servile opus revertebatur. Cum ergo ultimo die Scenophaegiae praedicasset in templo, vespere perrexit in montem. Haec ille.[19]

The Gloss has only:

Quia mos erat ei die docere in templo, vespere revertere in Bethaniam, quae est in monte Oliveti.

Et sedens docebat eos (John 8.2) quae sessio signabat humilitatem incarnationis, prout ait Glossa, et idem Anselmus: Sessio, inquit, humilitatem incarnationis, per quam misereri nobis dignatus est, insinuat.[20]

The Gloss reads:

Sessio est humilitatem incarnationis qua miseretur et docet.

John must have had some abbreviation of Augustine's *Tractatus* circulating under the name of Anselm; probably Anselm of Laon was meant; the quotations sound unlike anything that St. Anselm of Canterbury would have written and no such work is ascribed to him.

The other puzzle is *quidam expositor*, quoted on John 19.26–27 and 21.19.[21] Could it be the same as Bonaventure's and Alexander's?[22] Since John quotes it on different texts, one cannot answer the question. Irritatingly John gives no exact references to Anselm or to his *expositor*, contrary to his custom when quoting authors.

[17] Bon. 466.
[18] See Bon. 391; 392; 397; 427. Could he mean the commentary ascribed to Anselmus Anglicus in a Bâle manuscript; RB 1349 (Supplement)?
[19] Bon. 383–384.
[20] Bon. 384.
[21] Bon. 453; 466.
[22] Above, pp. 209; 154–155.

His outstanding trait is his habit of quoting in his comments and in his digressions from a multiplicity of sources, as he did in his preaching aids. Bonaventure had strung texts together, but mainly from the Bible; John went further, outstripping any commentator known to me in the range and variety of his sources. Moreover, again as in his preaching aids, he generally gave exact references to book and chapter, where they existed, and added 'near the beginning', 'about the middle' or 'near the end', to help his reader to look them up if he wanted to. The printed edition has them in the margins for the commentary and collations on St. John; the Magdalen manuscript of the collations on St. Matthew has them in the text. Mrs. Swanson has found that his references are nearly always exact in his preaching aids; a spot check of those in his biblical works brought a similar accuracy to light. He takes care to mark the end of a quotation by 'haec ille'. Sometimes he noted the volume of the *Opera* of Augustine or Ambrose: 'Augustinus *in Ps. 108*, tom. 8'; '*Tract. 50 in Ioannem* post medium tom. 9'; '*De natura boni* cap. 32, tom. 6'; 'Ambrosius *Liber de Isaac et anima* cap. 5 ante medium tom. 1'.[23] These volume numbers suggest that he had *Opera* to hand, probably in the Oxford Greyfriars library. They would have helped students at Greyfriars, but would hardly have applied to all copies of all Augustine's or Ambrose's works. Such precision of reference was unusual and underlines John's method.[24]

He sought to capture his public's attention not by diversion, after the manner of the 'biblical-moral school', but by diversity of quotation. A full list of his sources would be out of place here. I shall mention John's favourites and then the rarer, less familiar ones. Augustine easily heads the list. John quotes from the full range of his works, not only from the expected *Tractatus, De verbis Domini in sermone in monte* and *De consensu evangelistarum*: *De civitate Dei* is favourite. The only omission, as far as I can see, is the *Quaestiones* on various biblical books. Pseudo-Augustine, *De spiritu et anima* appears interestingly without ascription to Augustine.[25] St. Jerome's commentaries and letters occur, though less frequently. John knew the three most popular of Ambrose's works: *Hexaemeron*, the commentary on St. Luke and *De officiis*. He also quotes from the lesser known *De fuga saeculi* and *De Isaac vel anima*.[26] St. Gregory approaches most closely to Augustine in number of quotations from the *Moralia, Homilies* on Ezechiel and the Gospels, *De cura pastorali* and *Registrum*. Gregory's exposition of the first book of Kings is omitted;

---

[23] Bon. 351; 409; 450; 381.

[24] A copy of Peter the Chanter on the Psalter, MS Oxford, Bodl. e Mus. 30, SC 3580, has notes in an English-looking hand of the early 13th cent., quoting from *Quaestiones* of an unidentified Magister W. by quire, folio and opening words or paragraph (pp. 5–17). But the annotator was scribbling notes for his own use, while John of Wales wrote for a public.

[25] M, fol .78.

[26] Bon. 329, verified from CSEL 32, 2, 184; Bon. 381, verified from ibid.1, 665.

but John quotes once from Pseudo-Gregory on the Canticle 7.1.[27] Robert of Tomberlain on the Canticle had supplemented or replaced the genuine Gregory on Cant. 1. 1–8 in some manuscripts;[28] John could easily have mistaken it for Gregory. He seems to have quoted from the originals; there is no trace of Paterius, whose excerpts from Gregory proved such a boon to medieval scholars.[29]

Boethius' *De consolatione Philosophiae* keeps recurring, in one place supplemented by an unnamed *expositor*, William of Conches: Boethius chose a woman to personify Philosophy because she softens her own and others' fierceness and knows how to feed with milk and tend the sick.[30] John quotes Pseudo-Boethius, *De disciplina scolarium* in a *distinctio* on wine: too much of it disturbs the reason and leads to ignorance. The *De disciplina*, produced 1230–1240, probably at Paris, was popular in England.[31]

A quotation from 'Maximus in sermone de Nativitate beati Ioannis' has some resemblance to Pseudo-Maximus of Turin, sermon 65, on the same feast:

Sicut sermo vocis quodammodo ministerio et vehiculo ad audientem transmittitur, ita Ioannes Christum sonans, ut verbi minister et portator fuit.[32]

I have not traced a quotation from Pope Leo in his authentic sermons:

Et verbum est quod intra animi silentium mente concipit vox, per quam verbum in medium profertur. Sonus enim, index cognitionis est cognitio verbi [MS verbum], ait Leo papa in sermone de nativitate beati Iohannis.[33]

---

[27] Bon. 329, verified from PL 79, 533.

[28] P. Verbraken, *Sancti Gregorii Expositio in Canticis Canticorum*, CCSL 144, vii–ix.

[29] R. Wasselynck, 'L'influence de l'exégèse de S.Grégoire le Grand sur les commentaires bibliques médiévaux (VIIe–XIIe siècles)', *Recherches de théologie ancienne et médiévale*, 32 (1965), 157–204.

[30] M, fol. 79: 'Unde super prologum Boetii de consolatione dicit expositor quod philosophia describitur in forma mulieris, quia mollit ferocitatem tam suam quam aliorum animorum, quia lacte mulieris ac [*sic*] fovet, quia assidere scit egris.'

Mlle. d'Alverny kindly sent me transcripts of the two versions of William's commentary from MSS, Paris, Bibl. nat. lat. 13334, fols. 45–46^v and 14380, fol. 67 on *mulier* in the prologue. They both correspond roughly with John's quotation; but it is uncertain which version he used. On the popularity of William of Conches as a commentator on Boethius, see P. Courcelle, *La Consolation de Philosophie dans la tradition littéraire* (Paris, 1967), 302–303.

[31] Bon. 471–472; from *De disciplina* ii, 11, ed. O. Weijers (Leiden, 1976), 102 and 7–11.

[32] Bon. 469. See PL 57, 664: 'Se enim dicit esse vocem, quia Verbi annuntiator erat et praedicatator'.

See *Clavis Patrum Latinorum*, ed. E. Dekkers, *Sacris Erudiri* 3, 2nd ed. (1961), 54–56.

[33] M, fol. 6^v.

Cassian rates one entry, a summary of a passage in his *De institutione coenobitarum*.[34] As might be expected, Isidore's *De summo bono* and *Etymologies* appear.[35] There is plenty of Bede on St. Luke both from the original and from the Gloss, but no other of his works.

Of Greek Fathers in Latin translation, Origen had little appeal for John. His quotation from the widely read *Homilies* on Numbers is banal:

. . . ut enim ait Origenes: Cibus verus animae rationalis est sermo Dei.[36]

He alludes to Gregory of Nazianzus, whose work was also current in the West:

Et de hoc bene Gregorius Nazianzenus, ubi ait quod ante passionem et post resurrectionem et post ascensionem adfuit eis Spiritus sanctus. Et ibi bene de hoc.[37]

We have already noted his reliance on Chrysostom. He was unusual in distinguishing him from Pseudo-Chrysostom, *Opus imperfectum* on Matthew, an Arian work written originally in Latin, but supposed to be genuine Chrysostom in translation. John makes two correct references to it.[38] We are not surprised to find many quotations from St. John Damascene's *De fide orthodoxa*.

John's most enterprising efforts centre on the Pseudo-Dionysian corpus. He quotes Grosseteste's translations of *De divinis nominibus*, *De mystica theologia* and the *Celestial* or *Angelic* and the *Ecclesiastical Hierarchies*. His quotations can be checked from Ph. Chevallier's edition.[39] The *Angelic Hierarchy* seems to have had a special fascination for him; he quotes from three commentaries on it. First comes Hugh of St. Victor.[40] Second comes the Victorine, Thomas of Vercelli, referred to as 'the Abbot'. Thomas's commentary is still unprinted; but fortunately one of John's quotations can be verified from an extract printed by J. Châtillon, where Thomas praises St. Antony of Padua. John dedicates one of his collations on St. John to St. Antony, a saint of his Order:

---

[34] Bon.472 (*sic, recte* 480); from *De institutione* v, 21, CSEL 17, 98–99.

[35] M, fols.11; 63ᵛ.

[36] Bon. 472 (*sic, recte* 480); from *Homilia* 27, 1; PG 12, 780.

[37] Bon. 459, from *Oratio iv de Pentecoste et de Spiritu Sancto*, CSEL 46, 154. I have not identified another quotation ascribed to Gregory in a *distinctio* on a ship, Bon. 370: 'Et de gubernatione istarum navium Gregorius Nazianzenus bene, ubi ait: Mos navigantibus est semper caelum intendere, et inde vias sui cursus agnoscere, per diem solis indiciis, in noctibus astrorum signis: sic debet iustus respicere ad solem iustitiae et ad stellas, id est ad exempla sanctorum.'

[38] Bon. 315; PG 56, 612; M, fol. 12ᵛ; PG 56, 675. Fr. J. H. A. van Banning discusses the significance of John's quotations in his thesis on the *Opus imperfectum*.

[39] Bon. 408; 450; 316; 468; 492; see Ph. Chevallier, *Dionysiaca. Recueil donnant l'ensemble des traductions latines des ouvrages attribués à Denys de l'Aréopage* (Bruges, 1937–1950).

[40] Bon. 454; M, fol. 69ᵛ; these can be found in Hugh's commentary, PL 175, 1037.

Ille erat lucerna ardens (John 5.35) . . . istud verbum fuit verificatum in sancto Antonio de ordine fratrum minorum, ut ait commentator, scilicet Abbas: Ideo sibi possit adaptari convenienter. Etenim fervore amoris et ardore devotionis et sublimitate contemplationis ipse fuit illustratus et illuminatus in divinis theoriis et arcanis scripturarum mysteriis, prout ait commentator ibidem.[41]

Grosseteste's commentary is quoted most often. I was able to make a spot check of his quotations of Grosseteste on chapter 15 from Professor James McEvoy's edition in his thesis, kindly lent to me from the University Library, Queen's University of Belfast.[42] I set them out in the order of the *Angelic Hierarchy* text: (1) 'Ut enim ait Commentator scilicet Episcopus super Angelicam Hierarchiam: Homo convenit cum angelis et superat bestias. Est enim intelligibilis, habens virtutes visivas ad superius, et formam erectam et principatum super irascibile et concupiscibile, et minimum habet de sensu respectu brutorum, et superatum in virtute intellectiva. Et sic de aliis quae ibi enumerat' (Bon. 468). This is a summary with some verbal echoes of Grosseteste on *Sed et humaniformis ipsas rescribunt* (McEvoy, 160–162). (2) 'Unde angeli depinguntur discalceati: ubi Commentator scilicet Episcopus: quod hoc in angelis signat dimissum, et facile solubile et irretentibile, et purgativum ab ea, quae exteriorum oppositione, et ad simplicitatem divinam, ut possibile assimulativum. Haec ille' (Bon. 329). A shortened version of Grosseteste on *Nudum autem et discalceatum dimissum* (McEvoy, 179). (3) 'Commentator super angelicam ierarchiam cap xv° quod nubes habet in se occultum lumen et habet naturam luminis [nobis] occultam, ex qua emicant corruscationes ymbrium . . . nascentium' (M, fol. 83). Again a summary with verbal echoes of Grosseteste on *Sed et nubis ipsis speciem* (McEvoy, 199). (4) 'Albedo materialis est lux multa clara et incorporata in perspicuo puro et inter colores est similior luci, ait commentator super angelicam ierarchiam, cap xv' (M, fol. 56). An almost verbal quotation from Grosseteste on *et albis quidem existentibus* (McEvoy, 217). The only quotation which cannot be traced exactly is: 'Super angelicam hierarchiam cap. xv commentator: Est claritate splendidum et calore flammeum, quia eius proprietas splendor et eius calor flammeus. Commentator, ubi supra, unde aurum dicitur ab aura, id est splendore' (M, fol. 5). This might come from a *résumé* of Grosseteste on *Igneum quidem manifestare existimo* (McEvoy, 139; 144).

These quotations are interesting as pointing to the use of Grosseteste's commentary in Oxford not long after his death and as attesting John's capacity to understand and to reproduce a difficult text with an unfamiliar terminology. John may well have known the bishop of Lincoln personally and have learnt from him.

---

[41] Bon. 479; see J. Châtillon, 'Saint Antoine de Padoue et les Victorins', *Le Fonti e la Teologia dei Sermoni Antoniani*, ed. A. Poppi (Padua, 1982), 184.

[42] J. J. McEvoy, *Robert Grosseteste on the Celestial Hierarchy, an edition and translation of his commentary, chapters 10 to 15,* M.A. thesis, 1967.

John used Rabanus Maurus on St. Matthew in the original as well as in the Gloss. St. Anselm's *Monologion, Proslogion, Cur deus homo, De veritate* appear with the derivative *De beatitudine, De similitudinibus* and *Meditationes.* St. Bernard had been a favourite with his predecessors; John outdid them in the number of Bernardine quotations. He was fond of Hugh of St. Victor, quoting not only *De sacramentis* and *Didascalicon*, but Hugh's Ecclesiastes commentary,[43] his *De arrha animae,*[44] *De arca Noe morali*[45] and *De laude caritatis.*[46] Richard of St. Victor stays out in the cold. Perhaps John found the Victorine's mystical theology too exotic for his purpose. Surprisingly he quotes Andrew of St. Victor on Ezechiel in a string of texts to illustrate *in medio*, on Christ's crucifixion between two thieves (Matt.27.38). Among them is Ezech.8.11: *Et Iezonias . . . stabat in medio eorum stantium ante picturas.* John writes:

Iechonias *in medio*, ibi Andreas: Principantium solet esse locus medius, secundum illud poetae: Et celsus medio est aspectus in agmine Caesar [Lucan, *Pharsalia* i, 245].[47]

It is a summary of Andrew's comment, pointing out that 'the midst' is a place of honour, and quoting the same verse from Lucan.[48]

Pagan authors are represented by Aristotle's *Libri naturales* and Pseudo-Aristotle *De vegetabilibus.* The absence of his *Physics* and *Metaphysics* from the list brings out John's lack of interest in philosophy as such. Aristotle is often quoted as *Philosophus* or *Sapiens.* John quotes the *Nicomachean Ethics* from Grosseteste's translation with its 'Commentator' (Grosseteste). Grosseteste's translation of ix, 9, 1169b, 15–20 reads:

Inconveniens autem forte et hoc, solitarium facere beatum . . . Politicum enim homo et convivere aptus natus, et felici utique hoc existit. Que enim natura bona, habet.[49]

John enlarges on the theme of man as a political animal on Caiaphas' prophecy (John 11.50) *ut unus moriatur homo*:

Homo, inquam, socialitate polyticus, benignitate benevolus, largitate munificus, omne virtute magnificus. Talis enim est homo naturaliter et ipse [Christus] multo

---

[43] Bon. 484; PL 175, 180.
[44] Bon. 338; PL 176, 965–966.
[45] Bon. 471; PL 176, 619; M, fol. 57; PL 176, 673.
[46] M, fol. 68; PL 176, 973.
[47] Bon. 451.
[48] Dr Michael Signer kindly verified the quotation from his edition of Andrew on Ezechiel for CCSL, contin. med., not yet in page proof:
   'Dicendo Iezoniam in medio stantium ante picturas stare, principem illorum eum fuisse significat. Is enim principantium et venerabilium virorum locus esse solet iuxta illud: Et celsus medio conspectus in agmine cesar.'
[49] 'Translatio Grosseteste textus purus', ed. R. A. Gautier, *Aristoteles Latinus*, 26, 1–3, fasc. 3 (Leiden, 1972), 337; 'Recensio recognita', ibid. fasc. 4 (1973), *ad loc.*

magis. Ut enim ait Commentator: Homo est animal polyticum, non solitarium, et communicativum.[50]

He quotes the same text of the *Ethics* on Matt. 12.35: *bonus homo*, with another reference to the Commentator:

. . . Commentator: Est ad futura creatus. Homo enim [est] creatus ut Deo placeat et ut futuris fruetur.[51]

A full edition of Grosseteste's commentary on the *Ethics* is being prepared, but is not yet ready for press.[52]

Arabic and Jewish sources appear occasionally. There are some four quotations from Avicenna's *De anima*, on prudence and discretion as the qualities proper to man, on Matt. 12. 35, and on the trouble which darkness causes to the mind.[53] John also quoted his *De medicina* on the healing properties of metals and ointments on the gifts of the Magi, and on sulphurous, muddy and turgid waters as the cause of fevers on John 4.52.[54] Pseudo-Isaac [Israeli] gives a medical account of a woman's issue of blood, on Matt. 9.20–22.[55] So John shows traces of the interest in natural science which marked Oxford scholars in the thirteenth century.

Latin classical poets are quoted sparingly. I noted only one from Virgil, *Aen.* 4, 449, and one from Juvenal, *Sat.* 8, 269–271.[56] Latin classical prose writers have a larger share. John admired Vegetius for recommending humility before a prince, who must be allowed to know better:

---

[50] Bon. 490. 'Aristoteles over de Vriendschap Boeken VIII en IX van de Nicomachische Ethiek met de commentaren van Aspasius en Michaël in de Latijnse vertaling van Grosseteste', ed. W. Stinissen (*Verhandeligen van de Koninklijke Vlaamse Academie voor Wetenschappen, Letteren en Schone Kunsten va Belgie*, kl. der Letteren, 45, 1963), 153.

[51] M, fol. 48. Mrs. Swanson has found another reference to this text and its Commentator (*Communiloquium*, Pars 2, Dist. 8, cap. 1) on man as a social animal. She points out that in all three cases John would have been writing before the *Politics* with Aquinas' commentary became available. It would have interested him and he does quote it in a later book.

[52] McEvoy, *The Philosophy of Robert Grosseteste*, op. cit. 473–474.

[53] M, fol. 48; Bon. 467; see *Avicenna Latinus Liber de Anima* 1–3, ed. S. Van Riet (Louvain, 1972), 130–132; 4–5, ibid. (1968), 17. I have not traced the other two, M, fols. 9ᵛ; 68.

[54] Bon. 358; see Avicenna, *Canon Medicinae*, Lib. II, tract. ii, cap. 59.

[55] M, fol. 35ᵛ; see the *Viaticum* printed in *Omnia Opera Isaac* (Lyons, 1515), Lib. VI, cap. 10; the *Viaticum*, really the work of ibn al-Jazzar, was usually attributed to Isaac or to the translator, Constantinus Africanus. I am most grateful to Mr. Charles Burnett and Mlle. Danielle Jacquart for identifying this and the previous quotation.

[56] Bon. 423; 389.

Ideo ait ille nobilis, scilicet Flavius Vegatus: Neque quemquam [magis] decet, vel meliora scire, vel plura quam principem, cuius doctrina omnibus potest prodesse subiectis.[57]

In only one case does John quote through an intermediary, John of Salisbury's *Policraticus*, for Apuleius *De deo Socratis*.[58] Cicero's *De amicitia*, *De divinatione*, *De finibus*, *De officiis*, *De natura deorum*, *De senectute* and *Tusculanae Quaestiones* are all quoted. Seneca leads by a long head in this group. John summarises his *Naturales Quaestiones* on the twelve causes of earthquakes on Matt. 27. 51.[59] Copious quotations from his *Epistolae morales* include some of the less widely distributed part of the collection, 89–124,[60] and the rare *De consolatione ad Marciam*.[61] John took from Aulus Gellius, *Noctes atticae*, another fairly rare author, the opinion of a philosopher who held that babies breast-fed by their own mothers were healthier than those put out to nurse.[62] Macrobius *De somnio Scipionis* supplies a comment on prophetic dreams.[63]

There is one local legend concerning Glastonbury abbey; John writes apropos Joseph of Arimathea:

Concerning him it is read in an old book that he was sent to Greater Britain with others, and is said to be buried in an old monastery called Glastonbury, where Arthur is buried too.[64]

The supposed body of King Arthur was exhumed at Glastonbury in 1191; the legend that Joseph of Arimathea was buried there dates from the mid-thirteenth century, not long before John of Wales was writing.[65]

His quotations are the result of thirteenth-century efforts to make texts available by way of concordances, tables, indexes and *distinctiones*. John would have had a team of friar helpers. Even so his industry, ingenuity and accuracy in making his lists amaze. 'What was it all for?' a reader may well ask. Certainly it did not serve exegesis as such: the quotations clog the exposition of the text and often have little, if any, relevance to it. Further,

[57] Bon. 344; *Epitoma rei militaris*, preface (Teubner ed. C. Lang, Leipzig, 1885, 4).

[58] M, fol. 72ᵛ: '. . . sicut recitat Policraticus lib. 6, in fine'. See *Policraticus*, ed. C. C. I. Webb, 2 (Oxford, 1909), 83. John's reference is exact.

[59] M, fol. 86ᵛ; vi, 5–16 (Teubner ed. A. Gercke, Stuttgart, 1970, 200–214).

[60] Bon. 479. John quotes *Ep.* 108 and *Ep.* 110 correctly.

[61] Bon. 340: 'Coram enim Catonem nullus est ausurus peccare, ait Seneca.' The reference, 'De Consolatione ad Marciam c.20 circa med.', is given correctly in the margin; see *Dialogi* VI, xx, 6 (Teubner ed. L. Hermes, Leipzig, 1905, 183). Mrs. Swanson examines the problems arising from these and the following quotations from works not easily available everywhere at the time.

[62] Bon. 481, with correct marginal reference to 'lib. 12, cap. 1'.

[63] Bon. 408, again with correct reference 'lib. 1, cap. 3 post medium'; see Teubner ed. (J. Willis, Leipzig, 1970), 11–12.

[64] Bon. 455.

[65] A Gransden, 'The Growth of the Glastonbury Traditions and Legends in the Twelfth Century', *Journal of Ecclesiastical History*, 27 (1976), 349–358.

they get in the way of any attempt to distinguish between the senses, since some quotations could be applied equally well to literal or spiritual. John knew the difference, but did not give it much consideration. My tentative answer to the question would be that he had the preacher's needs in mind, as he had in his preaching aids. A man who needed to preach on a particular gospel text could find a choice of quotations to help him develop his theme, by this time far removed from any straightforward exposition of the texts cited in theme or pro-theme. John sometimes follows the school practice of suggesting a sermon for a named type of audience in his commentary, as 'for St. Andrew's day', 'to religious' or 'for the election of prelates'.[66] He does the same in taking an occasional swipe at bad teachers, at ecclesiastics and religious who pride themselves on holding high office and doing good works, at heretics who suffer burning, but are not true martyrs, and at the error of the Greeks who say that the Holy Spirit does not proceed from the Father and the Son.[67]

Yet a personality shines through chinks in the conventional, borrowed matter and the appended quotations. He could be more down-to-earth than Bonaventure. On the miracle at Cana Chrysostom explained that the host had kept his inferior wine to the last, because by that time the guests would have been too drunk to notice. How then did God's son come to be present at a drinking bout? John adds to the stock answer, that Christ condescended to sinners, by adding that the Galileans were fishermen and countryfolk; hence it must be supposed that they got drunk rather from being unused to strong drink, or from drinking too fast or from ignorance of the effects of wine than from eagerness to drink too much. Typically John goes on to list three kinds of drunkenness and to classify them according to their degrees of sin.[68]

He went further than Bonaventure in his more polemical defence of gospel poverty of the Franciscan type. He denies time and again that Christ and the apostles owned anything. When their having money is mentioned, it was given to them as alms; they had nothing of their own; God's son was a beggar.[69] Holy women went round with them, ministering to them, which would account for Philip's implication that they had money to buy food (John 6.7);[70] Christ had no house of his own, but lodged with Lazarus' sisters (John 8.1).[71] Bonaventure had confuted 'the false opinion' that Christ's seamless robe was silken;[72] John repeats his argument that if it had been, Christ would not have been mocked by being clad in silk, and adds a second: the soldiers

---

[66] Bon. 333; 389; 430.
[67] Bon. 365–366; 389; 420; 432.
[68] Bon. 338; see below, pp. 232–233.
[69] Bon. 351.
[70] Bon. 368.
[71] Bon. 383–384, partly derived from Bonaventure, 6, 353; see above p. 217.
[72] *Expositio in Regulam*, Quaracchi ed. 8, 402–405. This was a common theme in polemic; see D. L. Douie, *Archbishop Pecham* (Oxford, 1952), 29.

would have sold it and divided the money between them instead of casting lots.[73] Joseph of Arimathea, a rich man, was converted later.[74] On the Franciscan practice of wearing sandals instead of going barefoot John borrows arguments wholesale from Bonaventure's *Apologia pauperum*. This is dated 1269; John may have added it later or else have seen some early draft or had advance knowledge of the gist. He took even more from the undated spurious *Epistola de sandalis apostolorum*.[75] Praise of Christ's poverty and exhortation to imitate its perfection is a constant theme; even the philosophers chose poverty and poor companions, the better to study philosophy; the Baptist's nakedness marked a return to man's pristine nobility in paradise, before the fall, a theme dear to the heart of an Order whose founder was believed to have returned to that blessed state.[76] One of the collations, on John 21. 18, is dedicated to St. Francis and another to St. Antony of Padua.[77]

Like Bonaventure John was a loyal papalist. It came naturally to him to cite 'the pope in the midst of his cardinals for all governance of all men', as an example of 'the midst's' being the place for the highest, and to compare the Baptist, sent by God, to a papal legate.[78] In a *quaestio* on the remission of sins (John 20.22) he seems to give the whole authority of the keys to the pope, delegated to him by God, and delegating it to those under him.[79] On the other hand, he held back on questions concerning the relationship between the temporal and spiritual powers, as we might expect of a friar thought suitable for royal government service. He omits the sword text from his collations on St. Matthew and St. John. In his commentary on St. John he quotes Chrysostom to the effect that St. Peter had a sword because he was not yet perfect, and goes on to make him signify the prelate, who ought to draw the sword of the divine words from Scripture, signified by the sheath.[80]

Though the whole effect is of artificiality, redeemed by personal Franciscan notes, John was capable of a piece of glowing devotion. One of his collations, on *consummatum est* (John 19.30), Christ's last words on the cross, dispenses with a rigid schemata and brings together Old and New Testaments and the present. The words, short and plain, but containing deep mysteries, teach that the saving immolation of God's Son was indeed the consummation of the sacrifices of the Old Law, of the deeds and martyrdoms of the prophets and of the mysteries of Scripture. Again this

---

[73] Bon. 451–452.

[74] Bon. 455.

[75] On John 1.27, Bon. 329; see parallels in Quaracchi ed. 8, 306–307; 386–390.

[76] Bon. 451; M, fols. 2; 12ᵛ; 14ᵛ; 43.

[77] Bon. 504 (*sic, recte* 510); 479.

[78] Bon. 460; 468.

[79] Bon. 460. This *quaestio* is not taken from Bonaventure. Another on a theological point, whether charity in a man can be greater or less (John 15. 13), is also John's own, as is indicated by his: 'et ad istud respondendum sine praeiudicio', Bon. 430.

[80] Bon. 443–444.

saving passion was the consummation of all passion. John recounts Christ's passion: he toiled from his youth onwards; it was universal, since his whole body was stretched out on the cross; it was intensified by his good health and strength; it was greater than any other by reason of ignominy before and after, as is plain to one who considers its stages. It consummated all his works on earth; it perfected his teaching. Similarly we must consummate the passage of our lives by perseverance in doing his will. The supporting texts here are not set out for display, but are really woven into the texture of the collation. It gives us the measure of John's capacity as a devout preacher.[81]

A gulf separates Bonaventure and John of Wales from the 'pre-war' generation of friar doctors. Anti-mendicant polemic sharpened their self-awareness and led them to infuse into their gospel commentaries and collations the spirit of St. Francis, if not as his first companions understood it, at least as it was perceived by university friars. Instead of imitating the 'biblical-moral school', they defended themselves and met attacks from the seculars by counter-attacks. The change of content appears even more striking in that it comes through to us despite increasing artifice in dividing the text and despite floods of quotations, mainly from Scripture in Bonaventure's case, from any and everywhere in John's. The latter also shows how soon and how pervasively Bonaventure's influence spread to Oxford. On the other hand, the two of them mark a step backward in school exegesis. Though aware of distinction between the literal and spiritual senses, they played it down: either the evangelist intended all edifying meanings, or the spiritual sense included all that edified. Would their successors pursue their positive aim and at the same time take a more scientific approach to the senses?

[81] Bon. 506–501 (*sic, recte* 507).

III. JOHN PECHAM

Pecham was the third and last of the Oxford/Paris Franciscan friar doctors to leave a surviving commentary on the fourth Gospel. Its form labels it as a lecture course, although I have found no signs that it was a *reportatio* rather than the master's own notes. He is best known as a religious poet, as a scientist and mathematician, as a defender of the mendicants against the seculars, as a doughty opponent of the doctrine of the plurality of forms, and finally as a would-be reforming but frustrated archbishop of Canterbury.[1] His exegetical works have received much less attention. The late Professor

[1] Decima L. Douie, *Archbishop Pecham* (Oxford, 1952); Emden, op. cit. 3, 1445–1447. For a recent account of the philosophical discussion, see *Expositionis D. Thomae Aquinatis in libros Aristotelis. De Generatione et Corruptione continuatio per Thomam de Sutona*, ed. F. E. Kelley (Bayerische Akademie der Wissenschaften, 6, 1976), 1–45.

F. Stegmüller edited the prologues to St. John and the commentary on 1.1–5.[2] I printed two lone quotations from the Cambridge Franciscan John Russel's exposition of the Canticle; Pecham is said to have lectured on this book at the papal Curia.[3]

Stegmüller used only MS Schaffhausen, Ministerial-Bibliothek 84, although he also mentioned MS Prague Kapitel A 108 and a Bruges MS. The latter is by Nicholas of Lyre, not Pecham. There is another genuine copy at Casale Monferrato, Seminario C 14, according to the Supplement to the *Repertorium Biblicum* (no.4852). I have read Pecham on St. John in a microfilm of the Schaffhausen copy. The hand is late thirteenth to early fourteenth century, perhaps French. Many marginal glosses have been added, some by nearly contemporary hands, others later. The volume belonged to the Swiss Benedictine abbey, All Souls, near Schaffhausen.[4] We do not know how or when it got to All Souls, since no late medieval library catalogue survives. I quote from a microfilm of it, unless otherwise noted, and Stegmüller's edition as far as it goes. The microfilm is so blurred as to be illegible in many places; hence I am conscious of having done the author less than justice.

Given the dates of Pecham's teaching as a friar doctor, we have three options for his commentary: his Paris lectorship 1269–1271 (he studied arts at Oxford and theology at Paris); his lectorship at Oxford c.1272–1275, and at the papal Curia on the invitation of John XXI 1277–1279. Pecham acted as Provincial of the English Franciscans 1275–1277 and was provided to the see of Canterbury in 1279; he died as archbishop in 1292.[5] Stegmüller decided on the Paris lectorship and with reason. We know that his commentary on the Canticle dates from his two years at the Curia; so we should probably have been told that his lectures on St. John were given there too, if they had been. Proof that he wrote out of England appears in the fact that he never quoted Pseudo-Dionysius in Grosseteste's translation, as did John of Wales. Of his two quotations the first seems to come from Erigena's: 'forma aquilae . . . contemplativum' (ed.Stegmüller, 401),[6] the second from John Saracen's:

Unde Dionysius ecclesiastice yerarchie 1.c[ap?]: deificantur qui salvantur. Deificatio autem est ad Deum, ut est possibile, unitio. Universe autem ierarchie finis est ad divinam intentam dilectionem. Hoc Dionysius (fol.106rbon 17.3).[7]

---

[2] 'Der Johanneskommentar des Johannes Peckam O.M.', *Franziskanische Studien*, 31 (1949), 396–414.

[3] D. L. Douie, op. cit. 43; B. Smalley, 'John Russel O.F.M.', *Recherches de Théologie ancienne et médiévale*, 23 (1956), 294–295.

[4] See L. H. Cottineau, *Répertoire topo-bibliographique des Abbayes et Prieurés*, 2 (Mâcon, 1937), 2973–2974.

[5] See above, n.1.

[6] ed. Chevallier, op. cit. 2, 1026–1027.

[7] ibid. 1090–1091.

H. F. Dondaine has shown that John Saracen's translation superseded Erigena's only gradually in the Paris schools. Hence it is not surprising that Pecham used Erigena's near the beginning of his commentary and Saracen's later.[8] He quotes no commentary on Pseudo-Dionysius here, although he did quote from one on the *Angelic Hierarchy* in a Paris collation. It is not Grosseteste's.[9] Hence we are left with the Paris period, 1269–1271. The commentary fits easily into the Paris type, except that Pecham had caught the English habit of discursiveness, as opposed to the brief and brisk method of Bonaventure. Nor does he bunch his *quaestiones* neatly together, as Bonaventure does. In that he resembles John of Wales. Like the latter, too, he has no scruples about the relationship between the senses, seeing no need to make the spiritual inhere in the literal. In the absence of any signs of a *reportatio* we must suppose that the lecture course represents the master's own version.

A search for his major source ran into problems. Stegmüller observed that if Pecham had read Bonaventure, he also added much of his own. To that may be added 'if he had also read John of Wales'. In fact a collation of John 1.1–5 in Stegmüller's edition with Bonaventure and John of Wales shows no verbal borrowing from either, not even from their quotations from Chrysostom. Of some twenty quotations from Chrysostom in Pecham on the whole first chapter, only one could be found cited by his two predecessors. Later on, however, there is clear evidence that he consulted both, though without naming either. Bonaventure on St. John could hardly have been excluded by a friar teaching at the Paris *studium*; John of Wales had it at Oxford. The Oxford friar comes less expectedly. It occurred to me that it might have been John of Wales quoting Pecham instead of *vice versa*. Collation of similar passages suggested rather that Pecham was using and tidying up John of Wales. John's book was the earlier, if it is rightly assigned to Oxford, 1257–c.1262 or even rather later. The links between Paris and Oxford were close enough for it to have crossed the Channel. Further, Pecham knew John of Wales well enough to send him as an envoy to the Welsh prince Llewelyn twice in 1280 in the archbishop's attempt to mediate between Llewelyn and Edward I.[10] The two friars would have met at the Oxford convent, perhaps as early as Pecham's novitiate there; he entered the Order between 1250 and 1259. In any case, he used the two commentators directly and independently of each other. For instance on the baptism of St. John Baptist Pecham divides the power to baptize into

---

[8] H. F. Dondaine, *Le Corpus dionysien de l'Université de Paris au XIIIᵉ siècle* (Rome, 1953), 114–115. The author is mistaken in stating that Pecham *always* used Saracen's translation, since he did not know of this exception to the rule.

[9] Decima Douie, 'Archbishop Pecham's Sermons and Collations', *Studies in Medieval History presented to F. M. Powicke*, ed. R. W. Hunt, W. A. Pantin, R. W. Southern (Oxford, 1948), 277.

[10] Douie, *Archbishop Pecham*, op. cit. 238–248.

five parts (fol.13va) according to Bonaventure's fivefold division (*Opera* 6, 261). This did not occur in John of Wales. On St. John Baptist's recognition of Christ, 1.34, John of Wales quotes a view ascribed to *quidam*:

Vel aliter, ut quidam aiunt, neque omnes consideraverunt . . . sed solum Johannes . . . (Bon.331).

Pecham copied the view almost *verbatim*:

Quidam dicunt non omnes eos considerasse, sed solum Iohannem . . . (fol.14rb).

This did not occur in Bonaventure. The most interesting parallel is on Joseph of Arimathea. John of Wales, as we have seen, brought up the Glastonbury legend:[11]

Et de isto legitur in antiqua historia, quod fuit missus in Britanniam maiorem cum aliis, et dicitur esse sepultus in antiquo monasterio, nomine Glastimbriae, in quo et Arturus est sepultus (Bon.455).

In Pecham this becomes:

Unde missus est in Angliam, tunc in [?] Germaniam et sepultus dicitur in monasterio quodam antiquissimo dicto Glastenburch (fol.121ra).

Pecham omits Arthur from the legend. The 'tunc in [?] Germaniam' may be an interpolation; there is no evidence that Joseph went on to evangelise Germany in the literature on his cult. Bonaventure makes no mention of the story. Pecham mentioned it, but pruned off an extravagance in John of Wales.

Two examples of parallel passages in John of Wales and Pecham will show how both start off from a short statement of Bonaventure, their common source, and then go off each on his own, though in the first case there is some identity of wording.

The first question concerns the miracle of water turned to wine at the wedding feast at Cana. The chief steward said to the bridegroom: *Every man at first setteth forth good wine, and when men have well drunk, then that which is worse* (2.10). It appears from this that the guests were already drunk, and so unable to distinguish good wine from bad. Bonaventure contents himself with a stricture: 'that was a bad habit, since it contravened truth and sobriety'; he quotes St. Paul: *And be not drunk with wine, wherein is luxury* (Ephes. 5.18); Pecham enlarges on this. Both he and John of Wales trace the statement that the guests were drunk to Chrysostom; hence the problem poses itself to them both: how did Christ come to mix with drunkards, against the saying of Proverbs: *Be not in the feasts of great drinkers*? Pecham answers this question by explaining that the wedding feast was for poor shepherds unaccustomed to strong drink. They must have

[11] Above, p. 224.

sinned rather from weakness than from bad habit; although they got drunk here, it does not follow that they were habitual drunkards, just as Noe got drunk from ignorance. He goes on to ask whether they sinned mortally. John of Wales adds to his first question a slightly different one, whether drunkenness is always sinful and in what case it is sinful and in what case it is excusable. He answers the first by saying that Christ deigned to eat and drink with them so as to cure them: *They that are in health need not a physician*. An argument similar to Pecham's follows, differently worded: the guests were poor fishermen and countrymen, who got drunk rather through inexperience and haste than through desire to get drunk (*ex studio bibendi*). Both commentators go on to give the same answer to the second question on whether drunkenness is a mortal sin (Pecham), or whether it is always a sin (John of Wales). There are three stages of drunkenness: the first fuddles the reason; the second impedes or disturbs tongue and members (Pecham) or members and heart (John of Wales); the third overcomes the reason totally and impedes the whole body. Both classify the first stage as venial sin except perhaps when the occasion requires total abstinence, as when the priests of the Old Law went into the tabernacle. Pecham adds the Gloss on the Leviticus text forbidding drink on such an occasion: the Church observes this precept up to this very day. John of Wales classifies the second stage as dangerous, quoting St. Luke: *Let not your hearts be overcome with surfeiting and drunkenness*. Pecham also allows that the second stage, from natural weakness, is not mortal sin either, unless the third stage follows. Both Johns agree that the third stage is mortal sin. Both cite the Gloss on Leviticus 10. 9, defining drunkenness, though John of Wales does not name it and Pecham does. John of Wales calls it mortal sin as such, if the sinner knowingly seeks to get drunk, and quotes two texts against heavy drinking. Pecham softens his classification of the third stage as mortal sin. It is excusable if someone maliciously makes another drunk, or if it is recommended for medical reasons. Heedlessness and weakness excuse, but not if drinking has become habitual, since habit teaches the danger, which would be unknown otherwise.

Our two commentators depart from Bonaventure's brief statement to ask much the same questions and to give much the same answers. But they quote different texts in some places, do not follow the same sequence in all their arguments, and expand or compress at different points. My overall impression is that Pecham has taken the gist from John of Wales, has put it into more logical order, and has slightly expanded it so as to make it more comprehensible.

BONAVENTURE, *Opera* 6, 270: . . . *id quod deterius est*, quia tunc non valent diiudicare, sed omne vinum dicunt bonum . . . Malus mos erat iste, quia contra veritatem et contra sobrietatem; unde ad Ephes.quinto [18]: *Nolite inebriari vino, in quo est luxuria* . . .

PECHAM, fol.23ra
Item ad commendationem prudentie et

JOHN OF WALES, 338
Quaerunt aliqui hic, ex quo nonnulli
convivantes in his nuptiis fuerunt ebrii,
ut ait Chrisostomus: qualiter filius Dei
fuit cum eis in convivio, cum dicatur:
Noli esse in convivio potatorum?

Item quaeritur tum etiam an
ebrietas semper sit peccatum, et in quo
casu est peccatum et in quo
excusabile. Et ad primum respondendum, ut supra, quod Christus dignatus est
comedere cum eis et bibere, ut sanaret
eos, quoniam *non est opus valentibus
medicus* [Mt. 9. 12]. Et quia in Cana
Galilaeae erant piscatores et homines
rusticani, ideo credendum est eos magis
fuisse ebrios ex desuetudine bibendi
vinum, vel ex praecipitatione, vel ex
infirmitate, vel ex ignorantia virtutis
vini, quam ex studio bibendi. Ad aliud
respondetur consequenter quod in
ebrietate sunt tres gradus, sumendo
eam large. Prima enim ebrietas est
ad rationis aliqualem obnubilationem.
Secunda est ad organorum et cordis
aggravationem et disturbationem.
Tertia est ad rationis subversionem et
membrorum et organorum ligationem.
Prima dicitur esse venialis, nisi forte
ratione circumstantiae ex parte personae
vel officii vel temporis, sicut in
sacerdotibus legalibus tempore sui
officii, ubi cum prohibetur sacerdotibus
bibere vinum, tempore quo debebant
intrare tabernaculum testimonii.

circumspectionis dicit: *cum inebriati
fuerint*. Si inebriari contingat, tunc *id
quod deterius est*, quia remedium est
ebrietatis vinum debilius, quia etiam
augmentari posset periculose ebrietas,
nisi potio peccatum vitaretur. Sed tunc
videtur quod isti fuerint ebriosi et
videtur innuere Cristostomus quod ad
litteram fuerunt ebrii.[12] Ergo fecit
Dominus contra illud preceptum Prov.
23 [20]: *Noli esse in convivio potatorum*.
Respondeo quod nuptie pauperum
erant, id est pastorum, et credibile est
eos magis ex infirmitate peccasse quam
ex prava consuetudine. Unde et licet
ebrii fuerint, non tamen sequitur quod
ebriosi, quia pauperes erant et infirmitate et ignorantia peccaverunt, sicut
Noe, de cuius ebrietate legitur Gen. 9
[21] quod *bibens vinum inebriatus est*.
    Sed queritur si peccaverunt mortaliter.

Respondeo: ebrietas
tres habet gradus.
Prima pervenit ad rationis
obnubilationem, secunda ad lingue et
organorum disturbationem, tertia ad
plenam rationis subversionem et corporis omnimodo impedimentum. Prima
est veniale, ut credo, nisi sit in casu in
quo exigitur rationis perfecta serenitas,
Levit. 10[9]: *Vinum et omne quod
inebriare potest non bibetis tu et filii tui*
etc. Hic dicit glosa: Usque hodie in
ecclesia servari moderate utendo vino
[*sic*].[13]

[12] PG 59, 135: '. . . nam quod ebrii essent, ipse architriclinus declaravit . . . Non
enim convivas ait de re illa sententiam tulisse, sed architriclinum, qui sobrius adhuc
nihil gustaverat.'

[13] Gloss on Lev. 10. 9: 'Usque nunc hanc legem ecclesia custodit. Neque enim
omnino a vino abstinere praecepit, sed quando ad tabernaculum testimonii . . .'

Ebrietas vero secundo modo est periculosa, propter quod ait Salvator: *Non graventur corda vestra crapula et ebrietate* [Lc. 21.34].
Tertia vero, quae sobrietatem subvertit, mentem pervertit, ut non intelligat quae agit, videtur esse

mortale peccatum, quantum est de se, si scienter et studiose se quis inebriaverit, et inebrietantibus isto modo comminatur scriptura poenam aeternam. *Cui vae? Cuius patri vae* etc? *Nonne his qui commorantur in vino?* [Prov. 23.29–30] Et: *Vae qui potentes estis ad bibendum vinum* etc [Isa. 5.22].

Sed in genus ebrietatis secunda in lingua . . . ex infirmitate naturali [est]. Unde nec hoc mortale est, nisi [sequitur?]
tertia, scilicet mentis subversio et iudicii, unde in illa glosa Levitici dicitur ebrietas sobrietatem subvertit, mentem pervertit, ut non intelligat que ait.[14]
Ergo hec ignorantia ex genere est peccatum mortale.

Si tamen quis inebriat alium ignorantem per malitiam et etiam si propter medicinam indicetur necesse ut inebrietur, adhibita cautela necessaria, non peccatum mortale [est]. Si autem aliquis illectus ex inconsideratione et ex infirmitate sic inebrietur per ignorantiam, excusari posset a peccato sceleris, sed non si consuetus facit. Consuetudo docet periculum, quod aliter scire non potest a quolibet.

The second example concerns St. Augustine's treatment of the last verses of the Gospel, 19–25. Briefly put, he compared the relations of St. Peter and St. John to Jesus. It can be shown from 'many documents' that St. Peter loved him more than did any other of the disciples, yet it is clear too that Jesus loved John more than he loved Peter. If we ask which of the two disciples was better, we must answer: 'he who loved Jesus more', although, if we put the question the other way round, we must answer 'he who was more loved by Jesus'. Augustine gave his own opinion, 'as far as I know': he who had more love for Jesus was the better; he whom Jesus loved more was the happier. He works out a figurative interpretation of the comparison, which illustrates the open mercy of God whose justice is hidden. Peter, foundation of the Church and receiver of the keys, figures her active life in her wretched pilgrimage through time. John figures that other blessed and immortal life hereafter, the reward of contemplation. Let Peter love Jesus so as to free us from our present mortality; let John be loved by him so that we may be kept safe in later immortality.[15]

Bonaventure schematises the passage as *quaestio* no. 4 in his exposition of 21.20. First, since Christ loved all his disciples, why did John claim for himself that he was the more loved? It seems false, because Peter loved

---

[14] Gloss on Lev. 10. 9: 'Ebrietas quoque sobrietatem subvertit, mentem pervertit, ut non intelligat quae agit.'
[15] *In Iohannis Evangelium Tractatus* cxxiv, 4 (CCSL 36, 682–683).

more; therefore he was the better; but God loves better men more. Therefore he loved Peter more than John. To this it may be replied that John knew himself to be loved by revelation or by certain signs. Secondly, Augustine seems to say that John was loved more, but that Peter loved more. Hence he asks which of them was the better, and says that Peter was the better, but John the happier; he turns (*retorquet*) these words into an allegory, saying that the contemplative life is signified by John, the active by Peter. 'But this only enlarges the question' (an unacknowledged quotation from Augustine). Augustine himself says that here justice is hidden and mercy appears. Bonaventure finds his answer in a scholastic distinction. There are two ways of loving more, one in giving greater reward, as Jesus loved Peter more, on the understanding that Peter always had the more love for the Lord; the other way of loving more relates to its greater outward showing. The Lord showed more signs of love to John, and so loved him more.[16]

John of Wales anticipates Bonaventure's first question, 'how did John know that Jesus loved him more?', by setting out John's 'privileges' at length. Then he adapts and expands Bonaventure on the second question: God's son should have loved more him who loved him the more, hence he should have loved Peter more than John. John of Wales accepts Bonaventure's solution, but refines on it, quoting a distinction from St. Bernard (unspecified) between *affectus* and *effectus*, which corresponds to the contrast between *in via* and *in patria*.[17] He then distinguishes, not between these two states, but between love shown *in via* as regards substantial reward, in which respect Christ loved Peter more, if he was the better, and what was made known *in via*, such as revealing of secrets, intimacy in speaking, and special actions or honours. According to the Gloss here, Jesus loved them all, but John more intimately (*familiarius*) as the virgin of his choice.[18] Or it is said that he loved John more in respect of the mode of death, allowing him to die in peace rather than in passion.[19] That answers objections, but Augustine expounds it of the two lives, Peter figuring the active, John the contemplative. Christ loves us less as we now are; hence he frees us from being forever as we are now, hence loving us more abundantly.[20] John of Wales betrays a personal preference for St. John by dwelling on his special place among the disciples, though he says nothing to prejudice St. Peter's primacy.

John Pecham quotes from Augustine in the original, as neither Bonaventure nor John of Wales had done. Certain it is that the happiness of

---

[16] *Opera* 6, 528.

[17] The only distinction between *effectus* and *affectus* that I can find in Bernard is in Sermo 29, *De diligendo Deo*, *Opera* 3, 211: 'Videns enim Deus homines omnino carnales effectos, tantam eis dulcedinem exhibuit in carne, ut durissimi cordis sit quisquis eum toto affectu non diligat.'

[18] Gloss on 21.20.

[19] Gloss, ibid.

[20] Bon. 465–466.

which St. Augustine speaks can refer to none other than that of life eternal. The Gloss says that it is doubtful which of the two disciples he loved the more after the descent of the Holy Spirit.[21] This and other like authorities must be referred to that time (that is to the converse between Jesus and the two disciples after his resurrection). But, Pecham objects, John lived for a long time afterwards and garnered many merits for himself. Further, it seems from the sequel that the questioning of Peter (whether he loved Jesus) and not of John did not advantage Peter. Hence it is added: *Peter turning about saw that disciple whom Jesus loved following.* This text shows that Jesus was not speaking to all his disciples, but to these two only. Pecham now felt himself to be on dangerous ground. He may have thought that John of Wales favoured St. John to the detriment of St. Peter. His exposition ends with the comment that nothing should be asserted rashly:

God forbid that I should presume to define anything concerning the primacy of St. Peter. If anyone should wish to uphold the contrary, it is easy to reply to his objections.

The Latin of the passage is compressed. In transcribing it I have put the quotes directly from Augustine in quotation marks.

Hoc videtur sentire Augustinus, dicens quod apostolus Petrus plus aliis dilexerit Christum, 'possunt documenta multa proferri' et 'satis evidenter'. Ideo dixit: '*Diligis me plus hiis*? quod utique sciebat et tamen interrogabat,' et ita 'quantum ipse sapio, melior est qui plus diligit Christum, felicior est quem plus diligit Christus' secundum Deum. Hoc Augustinus. Certum est quod ista felicitas nulla esset nisi ad futuram vitam refertur. Item glosa dicit post missum Spiritum sanctum [*sic*] dubium est quis horum magis dilexeret. Ita etiam consequenter dicit de vita contemplativa [que] per Ioannem signatur. Unde subdit Augustinus: 'Ipse Dominus illam que futura est vitam nostram, qualis in nobis futura sit sciens, praedestinatione plus amat ut ad eam amando nos perducat.' Illa ergo et alie consimiles auctoritates referende sunt ad illud tempus; sed Ioannes postea supervixit longis temporibus et multa sibi merita cumulavit. Amplius videtur ex sequentibus textus quod nulla interrogatio Ioannis non fuit in profectum Petri. Unde subditur: *Conversus Petrus vidit discipulum etc.* Unde etiam non dixit Salvator hiis omnibus, sed hiis tantum. Circa hoc tamen nichil est temere asserendum. Absit enim michi ne presumam contra Petri primatum aliquid diffinire, quod si quis velit contrarium sustinere, facile est respondere ad obiecta (fols. 129vb–130ra).

Pecham forbad his friars 'not only immoderation (*enormitas*) but any empty or mirth-provoking word' in their preaching. He followed this rule in his own sermons and collations.[22] It supplies a key to his Gospel commentary. He refrains from the *exempla* and jokes with which Hugh of St. Cher and some of Hugh's predecessors had enlivened their lectures. The customary sharp satire on current abuses makes few appearances: the merchants and money-changers in the temple, 2.14, signify courtier clerks

[21] I have not found this in the Gloss *ad loc.* or on the descent of the Holy Spirit in Acts.

[22] Decima Douie, 'Archbishop Pecham's Sermons and Collations', op. cit. 271.

struggling to get benefices (fol.24ʳᵃ); the crown of thorns, 19.2, signifies the 'greater prelates' who today, though unworthy, are set up in the Church (fol.115ᵛᵇ); Christ's questions and behest to St. Peter, 21.16, signify that suitable, not bad men, should be chosen as prelates (fol.129ʳᵃ⁻ᵇ). That is a meagre harvest of criticisms. Pecham must have thought the technique irrelevant. Neither did he follow John of Wales in keeping his hearers alert by diversifying his quotations. I have not noted the name of any philosopher or poet, whether pagan or Christian, in his commentary. Even the little jingles quoted by Bonaventure and John of Wales on 6.26 and 7.24 are omitted. The latest theological work to be quoted by name is the standard Peter Lombard's *Sentences*. Pecham quotes it four times on texts where it is not mentioned by Bonaventure or John of Wales.[23]

His policy on quotations, and a policy he had, was to eschew any which did not bear directly on an edifying understanding of his text. He inveighs against philosophers who rely on reason and praises 'the simplicity of faith', on 5.44(fol.51ᵛᵃ⁻ᵇ). His patristic sources are too ordinary to be worth listing. Chrysostom and Augustine of course were his main guides. Augustine predominates among the other Fathers, quite apart from his *Tractate* on St. John. The most arresting of the early authors quoted is Pseudo-Augustine *De mirabilibus sacrae Scripturae*, referred to on the miracles said to have accompanied the crucifixion: eleven cities of Thracia collapsed. Pecham ascribes it to 'Augustinus, secundo de mirabilibus, ca.iii' (fol.119ᵛᵃ). It was written by an Irishman in 655 with the aim of rationalising biblical miracles,[24] though Pecham used it to extract what he took for an otherwise unrecorded one.

John of Wales had often referred to 'Papias', author of a dictionary variously called *Elementarium*, *Vocabularium* etc., of the mid-eleventh century;[25] his entries are correct.[26] Pecham does the same, though on different texts, as on *triclinium*[27] (fol.22ᵛᵃ). It seems, however, that Pecham may have fallen into the trap of confusing the medieval lexicographer with Papias, bishop of Hierapolis, who claimed to be 'auditor Ioannis', and whose book survives only in fragmentary quotations, mainly from Eusebius. He was sometimes mistaken for the lexicographer.[28] In his prologue Pecham lists 'Papias Hieropolitanus episcopus' among early writers on the New Testament, drawing on Jerome's *De viris illustribus*, where this Papias is said to have left 'five volumes which he entitled *Explanatio sermonum Domini*' (Stegmüller, 403). On the text *Erat mater*

---

[23] II, d.13, n.10; II, d.13, n.8–10 (Stegmüller, 410); IV, d.5, summarised (fol. 13ᵛᵃ); III, d.23,n.4 (fol. 30ʳᵃ).

[24] PL 35, 2174; B. Bischoff, 'Wendepunkte in der Geschichte der lateinischen Exegese in Frühmittelalter', *Sacris Erudiri*, 6 (1954), 198.

[25] *Papiae Elementarium littera A, 1, A-Aequus*, ed. V. de Angelis (Testi e Documenti per lo studio dell'Antichità, 58, 1, Milan, 1977), i-x.

[26] e.g. on *mirra* and *thus*, MS Magdalen 27, fol. 5, from *Papias vocabulista* (Venice, 1496), fols. [103]ᵛᵇ; [179]ᵛᵃ; on *caliga*, Bon. 329, Papias, ed. cit. fol. [23]ᵛᵇ.

[27] Papias, ed. cit. fol. [177]ᵛᵃ.

[28] *Lexicon für Theologie und Kirche*, 8 (1963), 34–36.

Jesu ibi, 2.1, Pecham wants to refute arguments against Mary's virginity. He quotes 'Papias' as saying that *mulier* applies to sex and not to non-virginity, as when Eve was called a woman at her creation, before her marriage to Adam (Gen. 2.22), and ends: 'Hoc probat Papias', as though Papias was taking part in a theological argument (fol.20[ra]).[29] But one cannot be sure.

Of medieval writers we find the expected sprinkling of St. Anselm and St. Bernard. Pecham was one of the first, as far as I know, to quote 'the Master of the Histories' as 'Comestor' instead of 'Manducator'. He refers to the normal title, 'the Master', but often quotes 'Comestor' as well, never 'Manducator' (fols.11[ra], 79[va], 115[ra], 118[va], etc.). I have not noticed any mention of the mysterious 'Victorinus', quoted by Bonaventure and others at Paris, or of John of Wales' 'Anselm'.[30]. On the other hand, Pecham resembles them in using an unnamed 'quidam expositor', unfortunately on a different text, so that one cannot tell whether it was the same as that quoted by Alexander of Hales, Bonaventure and John of Wales, if they were all using the same, which is unverifiable. Pecham takes over as an alternative his expositor's conjecture on what Jesus wrote on the ground, 8.6: there are four books of life, the first of reason, the second of correction, the third of grace, the fourth of divine wisdom. The Saviour here began the book of grace, being the first to allow that repentance brought pardon, as to the adulteress led before him by the scribes and Pharisees (fol.67[vb]). I have not identified this comment.

Quotations of 'Hugo' are baffling. The first, on 1.9, *That was the true light, which enlighteneth every man that cometh into this world*, seems to give a rough summary of Hugh of St. Cher's postill. Hugh raised the question why so many men are not enlightened. He answers from Chrysostom that the light enlightens every man as far as pertains to him:

Sed incidit quaestio. Si ipse illuminat omnem hominem, quomodo tot sunt non illuminati? Ad hoc respondetur multipliciter Chrysostomus in 8.Homil.: Ille omnem hominem illuminat quantum ad eum pertinet.

Pecham quotes Hugh as giving 'another exposition', after having himself given several: this light enlightens all men capable by nature of reason and of perceiving it:

Unde addit Hugo aliam expositionem, dicens hoc lumen omnes illuminat in quantum omnes natura rationis capaciter [*sic*] facti sunt et lumen intelligere [*sic*] perceperunt (fol.7[va]).

[29] Papias, ed. cit. fol. [106][vb]: '. . . Dicta est igitur secundum foemineum sexum, non secundum corruptionem integritatis. Et haec ex sacra Scriptura, nam statim, facta de latere viri sui nondum contacta a viro, dicta est: et formavit eam in mulierem.'
[30] See above, pp. 208; 217.

Pecham adds: 'Hec ergo fons est universalis luminis' and quotes Hugh again:

Unde Hugo ibidem: Omnis illuminatio est a Patre, sed sine Iesu mediatore illuminatio nulla haberi potest. Ergo nos qui illuminari possumus Iesum invocamus (ibid.).

Something of the kind appears in Hugh of St. Cher on 1.8 above: *He* (John Baptist) *was not the light*, where he explains the difference between *lux* and *lumen:*

Divinitas in se lux est . . . divinitas in carne lumen.

Pecham's use of Hugh's postill on St. John would strengthen the evidence that he was lecturing in Paris, where it was at hand for Bonaventure, and not in Oxford, where it was scarcely known.[31] Alas! the remaining quotes of 'Hugo' bear no resemblance to the postill. A good test case is a reference to Hugh on Ps. 9.4: *When my enemy shall be turned back* . . . Pecham makes Hugh expatiate on the role of the devil:

Hugo super Ps. 9: Tres in causam venisset, diabolus, homo, Deus. Diabolus Deo inimicitiam fecisse convincitur . . . Item diabolus homini inimicitiam fecit . . . (fol.83[rb]).

Hugh has only: *'inimicum meum* diabolus' with a quotation from Matt. 13.28. Either Pecham had a copy of the postill widely different from that printed and used by Bonaventure or he quoted from another Hugh, possibly Hugh of St. Victor. A passage on contemplative prayer, leading to forgetfulness of self and of all business, and being raised up by God's love, may perhaps represent the gist of Hugh of St. Victor's teaching on 'pure prayer' in his *De virtute orandi* (PL 176, 979–985), a genuine work of the Victorine.[32] Another sounds like him; 3.29, *rejoices with joy*, suggests three voices speaking to us to give advice:

. . . et Hugo dicit: audimus omnem causam [?] nos tribus vocibus alloquentem. Prima dicit accipe; secunda dicit recide; tertia dicit fuge; accipe subsidium infirmitatis; recide obsequium maiestatis; fuge supplicium iniquitatis (fol.33[ra]).

However, since Pecham never gives the name of the work ascribed to Hugh, unlike the meticulous John of Wales, and in the absence of adequate indices to Hugh of St. Victor, it is impossible to find the sources of most of Pecham's quotes from him (others are on fols.122va, 123ra, 127va). Neither Bonaventure nor John of Wales quote a 'Hugh' on any of the texts where Pecham does; so the mystery remains unsolved.

[31] Above, p. 215.

[32] R. Goy, *Die Überlieferung der Werke Hugos von St. Viktor* (Monographien zur Geschichte des Mittelalters, 14, Stuttgart, 1976), 404.

In method his exposition belongs to the scholastic lecture type, marking a stage forward in the development of scholasticism. There is more division and subdivision of prologue and chapters. The prologue expands on the traditional comparison of the evangelist to an eagle and on the unity of the two Testaments; it goes on to describe the four faces of Scripture: *initialis, intellectualis, doctrinalis, sententialis*, with supporting texts (Stegmüller, 399–401). Pecham adds *quaestiones* to his sources of a more sophisticated type, but of about the same shortish length. He produces *distinctiones* on words and sometimes gets fired to a long devotional outpouring by a few words in one of his sources. John of Wales commented on the compassion of Christ's Mother for the poor bridegroom whose wine ran out at the wedding feast, 2.3–5; she is our advocate. Pecham takes off into praise of the *Virgo gloriosa* which fills almost the whole section of the chapter describing the water-into-wine miracle (fol.19ra). He resembles other masters in expecting that his lectures would help preachers. He notes that 1.3–4 of the Gospel is preachable (*praedicabilis*) at Christmas (Stegmüller, 412) and that 4.24 is 'a good theme [for preaching to] religious'; he then shows ways to apply it (fol.39ra). He expounds the literal sense industriously from his sources, afterwards adding allegorical and/or tropological interpretations, mainly standard ones. His originality appears neither in his use of sources, unless we stress his sobriety, nor in his mode of commenting; we shall find it elsewhere.

Pecham outstrips both Bonaventure and John of Wales in his praise of humility and poverty. That is the most striking feature of his lectures. Not only does he follow his two predecessors on the obvious texts, but he presses other texts into service. At the very beginning of the Gospel, 1.3 evokes a long discussion on the humility of Christ in his incarnation (Stegmüller, 412). On the wedding feast, Christ showed his humility in deigning to eat and drink with sinners in a small town; Cana was a *viculus*, not a city (fol.18va), and again on the meeting with the Samaritan woman, 4.7 (fol.35rb). Bonaventure mentioned humility briefly on 7.18: *He that speaketh of himself seeketh his own glory;*[33] John of Wales made no such comment, whereas Pecham dwells on it at great length (fol.63ra). He praises Mary Magdalen for her humility in bowing down to anoint Jesus, 12.3 (fol.76rb). He elaborates on John of Wales on Jesus' humility in laying aside his garments before washing his disciples' feet, 13.4 (fol.87ra).[34] Bonaventure has a *quaestio* on the problem of human passion on 13.21: *. . . he was troubled in spirit*, but does not bring humility into it.[35] John of Wales passed it over. Pecham dwells on Christ's humility in conforming himself to our human nature (fol.88^{va-b}). He alone takes the opportunity afforded by the interpretation of the names of those present when Jesus

---

[33] *Opera* 6, 344.
[34] Bon. 417.
[35] *Opera* 6, 431.

showed himself after his resurrection, 21.2, to bring in humility: 'Thomas interpretatur *abyssus* et significat humilitatem profundam' (fol.127^{ra-b}).

Pecham's teaching on poverty reflects a time when polemic had descended to niggling over certain texts, as we shall see. He refers to it where it had not occurred before: the statement . . . *as many as received him, he gave them power to be made the sons of God*, 1.12, is fulfilled *moraliter* when poor men come to a house of clergy; Christ said that he came in them, Matt. 10.40 (fol.8ra). The desertion of Christ by many disciples, 6.67, leads to a rebuke to those who attack poverty (fol.60va); Pecham meant the enemies of the friars. Again, the account of Lazarus' burial *moraliter* signifies 'bad men in the cloister who do not love poverty' (fol.74^{ra-b}). Two texts prove that Christ went barefoot: Mary Magdalen anointed Christ's feet which she must have found bare and sore (fol.79va);[36] the soldiers who divided his clothes among them did not take shoes, which he did not have, nor could have had, since he forbad them to his servants (fol.118va). Arguments against the silken, and therefore costly, cloth of the seamless coat, 19.23, are marshalled: had it been silken, the soldiers would not have mocked Jesus by clothing him in purple, and would have sold it so as to divide the price between them instead of casting lots (fol.118^{va-b}). John of Wales had both arguments[37] and Pecham also gave both. And why did Jesus have clothes in the plural, when he had ordered his apostles to have one coat only? Perhaps it was normally worn over other clothes (fol.118va).[38] Christ's commission from the cross of his Mother to St. John, who 'took her to his own', 19.27, led Bonaventure and John of Wales to deny that *to his own* meant that St. John had any property.[39] Pecham expands the argument from Bonaventure: St. John took her as an office (*officium*), and *his own* referred to his spiritual, not his earthly goods (fol.119^{rb-va}). Joseph of Arimathea must have been a rich man and yet he counted as a disciple, 19.38. Bonaventure did not comment on this. John of Wales argued that Joseph must have been converted to apostolic poverty later.[40] Pecham met the case by denying that he ever belonged to the seventy disciples (fol.121ra). The poverty question, which had led to careful examination of the text in its literal sense, now gave rise to trifling with it on minor points.

Political theory on the relations between *regnum* and *sacerdotium* tempted Pecham even less than it did Bonaventure and John of Wales. He upheld, indeed took for granted, the primacy of St. Peter, as we have seen in his discussion of his question on the mutual love of Christ, St. Peter and St. John,[41] but he did not single out St. Peter from the other apostles on the giving of power to remit sins, 20. 23, although he inserted a long *quaestio*

---

[36] On this text in polemic, see Douie, *Archbishop Pecham*, op. cit. 29.

[37] Bon. 451–452. See Douie, op. cit. ibid.

[38] Neither Bonaventure nor John of Wales gives this explanation.

[39] *Opera* 6, 498: Bon. 452. This derives from Augustine.

[40] Bon. 455.

[41] Above, p. 235.

on the nature of the power to remit sins (fols. 124rb–126ra), nor did he mention the pope in the discussion. Like John of Wales, he refrains from making St. Peter's sword, 18. 10, a principal argument for papal power. Instead he makes Christ's order to Peter to sheath it an indication that Christ sacrificed himself willingly and that his disciples had not yet acquired all Christian virtues, being still impatient. Then, ironically in view of the way in which papalists interpreted the text, he takes Peter to signify one who has zeal, but not according to wisdom, in God's Church. Such men, on seeing others inimical to Christ, immediately draw out the sword of excommunication and cut off their subjects' ear of obedience (i.e. make them worse). Then and only then does he quote Bernard's *De consideratione*, as Bonaventure had done, taking it in the sense of a warning to the pope not to abuse his power (fol. 111^{rb-va}). Pecham's pacific attitude must have been known. It would explain why Edward I received him graciously, although he had wanted the pope to nominate the royal chancellor Robert Burnell, and why king and archbishop remained on friendly terms throughout Pecham's tenure of office.[42]

The general impression given by his lectures is that he was a conscientious but uninspiring teacher of Scripture, a view corresponding to Decima Douie's account of him as a reforming archbishop. His other intellectual interests did not colour his exegesis. Nonetheless, his lecture course on St. John makes a good conclusion to our survey of the three Franciscans. It shows the links between them: John of Wales drew on Bonaventure; Pecham drew on both. The content in all three, developing in all three, points to Franciscan piety and unction finding a way through scholastic techniques into the classroom. Further, and again the trend develops, the three friar doctors rally in defence of their mode of life against attacks by the seculars by underlining Christ's poverty and humility. We can now speak of a distinctively Franciscan approach to the Gospel in the schools, as we could not do before Bonaventure. It remains to see whether the Dominicans lead us into a different climate.

[42] Douie, *Archbishop Pecham*, op. cit. 47–52.

IV. ALBERT THE GREAT

John Pecham as exegete concealed himself as poet and scientist, probably by deliberate intent. St. Albert, encyclopaedist *Doctor Universalis*, bursts out joyously from every page of his Gospel commentaries. The liberal Arts, now reinforced by Aristotle's *Libri naturales* and other material on natural science, were pictured as handmaidens to Theology. Never had the queen of sciences kept her servants so busy. To translate into our modern jargon: Albert saw exegesis as an 'interdisciplinary' subject.

The known facts about his life have been set down so often that I need only mention what is relevant to his Gospel commentaries.[1] He joined the Dominican Order when Jordan of Saxony visited Padua, where Albert had been studying the *Artes* (and Padua had a bias towards natural science) in 1223. He trained in theology and taught it as lector in *studia* of his native Germany, then went to Paris in 1240 to qualify as doctor of theology, and held a chair at St. Jacques 1245-1248. For the remainder of his life, that is up to 1280, he was occupied in installing, organizing and teaching in German Dominican *studia*, apart from a few years at the papal curia and from his unwilling tenure of the archbishopric of Regensburg, 1260-1262; he was allowed to resign but then had orders to preach the Crusade in Germany.

On the latest reckoning the Gospel commentaries belong to the most active years of his career, the 1260s.[2] He expounded them in their canonical order, Matthew to John.[3] They came before his exposition of the Greater, followed by that of the Twelve Lesser Prophets and of Job. Hence he began with the Gospels, probably thinking that this was his most urgent task. The commentary on Luke may perhaps from internal evidence be dated after his consecration as bishop, 1260, which could put those on Matthew and Mark either before or after that date. In his commentary on Matthew he refers to his commentary on *De animalibus*, probably finished soon after 1261. If we accept an incipit of his commentary on Luke, in a manuscript now in Würzburg, he produced it at Würzburg, where his helpmate Brother Theodoric of Würzburg had it written out with the help of his friends. Albert is called 'formerly bishop of Regensburg'; therefore we are after 1262. In view of the other books belonging to this period, Albert's energy as preacher, organizer and teacher, 'wandering' under orders, astonishes. And he was a man over sixty.

It is difficult to tell from the texts we have how his Gospel commentaries originated. They are not *reportationes*, but probably represent lectures, which he may have written up from his notes; he writes as a doctor, with a doctor's authority.

Albert outstripped John of Wales in the multiplicity of his sources owing to his absorbing interest in natural science as well as in classical writers. Unfortunately he lacked John's scrupulous scholarship: he seldom gives the

[1] J. A. Weisheipl, 'Albert the Great and Medieval Culture', *The Thomist*, 44 (1980), 481–501; *Thomas de Aquino and Albert his Teacher* (Etienne Gilson Series, 2), Toronto, 1980.

[2] For what follows see A. Fries, 'Zur Enstehungszeit der Bibelkommentare Alberts des Grossen', *Albertus Magnus, Doctor Universalis, 1280–1980*, ed. G. Meyer and A. Zimmermann (Walberger Studien, Philos. Reihe, 6, Mainz, 1980), 119–139.

[3] In addition to the arguments presented by Fries there are cross-references from Mark to Matthew (21, 467), from Luke to Matthew (22, 133) and from John to Luke (24, 436). The editor in the Borgnet edition (see below, p. 243) has verified the references. The figures in brackets refer to this edition.

locus of his quotations, sometimes putting them under the heading 'Aristoteles dicit' or 'Plato'. I have had to use the edition of Albert's *Opera* by Borgnet, 20–24 (1893–1899), for his Gospel commentaries, although in places the text seems to be corrupt and few references to quotations are given. To produce a new annotated edition from the manuscripts would be a long task, for which I have neither the competence nor the time. I can only list the rarest and most interesting of the sources mentioned; in many cases I have failed to find the original quoted. My references to Albert on the Gospels come from Borgnet.

To begin with proximate sources: Albert must have had Hugh of St. Cher's *Postilla* to hand, though he would not have named a contemporary, whom he knew personally; Hugh died in 1264.[4] Collation showed that he used Hugh on the Gospels. He took over Hugh's explanation of why Chrysostom in Burgundio's translation omitted the episode of the woman taken in adultery (John 8.3–11) and why the Latins expounded it as authentic (24,327–328). Hugh's comment on the meaning of Christ's title written on the cross (John 19.19–22) has a parallel in Albert (24,657), also the point that the grave cloths in the empty tomb helped to prove the truth of the resurrection (24,673).[5]

Elsewhere, however, Albert refers to the *Postilla* only in order to disagree with the author. Why is Joseph not mentioned in the account of the Magi's adoration of the Christ child? Hugh's explanation had been: because his presence might have aroused suspicion of Mary's virginity. Albert quotes it 'as some say' and adds that it seems frivolous to him. The true reason was that Joseph had nothing to do with Christ's divinity, whereas Mary had (20,74). Commentators had suggested various reasons for the drink given to Christ on the cross (John 19.29–30). Albert thought 'less probable' the opinion which Hugh had listed first, that it was meant to hasten Christ's death (24,661). Discussing the question as to how Christ could enter through closed doors after his resurrection, Albert states that none of the saints has said that glorified bodies could do so as such; no 'author' has said it either: 'Nec aliquis auctor dicit quod hoc sit de gloria gloriosorum corporum' (24,682). Hugh of St. Cher had quoted Augustine for this opinion: the weight of a body wherein dwelt divinity was no obstacle to entry through closed doors. Albert thought that Augustine's words could bear a different interpretation. When he denies that 'any author' had held (Hugh's) opinion he is excluding Hugh from 'authority'. Albert thought for himself. I have not found any one medieval writer behind his comments: there is no trace of Bonaventure on Luke and John.

That is not to say that he ignored current aids to study. Naturally he had

---

[4] J. A. Weisheipl, *Friar Thomas d'Aquino. His Life, Thought and Work* (New York, 1974), 49: A. Fries, op. cit. 139.

[5] A. Fries, 'Die Gedanken des heiligen Albertus Magnus über die Gottesmutter', *Thomistische Studien*, 7 (1958), 325, noted that Albert used Hugh of St. Victor on Luke without naming him.

244 *The Gospels in the Schools, c. 1100–c. 1280*

a glossed text and quoted the Gloss. He quotes Comestor as 'Magister in Historiis' sometimes, but often as 'quidam' or without mentioning his source.[6] There is a quotation from the Lombard's *Sentences*, IV, as 'magister in iv Sent.' on baptism (24,120, reference given by editor). On the question of remission of sins and the power of the keys to bind and loose, he raises the question whether only a priest having the Holy Spirit can remit sins, and answers from a Magister Gulielmus, that the power does not signify the holiness of the minister, but that of the Church, whose minister the priest is, since sins are remitted only in the framework of the Church's holiness. This solution he holds for true (24,687).[7] I have not identified this Master William; his opinion is not to be found in William of Auxerre or in William of Auvergne. Hugh and Richard of St. Victor and St. Bernard appear frequently. Anselm (of Canterbury) is referred to occasionally. On *hoc est corpus meum* (Matt. 26.26) Albert quotes Innocent on the ubiquity of Christ:

. . .sicut enim dicit Innocentius: Corpus Christi per figuram propriam est in coelo, sacramentaliter in altari et, ut Deus, est ubique (21,164).

That sounds like Innocent III, *De sacro altaris mysterio* iv,27 (PL 217,878), although neither words nor substance correspond exactly. He knows Grosseteste's translation of the *Nicomachean Ethics* with some of its Greek commentaries. The first chapter of St. Luke gives Albert occasion to write on adultery, which was punished by a law of the Athenians, unless forced upon a matron of the city by a tyrant:

Et condemnatur lex Atheniensium, quam in commento Ethicorum recitat Eustratius, quod scilicet semper punitur adulterium, nisi quando matrona civis admittit tyrannum adulterum ut in sinu suo capiatur (22,175).

Grosseteste translated Greek commentators, including Eustratius, as well as the text of the *Ethics*. Albert's reference cannot be verified at present; no complete edition of text and translation has been made. The latest

[6] For example, 'some say' that after Christ's cry on the cross he went on to recite 150 verses from the Psalter up to 30.6 *In Manus tuas* etc. (21, 212); see PL 198, 1633. The story that the woman cured of an issue of blood made a statue of Christ in her garden and its subsequent history (21, 452) comes from PL 198, 1569–1570.

[7] 'Ex quo ordine videtur quod peccata non dimittit qui Spiritum sanctum non habet . . . Ad hoc respondet Magister Gulielmus quod collatio praecedens Spiritus sancti non significat sanctitatem ministri, in qua sanctitate peccata remittuntur, sed potius sanctitatem Ecclesiae cujus ipse sacerdos minister est: quia non nisi in sanctitate Ecclesiae peccata remittuntur. Et haec solutio est vera.'

estimate puts it c.1236-c.1252 and Albert has already used it in his lectures on the *Ethics* and the *Sentences*.[8]

To turn to the rarer of his patristic sources: he quotes 'Origines in Periarchon' on Matt. 1.18 (20,42) on the meaning of *umbra* as likeness rather than shadow, and makes the same point in other works.[9] 'Chrysostomus' may mean either the genuine homilies on St. Matthew or the *Opus imperfectum*. Recourse to the latter may be implied, without verbal quotation, on Matt. 1.12 (20,29) and on Matt. 1.18 (20,35).[10] But some of the comments ascribed to Chrysostom cannot be found in either the genuine or the spurious work. We shall see that Albert could be careless in his references. He quotes much Pseudo-Dionysius and also his own commentary on it (20,79). The Pseudo-Clementine homilies appear (20,145). Albert had read of some wonderful sayings and deeds of the apostles, but admits that these books (the apocryphal *Acta apostolorum*) are not authentic (20,189). I do not know what he meant by the history 'which is called *Euthimiatha*' which tells that St. John took the Virgin into his home and supported her 'with other girls' from the alms of the faithful (24,660). It must have belonged to apocryphal *Acts of the Apostles*. His quotation from Epiphanius is mysterious. Christ charged the Jews with killing their prophets: *Zacharias . . .whom you killed between the temple and the altar* (Matt. 23.35). The comment that from then onwards divine answers in the temple ceased to be given on the propitiatory is ascribed to Epiphanius without reference (20,25). It does not come from *Cassiodori Epiphanii Historia*[11] or from the *Sancti Epiphanii Episcopi Interpretatio Evangeliorum*.[12]

Albert normally took little interest in rabbinics; there are only two references to *Hebraei* in his commentary on Isaias.[13] To my surprise he suddenly quoted a Jewish tradition with named rabbis on Matt. 5.43: *You have heard that it has been said: Thou shalt . . . hate thy enemy.* 'They (the Jews) hold this for a divine precept, for Rab. Vasse, and Rab. Josue and

---

[8] J. McEvoy, *The Philosophy of Robert Grosseteste*, op. cit. 471–477. The quotation from Eustratius does not appear in the early part of Grosseteste's translation of Greek commentaries; see *The Greek Commentaries on the Nicomachean Ethics of Aristotle in the Latin Translation of Robert Grosseteste: Eustratius on Book 1*, ed. H. P. F. Mercken (Corpus Latinum Commentariorum in Aristotelem Graecorum 6, 1, 1973). See also J. A. Weisheipl, 'Albert the Great', op. cit. 492–493.

[9] A. Fries, 'Zur Entstehungszeit', op. cit. 129–134, gives the references.

[10] PG 56, 628; 631.

[11] ed. W. Jacob and R. Hanslik, CSEL 71 (1952).

[12] ed. A. Erikson (Lund, 1939); see RB 2245, 1 Suppl. and A. Siegmund, *Die Überlieferung der griechischen christlichen Literatur in der lateinischen Kirche bis zum zwölften Jahrhundert* (Leiden, 1949), 171–173.

[13] *Alberti Magni O. F. P. Postilla super Isaiam*, ed. F. Siepman (Aschendorff, 1952), 221; 250. I relied on the index. Neither of them gives a name to the *Hebraei*, though elsewhere he quotes Rabbi Moses (Maimonides) and his *Guide of the Perplexed*, 3; 181.

Rab. Joanna and other Scribes used to say that God gave two laws, one written on the hearts of the wise and one on stone.' According to this one should first love a person who approaches one in a friendly way and then hate him who withdraws his friendship. The reference has not been traced; it illustrates Albert's knack of picking up odd bits of information or misinformation wherever he could find them (20,222-223).

The obvious Latin doctors of the Church are well represented, with Isidore, Boethius, Cassiodorus, Cassian and Bede. The unidentified Victorinus, quoted by Paris lecturers, appears once. This time it is on the question whether the bridegroom at the wedding feast at Cana was St. John the Evangelist. Jerome and Augustine agree that he was; Victorinus, Chrysostom and Origen say not:

Dicit enim sic Victorinus: 'Cum virginitas sit in carne corruptibili incorruptionis perpetua meditatio, non est credendum quod Ioannes, cum de virginitate testimonium perhibet, unquam in nuptias consenserit' (24,99).

St. John the virgin would not have contemplated marriage. Belief in his virginity went back to the second century.[14]

Pagan classical literature attracted Albert less than works on science. Of writers on other subjects Cicero was his favourite. I have found no mention of Seneca. He quotes the poets rarely. Macrobius *De somnio Scipionis* makes one appearance (20,49). Quotations from early Greek writers must be spurious and/or handed down through intermediaries. Pythagoras keeps cropping up, as he does in other medieval books; Albert quotes him in his Gospel commentaries. Here he cites him on the virtue of names (22,13) and ascribes to him a saying in the context of praise of Mary's virginity: a flower has a father in the sun and no mother in heaven, but a mother and no father on earth (20,37); the same saying by 'Pythagoras' is repeated later (22,52).[15] 'Plato in Politegiis' or 'Politegnis' (21,585) on the nature of family attachment (Mark 10.6–9) might perhaps have come from Cicero, though I have not found it in the indexes; nor is it a mistake for something in Aristotle's *Politics*. Albert drew on the whole range of the *Libri naturales*, the *Physics* and *Metaphysics*, as then known in Latin translations (apart from the *Politics*) and the spurious *De caelo et mundo*. Avicenna and Constantine (Africanus) supply information on the effects of food apropos Christ's fasting in the desert (20,309). We meet geometers, *mathematici* and alchemists (22,102; 20,61; 21,161). Discussing the incarnation, Albert compares Galen to Aristotle 'and the philosophers' on woman's role in

[14] B. Capelle, 'La fête de l'Assomption dans l'histoire liturgique', *Ephemerides theologicae Lovanienses*, 3 (1926), 41–42.
[15] The saying must have been current. St. Thomas applies a version of it to Christ: 'For in heaven the Lord has a Father without a mother; and on earth a mother without a father'; here it is not ascribed to any author. See *Commentary on the Gospel of St. John*, English translation by J. A. Weisheipl and F. R. Larcher (Aquinas Scripture Series 4), Part 1 (New York, 1980), 161.

conception (22,72). The words *Nolite possidere* (Matt. 10.9) call for a definition of possession. Albert quotes 'Trismegistus':

Et ideo *possidere* dicit quietem in eo quod possidetur secundum Trismegistum (20,449).

This comes from the *Liber XXIV philosophorum*, a collection of statements about God, ascribed to 'Termegister the philosopher'; Albert has adapted it:

Deus est semper movens immobilis . . .Immobilis dicitur Deus, quia est semper secundum unam dispositionem; et hoc est esse in quiete.[16]

Albert's 'Cestabon' or 'Castabon' on melancholics suggests a corrupt text used by the editor (20,394). The name is otherwise unknown.

Grammar is not forgotten: we find an excursus on *ecce* as an adverb (20,45) and another on *ut* (20,81). Albert happily pairs *exempla* from Scripture with those from 'the histories of the gentiles'. Both condemn frivolous women who wander away from home as did Dinah and Helen of Troy. He contrasts their misdeeds to Mary's long stay with Elizabeth (22,88;151).

Lastly we have scraps of history, some admittedly apocryphal. The Fathers hand down the statement that Christ's executioners stripped his body wholly naked in the public sight. Pictures of him on the cross, however, show a cloth bound round his loins; it is said that his Virgin Mother covered them with her head-veil (21,735).[17] Albert criticized a statement, 'ut dicunt', meaning Hugh of St. Cher, that the Roman Church made Simon's change of name to Peter (John 1.42) a precedent for the pope-elect to change his name:

But that is untrue, because the name of the elected pope was not changed until long afterwards, when a certain man was elected who had a dirty name, being called 'Pigsmouth' (*os porci*); from his election as pope henceforward the pope's name began to be changed (24,79).

Only a scholar matching Albert's knowledge of medieval lore would be in a position to identify all his sources.

His carelessness would make it all the more difficult. Here are just two instances where he misnamed or misremembered his authors. He quotes 'Alexander in libro *De motu cordis*' on Matt. 1.20, comparing the human and angelic concepts of the soul:

---

[16] ed. C. Baeumker, *Beiträge zur Geschichte der Philosophie des Mittelalters*, 25, 1–2 (1928), 212. Alexander Nequam ascribed the *Liber* to Hermes Trismegistus, see R. W. Hunt, *The Schools and the Cloister: the Life and Writings of Alexander Nequam* (Oxford, 1984), 70.

[17] A. Fries, 'Die Gedanken', op. cit. 326–341, does not mention this legend in his chapter on Albert on St. John.

Et ideo dicit Alexander in libro *de motu cordis* quod anima humana illuminationum quae sunt a primo ultima relatione est perceptiva (20,46).

Alfredus Anglicus dedicated his *De motu cordis* to Alexander Nequam probably towards 1217. It had come to be used as a philosophic text-book in the Arts course at Paris by 1250.[18] The mistaken ascription to Alexander was common; but Albert ought to have noticed the prologue. A second blunder: he ascribes to Augustine an incorrect version of a common *exemplum*. Christ's second cry of anguish from the cross raised the question of fear of death (Matt. 27.50). Albert tells a story about a stoic philosopher, who showed visible signs of fear during a storm at sea; a 'slave sailor' twitted him afterwards because he himself had not feared at all. The philosopher excused himself on the ground that he had many good things to lose by death, whereas the slave sailor might as well have thrown himself overboard to end his wretched life (21,213). The correct version of Augustine's story was more suited to the case: the stoic's excuse for his fear was that *he* stood to lose a philosopher's soul; his mocker risked only a rascal's. This correct version was current; Albert garbled it.[19] After all, he was itinerant and busy in the 1260s and may not always have had access to good libraries. He would not let that hinder him from making his abundant quotations, perhaps from memory or from unreliable notes. He sometimes quotes without acknowledgement too.[20]

He does show some restraint, however. Sometimes he passes over a problem as irrelevant at the moment. He will not discuss 'fate' apropos the Magi's star (20,65) nor usury apropos Matt. 5.42 (20,221) nor the role of the agent and passive intellect in sense perception on Luke 1.13 (22,23).

All his rich store of learning is poured into *distinctiones* on words and descriptions of states or actions. A mention of sickness will release a mass of information on medical teaching or advice. When Jesus sits on the Mount (Matt. 5.1) we get an excursus on the physical benefits of the sitting position; doctors have chairs and Aristotle notes them (20,146). Not surprisingly, the reference to Aristotle is imprecise; it seems to depend on his account of bodily states and excellences and of motion coming to rest (*Physic.* vii,3, 246^b–248^a).

Much of this matter may seem irrelevant and distracting. Nonetheless Albert gives the impression that he is not showing off or keeping his hearers' or readers' attention by diversification of sources, as one suspects

[18] ed. C. Baeumker, *Beiträge zur Geschichte der Philosophie des Mittelalters*, 23 (1923), 2: '[Anima] in se enim considerata substantia est incorporea, intellectiva, illuminationum quae a primo sunt ultima relatione perceptiva.' Albert's following note on angels is not from *De motu cordis*. On Alfred see J. K. Otte, 'The Life and Writings of Alfredus Anglicus', *Viator*, 3 (1972), 275–291.

[19] Augustine, *De civitate Dei* i,22. For transmission of the story see B. Smalley, 'Oxford University Sermons', *Medieval Learning and Literature. Essays presented to Richard William Hunt*, ed. J. J. G. Alexander and M. T. Gibson (Oxford, 1976), 323.

[20] His comment on the ascent to the mount (20, 145) is a paraphrase of Pseudo-Chrysostom, PG 56, 679.

was the case with John of Wales. Rather he was putting his encyclopaedic knowledge at their disposal in order that they should understand every word of the text and the clarification that science could bring to it.

In handling his material Albert broke free from the rigid Paris model. He knew it, of course: his *Principium biblium* follows the rules;[21] his prologue to St. John is constructed on the usual theme of the four causes. On the contrary his prologue to St. Matthew has no causes. These are kept for his commentary on the Gloss prologue: material, formal and final; the efficient appears on Matt. 1.1. The prologue to St. Mark makes the traditional identification of St. Mark with the lion, but does not explain or adapt it there. The reasons are given in Albert's commentary on the Gospel text, where in various places the traits of the evangelist are shown to correspond with a lion's. St. Luke's Gospel has no prologue; the verses of the evangelist's own prologue, 1.1–4, carry a commentary setting out *necessitas scribendi, materia, forma, finis*. Similarly the subdivisions of each chapter are not uniform; sometimes they are applied not to individual chapters but to whole blocks of the Gospel in hand. Writing in and presumably for a German rather than a Paris milieu, Albert preferred to modify the rules of exegesis when and as it pleased him.

His exposition according to the four senses also varies. One has the impression of new grass growing up among the stubble of the old. His *Principium* touches on the vexed question of the status of the historical books of the Bible, which could not pass the test of true science according to Aristotle, because they dealt with particulars, not principles. Albert taught that their science (he calls it *scientia*) differed from the others', since it mixed mysteries and instructive examples; accordingly 'particular history' receives the status of 'universal'. But that is to be inquired into elsewhere:

Non enim sic est in hac scientia sicut in aliis, quia ista in particularibus colligit mysteria et exemplares instructiones, et secundum hoc particularis historia accipit vim universalis. Sed de hoc alias est inquirendum.[22]

The 'elsewhere' is not in his Gospel commentaries.

Two definitions of the senses are set out near the beginning of his commentary on Matthew. Two things must be kept in mind for our understanding: the letter and the letter's intention. Three things must be understood in the letter; the first pertains to [Christ's] assumption of humanity; the middle to the enlightenment of those called [to perfection]; the [third and] perfect to the redemption and glorification of the enlightened. *Or (vel)* Albert gives the conventional four senses: historical, allegorical, tropological, anagogical. These four expositions of Scripture correspond to the *four very little things of the earth, and they are wiser than*

---

[21] ed. A. Fries, *Beitr. zur Gesch. Phil. Theol. Mittelalters*, Suppl. iv (1952), 128–147.

[22] *Principium,* ed. cit. 139.

the wise (Prov. 30.24) on account of their lowliness (20,13). Thus he does not grade the senses but calls them all 'lowly' (*propter humilitatem*). The letter's intention is to teach us to understand from the written word the Apostle's wondrous calling from being a publican to the throne of majesty among God's animals (alluding to the four of Ezechiel's vision).

Albert has at least put the historical sense on a level with those generally called 'higher'. How does that affect his practice as a commentator? He certainly gives a background of Old Testament history to St. Matthew's genealogy. On a few texts he prefers a literal exposition to the traditional spiritual. Although he has given the Saints' exposition of Matt. 5.26, it can be expounded more literally as metaphorical (20,195). *His face did shine as the sun and his garments were white as snow* (Matt. 17.2) at the transfiguration had been interpreted as meaning that the garments signified Christ's humanity. Albert did not think so (*quod ego non puto*); it was Christ's human face which shone like the sun. Literally his garment seems to have been a white cloud (20,652). St. Peter's remembrance of Jesus' saying that Peter would betray him before the cock crowed thrice (Matt. 26.75) recalls the text of St. Luke *And the Lord turning looked on Peter* (Luke 22.61). Augustine interpreted the look as meaning 'inner mercy'. Albert, speaking in the first person and without prejudice, held that the look was both outward and inward (21,190).

Yet here again Albert's thought moved too fast to flow in conventional channels. He did not expound each passage tidily according to the four senses, but would sometimes put the mystical first and the literal second as on *Bethlehem* (20,60). On the *narrow gate* (Matt. 7.13) he says, after giving spiritual interpretations, that literally it seems to mean 'gate of virtue'; in other words the literal sense is expressed in a metaphor (20,351). The raising of Lazarus provides an acid test on whether a commentator distinguished between the biblical story and the raising up of a mortal sinner by penance. Albert passes it easily. The spiritual interpretation that Lazarus signifies a sinner's life of penance comes well after exposition of the history (24,435). As an exegete Albert understood the principles of distinction between the senses; where the literal meaning was in doubt he probed it, to see whether it was probable historically or else metaphorical, rather than making the literal sense depend on a spiritual interpretation as the first meaning. The question of relations between the senses lay in the background of his thinking. He had intuitions on the subject, but no time to explore them. In keeping with this he was ambivalent on the problem of what must be left to the text itself without addition and what could legitimately be deduced from it. The speed of the Magi in reaching the Christ child cannot be classed as miraculous, surprising as it sounds, because Scripture does not say so (20,66). On the other hand it was miraculous that the Virgin did not have a miscarriage, since by visiting Elizabeth she flouted physicians' advice to pregnant women to avoid movement at the beginning and then after five months of pregnancy (22,115).

Albert raises and discusses *quaestiones* briefly, according to Paris custom. He differs from his predecessors in dismissing as frivolous questions on the nature of the dove, seen as signifying the Holy Spirit (John 1.32): 'It is asked by the curious rather than the devout' whether others than the Baptist saw it and heard the Father's voice. 'The curious also ask' what became of the dove after its appearance (24,72). Albert marks a shift of emphasis that must have come quickly in the schools. Problems touching on physics, such as the nature of Christ's body after the resurrection, interested him more than what he regarded as trivial.

His treatment of allegories and moralities marks another departure. They tend to be abstract and traditional, whereas his own moral teaching depends on the literal sense: *moralitas secundum litteram*, as Langton would have called it. The apostles' dispute on who should be greater and Christ's rebuke to them (Mark 9.33–34) is against prelates who proceed pompously (21,564). Many prelates keep for themselves money intended for the poor, as did Judas Iscariot (24,472). Such contemporary allusions are few, suggesting that Albert did not mean to give guidance to future preachers on satire and on attacks on abuses. Perhaps the proliferation of aids to preaching had made moralities on the bad conduct of clerks and laymen unnecessary in commentaries. He had a personal message of a different type, which he could express better in comments on the letter of the Gospel than in tropologies.

The forefront of Albert's thinking was the needs of man in society. Men needed laws to enable them to live civilly. He did not see law as a punishment for sin nor as mainly directed against criminals, but rather as regulating necessary institutions, such as marriage, and the various kinds of contract between parties. Tyranny, which allowed the ruler to legislate for his own, not the public good, was Albert's bugbear.

He chose as the opening text of his *Principium*: *Moses commanded a law in the precepts of justices and an inheritance to the house of Jacob, and the promises to Israel* (Ecclus. 24.33).[23] This leads to an analysis of the kinds and functions of law. A supporting text from Isaias: *The Lord is our judge, the Lord is our lawgiver, the Lord is our king* (Is. 33.22) introduces a distinction between a king and a tyrant. The king's orders become law especially if they have respect to usefulness common to all, and not to their usefulness to himself only. The difference between a king and a tyrant is that the latter considers what is useful to him, whereas the former considers what is useful to all. Albert explains the difference between natural and written law before going on to the fulfilment of the Old Testament promises in the New and the contents of the Gospels.

The same interest governs his treatment of the Gospel text. At the very beginning of the Gospel according to St. Matthew the marriage of Mary and Joseph sets him off on the necessity of its institution and the canon law rules on how marriage is validated (20,34). His concept of law and of the

---

[23] ed. cit. 128–131.

difference between Old and New provides him with a neat solution to the vexed question whether to identify St. John the Evangelist with the bridegroom of Cana. We have seen that he quoted conflicting authorities on the subject. The general opinion among Latin exegetes was that the identification should stand. Against that was the objection that a man dedicated to virginity would never have thought of marriage or needed to be converted from the planned wedding. Albert supports the received opinion, giving a new and typical reason for it. St. John at the time of the wedding feast was still living according to the rules of the Old Law, which encouraged marriage. Therefore he might well have prepared for marriage before receiving instruction from Christ (24,99–100). On the Sermon on the Mount, the command not to commit perjury introduces a detailed description of the different sorts of oaths, since we cannot know the meaning of perjury unless we understand what an oath is. But Albert warns us: 'we speak of these things defining rather than disputing.' Law (*ius*) is needed because men cannot live together civilly without contracts and pacts. To make them belongs to the will, which can be expressed in words only, as indicative of will. Since will is subject to instability and ignorance, its expression must be supported by what is stable and all-knowing. Hence the oath is taken in the name of God. The Church admits swearing on the Gospels and relics of saints because they have some divinity in them (20,208–210).

A later text, *Judge not that you may not be judged* (Matt. 7.1.), evokes a distinction between 'judgment of reason' and 'judgment of jurisdiction' and a long account of modes of judgment and of the ways of advocates. On Peter's sword Albert explains that self-defence is allowable to both clergy and laity in private; but if the quarrel is public and an army is raised, then laymen, but not clerks, may take part in it. Only a judge having 'ordinariam ultionis potestatem' may promote just wars against wrongdoers (20,179–180). A relevant text, *Be ye not many masters* (James 3.1) instructs us to respect authority's magisterial power to judge, a magistery which prelates have. In judgments of men the inferior judge is an intruder unless he has been appointed by the pope, the emperor or the king in his kingdom; just so the prelate is an intruder unless God has called him to exercise the power to make judgments. Albert is taking a moral rather than a legal stance on prelates here, only to end on a legal note: a judge must be appointed (*constitutus*); he cannot take office just by himself. His judgments must be guided by will and by reason (20,330–332).

The command 'do as you would be done by' (Matt.7.12) raises a question much debated in the schools. Schoolmen asked whether biblical precepts only were contained in the law of nature. The two precepts came from Tobias 1.10: *fear God and abstain from all sin*; Christ completed them by his command to love one's neighbour also. Albert's opinion here on the character and scope of the law of nature in relation to positive law corresponds to a much fuller discussion of the same subject in his *Summa de bono*.[24] In his commentary he cites a standard text from Cicero and another usually supposed to come from St. Basil,[25] adding a new one from Boethius, *De consolatione*.[26] Even this shortened answer to the question contains a reference to the community: what is said of all men applies especially to those who commune with one another in the unity of one charity and one law. The second half of the verse, *For this is the law and the prophets*, brings out the point of the first half. Christ gives this precept concerning communication and goes on to stress its usefulness by appealing to the law and the prophets (20,350).[27]

Given his focus on man as a member of a society, it is not surprising that he felt no guilt or scruple in adapting the Sermon on the Mount to men as they were living at the time. *Give to him that asketh of thee* (Matt. 5.42) carries the rider that it is indiscreet to impoverish oneself. One must uphold one's dignity as a spiritual or temporal ruler or as head of a family. The petitioner would be dishonest if he asked for more. The same applies to lending as to giving (20,220). Do not go to law unless it is really necessary. If it comes to blows, outside the courts, you may defend yourself against harm, but without counter-attacking, unless forced to do so in self-defence. Even then one must not seek revenge nor continue fighting when the danger is over (20,215–216). An account of the four cardinal virtues which prefaces his commentary on the Sermon relates them to *virtus*, *felicitas* and *beatitudo*. Civic virtue comes into the virtues (20,148–149). Gone is any hesitation on war against non-Christians: Christ commands us to do good to our own enemies but not to God's, who should be exterminated without mercy (20,223).

The title *Rex Iudaeorum* set upon Christ's cross evokes an excursus on the qualities of a good king 'secundum diffinitiones eorum qui de urbanitatibus tractaverunt' (21,737). *Herod the king of Judaea* should properly be called a tyrant, not a king, but the evangelist conforms to common usage, whereby those who reigned tyrannically were called 'kings'. A true king works for the people's benefit, a tyrant only for his own (22,11). The wedding feast at Cana serves as a starting point for the reasons why marriage was instituted, one of which is the needs of civil society (24,89). The liberation of the woman taken in adultery raises the problem: if no sinner could ever act as judge, then all sinners would go unpunished, seeing that many ecclesiastical judges are sinners. Albert

[24] O. Lottin, *Le Droit Naturel chez Saint Thomas d'Aquin et ses prédécesseurs*, 2nd ed. (Bruges, 1931), 41–48.

[25] ibid. 10; 14.

[26] *Consol.* 5, m.3, 24: 'Summamque tenet singula perdens.' The context is the limits of the human intelligence in seeking truth.

[27] 'Quidam dicunt in his duobus jus naturale contineri; quod nullo modo est verum. Quia illud quod hic dicitur utiliter de omnibus praeponitur illis in quibus sibi mutuo communicant homines secundum formam unius charitatis et juris . . .

Posito igitur huiusmodi praecepto communicationis, adjungit utilitatem ejus, cum dicit *Haec est enim Lex et Prophetae*.'

answers that such a sinner cannot judge if his sin is notorious; if it is private, then at least he can judge without scandal, although, 'I think', he sins in judging, unless he has no other judge at hand and judgment is needed on account of the accuser's insistence; in that case a judge who holds the office of judging may dispense justice, while fearing for himself (24,332).

Albert mentions the Petrine supremacy once only and here again he shows tactful moderation. He says on Matt. 16.19, *I will give to thee the keys of the kingdom of heaven*:

I will give thee singly, not [meaning that] Peter should receive them as a single person, but because there is one in the unity of the Church's order who receives plenitude of power; he is Peter's successor and Peter in power. Others receive partial power in the same unity, since they are called to [pastoral] care in part (20,642).[28]

The papal and episcopal powers are nicely balanced. St. Peter wielded his sword of his own accord, without its having been given to him as an 'ordinary' power (*ordinarie*); it follows from Christ's rebuke that he incurs guilt who takes up the sword when he has not received it as part of his office (21,179–180). Albert avoids discussing the relations between *regnum* and *sacerdotium*.

His background, the more or less autonomous free cities of the Rhineland and other parts of Germany, may explain his view of 'civics' and his political realism. We have seen that he cites 'pope, emperor *and king in his kingdom*' as having power to appoint officials. That means that he had shed any illusions about the empire as supreme secular power.

What was his attitude to poverty and mendicancy? First, he had no use for the Franciscan claim to own nothing; he thought it a mere quibble. The friars Minor in theory lived on the proceeds of funds donated to them as bequests or as the result of begging. These proceeds were vested in a 'spiritual friend', by this time the papacy. Hence the friars did not own them. Albert gives his opinion on this in a discussion of the Lord's command not to reclaim one's belongings in a law suit. He allows that even they who have put on the 'habit of perfection' (religious) may seek to reclaim their own, not by contentious judgment, but by a just and pious one, without cost to their perfection. Nor did he think that it mattered (*nec facio vim*) whether they held property not individually, but in the name of a chapter communally. It struck him as fraud and trifling on the part of certain persons who pretended to reclaim goods in the name of a third party, who was supposed to have ownership, while they had the use. Such practice was that shadow of which it is written: *The shades cover his*

[28] '*Dabo tibi* singulariter, non quod singulariter acceperit Petrus, sed quia in unitate ordinis Ecclesiae unus est qui accipit in plenitudine potestatis, qui est successor Petri, et Petrus in potestate. Alii autem in eadem unitate accipiunt in parte potestatis, eo quod vocantur in partem sollicitudinis.'

shadow (Job 40.17). The general conclusion is that to reclaim one's goods 'cum contentione et clamore' is forbidden to all. Without them, all may reclaim their own. He who does so is harming no one, unless he knows that great evil may arise from his action; he should desist if it is leading to general strife (*contentio communis*). Again, Albert speaks as a man familiar with city feuds and tumults (20,218–219). He takes the whole apparatus of justice for granted; it protects weak laymen, who depend on the comforts of good fortune to prop them up. They too may reclaim their own without contention making for scandal (ibid.). Albert tried to take a realistic view of men as they were; but his distinction between lawsuits conducted 'with contentious clamour' and those managed peacefully might be a fine one in practice.

Secondly, he pictures the Gospel characters as more comfortably off than they had sometimes been presented by commentators. The reason why Jesus was tired on his journey through Samaria was that he preferred to travel on foot rather than by carriage for fear of burdening those who gave him hospitality (24,157). He had money in case no hospitality was available (24,159–160). He kept it for future needs (20,327; 21,468). The question why St. Peter had a sword, although the apostles had been sent on their mission without any provisions, rather annoyed Albert: he had answered repeatedly that the ban applied only to their first mission, which took place in peacetime, and not to the later time of trouble (24,631).

Peter the Chanter had noted the humble life-style of Martha and Mary, holding it up as a shaming contrast to modern prelates'. Albert, a noble himself, could not imagine the inhabitants of a castle (*castellum*, John 11.1;30) living without servants. Martha, Mary and Lazarus lived together on their joint heritage; the last two left its management to Martha, because she was the best administrator. Her 'ministry' to Jesus consisted not of personal service but of management of the expenses involved (24,435). Many Jews came to condole with the sisters on the death of their brother because they were noble persons (24,445). Albert never considers the question whether Christ wore shoes or went barefoot. When the soldiers at the crucifixion divide Christ's garments among themselves and cast lots for his seamless coat (John 19.23–24), Albert cheerfully admits that he probably had four pieces of clothing, nor could they have been squalid, or the soldiers would have thrown them away. The evangelist describes the precious workmanship of the seamless coat such as cappers and glovers (*birreti et chyrotecae*) make (24,658). Albert saw the apostolic life as not excluding decent clothing.

However, he would defend the Preachers' right to go begging. The mission of the disciples without money 'is strongly against the dogma of those who condemn mendicancy in Preachers' (20,449). The word *dogma* points to the fixed principle of anti-mendicant polemicists. He stressed the poverty of Christ and his milieu. His Mother wrapped the Christ child in rags, since *pannis* denotes cloths old and ragged, to teach us poverty, humility and austerity (22,199). That wine ran out at the wedding feast at Cana demonstrates the poverty of the host, since wine would have been cheap and plentiful at that time of the year (24,91). Albert sees 'the highest poverty' as the state of perfection, which is not for everyone. The young man who was saddened by the command to leave all and follow Jesus felt sad at the thought of rejection of all and of mendicancy (Mark 10.22). That was not against his salvation, but pertained to perfection according to the state of highest poverty (21,598). A certain sympathy for Martha comes through the exposition of the contrast between the two sisters. The text *But one thing is necessary. Mary has chosen the best part* (Luke 10.42) is expounded diversely:

According to my opinion it should be expounded in praise of the active life or Martha's, thus: 'You, Martha, are troubled about many things, *but one thing is necessary*, and required by the needs of this life, and so acceptable to me and to the saints, since without it Mary could not engage in contemplation. Augustine, however, seems to take Mary's side in expounding the text (23,88).

Inevitably in comparing the two types of life, the active and the contemplative, Albert takes the traditional view that the latter is better: the active life often brings venial sins; some say that contemplatives' behaviour excels in virtue. And indeed contemplation is a good in itself; action is directed to an end (23,89–90). But recognition of the contemplative's dependence on the work of others tended to be overlooked in religious literature: Albert was more perceptive.

On the whole he stresses humility more than poverty. *Blessed are the poor in spirit* (Matt. 5.3) refers to those who think themselves insufficient: 'and so I call this the literal exposition' (*Et ideo dico litteralem esse expositionem*). There follows a long discourse on humility. It consists of rejection of all things which might make one think oneself self-sufficient (20,149). Jesus showed his humility by charging the healed man not to make him known (20,520) and by bowing down to write (24,331).

Albert's Gospel commentaries differ from the Franciscans' in being less defensive and polemical. He does not mention his Order and touches on subjects debated with the seculars only where they bring his values under direct fire. In such cases he answers them back. But his main object seems to be to explain his text to a sympathetic audience, without pathos or confrontation. That would be characteristic of him.

V. THOMAS AQUINAS

In order to tackle St. Thomas as an exegete one would have to be both a theologian and a Byzantinist. He approached his text as a theologian and he drew on Greek sources in translation, which have not yet been identified.[1] Being neither, I can only compare his expositions with his predecessors' to note what was traditional and what original and personal in Thomas. I have had to exclude the *Catena aurea* from my study, although it was one of the most popular of his books. It took the form of a collection of extracts from the Fathers and Church councils, both Latin and Greek in translation, on all four Gospels, with the aim of providing a much more thorough aid to study than had been available hitherto on both literal and spiritual senses. A fuller knowledge of patristic teaching on the whole Gospel text would disarm heretics and strengthen the faith of believers. We know that Thomas's unnamed Greek helpmeet used one of the best of Greek compilations of this kind, by Nicetas of Herakleion; but once the great names have been listed, we know little of other contributors. Thomas worked on this enormous task 1263–1267.[2]

It seems certain that his *Catena* underlies many later medieval Gospel commentaries. It could arouse mixed feelings: the English friar William of Nottingham, writing in the early fourteenth century, attacked the over-imaginative literal sense put forward by 'Theophylus', who stated that the Virgin for reasons of modesty left St. Elizabeth before the birth of the Baptist, her son. William wondered by what authority friar Thomas Aquinas quoted Theophilus so frequently.[3] The Leonine Commission has a critical edition of the *Catena* in hand. Until this appears it would be waste of time to study it in depth.

Its omission leaves us with Thomas's lectures on St. Matthew and St. John. The former survive in an incomplete form: the commentary on Matt. 5. 11–6.8 and on 6. 16–18 is missing. The blank was filled in spuriously by a later Dominican, but has been printed as genuine in all existing editions. Fr. H.-V. Shooner discovered a missing fragment on 5. 13–16, and also showed that the lectures represent *reportationes* made by two friar students.[4] Now Fr. J. P. Renard has given us an annotated edition of Thomas on Matt.5. 20–48 from the Bâle manuscript used by Fr. Shooner. This lecture course is now dated to after 1263 and probably to Thomas's second regency at Paris, 1269–

---

[1] J. A. Weisheipl, 'The Johannine Commentary of Friar Thomas', *Church History*, 45 (1976), 185–195.

[2] J. A. Weisheipl, *Friar Thomas d'Aquino. His Life, Thought and Work* (New York, 1974), 171–173; 370–371; R. Devreesse, 'Chaînes exégétiques grecques', *Dict. de la Bible*, Suppl. 1 (Paris, 1928), 1084–1233; M. Geerard, 'Concilia. Catenae', *Clavis Patrum Graecorum*, 4 (Turnhout, 1980).

[3] B. Smalley, 'Which William of Nottingham?', *Mediaeval and Renaissance Studies*, 3 (1954), 235; reprinted in my *Studies*, 284.

[4] 'La *Lectura in Matthaeum* de S. Thomas', *Angelicum*, 33 (1956), 121–142.

1272.[5] The lectures on St. John belong to the same period, probably to the years 1270–1271.[6] I have used the editions in the Marietti series by Fr. R. Cai on Matthew (1951) and on John (1952), and that of Renard on Matt. 5. 20–48. I refer to them as 'M', 'J' and 'R' respectively, giving the page numbers.

To begin with the sources: naturally Thomas used the standard glossed text and quoted from the Gloss; but he did not regard it as authoritative. He criticises the gloss on John 6.47 as going against the context (J,180) and notes that on one text the author of the gloss is unknown (M,245). His proximate source has eluded me. Thomas probably consulted Hugh of St. Cher's postills, though he would not have mentioned a contemporary by name. There are many parallels, though Thomas does not quote verbatim. Hugh seems to represent some of the *aliqui* whose opinion is quoted on the reasons why the Pharisees built tombs for the prophets (Matt. 23.29), which Thomas disagreed with (M,291), and again *secundum alios* on what Jesus wrote on the ground (John 8.8); here he approves it as a better suggestion than others, though there is no certainty (J,213). Collation makes it clear that he did not have Hugh's postills as a constant guide to study on his desk. The number of differing opinions of unnamed commentators which Thomas mentions shows that he had access to some whose work is anonymous or which have not survived. The 'Master of the Histories' is named once, and only for blame: he suggests that Salome may have been the name of one of the Marys' husbands, a patent error, says Thomas: in Greek we have Solomei, which is a feminine ending and can never be found in the masculine (M,368). This was unfair; Comestor did not commit himself to such a view.[7] Thomas must have had more recent guides; perhaps he used some collection of authorities on the Gospels; perhaps he used the fruits of his own labours in compiling the *Catena aurea*. The Greek Theophilus appears again on John 11.10, quoted by name (J,278); it is the same quotation as in the *Catena*.[8]

Thomas liked to use Greek Fathers in translation. It was unusual to quote Origen's work on Matthew as Thomas constantly did. He made much use of the homily beginning 'The spiritual voice of the eagle', which he said was 'ascribed' to Origen, showing commendable doubt on a widespread mistake of ascription.[9] The homily's author was John Scot Erigena. Thomas knew John's incomplete commentary, as distinct from his

[5] 'La *Lectura super Matthaeum* V, 20–48 de Thomas d'Aquin', *Recherches de théologie ancienne et médiévale*, 50 (1983), 145–190.

[6] J. A. Weisheipl, *Friar Thomas*, op. cit. 121–123; 371–372. I quote from the translation into English by J. A. Weisheipl and F. R. Larcher, cited above p. 246, n.15, up to where the first part ends on John 7.53.

[7] PL 198, 1631.

[8] *Catena aurea*, ed. A. Guarienti, 2 (Turin/Rome, 1953), 483.

[9] J. McEvoy, 'The Sun as *res* and *signum*: Grosseteste's commentary on *Ecclesiasticus* ch. 43, vv. 1–5', *Recherches de théologie ancienne et médiévale*, 41 (1974), 47–48.

homily, only through its quotation in the Gloss on St. John.[10] Pseudo-Chrysostom's *Opus imperfectum* plays more part in his lectures on Matthew than the genuine Chrysostom's homilies, as it does in his *Catena aurea*; Thomas, like his contemporaries, believed that it had been translated from Greek. It was really written by an Arian in the fifth century. Very likely it was the book which Thomas was recorded to have said he would prefer to the whole town of Paris; he would like better to have 'Chrysostom on Matthew'. Doubtless he thought that a complete copy of the *Opus imperfectum* existed somewhere or other and he already had Chrysostom's genuine homilies.[11] Chrysostom on St. John with Augustine were his basic patristic sources on the fourth Gospel. All the established Latin Fathers and early medieval commentators down to Rabanus and Remigius appear, except for 'Victorinus', who seems to have found special favour with the Franciscans.

Thomas often strings his quotations one after the other without choosing between them. His preference, when expressed, has nothing to do with degrees of authority, but depends on whichever explanation to his mind makes better sense of the text; his choices generally reflect what strikes him as the least far-fetched. Augustine is often preferred, but may be criticised alongside other Fathers, as on John 1.14:

For the early doctors and saints were so intent upon refuting the emerging errors concerning the saints that they seemed meanwhile to fall into the opposite ones. For example, Augustine, speaking against the Manichaeans, who destroyed the freedom of the will, disputed in such terms that he seemed to have fallen into the heresy of Pelagius (J,35).

Here as elsewhere Thomas's flair for nosing out spurious ascriptions appears in his statement on John 10.9–10: 'Fourthly it is expounded in the book *De spiritu et anima*, which is attributed to Augustine, but is not his' (J,260). The *De spiritu et anima* circulated under cover of Augustine, but was really a twelfth-century *pastiche* of disputed authorship. Thomas had earlier accepted the wrong attribution, which he denies here.[12]

Ancient philosophers receive better treatment from him than they got from Bonaventure and Pecham and even from Albert. Even in the prologue to his lectures on John he explained the four ways by which ancient philosophers attained to a knowledge of God (J,1). Their ignorance of revelation led them to error and the light they prided themselves on having was false (J,26). That did not stop Thomas from appreciating their

---

[10] See *Jean Scot Homélie sur le prologue de Jean*, ed. E. Jeauneau (SC 151, 1969), 140–141, and his edition of John Scot's commentary (SC 180, 1972), 62.

[11] Joop (J. H. A.) van Banning, 'Saint Thomas et l'Opus Imperfectum in Matthaeum', *Atti dell'VIII Congresso Tomistico Internazionale*, 8 (*Studi Tomistici*, 17, 1982), 73–85.

[12] Weisheipl, op. cit 439.

mode of reaching and achieving such truth as natural reason permitted them.

Aristotle predominates among 'early philosophers', as might be expected, not only in explicit quotations, but in the workings of Thomas's mind. As expected, too, he preferred the metaphysical, ethical and political books to those on natural science so dear to Albert. He quotes the *Politics* to justify hunting animals for food, for example (R,156). Two quotations from the *Rhetorics* (Philosophus in Rhetoricis) are brought forward: 'Timor facit consiliativos' (J,310), and a remark on the calming of anger (J,443). Thomas seems to be referring to the gist of ii,5, on the causes of fear, and of ii,3, on calm after wrath. The *Rhetorics* was not translated into Latin until the mid-thirteenth century, by whom is unknown. Its survival in five manuscripts only suggests that it was not read widely.[13]

He seldom quotes Latin classical authors; but his quotation is apt and not a mere frill when he does so. He does not often give a precise reference, nor quote verbally; hence he must have relied on his memory or used some collection of sayings. He quotes Seneca on how to expose hypocrites (on Matt. 7.16): 'Nemo potest diu fictam ferre personam'; they will show their true selves in the long run (M,103).[14] Vegetius' advice to a general supports Christ's refusal to obey Satan at his temptation, even though the act itself may have been good:

Nihil umquam sapiens dux debet facere ad arbitrium sui hostis, etiam si bonum videatur (M,51).[15]

Boethius 'in musica' cites Pythagoras' opinions on music (M,146) on the text *we have sung to you* (Matt. 11.16–17).[16] Thomas could also adduce Roman history to illustrate the waning of the Baptist's power after Christ's coming:

For this custom was observed by ancient powers, that the lesser power should not wear the insignia of his power in the presence of a greater; hence the consuls would lay aside their insignia in the presence of the Dictator (J,274).

He could use shrewd observations of his own to perform the same function; the 'dumb ox' was not always abstracted by higher thoughts. Why did the disciples need to be taught humility, when they were humble poorfolk already (John 4.8)? Because they had received the gift of wisdom, and persons promoted suddenly tend to be proud (J,109). The Samaritan woman at the well showed good knowledge of the details of religious

---

[13] *The Cambridge History of Later Medieval Philosophy*, ed. N. Kretzmann, A. Kenny, J. Pinborg (Cambridge, 1982), 78.

[14] *De clementia* i.1 (Teubner ed. C. Hosius, Leipzig, 1914, 212).

[15] *Epitoma rei militaris*, iii.26 (Teubner ed. C. Lang, Leipzig, 1885, 120).

[16] *Inst. Music.*, ed. G. Friedlein (Leipzig, 1867), 185–186.

differences between the Samaritans and the Jews: 'It is not surprising that she was taught about this, for it often happens in places where there are differences in beliefs that even the simple people are instructed about them' (J,114). This must have been true of the mixed population in many Mediterranean areas. On Christ's comparison of his generation to children playing (Matt. 11.16–17) Thomas remarks that it is natural for boys to play, since, unlike adults, they have no cares:

And be it noted that it is natural for man to take pleasure in some likeness; hence if we see something well sculptured, which has a good resemblance to what it should, then we are pleased. Just so boys who take pleasure in games always make play with something representing war or suchlike (M,145).

Thomas had watched children playing.

What characteristics does he show as an exegete? Thomas distinguishes himself from most earlier commentators by keeping to the point, concentrating with a fierce singlemindedness on the text in hand. To read him after Albert is like passing from a Victorian salon, littered with furniture and ornaments, to a white-washed 'functional' living room. Thomas ignored what struck him as irrelevant. He omits discussion of the identity of St. John and the bridegroom at Cana, and of the guests' alcoholism. He does not mention the absence of the 'woman taken in adultery' episode in Burgundio's translation of Chrysostom. He had no use for the colourful legends which must have made the *Historia scholastica* such good reading. Comestor gives the names of the three Magi;[17] Hugh of St. Cher repeats them.[18] Thomas says that the evangelist does not tell us how many Magi came to adore the Christ-child (much less names them). It seems from the gifts they offered that there were three, although they represented some others (M,26). His predecessors had alluded to the content of the apocryphal *Liber de infantia Salvatoris*, while warning that it was not authentic. Thomas exposes its falsity twice: it contradicts St. John's statement that the turning of water into wine was the first miracle worked by Jesus, since it recounts many other miracles worked by him as a boy (J,53; 72).

There are no devotional interludes, no apocalyptic speculation and no casuistry on the Sermon on the Mount.[19] *Distinctiones* serve to clarify the meaning of the word in the text rather than to provide miscellaneous items of information. I have noted only one *exemplum* and that is used to illustrate rather than to edify: Thomas finds a grim parallel to Herod's mixture of pleasure and cruelty when he had the Baptist's head brought to him at a banquet. 'It is said that a certain bailiff loved a whore; she told him during an embrace that she had never seen a man killed. At lunch-time he

[17] PL 198, 1542.
[18] I quote Hugh of St. Cher *ad loc.* here as before: on Matt. 2. 1.
[19] Apart from a *quaestio* on the right or duty of a sinful judge to condemn a sinner (M, 100). See also J, 213.

had a man worthy of death brought in and had him beheaded before her. The Romans knew and exiled him from Rome' (M,191).[20] Thomas refined on the technique of division and subdivision. It fragmented the text even more, but it did enable him to give weight to each phrase. Some of his *quaestiones* seem wide of the mark, as when the text *But the very hairs of your head are all numbered* (Matt. 10.30) raises a long *quaestio* on the state of men's bodies after the resurrection (M,137). The reason was that school tradition had attached certain *quaestiones* to certain texts. Albert hinted at such a discussion. He described the nature and function of hair and added that it would be preserved so as to rise with man at the resurrection, by the Father's wisdom and care, in so far as it made for his adornment and eternal wisdom in disposing to contemplation (20,469). A master would have disappointed his pupils had he shirked from giving his own solution to these problems.

Another characteristic of Thomas is his relentless pursuit of heretics. All commentators agreed that the evangelists wrote in order to confute both heresies which had already arisen and those which would arise in the future; but they could be perfunctory in naming heretics and in underlining the texts thought to attack them. Thomas wins the prize as a heresiologue in his list of names and in his search throughout the Gospels for anti-heretical arguments. The named heretics belong to patristic tradition, while those of his day are comprised under the heading of Manicheans: *Do not think that I am come to destroy the law or the prophets* (Matt. 5.17) is very efficacious against those who condemn the Law as coming from the devil. A man was swayed by this argument and became a friar Preacher. Hence Manichees hold it in horror.[21] The convert must have been a former Cathar. Some men, Thomas says, hold falsely that secular judges are all murderers when they condemn criminals according to various laws (R,156). They may have been Cathars too. The prediction that false Christs would arise (Matt. 24.23–24) moved Thomas to describe the errors of those who heralded the false Christ's coming: 'and sometimes they want to confirm it from apocryphal scriptures, sometimes from secret senses of Scripture' (M,302). He could have been alluding to such texts as the *Interrogatio Ioannis* circulating among the Cathars and to speculation based on Joachim of Fiore or Pseudo-Joachim. The current heresies preoccupied Thomas little less than the ancient ones. He does not neglect the errors of ancient philosophers either. That Jesus is recorded to have groaned in the spirit, troubled himself and wept (John 11.33–35) contradicts the Stoics, who say that no wise man is ever sad. It is very inhuman not to grieve at the death of a friend (J,286).

Thomas also set his face against what seems to have been a tendency at Paris to rationalise Christ's miracles and make them more natural, of course against a background of his divinity and humanity. They said on the feeding of the multitude that it was a natural property of wheat seed to multiply;

---

[20] This story is not in the standard collections of *exempla*.
[21] Shooner, op. cit. 129–130.

Thomas stresses that Christ worked a miracle (M,193). His walking on water was possible, some would say, because he had the gifts *(dotes)* of impassibility, agility, subtility and clarity. Thomas gives their opinion, but adds: 'Sed hoc non credo; credo enim quod miraculose fecit' (M,195), a rare personal touch. Albert also rejected the explanation of *dotes* for walking on water in favour of a miracle (20, 602). On the transfiguration again, Thomas repeats that walking on water and shining all came from Christ's divine nature and not from his *dotes*. The gift of *glory* does not belong to the wayfarer on earth; but here it had some resemblance, since *His face was as the sun shineth in his power* (Apoc. 1.16). These actions were beyond human power to accomplish, even Christ's:

Ego autem hoc non credo, quia dos est quaedam proprietas ipsius gloriae. Unde quod super mare ambulavit, quod resplenduit, totum fuit ex virtute divina, quia dos gloriae repugnat viatori, sed habuit aliquam similitudinem, quia *resplenduit facies eius sicut sol* (M, 218).

The same doctrine is expounded at much greater length in the *Summa theologica* III, q.45, a 1–2. Current misbeliefs are noted from a theological point of view: laymen mistakenly receive the eucharist on behalf of those in purgatory (J,181).

On the contrary, there is little polemic against the Mendicants' enemies. Thomas must have thought that lectures on Scripture were not the place for it. He makes a few clear but oblique references to the friars' function, as teachers and preachers helping prelates, and depending on alms for their living:

The fact that Christ was not always baptizing gives an example to us that the major prelates of the churches should not occupy themselves with things that can be performed by others, but should allow them to be done by those of lesser rank (J,106).

Christ received food from others

. . . in order to give us an example that those engrossed in spiritual matters should not be ashamed of their poverty nor regard it as burdensome to be supported by others. For it is fitting that teachers have others provide their food, so that, being free from such concerns, they may carefully pay attention to the ministry of the word . . . (J,119).

Thomas insists on the need for study as a preparation for preaching:

. . . every teacher is obliged to possess the means of feeding spiritually the people who come to him. And since no man possesses of himself the resources to feed them, he must acquire them elsewhere by his labour, study, and persistent prayer (J,161).

He does not pay much attention to poverty. It was traditional to say that Jesus had no home of his own, but lived in lodgings on John 1.39 (J,59). It was traditional, too, to admit that he had money, but that he had used it to feed the poor (M,226). Discussing the relative merits of prelates and religious, Thomas states that a *prelate* should not 'sell all' as Jesus advised the young man seeking perfection to do. Sale of all one's possessions is a means to perfection, not perfection itself (M,244). The apostles wished to be poor, not for poverty's sake, but in order to devote themselves to contemplation (R,189). Thomas abstains from answering the debated question whether the seamless robe was cheap or precious; both sides of the argument are given; Thomas adds only that it could be both cheap and seamless because in Palestine tunics could be made by rags patched together (J,451). He takes the general view that the disciples' mission to preach without purse or shoes was *pro tempore*; the disciples were sent to the Jews, who were accustomed to support preachers; the poor in Palestine went barefoot and so the disciples had to conform to the local type of pauper (M,130). That Christ lived on alms does not detract from his perfection (J,300).

Views, expressed by Thomas as an exegete, on the papacy may be interesting for the light they throw on a much discussed problem. On Matt. 16.18–19, Thomas claims that the Roman Church has never been stained by heresies, unlike other Churches, especially Constantinople's. The 'Roman' applies to the whole Western Church: 'Hence I believe that westerners owe greater reverence to Peter than to the other apostles' (M,212). On the commission to remit sins (Matt. 16. 19–21), Thomas states that Christ gave it directly to Peter; the others received it from him. Lest it should be thought that he said this to Peter alone, he puts the commission in the plural, *quorum remiseretis*. For that reason the pope, who is in St. Peter's place, has plenitude of power, but others derive it from him (M,213). He says in his *quaestio* on tithes that decision belongs to any prince who has power to make law; hence it is in the Church's power to determine what tithes should be paid (M,289–290). Thomas held strongly to the pope's plenitude of power and the special reverence owed him by members of the Roman Church. A governor must excel in virtue as the soul rules over the body (J,482). However, Thomas does not discuss the relations between *regnum* and *sacerdotium* even on the episode of St. Peter's sword. Evidently he did not think it a suitable subject for exegesis, or for theological discussion for that matter. His commentaries show the same reticence as his works on theology and his *De regimine principum* (the authentic parts of it).

Some political theory we do find. It stems from his reading of Aristotle's *Politics*. He makes a specific quotation from 1,2,1253a (M,145) as well as that mentioned earlier. *Every kingdom divided against itself shall be made desolate* etc. (Matt. 12.25) prompts the comment that there are three kinds of community: the house, the city and the kingdom, which consummates the two former communities. The kingdom is necessary because it alone can protect all its citizens. Peace in a kingdom resembles life in a man. Bodily health is nothing more than the temporising of humours (the medieval physician's commonplace); just so is peace. Illness follows if the balance of humours is disturbed in a kingdom as in a man. Therefore each member of the kingdom must keep to his own order (M,158–159;70). More significant is Thomas's adaptation of Gospel teaching to Aristotle. The Fathers handed down a tradition of adjusting in practical terms commands such as *Take no heed for the morrow*; but it was accepted that such a code of morals would in any case apply only to an individual or to a group. At best the Christian was told to obey the State unless the order went against his conscience: the State was exterior. Thomas was probably the first exegete to realise and to state that what was enjoined on a private person did not apply to a public person or institution at all. Kings *must* store up treasure; it is no sin for a king to do so. He does it for the sake of many and has many needs. A sin for one person is a right for a royal government (M,94). Albert had underlined the social nature of man and his need for laws; Thomas took a long step forward in distinguishing between public and private and in insisting on the functions and legitimate claims of the former. It was all of a piece with his *De regimine principum* (1263–1267)[22] with its preference for monarchy.

I have left until now the subject of Thomas's treatment of the four senses in the practice of exegesis, in contrast to his theory on their functions. His principles are well-known. The literal sense included the inspired writer's whole intention, whether he used forms of speech such as metaphor or whether he prophesied. God, who inspired the writer, put spiritual significance into the events, persons and things mentioned by the writer of which he was not aware, for the benefit of readers living afterwards, recipients of a fuller revelation than God had vouchsafed to the human author.[23] It would seem to follow that the exegete ought to focus on the literal sense instead of downgrading it as a mere foundation or outer rind of spiritual sweetness. Thomas's brilliant literal exposition of the book of Job (1263–1264) underlined the point. I plead guilty to having drawn this conclusion, which goes much too far. Thomas gave spiritual senses to his text both in his *Catena aurea* and in his lectures on Matthew and John. Why then the exposition of Job *ad litteram*? The answer lies in his prologue to Job; I did not take it seriously enough.[24] St. Gregory had given such a thorough exposition of the spiritual senses that nothing more needed to be added.[25] Thomas expounded Job *ad litteram* as a supplement to the *Moralia*, also presumably because the literal content of a provocative book fascinated him. The Gospels had no such authoritative spiritual exposition as Job; therefore the exegete ought to supply one, if not as full as Gregory's, at least serviceable.

His lectures on the Gospels prove, if proof be needed, how much the

[22] Weisheipl, op. cit. 189–195; 388–389.
[23] *Quodlibet VII*, q. vi, ed. R. Spiazzi (Rome/Turin, 1928), 145–148; *Summa Theologiae* 1a, q.1, a. 8–10.
[24] In my *Study of the Bible*, op. cit. 300–306.
[25] *Opera*, Leonine ed. 26 (1965), 4.

spiritual exposition of Bible texts belonged to Christian doctrine in his eyes. To deny it would be to deny God's plan for mankind. The Bible was Christ-centred. The Gospel represented a middle state between those of the Law and of glory (R,154). Christ fulfilled the promises of the Old Testament in such a way that the spiritual exposition was needed to explain the promises:

Again he was *full of truth* (John 1.14) in so far as he fulfilled the figures of the Old Law and the promises made to the fathers . . . (J,38).

Christ told the Jews to *search the Scriptures* (John 5.39):

As if to say: You do not have the word of God in your hearts, but in the Scriptures; therefore you must seek for it elsewhere than in your hearts. Hence *Search the Scriptures*, that is in the Old Testament, but not on the surface, for it lay hidden in its depths under shadowy symbols: 'Even until this day, when Moses is read, a veil is over your hearts' (2 Cor. 3.15). Thus he significantly says *Search*, probe into the depths (J,155).

The clearest statement comes on Christ's entry into Jerusalem (John 12.12–15):

Know that Christ's deeds are as it were the mean between those of the Old and New Testaments. Therefore both the crowd which preceded him and that which followed him were praising him in so far as Christ's deeds are rule and example as performed in the New Testament and were prefigured by the fathers in the Old Testament (J,304).

Without Christ as a link the bond between Old and New would have snapped.

Commentators could find spiritual senses without difficulty in the Old Testament; but Thomas's definition of the literal sense as the whole meaning intended by the human writer only sharpened a problem which had vexed them ever since Andrew of St. Victor had given the Jewish interpretation of Isaias' prophecies of Christ's coming as the literal sense and had left the christological sense to be explained by others.[26] How could one distinguish a christological prophecy directly intended by the writer from prophecies or references which he directed to the Jewish people regarding their immediate or near future? The latter would express his direct intention; Christian expositors would have to deduce a spiritual sense from such passages to supply what the prophet himself had not foreseen. There was agreement in the schools that such passages existed: the problem was to distinguish between them.

The young Thomas wrestled with the question in his lectures on Isaias as a *cursor biblicus*. He was not yet a qualified doctor of theology and gave them either at Cologne under Albert before the summer of 1252 or else at

---

[26] B. Smalley, op. cit. 156–172; 295–299.

Paris in the academic year 1252–1253. The title should probably be *Postilla* rather than *Expositio ad litteram*.[27] He states on 1.2 that the author's principal intention refers to Christ's coming and the calling of the gentiles.[28] The key prophecies such as *Behold a virgin shall conceive* in the context of the whole of Is. 7 are recorded by the prophet as signs of the incarnation, as is also for instance 9.6: *For a child is born to us*. 'Here he describes the Saviour', Thomas says, and goes on to explain the prophecy.[29] All the same he persists in interpreting 8.1–3 as Isaias' literal meaning and answers the objections of those who hold that the text cannot be explained *ad litteram*. Their exposition lacks the authority of that of the other sign in chapter 7, because it is wrested by force (out of context) and has not such authority from Scripture as the earlier one cited by St. Matthew, 1.22–23. We can interpret it in the literal sense provided that the child is understood to prefigure Christ.[30] There are other places where Thomas rejects a direct christological reference as belonging to the prophet's first intention.[31]

By the time he came to lecture on Matthew, Thomas had realised that denial of certain direct christological prophecies of the Old Testament had been condemned as heretical. In fact the Council of Constantinople, 553, had condemned the denial with other errors ascribed to Bishop Theodore of Mopsuestia, although modern research has shown that Theodore had not really made such a clean sweep of Old Testament prophecies as members of the council claimed.[32] Thomas alluded to Theodore's teaching and its condemnation on Matt. 1.23: *Behold a virgin shall be with child . . . Emmanuel, which being interpreted is God with us*. Thomas lists three errors arising from this text. The second was Theodore's who said that none of those things which are put forward from the Old Testament concern Christ *ad litteram*, but are adapted, as when they bring forward the line of Virgil:

So he spoke, firm in his resolution and could not be shaken (*Aen.*2,650).

Presumably Anchises' refusal to be saved from the ruins of Troy was 'adapted' to Christ's refusal to avoid danger to himself. Thomas goes on to quote: 'for this was adapted to Christ, and so must be understood *Now all this was done that it might be fulfilled which the Lord spoke by the prophet*' (Matt. 1.22). He counters the argument by an appeal to Luke 24.46 and

---

[27] *Opera*, Leonine ed. 28 (1974); review by J. Weisheipl, *The Thomist*, 43 (1979), 331–337.

[28] ed. cit. 10.

[29] ibid. 68.

[30] ibid. 60–61.

[31] ibid. 11; 40; 67; 96.

[32] See *Dict. de théol. cath.* 15 (1946), 235–279; R. Devreesse, 'Essai sur Théodore de Mopsueste', *Studi e testi*, 141 (1948); R. A. Greer, *Theodore of Mopsuestia Exegete and Theologian* (London, 1961).

explains that some things in the Old Testament refer to Christ and are said of him only, such as Is. 7.14 and Ps. 21.2. If anyone put any other literal sense on this, he would be a heretic, and the heresy is condemned (M.21). We find a more explicit reference to the Council of Constantinople in Thomas's prologue to his Psalter-commentary (1272–1273):

Concerning the mode of exposition, know that both in the psalter and in other prophets we must avoid the error condemned in the fifth synod. Theodore of Mopsuestia said that in holy scripture and the prophets nothing is said expressly of Christ, but something about other things, but they were adapted to Christ, just as Ps. 21[19]: *They parted my garments amongst them* is said not of Christ, but literally of David. But this mode was condemned in that council, and he who says that the Scriptures should be expounded in such a way is a heretic.

Again on Ps. 21 he brings forward Theodore's condemnation at the Council of Constantinople for expounding the Psalm literally of David and for other errors. Therefore this psalm must be expounded of Christ.[33]

Neither the Latin record (no Greek survives) of the Council's decisions[34] nor any other source known to me mentions Theodore's posthumous condemnation, except that it is taken as an example of a ban on a dead man's teaching in 'Gratian's' *Decretum* (II, causa xxiv, q.2, cap.6, not enlarged by the Gloss on it). Had the condemnation been known earlier, Andrew of St. Victor's critics could have used it against him. Nor is the Aeneas verse quoted to illustrate Theodore's supposed doctrine of adaptation found elsewhere. The doctrine of adaptation is sophisticated and does not figure in medieval biblical exegesis. Thomas probably owed his knowledge of the conciliar ban to one of his Greek informants. It witnesses to his wide curiosity in finding new sources.[35]

Carefully orthodox as he was, Thomas did not interpret each single psalm as christological in its literal sense. He kept a balance, as in his early lectures on Isaias. It was a precarious balance: no authoritative criterion existed to enable the commentator to decide in which prophecies the psalmists and prophets had been granted a direct vision of the Christian faith. Classification had to be mainly subjective.

Application of the four senses to the Gospels posed an equally difficult, but less definable problem. The Gospels had an allegorical sense, in that they described promises fulfilled and figures realised. Certainly, too, they themselves promised the mission to the gentiles and the rise of the Church, while all was written for the Christian's instruction tropologically. But were the evangelists, recording the very words and deeds of Christ, left out

[33] *Opera* 13 (Antwerp, 1612), fols. 1ᵛ; 24ᵛ. The text of the second allusion to Theodore is corrupt; 'in synodo Toletana' and 'Monestenus' for Constantinople and Mopsuestia.

[34] J. D. Mansi, *Sacrorum conciliorum nova et amplissima collectio*, 9 (Florence, 1763), 211–215.

[35] On his use of conciliar documents at first hand, see G. Geenen, 'En marge du Concile de Chalcédoine', *Angelicum*, 29 (1952), 43–59.

of the secret? They benefited from the Christian revelation, so that their eyes were not veiled like the prophets, but wide open. Did they *intend* a spiritual sense as well as a literal? If so, according to Thomas's view of the writer's whole intention, the literal and spiritual senses would amalgamate. Both Bonaventure and Albert had been feeling the way to an answer. Without formulating a theory, they sometimes understood that literal and spiritual senses are identical.

There are a few clues to Thomas's thinking on this question. He draws out the significance of the number twelve on the calling of the disciples:

And why does he say twelve? In order that the conformity of New and Old Testaments should be shown . . . The second reason is that their future strength and achievement should be shown . . . Again it is to signify perfection (M,128).

St. Matthew surely seems to be writing deliberately on the significance of twelve. On *This happened in Bethany* (John 1.28) Thomas gives two reasons, literal and mystical, for the mention of *Bethany*, which means 'house of obedience'; the literal, ascribed to Chrysostom, is that 'John wrote this Gospel for certain persons, perhaps still alive, who would recall the time and who saw the place where these things happened . . .;' Thomas goes on:

The mystical reason is that these places are appropriate for baptism. For in saying 'Bethany', which is interpreted as 'house of obedience', he indicates that one must come to be baptized through obedience to our faith (J,50).

St. John is 'indicating'! On the well in Samaria (John 4.5–6):

The evangelist is so careful to record all these matters in order to show us that all the things which happened to the patriarchs were leading up to Christ, and that they pointed to Christ, and that he descended from them according to the flesh (J,107).

Here St. John carefully records data which have an allegorical sense for him and which he intends to be understood as such by his readers. More explicitly, Thomas states St. Matthew's intention in describing Christ's entry into Jerusalem riding upon an ass (on John 12.14–15), whereas the other evangelists call it *a colt of an ass*:

Because Matthew wrote his Gospel for the Jews, he mentions an ass, which signifies the synagogue of the Jews, which was as it were the mother of the gentiles in spiritual things, since *the Law shall come forth from Sion: and the word of the Lord from Jerusalem* (Is. 2.3). The other evangelists, because they wrote Gospels for the gentiles, also mention the colt etc. (J,304).

The evangelists intended a spiritual sense; Matthew mentions an ass, mother, as well as a colt, offspring, because the gentiles were children of the spiritual heritage of the Jews. The other evangelists, unlike Matthew, found it sufficient to mention a colt. Hence the whole intention covers the spiritual sense, and a rather subtle one too; hence the literal sense *is* the spiritual for the evangelists.

Thomas leads us to suppose that it was so; he does not discuss it. Otherwise he uses the conventional etymologies, number symbolism and properties as a vehicle for the spiritual senses. Like Albert he sometimes inverts the spiritual and literal senses, giving the spiritual first. Like Albert's, too, his few strictures on moral behaviour are evoked by examples given in the historical narrative. An often repeated formula: 'Here a literal question arises' nearly always points to some divergence in the Gospel accounts of what happened, to be solved by Augustine's *De concordia* or some other mode of ironing out 'apparent' contradictions. His ideas on the four senses as applied to the Gospels are hard to fathom. At least he bespeaks as keen an interest in actual historical detail as any of his predecessors. Commentators had puzzled over Jesus' presence at a wedding feast and over why his Mother was mentioned first. Some had postulated a family relationship with the hosts. Thomas put forward his own opinion:

. . . Or, perhaps his mother is invited first because they were uncertain whether Jesus would come to a wedding if invited, because of the unusual piety they noticed in him, and because they had not seen him at other social gatherings. So I think that they first asked his mother whether Jesus should be invited. That is why the Evangelist expressly said that his mother was at the wedding, and that later Jesus was invited (J,68).

It was in character for busy Martha to go to tell Jesus of her brother's illness, leaving Mary at home (J,282).

It is fashionable now to credit Thomas with a 'sense of history'. He did not think, it is claimed, of a renewal of the apostolic life as a backward-looking return, but as an ever-present ferment; reformers went not back to, but progressed *with* the New Law.[36] The truths perceived by our minds change. The only eternal truth belongs to the divine mind. Such truths as we can reach are achieved in time and through history.[37] Without contesting these statements, I can only note that the texts supporting it hardly ever come from his exegesis. His lectures on the Gospels lay no special stress on the New Law or on salvation history, even when he is claiming divine approval for his Order.

However, he did innovate. He was aware of the mind of his author, as his definition of the senses implied. St. John's practice in writing his Gospel is discerned. On the miraculous stirring of the water of the Sheep Pool (John 5.1–8) Thomas says:

First he sets forth a visible sign in which he shows Christ's power to produce and to restore life. This is the usual practice in this Gospel: always to join to the teaching of Christ some appropriate visible action, so that what is invisible can be made known through the visible (J,131).

[36] E. Panella, 'La "Lex Nova" tra Storia ed Ermeneutica. Le occasioni dell'esegesi di S. Tommaso d'Aquino', *Memorie Dominicane*, NS 6 (1975), 68; 92–93.

[37] A. Maurer, *St. Thomas and Historicity* (Milwaukee, 1979), 26–33.

Jesus' grief at the death of Lazarus, followed by his raising of Lazarus from the dead, denotes St. John's method, always making a sign of humanity in Jesus precede a sign of his divinity (J,282). 'Note the wonderful variety of expressions,' Thomas explains when he lectures on John 5.20–23: he honours the evangelist's power to express the relationship of Father and Son in fitting terms (J,144). Finally, Thomas nowhere calls the literal sense inferior to the spiritual.

While embracing current teaching on the senses with heart and mind, he enlarged it to demand a new, and occasional, look at the *mens auctoris*. The evangelist's intention might amalgamate literal and spiritual meanings. Thomas could perceive the human, inspired writer as having his own individual gifts and purpose. In doing so he crossed over a border within which earlier commentators on the Gospels had been happy to stay.

6
Conclusions

We have come a long way from the formless compilation of excerpts connected with the school at Laon to the scholastic lecture course with its opening text from Scripture, its chapters, its divisions, its *distinctiones* and its *quaestiones*. Yet several threads of continuity run all the way through because almost every master chose an earlier commentary as his basic source, sometimes naming its author, more often quoting anonymously. This practice prolonged the Laon habit of expanding earlier sets of glosses.

The anonymous exposition of St. Matthew in MS Alençon 26, copied by the historian Orderic Vitalis at St. Évroul, whose author I call *A*, is the first compilation from the Laon circle to deserve the title of 'commentary'. *A* served as basic source for a second anonymous commentator, whom I call *B* without prejudice to his proposed identification with Geoffrey Babion, which is most unlikely. *B* was a religious who had probably studied in some school in northern France, perhaps Laon, and was writing in the 1140s. His commentary passed into the Paris schools owing to Peter Comestor's use of it. A parallel link between Paris and Laon appears in the transfer of the Laon Gloss to Paris. Peter Lombard lectured on a glossed text of St. Luke; so did an anonymous lecturer on Luke whom I call *L*, teaching at Paris probably in the 1160s. Comestor and his successors at Paris all lectured on the glossed text. Peter the Chanter, lecturing on a conflated text of the Gospels, also made some use of *B*.

The Dominican Hugh of St. Cher bridged a long time span by taking Comestor as his basic source on the Gospels, as well as quoting less frequently from the Chanter. Alexander of Hales, it is now clear, borrowed from Hugh of St. Cher. Here we have a loop instead of a straight line: Alexander also went back to *A*, calling him 'Anselm' and probably meaning Anselm of Laon, a false attribution. John of La Rochelle used both Hugh and Alexander. Now comes another loop: Alexander and John of La Rochelle probably both taught Bonaventure; but he seems to have passed them over; he went back to Hugh of St. Cher in his commentaries on St. Luke and St. John. The English friar John of Wales used Bonaventure as his basic source when lecturing at the Oxford Greyfriars. John Pecham, lecturing at Paris, used both Bonaventure and John of Wales. John of Wales and Pecham witness to the close link between the Franciscans at Paris and Oxford, since John of Wales could use Bonaventure and Pecham John of Wales so soon.

Tentatively I suggest the following sequence of 'borrowed from' and borrower. I list only main sources; occasional allusions and quotations are not counted. *A*–*B*–Comestor and Chanter–Hugh of St. Cher (making more use of Comestor)–Alexander (who also went back to *A*)–John of La Rochelle (using both Hugh and Alexander); Hugh of St. Cher–Bonaventure–John of Wales–John Pecham (using both Bonaventure and

John of Wales). *B*, Comestor, Hugh of St. Cher and Bonaventure are the oustanding names.

Now the trail breaks off. I have found no principal source for either Albert or Thomas. My failure reflects either their originality or my ignorance of anonymous unprinted commentaries of the mid-thirteenth century. Two lines only go straight through: the Gloss and after its production Comestor's *Historia scholastica*.

The whole period saw an expansion of the range of patristic authors in Latin or in translations from Greek, and of earlier medieval writers. The friar doctors enjoyed new resources in the shape of teamwork, indexing and general preparation of material for study and classroom. Hugh of St. Cher seized upon Chrysostom's homilies on St. John when Burgundio of Pisa had translated them. Henceforward Chrysostom became a standard guide to St. John, taking his place beside Augustine. Thomas drew on fresh Greek sources, which he deployed mainly in his *Catena aurea*, but also brought into his lectures. To give one example of a rare Latin text quoted: Pecham quotes from Pseudo-Augustine *De mirabilibus sacrae Scripturae*. Such quotations raise up puzzles and show how little we still know of the contents of medieval libraries in spite of modern intensive work on them, whether finished or in progress. What book is quoted as 'Victorinus' (of Pettau?)? Who were Alexander's Gilbertus and Gaufredus? What were the nature and contents of an *expositor* (not the Gloss) quoted by Alexander, Bonaventure and John of Wales, not necessarily the same in each case? If we look at twelfth-century non-scholastic writers, St. Bernard tops the list. Hugh's postills might be described as 'Bernardizing'. Their popularity brought Bernard into the schools. The Franciscans especially felt an affinity with Cistercian piety.

Use of pagan authors will vary with each separate commentator. Aristotle's *Libri naturales*, Pseudo-Aristotle and books on medicine and natural science penetrated slowly. Their full impact was not felt until Albert and Thomas.

Stripped of his sources, each commentator had to face the distance between gospel teaching and present-day practice. How could he square the precepts of the Sermon on the Mount with men's current approved behaviour? Disapproved behaviour could well be denounced; but what of approved, such as litigation? The Fathers had given answers to some of the problems, but in very different historical circumstances. In tackling his problems each commentator discloses something of his personality. It could not be otherwise; he had to deal with facts and people rather than with abstractions.

A partial solution, commonly held, was to distinguish between the ordinary Christian, a layman or secular clerk, and the would-be perfect, members of religious Orders or hermits. Even so, religious would be hard put to it to claim that they conformed exactly to the pattern of the primitive Church. Already by the thirteenth century the terms 'gloss' and 'postill' had acquired overtones of 'glossing *over*' or adulteration.

To begin with *B*: he emerges as positive and decided, anxious to uphold discipline at any cost. Litigation and punishment of criminals were quite compatible with the command *Judge not*. That Christ and the apostles lived in utter poverty never crossed his mind. Indeed, he imagined Jesus as the apostles' steward, managing their property for them, so as to free them for their mission while he remained on earth. The precepts in *B*'s hands reduced themselves to such *trivia* as whether the command to take no thought for the morrow allowed an abbot to store up grain from one harvest to the following. The same type of casuistry continued. Peter Comestor, as befitted the author of the *Historia scholastica*, wanted to bring gospel history to life by setting it in its historical and geographical context and by drawing parallels with contemporary customs. On the precepts he was sensible and reasonable. While attacking current abuses, he explained that the precepts were not absolute. The Church had to reckon with changed circumstances in order to survive. What would happen if we turned the other cheek to the Saracens? They would overrun Christendom; hence crusading warfare was a duty. Peter the Chanter, on the contrary, deplored what he saw as a decline from primitive standards, in uses as well as abuses, although uses were tolerated and established by the Church. One means to improve, if not cure, current ills was more preaching to clergy and people. The Chanter inspired a group of Paris masters to reform society by preaching. They transformed lecture courses by inserting instruction to pupils on their own conduct and on the message they must go on to preach outside the schools. The preacher must satirise all ranks of society and particularly prelates. The tropological sense favoured this kind of matter. Comic touches and *exempla* were recommended as a means to captivating the audience. Satire was not new, of course. *L* had denounced the vices of religious as seen by a jealous secular; but the bulk and purpose expanded.

The friars gave new life to the drive to reform by preaching and by the example of men who vowed themselves to the *vita apostolica*; they aimed at following the gospel example literally. I expected, therefore, that friars would put new content into their lectures on the Gospels, even though they kept to traditional ways of interpreting the Old Testament. I was wrong in respect of the first three friar doctors. The Dominican Hugh of St. Cher and his team of helpers simply prolonged the biblical-moral school. Hugh never mentioned the founder of his Order or its new way of life. His personality as a postillator is obscured by the fact that he presided over a team and that they busied themselves with piecing together excerpts. At least we know that he had a sense of humour; otherwise he would not have allowed so many jokes to pass. He also shows more tenderness to involuntary poverty than earlier commentators had done and that suggests a personal influence. Alexander of Hales is now known to have lectured on the Gospels when he was at the Franciscan *studium* at Paris. He shows no more consciousness of being a Franciscan than Hugh showed of being a

Dominican. He was analytical and impersonal as a postillator. John of La Rochelle gives some hints that he belonged to an Order vowed to poverty; he defends study by religious and allows himself one piece of eschatological speculation, marking himself out as a friar of the second generation of friars Minor. But one has to read him carefully to find the marks. Much more evident is his interest in law and theology as applied to Bible study.

A dramatic change takes place from the mid-thirteenth century onward. The secular masters' attack on the mendicants led to a counter-attack in lectures on the Gospels as well as in the abundant polemical tracts of the period. Bonaventure praises St. Francis by name, recalls stories of his Order's origins and defends its basic thesis, that Christ and the apostles owned absolutely nothing. He comes through as a Franciscan first and foremost. John of Wales and John Pecham follow suit and surpass him. Items of gospel history which figured in polemic, such as the quality of Christ's seamless tunic (cheap or costly?), get into their lectures. Both men are as serious as Bonaventure: no jokes. John of Wales, however, bids for attention by amazing rather than amusing through his record number and variety of quotations. Pecham remains oddly faceless in spite of his prayerful effusions.

Albert and Thomas are less concerned with poverty; they prefer to stress humility, though both uphold the right of religious preachers and scholars to live on almsgiving. Albert resembles John of Wales in pouring out a cornucopia of learning whenever his text gave him an opportunity; unlike John, he had no time for precise references. A warm, exuberant character, he minimised misery and wretchedness in the Gospels. Some of those frequented by Jesus were comfortably off. Ironically Peter the Chanter, a well-to-do secular master, noted that the sisters Martha and Mary were too poor to pay servants to help them entertain visitors. Albert imagined that Lazarus and Mary left Martha to manage their joint property because she was so practical; she ran a household staff, which she supervised, instead of doing the cooking herself. Thomas, astringent and ruthless pruner as he was, seems less remote and more aware of the life around him than he does in his philosophical and theological books.

Changes of interest make themselves felt. Exposition of the Sermon on the Mount becomes less entangled in pettifogging detail. The precepts are interpreted more largely and a new factor introduces itself. The concept of 'the community of the realm' and its corollary 'the common good' took shape in secular society outside the schools. It carried as its consequence that a code of morals enjoined on the individual could not bind the corporate body to which he belonged. Hugh of St. Cher made a beginning when he allowed litigation, reluctantly, as had been done earlier, but with the new proviso that it should not prejudice a person in authority or the commonwealth. Alexander made 'the common good' a criterion for action in his *quaestiones disputatae*, but not in his postills. Albert was the first of them to consider man as a social being and to recognize the claims of society upon him. Thomas made the break-through. He separated precepts enjoined on a private person from those applying to governments. An individual ought not to store up more treasure than he needed for himself and his household. A king *must* store up treasure, since he has more needs and should use it for his subjects' benefit. That goes further than *Render unto Caesar*; it gives a positive role to the secular power.

Another change appears after c.1250, this time in the purpose of the lecturer; it narrows. He contents himself with expounding his text for his pupils' understanding. He no longer thinks it his duty to provide them with sermon material. John of Wales is the exception to prove the rule. He seems to have meant his commentaries as preaching aids. But John at Oxford may have been old-fashioned. The reason for the change was probably that the production of handbooks on preaching, with model sermons and the like, equipped the pupil to preach and so lessened the burden on the lecturer and made his course more functional.

The Gospels invited discussion on the primacy of the papacy and the relations between *regnum* and *sacerdotium*. Our lecturers pronounce strongly in favour of papal primacy over the Church and generally in favour of the pope's supremacy over temporal rulers. Comestor is the most moderate on the second point and Hugh the most hesitant. None of them use the mention of St. Peter's sword or of the two swords as an occasion to belittle the temporal power or to dwell on the liberties of the Church. The mendicant Orders relied on support by secular rulers as much as they did on papal privileges. It would have been foolish to stir up an old quarrel needlessly.

Increasing discrimination against the Jews and their sacred writings, such as the burning of the Talmud, lead one to expect that masters would step up their anti-Jewish polemic in the thirteenth century. The Gospels lent themselves to it even more than the Old Testament. Surprisingly the commentators do not sharpen much, if at all, the polemic handed down by the Fathers. The old stereotype of the blind and guilty Jew of the Bible persists. Thomas's lectures have all the ingredients of an anti-heretical tract, the Jews included; but he does not single them out for special attack. The lecturers' indifference to 'the Jewish question' probably sprang from conservatism rather than tolerance. Enough was being done against the Jews without bringing more into the classroom. The same conservatism appears in exegesis of the Cain and Abel story, where Cain signifies the Jews allegorically![1]

Did the masters make any change in their handling of the four senses and their inter-relationship? The answer to that question is elusive, but it turns out to be 'yes'. Twelfth-century commentators for the most part dropped the idea that they should introduce a spiritual sense in place of the literal, if 'the letter' struck them as unsuitable or nonsensical. 'The letter'

[1] G. Dahan, 'L'exégèse de l'histoire de Cain et Abel du XIIe au XIVe siècle en Occident', *Recherches de Théologie ancienne et médiévale*, 49 (1982), 80–87.

had to be explained and understood before spiritual senses could be built on it. The masters did something to clear up the muddle inherited from the Fathers. Better still, the thirteenth century brought at least a dim perception that the inferiority of the literal sense, so obvious to them in the Old Testament, did not apply to the Gospels so well. Allegory, that is the realisation of Old Testament figures and promises, and tropology, or moral teaching, might belong to the literal sense instead of being superimposed as superior to inferior. The outward sign of this perception appears in the fact that spiritual senses are often given before the literal, or the literal may be sandwiched in between two spiritual senses. Bonaventure often made the spiritual sense inhere in the literal. Albert again made no clear discrimination between them. Thomas gives reason to suppose that he judged the evangelists to be expressing a spiritual as well as a literal sense. That would have been a logical sequel to his view that the literal sense included the writer's whole intention. The evangelists' knowledge stretched to an understanding of the vital link between Old and New Testaments and the novelty of the New Law. Nor could they have been strangers to the moral teaching of the latter. Thomas often gives a literal plus a spiritual 'reason' for an event, as though he thought that the evangelist saw God's intention in bringing that event to pass. I have said that the answer to my question is 'elusive' because the problem of the evangelists' participation in the divine secrets which they revealed to their readers never came under discussion, as far as I know. Only hints are available to enable one to guess what the schoolmen made of it.

A reinstatement of the literal sense as including the spiritual, if it really happened, did not lead to fresh probing of the historical setting of the Gospel story. Peter Comestor's researches on the history, geography and archaeology of Palestine died with him. His comments were repeated, but not improved on. Indeed Peter the Chanter roundly blamed such research as frivolous and time-wasting. Comestor marked the impact on Bible study of the Victorine stress on history as a part of learning and of the flourishing of history writing in the twelfth century.[2] It was short-lived. Thirteenth-century masters of *sacra pagina* preferred the discussion of timeless questions as more rewarding. They had a tool in logic for that activity, wholly lacking in Comestor's type of research, where he had to make do with scanty evidence. Masters, perhaps wisely, avoided entry into a blind alley.

But there was innovation of a more promising kind. Thomas followed through his view of authorship, expressed elsewhere, in his lectures on the Gospels. He pointed to characteristics of St. John as a writer. Medieval writers were generally too keen to grasp the wisdom set down on the page to bother about the writer, as writer, and why he expressed himself as he did. A brief note on his name and life (if known) and purpose in the first

---

[2] R. W. Southern, 'Hugh of St. Victor and the Idea of Historical Development', *Transactions of the Royal Historical Society*, 5th series, 21 (1971), 163–177.

lecture satisfied their curiosity. St. John resembled an eagle in peering up into the mysteries of heaven. Now Thomas fastened on his use of words and content. Similarly he explained a text of St. Matthew, with its accompanying spiritual sense, as addressed particularly to the Jews, because St. Matthew was writing for them, not for gentiles. A new dimension opened up when the sacred writer stepped out of his page. It would be exploited by commentators of the later middle ages.[3]

Thomas's lectures, traditional at first sight, mark a new sense of direction, hence a new beginning, and so a good place to stop.

---

[3] A. J. Minnis, 'Discussions of "Authorial Role" and "Literary Form" in Late-Medieval Scriptural Exegesis', *Beiträge zur Geschichte der deutschen Sprache und Literatur*, 99 (1977), 37–65; *Medieval Theory of Authorship. Scholastic literary attitudes in the later Middle Ages* (London, 1983).

Index of Persons

Index of Manuscripts

ALENÇON, Bibliotheque municipale

26	15, 17, 20, 35, 48, 49 n. 44, 56 n. 63, 151-3, 190, 273

ASSISI, Biblioteca Comunale

138	177
182	177
355	144-6, 149-50, 151, 153, 154, 155 n. 12, 156-7, 158-9, 161-2, 163, 164, 168, 170, 180-1

BASEL, Universitätsbibliothek

B. VI. 17a	30 n. 64

CAMBRIDGE, Pembroke College

7	58
75	4-5, 8-9, 58, 60-2, 67, 69 n. 91

CAMBRIDGE, Trinity College

9 (B. 1. 10)	18 n. 42
70(B. 2. 27)	20-1, 50 n. 46

CASALE MONFERRATO, Biblioteca del Seminario Vescovile

C 14	228

DURHAM, Cathedral Library

A. I. 9	4-5, 32 n. 69, 59-61, 64, 67, 68 n. 90, 69, 70, 71, 72, 77, 79, 80, 83
A. II. 17	146
A. II. 22	20 n. 48, 146-51, 152-4, 155 157, 158, 166-7, 168, 169-70

HEREFORD, Cathedral Library

O. vi. 12	3 n. 12

LONDON, British Library

Royal 2. C. ix	7 n. 24, 108
− 4. C. viii	153-4

MONTECASSINO, Biblioteca Monastica

240	87-8

OXFORD, Bodleian Library

Bodley 412 (SC 2308)	173-4, 177, 178, 179, 180, 181, 183
− 494 (SC 2108)	4-5, 31 n. 67, 58, 59, 61-2, 64, 69, 77
− 729 (SC 2706)	51 n. 47
e Mus. 30 (SC 3580)	218 n. 24
Hatton 37 (SC 4091)	7 n. 24
Lat. d. th. 45	85-97
Laud. misc. 5	19
− 69	14, 21
− 87	12, 19, 22-4, 33, 56 n. 64
− 221	177, 188
− 291	4-5, 6, 10, 11, 13, 16 n. 36, 25-6, 28, 32 n. 69, 58, 59, 62, 64, 65, 66, 67, 68 nn. 89 & 90, 69, 70, 72, 73, 75, 76, 77-8, 79-80, 81, 110, 114, 116 n. 32, 127 n. 1
Lyell 66 (Phillipps 438)	21, 56 n. 64
Rawl. C. 46	160 n. 22

OXFORD, Magdalen College

27	214, 218 n. 25, 219 nn. 30 & 33, 220 nn. 35, 38 & 40, 221, 222 nn. 45 & 46, 223 nn. 51, 53 & 55, 224 nn. 58 & 59, 226 n. 76, 236 n. 26

OXFORD, Merton College

80	174-5, 179, 181, 188
212	7 n. 24, 9, 25-6, 32, 107-8, 110 n. 20, 111-14, 126, 140

OXFORD, New College

48	150, 172-3, 176, 180, 181, 182, 184, 188, 189